THE UNITED STATES AND EUROPE: POLICY IMPERATIVES IN A GLOBALIZING WORLD

Global Interdisciplinary Studies Series

Series Editor: *Professor Sai Felicia Krishna-Hensel, FRGS*
Auburn University Montgomery, USA

The Global Interdisciplinary Studies Series reflects a recognition that globalization is leading to fundamental changes in the world order, creating new imperatives and requiring new ways of understanding the international system. It is increasingly clear that the next century will be characterized by issues that transcend national and cultural boundaries, shaped by competitive forces and features of economic globalization yet to be fully evaluated and understood.

Comparative and comprehensive in concept, this series explores the relationship between transnational and regional issues through the lens of widely applicable interdisciplinary methodologies and analytic models. The series consists of innovative monographs and collections of essays representing the best of contemporary research, designed to transcend disciplinary boundaries in seeking to better understand a globalizing world.

Also in the series

The New Millennium: Challenges and Strategies for a Globalizing World

Edited by Sai Felicia Krishna-Hensel

ISBN 0 7546 1391 7

The United States and Europe: Policy Imperatives in a Globalizing World

Edited by
HOWARD M. HENSEL

Routledge
Taylor & Francis Group

LONDON AND NEW YORK

First published 2002 by Ashgate Publishing

Reissued 2018 by Routledge
2 Park Square, Milton Park, Abingdon, Oxon OX14 4RN
711 Third Avenue, New York, NY 10017, USA

Routledge is an imprint of the Taylor & Francis Group, an informa business

Copyright © Howard M. Hensel 2002

The editor and contributors have asserted their moral right to be identified as the the authors of this work in accordance with the Copyright, Designs and Patents Act, 1988.

All rights reserved. No part of this book may be reprinted or reproduced or utilised in any form or by any electronic, mechanical, or other means, now known or hereafter invented, including photocopying and recording, or in any information storage or retrieval system, without permission in writing from the publishers.

Notice:
Product or corporate names may be trademarks or registered trademarks, and are used only for identification and explanation without intent to infringe.

Publisher's Note
The publisher has gone to great lengths to ensure the quality of this reprint but points out that some imperfections in the original copies may be apparent.

Disclaimer
The publisher has made every effort to trace copyright holders and welcomes correspondence from those they have been unable to contact.

A Library of Congress record exists under LC control number: 2002074454

ISBN 13: 978-1-138-72066-4 (hbk)
ISBN 13: 978-1-138-72064-0 (pbk)
ISBN 13: 978-1-315-19495-0 (ebk)

Contents

List of Contributors vii
Introduction ix

1 American National Interests and Objectives
   Howard M. Hensel 1

2 Understanding the European Union's Enlargement:
   The International Society Approach of the English School
   Yannis A. Stivachtis 55

3 NATO After the Cold War
   Joyce P. Kaufman 79

4 NATO, the European Union, and European Security
   Roger E. Kanet and Nouray V. Ibryamova 99

5 Squaring the Circle? British Defence Policy
   in a Changing World
   Andrew Dorman 123

6 The Core and the Periphery of European Security Policy
   Glen M. Segell 143

7 The Multi-Dimensional Approach of the OSCE in Estonia:
   Assessing the Organization's Preventive Diplomacy Role
   Maria Raquel Sousa Freire 159

8 Non-Governmental Organizations and the Liberalization
   of Global Trade Policy Under GATT/WTO
   Zdzislaw W. Puslecki 183

9 Critiquing Traditional Responses to Cocaine
   and Heroin Trafficking
   Joseph E. Vorbach III 205

10 Conclusion: The United States and Europe in a Globalizing World
   Daniel S. Papp 231

Index 249

List of Contributors

Andrew Dorman, Lecturer in Strategic Studies; Joint Services Command and Staff College, United Kingdom

Maria Raquel Sousa Freire, Professor, Universidade Lusiada, Portugal

Howard M. Hensel, Professor of Politico-Military Affairs, Air War College, United States

Nouray V. Ibryamova, School of International Studies, University of Miami, United States

Roger E. Kanet, Professor, School of International Studies, University of Miami, United States

Joyce P. Kaufman, Professor of Political Science, Whittier College, United States

Daniel S. Papp, Senior Vice-Chancellor for Academics and Fiscal Affairs, University System of Georgia, United States

Zdzislaw W. Puslecki, Professor, Institut of Political Science and Journalism, Adam Mickiewicz University, Poland

Glen M. Segell, Director, Institute of Security Policy, United Kingdom

Yannis A. Stivachtis, Professor of International Relations, Schiller International University, Switzerland

Joseph E. Vorbach III, Assistant Professor of International Relations, U.S. Coast Guard Academy, United States

Introduction

Howard M. Hensel

Relations between the United States and Europe have been inextricably intertwined since the birth of the American republic over two and a quarter centuries ago. From its inception, the principles and values that served as the foundation for the United States' identity were rooted in the ideas of the Enlightenment. Similarly, from colonial times forward through the 225 years since independence, socio-economic bonds have continuously linked America with Europe. Moreover, throughout most of the 20th Century, the political fate of Europe has been closely tied to, and even hinged upon, the politico-military involvement of the United States in European affairs. Between 1917 and 1918 and again between 1941 and 1945, the United States intervened in the two most destructive wars in recorded history in order to prevent Germany from dominating the continent and to protect the independence, territorial integrity, and socio-politico-economic freedom of the European peoples. For four and a half decades following victory in the second of these conflicts, between 1945 and 1991, the centerpiece of U.S. foreign policy was the protection of European independence and socio-political freedom against the threat of Soviet continental domination. Simultaneously, in the aftermath of World War II, the United States dedicated significant American resources to rebuilding Europe's shattered economy and, throughout the remainder of the 20th Century, continuously sought to promote European economic prosperity. Today, at the dawn of the 21st Century, political, military, economic, and socio-cultural ties between the U.S. and Europe are not only central to both Americans and Europeans, the course of events throughout Europe and, indeed, the remainder of the international community will be heavily, if not decisively influenced by the relationship between the United States and its European partners.

The purpose of this work is to frame the context and explore aspects of the contemporary relationship between the United States and the European powers as they attempt to address common challenges and opportunities as the international community enters a new millennium. Most of the material embodied in this work was prepared for and presented at the annual Millennium Conferences of the Comparative and Interdisciplinary Studies Section of the International Studies Association. These annual events represent an effort by academic scholars and policy makers, drawn from a variety of backgrounds and bringing with them varying perspectives, to apply the various methodological approaches of diverse disciplines to better conceptualize and analyze contemporary policy challenges and opportunities and to formulate effective policy responses within the international arena.

Chapter 1 attempts to define the sources, evolution, contemporary context, and parameters for American foreign policy, as applied throughout the international arena. Specifically, it attempts to define and analyze the principles and values which underpin American foreign policy, delineate the national interests pursued by the United States since the inception of the republic, trace patterns of continuity and change in American foreign policy as these interests have been prioritized and translated into national objectives during the two and a quarter centuries since American independence, and, finally, outline and assess contemporary U.S. national objectives, as they apply generally throughout the entire international system, as well as, specifically, within the individual regions and sub-regions of the international arena. The chapter serves to set the stage for an analysis in subsequent chapters of some of the contemporary challenges and opportunities confronting the United States and the European powers. In addition, it provides historical and global perspective for their assessment of the U.S.'s strategic initiatives and responses, utilizing a variety of policy instruments, to individually and, in concert with its European partners, address the challenges and capitalize upon the opportunities that characterize the global and European regional environment at the outset of the new century.

Chapters 2 and 3 provide further perspective by amplifying upon the European context of contemporary American and European policy. Chapter 2, by Yannis Stivachtis discusses various politico-economic motivations, processes, and dynamics inherent in the enlargement of the European Union. In chapter 3, Joyce Kaufman examines the question of role redefinition and expansion of mission by the North Atlantic Treaty Organization (NATO), focusing on developments between 1991 and the end of the decade, and the implications of this transformation for the alliance's ability to effectively deal with the challenges and opportunities in the decades ahead.

Chapters 4, 5, and 6 focus specifically on contemporary security oriented issues and dilemmas confronted by the European powers and the United States. In chapter 4, Roger Kanet and Nouray Ibryamova explore the dimensions of United States and Russian coincidences and conflicts of approach and policies in dealing with European security challenges. Central to their discussion is an analysis of the Russian, European, and American approach to NATO expansion and its impact, specifically, on Russo-European-American relations. Chapter 5, by Andrew Dorman, examines patterns of change and continuity in British defense policy, as well as assesses the direction of the security policies of the contemporary United Kingdom. In chapter 6, Glen Segell concludes the section of the book dedicated specifically to security-oriented issues by analyzing domestic and transnational/international sources of European security policy.

Chapters 7, 8, and 9 focus on some of the economic, political, and non-traditional problems confronting the United States and the European community, as well as assess some of the institutions and methods used by the U.S. and Europeans in an attempt to successfully address these problems. In chapter 7, drawing upon the case study of post-Soviet Estonia, Maria Raquel Sousa Freire examines the role and mission of the Organization for Security and Cooperation in Europe (OSCE) and assesses the organization's ability to respond successfully to the often varied socio-political challenges, especially those within post-Soviet Central and Eastern Europe. Chapter 8, by Zdzislaw Puslecki, focuses on global and European economic issues by analyzing various motivations, constraints, and dilemmas associated with international trade liberalization under the auspices of the World Trade Organization. In chapter 9, Joseph Vorbach turns to an analysis of a non-traditional threat to both European and American society - the global threat posed by illicit drugs. In the chapter, he critiques contemporary policies aimed at halting cocaine and heroin trafficking and calls for new approaches in dealing with this modern scourge.

Finally, the work concludes with Daniel Papp's chapter 10, which assesses the various points raised within the preceding chapters and examines their implications for both American and European security, economic, and political responses and initiatives in addressing the challenges and opportunities of the 21st Century.

In short, the following chapters represent a diversity of perspectives, opinions, analyses, and recommendations regarding the regional and global problems and opportunities confronted by both the United States and the Europeans as they enter the new century.[1] Hopefully, the material presented will prove to be suggestive to both scholars and policy makers alike, and contribute to ongoing discussions concerning American and European regionally and globally oriented foreign policies. A number of individuals helped to produce this volume. I would particularly like to thank the contributors to this book, as well as the members of the editorial and production staff of Ashgate Publishing Ltd. Most of all, however, I would like to thank my family, especially my wife for encouragement, as well as invaluable support and assistance in producing this work.

Note

[1] The opinions, conclusions, and/or recommendations expressed or implied within this book are solely those of the authors who are entirely responsible for the contents of their works and do not necessarily represent the views of any academic institution, the Air University, the United States Air Force, the Department of Defense, any U.S. government agency, any other government, or multinational organization.

Chapter 1

American National Interests and Objectives

Howard M. Hensel

Over five hundred years ago, Europe suddenly awoke to the existence of a "new world" - the previously unknown Western Hemisphere. In the eyes of both those Europeans who first beheld this new discovery, as well as in the eyes of those Europeans who would ultimately settle in this virgin wilderness, the New World provided mankind with a unique opportunity to construct a new society, a new economy, and a new political system, unencumbered by the social, economic, and political constraints which restrained "progress" in the Old World. Hence, armed with confidence in man's power to understand and shape his environment along desired lines, the early Americans viewed the untamed wilderness of the New World as a place where man might be able to approximate paradise on earth. It was in this context that the new experiment in freedom and liberty was undertaken and the United States was born.

This chapter[1] will attempt to: (1) delineate the values and ideals which underpin the principles and purposes that shape the American national identity; (2) define the United States' national interests and introduce some of the dilemmas associated with translating the national interests into specific national objectives; (3) trace the evolving ways in which these national interests have been translated into specific objectives and analyze the order of priority assigned to the various component parts of the national interests and objectives since the founding of the republic and, finally, (4) outline, prioritize, and analyze the relationship between the various, contemporary, global and regional foreign policy objectives of the United States, as interpreted by this author, as the republic enters the 21st Century.

Principles and National Interests[2]

On July 4, 1776, the delegates to the Second Continental Congress stated in the Declaration of Independence:

> We hold these truths to be self-evident, that all men are created equal; that they are endowed by their Creator with certain unalienable rights; that among these, are life, liberty, and the pursuit of happiness. That, to secure these rights, governments are instituted among men, deriving their just powers from the consent of the governed;

that, whenever any form of government becomes destructive to these ends, it is the right of the people to alter or abolish it, and to institute a new government, laying its foundations on such principles, and organizing its powers in such form, as to them shall seem most likely to effect their safety and happiness.[3]

Throughout the subsequent two hundred and twenty five years, Americans have further developed these principles. For example, the Bill of Rights to the U.S. Constitution delineated the basic rights that are guaranteed to all Americans.[4] Over a century and a quarter later, against the backdrop of World War I, President Woodrow Wilson articulated his celebrated Fourteen Points which called for the establishment of a new world order based upon such principles as: national self-determination of peoples, democratically elected governments, freedom of navigation, and free trade.[5] Less than a quarter century later, within the context of the most devastating international conflict in recorded history, President Franklin Roosevelt enunciated his "four freedoms:" freedom of speech and worship and freedom from want and fear. Subsequently, in the Atlantic Charter, he and British Prime Minister Winston Churchill agreed upon the common principles governing American and British foreign policy.[6]

Based upon the concepts presented in these and similar documents, it is possible to compile a list of some of the most basic principles that serve as the foundation for U.S. foreign policy.

1. Principles which pertain to the relationship between the peoples and their government, including:
   a. The right of all peoples to collectively select their own government and, if necessary, to replace or abolish that government should it violate this right or any of the other rights listed below.
   b. Government, which maximizes individual liberty by remaining limited in size and scope.
   c. Respect for the basic "human rights" of peoples, including:
      (1) The right to life and physical security;
      (2) The right to freedom of religion, speech, assembly, and the press;
      (3) The right to petition for the redress of grievances, to keep and bear arms, and security from unreasonable searches and seizures of private property;
      (4) The right to due process of law as outlined in the 5th, 6th, 7th, and 8th amendments to the U.S. Constitution;
      (5) The right to equal opportunity under the law;
      (6) The right to emigrate.
   d. A free market economy devoid of unnecessary government regulation.
   e. Protection of private property
2. Principles pertaining to the American conception of the international order, including:
   a. The right of all peoples to political independence within borders determined on the basis of nationality, with the right of autonomous development for national groups within multinational states.

b. The right to security from the threat of physical attack, as well as security from territorial change and/or foreign domination against the will of the peoples concerned.
c. Freedom of navigation on the high seas.
d. Free international trade.
e. Peaceful resolution of disputes.
f. The right of all states in the international system to individually act, by whatever means they deem necessary, in their own self-defense against any power or coalition of powers which threaten their independence and/or security or to collectively unite and suppress any power or coalition of powers which threaten the international peace.

These principles, in turn, serve as the foundation for the national interests[7] consistently pursued by the United States since the establishment of the republic two and a quarter centuries ago. These interests could be categorized as follows:

1. Security Interests – Protection of the political independence and territorial integrity of the United States; preservation of the freedom and security of the American people; maintenance of the socio-economic-political principles underpinning American society, the American economy, and the American political system; and guaranteed access to those areas abroad which are deemed to be vital to the political and economic survival of the United States.
    a. Deter any hostile power from launching an attack upon the territory of the United States and/or those areas abroad deemed to be vital to American economic and/or military security.
    b. Reduce and optimally eliminate altogether the prospects of any hostile power establishing staging areas abroad from which to launch an attack against the territory of the United States and/or against those areas abroad deemed to be vital to the United States' economic and/or military security.
    c. Defend the territory of the United States and/or those areas abroad which are deemed to be vital to American economic and/or military security in the event of hostile attack so as to successfully:
        (1) Guarantee the territorial integrity and politico-economic independence of the United States;
        (2) Prevent hostile domination of areas vital to American economic and/or military security; and
        (3) Reestablish peace on terms consistent with American security interests.
    d. Prevent any hostile power from establishing hegemony over areas abroad deemed vital to American economic and/or military security by means other than overt military attack.
    e. Guarantee secure access to necessary overland, maritime, and air transit routes linking the United States with those areas abroad deemed to be vital to American economic and/or military security.
    f. Guarantee secure access to those areas abroad deemed to be vital to American economic and/or military security.

2. Commercial Interests – Promote the prosperity of the American and world economy beyond that which is necessary for the minimal maintenance of American economic security.
   a. Promote the establishment of free market economies abroad.
   b. Guarantee the freedom of all air and maritime transit routes for all international commercial shipping.
   c. Guarantee the physical safety of all American citizens living or traveling abroad.
   d. Guarantee the security of American property abroad.
   e. Promote free access to all foreign commercial markets.
3. Political Interests – Promote the establishment of democratically elected, limited governments which endorse and comply with:
   a. The principles of "human rights;"
   b. National self-determination of peoples and the right of autonomous development for those peoples residing in multi-national states;
   c. The peaceful resolution of international disputes, based upon respect for the principles of sovereignty and territorial integrity.

In compiling this list of principles of American foreign policy and deriving from it the definition of American national interests, it is recognized that Americans have often sharply disagreed, not only as to their scope and specific definition, but also as to whether they are absolute concepts or are subject to some measure of qualification in practice. If, indeed, they are subject to qualification, to what extent is that possible without subverting the concepts themselves? Moreover, questions have been repeatedly raised as to whether each of these interests are co-equal or whether some are more basic and, therefore, inviolable that others. Among those Americans who maintain the latter position, there has been considerable controversy concerning the delineation of priorities among the various national interests. For example, in some situations, a policy designed to promote American political interests can serve to advance not only the United States' long-term security and prosperity by contributing to the establishment of a freer and more peaceful world community, it can also help consolidate America's immediate security interests. Conversely, however, in other cases, a policy designed to promote American political interests, while perhaps contributing to the long-term security of the United States in a general sense, may be incompatible with efforts to promote or even maintain its immediate security. Indeed, in extreme cases, American efforts to promote political interests may seriously jeopardize, even to the extent of totally undermining the immediate security of the United States. The reverse is, of course, also true; a policy designed to promote the immediate security interests of the United States in a particular context may necessitate overlooking human rights violations by governments sympathetic to those security interests and, therefore, clash with American political interests. Fortunately, there are often situations in which immediate American security interests are not involved. In these situations, a policy designed to promote American political interests, while having little or no effect upon the immediate security of the United States, may enhance America's long-term security by helping to create a better world order.

Apart from the problems associated with the determination of priorities among the relatively unchanging national interests pursued by the United States, Americans have often disagreed concerning the delineation of specific national objectives[8] appropriate to the opportunities and challenges presented within the international environment at a given time. They have also often sharply disagreed concerning the specific goals and methods embodied within the national security strategy as the United States attempts to utilize diplomatic, political, economic, military, and informational instruments in order to secure its objectives. For instance, there has often been sharp disagreement even among those Americans who emphasize the paramount importance of American political interests. Some Americans have argued for an active, interventionist crusade designed to directly promote the establishment of a world order based upon the principles underpinning American foreign policy. Conversely, however, notwithstanding agreement concerning the emphasis placed upon American political interests, others have argued in favor of a relatively passive foreign policy that would attempt to promote those political interests by example, rather than by direct intervention. Obviously, between these two extremes, a variety of possible policy actions are, of course, possible. In any case, even among those Americans who have agreed upon a particular set of priorities among the component parts of the national interest, there has often been sharp disagreement as to appropriate policy actions.

The United States' Rise from Regional to Global Power

While American national interests are global in scope and, if realized, they imply a significant revision in the nature of the entire international system, throughout the first century and a quarter after independence, the United States' interpretation of and the emphasis placed upon the component parts of its national interests, as well as the national objectives and strategies which it adopted in policies in pursuit of its national interests, differed significantly between the geographic areas contiguous to the United States, gradually expanding to encompass the whole of the Western Hemisphere, versus American policies pursued toward the Eastern Hemisphere. Within the geographic areas initially contiguous to the United States, but gradually expanding to include the entire Western Hemisphere, the United States implicitly delineated, as its national objectives, goals which were designed to: (1) protect and enhance American security interests and, (2) while promoting the United States' non-essential commercial interests and political interests, these interests were subordinate to U.S. security interests. Hence, when U.S. non-essential commercial interests and political interests were pursued, they were shaped to conform to, reinforce, complement, and even justify American security interests. Finally, in formulating its policies toward the geographic areas contiguous to the United States and, eventually toward the whole of the Western Hemisphere, the United States government actively adopted strategies directly designed to secure these national objectives. In contrast to its objectives and strategies toward the Western Hemisphere, in its policies toward the Eastern Hemisphere, (1) the United States' security interests were marginal or non-existent, and, (2) while its non-essential commercial interests and political interests were pursued, (3) these interests were only indirectly promoted by the U.S. government and were instead actively and directly pursued by American citizens on an individual basis.

Early American Foreign Policy Within the Western Hemisphere

During the early years of the new American republic, the United States concentrated much of its attention upon the Western Hemisphere, especially those areas immediately contiguous to the United States. Even during these early years, however, various Americans, such as Alexander Hamilton, looked forward to the eventual establishment of United States hegemony throughout the entire Western Hemisphere, not merely the areas bordering the new republic.[9] In any case, during the years immediately following the United States' independence, in areas adjacent to the United States, the British to the north and northwest and the Spanish to the south and southwest threatened American security interests, as well as its commercial interests. Hence, the administration of George Washington set as priority national objectives: the evacuation of the British military presence and the closure of those British trading posts which were still located on U.S. soil, cessation of British interference in relations between the United States and the Indians in the region north of the Ohio River, resolution of the boundary dispute with Spain in the region south of the Tennessee River, acquisition of secure rights of transshipment down the Mississippi River through the port of New Orleans, and Spanish agreement not to interfere in U.S.-Indian relations. By the conclusion of Mr. Washington's second term as President, his administration had successfully pursued an active, primarily diplomacy oriented strategy, supported by a growing and increasingly active military presence, and, as a result, had largely attained its priority national objectives.[10]

It was the Jefferson Administration, however, which was permanently able to secure the critical objective of guaranteeing freedom of navigation along the entire Mississippi and permanent access to the port of New Orleans. This, of course, was accomplished by a diplomatic strategy, culminating in the Louisiana Purchase of 1803.[11] Moreover, the ambitions of some Americans to expand in the direction of Canada, culminating in the abortive attempt during the War of 1812 to seize that region, could be interpreted within the framework of American ambitions to reinforce security, while, simultaneously, enhancing the U.S.'s power and position within North America.[12] Following that conflict, however, the United States set as one of its key foreign policy objectives the stabilization of Anglo-American relations along the U.S.-Canadian frontier, while, at the same time, reducing the British threat to American security from the north. Consequently, in order the neutralize British naval power on the Great Lakes, while avoiding a costly naval arms race, the United States' diplomatic strategy culminated in an agreement with the British which placed limits upon naval forces in the Great Lakes and on Lake Champlain. Meanwhile, in 1818, the U.S. and the British successfully negotiated an agreement clarifying the boundary between the United States and Canada from the Lake of the Woods westward to the crest of the Rocky Mountains. The agreement provided for joint British and American occupation over Oregon, a region of growing concern to the American people and their government.[13]

During this same period, the United States came increasingly to view Latin America as part of its primary zone of foreign policy concern, albeit of lesser importance than the areas immediately contiguous to the territory of the United States. Assessing American policy toward Latin America during this period, the U.S. strategy, in part embodied in the Monroe Doctrine, can be interpreted as having been designed to advance American political interests by promoting the objective of containing and undermining the European colonial presence in the Western Hemisphere, while, simultaneously, encouraging and supporting the establishment of independent, democratically oriented nation-states throughout Latin America. It also served to promote American military and economic security, as well as the United States' non-essential commercial interests by laying the foundations for subsequent efforts to actively establish U.S hegemony throughout the Western Hemisphere. Occasionally, however, policy considerations in areas immediately contiguous to the United States required a modification of U.S. strategy toward Latin America. For example, in the case of the relationship between the timing of recognition of the newly established Latin American republics and the conduct of territorial and border negotiations between the United States and Spain, U.S. territorial ambitions took precedence over American efforts to assert greater influence throughout the remainder of the Western Hemisphere.[14]

From the time of independence onward, however, most Americans agreed that the defense and promotion of security and commercial interests in North America would contribute significantly, though passively, to American political interests throughout the international system. It was commonly felt that merely by maintaining the United States' independence over a sustained period and, thereby, allowing the experiment in liberty and popular economic prosperity to develop, the United States would itself provide a shining example for the rest of mankind that such a government could, in fact, endure. Indeed, many Americans believed that the establishment of the American republic was the first step toward the realization of the golden age of man.[15] Beyond this, however, other Americans felt that a policy of passively and indirectly providing an example for mankind to emulate, though obviously important, was insufficient and that a more active, direct policy should be adopted. Prior to the 1840s, however, the promotion of American political interests does not seem to have been a principal cause of American territorial acquisitions.[16]

The 1840s heralded a new era in American foreign policy, associated with the concept of "manifest destiny" and characterized by aggressive expansionism within North America. This change of tone drew upon a number of trends that were present during earlier periods. The new orientation was consistent with the proposition that the United States' primary foreign policy focus ought to enhance U.S. power by pursuing national objectives designed to establish hegemony over the areas contiguous to the United States, and, to a lesser extent, throughout the entire Western Hemisphere. Second, such domination would, in turn, reinforce American independence and security, while, simultaneously, contributing to increasing U.S. prosperity. Third, it drew upon the concept of a unique American mission to spread its ideals by focusing that mission on a specific geographical goal.[17]

While the hegemonic character and aggressively expansionist national objectives toward contiguous territories, drew upon the older tradition of mission, the United States' new aggressiveness naturally tarnished the image of American selflessness and idealism. Indeed, "manifest destiny" transformed the notion that American principles should be exported peacefully into a doctrine of belligerent, territorial expansionism based upon the proposition that the United States possessed "special rights" over its neighbors and others within the Hemisphere. In any case, by the 1840s, many Americans had concluded that acquisition of Texas and the area beyond the Rocky Mountains was important, not only to promote U.S. security interests, they also argued that acquisition of these territories would bring to these regions the benefits embodied in the American system of government. The aggressive strategy designed to achieve these expansionist national objectives eventually led to war with Mexico and diplomatic confrontation with Great Britain.[18]

Following the military success against Mexico and the diplomatic compromise with Great Britain over the Oregon territory, U.S. power in North America reached unprecedented proportions. Consequently, many Americans entertained further regional expansionist designs in the direction of the Caribbean and Central America. It was the intensifying domestic crisis between the southern states and the remainder of the republic, however, which posed the greatest challenge to U.S. security interests since independence and, consequently, such expansionist projects were set aside, at least for the moment.[19]

During the first half of the 1860s, the great struggle for southern independence reached its terrible climax,[20] but with the successful attainment of the vital national objective of politically reintegrating the Union, the United States emerged in the aftermath of the war more powerful than ever. In the period immediately following the Civil War, American attention focused on reconstruction and industrial development, as well as the final, though tragic, resolution of the internal security problem posed by the American Indians that all U.S. administrations had confronted since independence.[21] Meanwhile, in an effort to promote its security, commercial, and political interests within North America, the Andrew Johnson administration availed itself of Russian eagerness to sell Alaska to acquire that vast region.[22]

By the latter part of the 19th Century, it was clear that not only had American industry grown enormously, the western frontier, which had heretofore been looked upon as a permanent feature of American life, was now rapidly disappearing. As a result of these and other factors, attitudes toward America's role in the world began to undergo a transformation. First, with respect to the enlarged potential to project power, the United States began to redefine the Monroe Doctrine so as to transform it into a justification for the active assertion of U.S. influence throughout the entire Western Hemisphere.[23] Second, America's expanded power potential made its projection outside the confines of the Western Hemisphere possible. Third, American business increasingly looked abroad for new markets.[24]

These factors, in combination with others, served to rekindle talk of "manifest destiny" and helped to create a new expansionist atmosphere in the United States. One result of this new expansionism was the American acquisition of Hawaii and a portion of Samoa during the final years of the 19th Century. Closer to home, longstanding American ambitions to control the Caribbean basin and its islands, especially Cuba, ultimately led to war with Spain and eventual control over Spanish possessions in the Caribbean and the Orient.[25] The acquisition of Puerto Rico and control over Cuba, combined with the American acquisitions in the Pacific and the Philippines, revived American ambitions to control Central America and construct a trans-isthmian canal. Following a series of diplomatic maneuvers, the United States undertook construction of the Panama Canal in 1904, completing the project ten years later. Henceforth, control and defense of the Canal and its maritime approaches would be a priority national objective of American foreign policy.[26] With unprecedented power to influence events globally, not just within the Western Hemisphere, what interests, national objectives, and strategies would the United States pursue in the 20th Century?

Early American Foreign Policy toward the Eastern Hemisphere

To gain perspective on this question, one must refocus attention back to the period of a century and a quarter earlier and analyze the direction of U.S. policy toward the Eastern Hemisphere. During the century and a quarter period following independence, in sharp contrast to its attitude toward the Western Hemisphere, successive administrations in Washington agreed that neither American security, commercial, nor political interests required the United States government to become actively and directly involved in the political affairs of the Eastern Hemisphere. Consequently, the founders of the republic and their successors sought to remain aloof from the political rivalries that characterized European international politics. The strategy adopted to facilitate attainment of this goal was embodied in the celebrated call for the United States to avoid "entangling alliances" with the European powers.[27]

Simultaneously, however, most American policy makers at the time of independence and thereafter enthusiastically sought to promote American non-essential commercial and political interests by encouraging privately conducted cultural and commercial relations with Europe and the remainder of the world. In encouraging these contacts, various administrations advocated commercial diversification to avoid becoming economically dependent upon a particular foreign power. Indeed, they feared that such a dependency could seriously undermine their strategy of avoiding political entanglements with the powers of the Old World. Conversely, broadly based commercial internationalism would complement and reinforce that strategy.[28]

Of course, encouragement of broadly based commercial internationalism would help promote U.S. commercial interests by contributing to the growth and prosperity of the American economy. Not only was this desirable as an end in itself, it would also help promote American political interests by providing mankind with an example of economic prosperity, buttressed by individual freedom and democracy. Similarly, many Americans believed that commercial internationalism, insofar as it promoted such principles as open markets, free trade, and freedom of navigation for commercial shipping, would, simultaneously, help advance U.S. political interests by contributing to a reduction of international tensions. This would, in turn, supposedly produce eventual advances toward realization of the other American national interests.[29]

In short, throughout the first century and a quarter of American foreign policy, the United States did not feel that its security interests extended into the Eastern Hemisphere. Successive administrations did feel, however, that the United States had political and non-essential commercial interests in that region, but these interests, and their specific expressions as national objectives should largely be pursued by Americans on an individual or group basis and not officially by the American government. Hence, while the instruments of American foreign policy, especially diplomacy and naval power, were regularly and often dramatically used by the United States government in order to negotiate commercial treaties with Eastern Hemispheric powers and to ensure the attainment of such objectives as freedom of navigation for commercial vessels traversing these distant waters,[30] the United States government consistently maintained a policy of non-involvement in the political affairs of the Eastern Hemisphere. At most, the government would, on occasion, express sympathy for a particular revolutionary movement that was seeking to advance "human rights", democratic rule, and/or the principle of national self-determination of peoples, but it would always refrain from officially intervening. Simultaneously, however, the U.S. government did not attempt to block the efforts of American citizens, individually or collectively, to assist these revolutionary movements.[31] Finally, while many high ranking members of the United States government endorsed and supported American missionary activities, as well as scientific and archaeological expeditions in Africa and Asia, the American government was quite slow to assume responsibility for the safety of U.S. citizens living and traveling in these areas.[32]

To sum up, throughout the first century and a quarter following its independence, as its military and economic power progressively increased, the United States adopted ambitious and often aggressive national objectives and strategies designed, in turn, to simultaneously promote American security, commercial, and political interests within the Western Hemisphere, especially the areas immediately contiguous to American territory. When there was a conflict of interests, however, the United States always gave priority to its security needs. Moreover, affairs in areas contiguous or in close proximity to the United States were given priority over those in Latin America distant from U.S. territory. Within the Eastern Hemisphere, American policy makers felt that U.S. security interests were not threatened and, therefore, the most appropriate policy was to remain officially aloof from the political affairs of the Old World. This policy stance was, in effect, the reverse side to the U.S. effort to reduce and, if possible eliminate European influence from the Western Hemisphere, thereby allowing the United States to dominate in the New World. Thus, the pursuit of American political and non-essential commercial interests was generally left to private individuals. Of course, it was felt that U.S. political interests would be passively promoted by the continued example of American political freedom and prosperity.

The United States as a Global Power

The Spanish-American War marked the beginning of a fundamental transformation in American perceptions of the international system. The war demonstrated that American power was now of sufficient scale to be applied outside the Western Hemisphere. This factor, combined with the impact of political developments within Europe and East Asia during the first four decades of the 20th Century, led the United States government to gradually and haltingly abandon its traditional reluctance to become officially involved in the political affairs of the Eastern Hemisphere that had underpinned American foreign policy during the preceding 125 years. Hence, the new century set the stage for what would initially prove to be a temporary and eventually a more lasting enlargement of the United States government's policy focus to global dimensions.

President Woodrow Wilson most fully exemplified the proposition that there was no incompatibility between actively promoting American political and non-essential commercial interests throughout the entire international system and protecting American security, now viewed in global dimensions. Hence, motivated by a willingness to use American power to actively promote the establishment of a new world order based upon the principles underlying American political and commercial interests. President Wilson abandoned the traditional reluctance to become entangled in European international politics and led the United States into World War I.[33] For the first time in American history, the U.S. government would actively and directly pursue American national interests on a global scale.

U.S. intervention in the war in Europe served, in part, to tip the military balance in favor of the Anglo-French allies and the resultant military victory seemed to clear the way for the establishment of a new international order, based upon the principles underpinning American foreign policy. Unfortunately, President Wilson's ambitions were foiled, in part, by the policies of the British and the French who were less committed to the principles underpinning American interests than to their own respective, immediate, security objectives. In the larger sense, however, as Professor Robert Osgood has noted, Mr. Wilson's exhortations to the American people, ". . . to subordinate their self-interest to abstract moral standards and welfare of the rest of the world" was unacceptable to many in the United States.[34] In the end, the Treaty of Versailles failed to embody many of the abstract values to which President Wilson adhered. Thus, the peace settlement was attacked by some for sacrificing U.S. security interests and by others for compromising American ideals.[35]

In short, the United States' crusade for a new international order ended in military victory and political defeat. Combined with the horrors of World War I itself, many Americans became disillusioned with the entire policy of actively using policy instruments to promote the establishment of a new global order based on the principles underpinning American foreign policy. Indeed, there was a strong pacifist feeling within American society during the interwar period. Hence, at the outset of the 1920s, while continuing its active involvement in political affairs within the Western Hemisphere and, since the turn of the century, the Philippines and the Pacific basin, the United States government attempted to return to its traditional policy of officially remaining aloof from the political entanglements within the Eastern Hemisphere. Of course, the United States still sought to promote its non-essential commercial and political interests in the Eastern Hemisphere, but, during the period between the World Wars, these interests were pursued by example and by privately undertaken commercial and philanthropic activities. Finally, the U.S. took the lead in a variety of efforts to secure legal sanctions against the use of war as an instrument of policy.[36]

By the 1930s, however, many Americans became increasingly disturbed by the rising threat to international peace emanating first from Japan and later from Italy and Germany. A difference of approach quickly developed among Americans as to the degree to which these developments constituted a threat to American national interests and how the United States should respond. Some Americans, influenced in large measure by the great disillusionment following U.S. participation in World War I, hoped to insulate the United States from the danger by redoubling the isolationist element of American foreign policy. Moreover, many felt that war was an inappropriate way to protect peace. Finally, others felt that the political affairs of the Eastern Hemisphere were not the concern of the United States. Conversely, however, another body of American opinion disagreed and argued that the United States should actively participate in a collective effort designed to reverse the policies of the aggressor states.[37]

Between the mid-1930s and December 1941, the administration of President Franklin Roosevelt gradually began to again globalize the United States' foreign policy focus. Initially, President Roosevelt increasingly embarked upon a policy designed to halt Axis aggression by means of an indirect strategy that made American material resources available to those states attempting to militarily resist the Axis powers. With the Japanese attack on American soil at Pearl Harbor on December 7, 1941, however, the United States abandoned this indirect strategy and, in concert with Great Britain, the Soviet Union, and a number of other powers, became militarily involved in the war. But once directly involved, the American people united in the effort to apply the now massive American military power on a global scale to attain the priority objectives of defeating the Axis and establishing a new world order based upon the principles underpinning American foreign policy.[38]

Following the defeat of the Axis powers in 1945, the post-war environment was dominated by two powers, the United States and the Soviet Union. Unfortunately, relations abruptly deteriorated between the two superpowers and American hopes for the immediate establishment of a new world order faded. Thus, with the breakup of the wartime alliance, international developments took place against the background of a protracted Cold War between the United States and the U.S.S.R.[39]

Consequently, in an effort to protect and promote its security, commercial, and political interests on a global scale, one of the key national objectives of American foreign policy in the post-World War II period became the containment of communist subversion and Soviet expansionism throughout the entire world. In pursuit of this overriding global objective, the U.S. adopted a multifaceted strategy that relied upon a blend of such policy instruments as direct American military power, military assistance, cooperation with interested states, diplomacy, and economic assistance.[40]

Over forty years after the Cold War began, in the late 1980s, President Reagan's administration provided one of the clearest and most comprehensive statements of American national objectives during the Cold War period. In that document, he stated that American national security objectives, which are, in turn, "refined from our national interests," serve to "provide a general guide for strategy in specific situations which call for the coordinated use of national power".[41] As such, President Reagan defined U.S. national security objectives as follows:[42]

1. To maintain the security of our nation and our allies. The United States, in cooperation with its allies must seek to deter any aggression that could threaten that security and, should deterrence fail, must be prepared to repel or defeat any military attack and end the conflict on terms favorable to the United States, its interests, and its allies. Specifically:
    a. To deter hostile attack on the United States, its citizens, military forces, or allies and to defeat attack if deterrence fails.
    b. To deal effectively with threats to the security of the United States and its citizens short of armed conflict, including the threat of international terrorism.
    c. To prevent the domination of the Eurasian landmass by the Soviet Union, or any other hostile power or coalition of powers.
    d. To prevent transfer of militarily critical technologies and resources to the Soviet bloc and hostile countries or groups.
    e. To reduce our reliance on nuclear weapons by strengthening our conventional forces, pursuing equitable and verifiable arms control agreements and developing technologies for strategic defense.
    f. To assure unimpeded U.S. access to the oceans and space.
    g. To foster closer relations with the People's Republic of China.
    h. To prevent the spread of nuclear weapons.
2. To respond to the challenges of the global economy. Our national security and economic strength are indivisible. As the global economy evolves in increasingly interdependent ways, we must be aware of economic factors that may affect our national security, now or in the future. Since our dependence on foreign sources of supply has grown in many critical areas, the potential vulnerability of our supply lines is a matter of concern. Additionally, the threat of a global spiral of protectionism must be combated, and the problem of debt in the developing world is a burden on international prosperity. Specifically:
    a. To promote a strong, prosperous and competitive U.S. economy, in the context of a stable and growing world economy.
    b. To ensure access to foreign markets, energy, and mineral resources by the United States and its allies and friends.

      c. To promote a well-functioning international economic system with minimal distortions to trade and investment, with stable currencies, and broadly agreed and respected rules for managing and resolving differences.
3. To defend and advance the cause of democracy, freedom, and human rights throughout the world. To ignore the fate of millions around the world who seek freedom betrays our national heritage and over time would endanger our freedom and that of our allies. Specifically:
      a. To promote national independence and the growth of free institutions worldwide.
      b. To encourage and support aid, trade, and investment programs that promote economic development and the growth of free and humane social and political orders in the Third World.
      c. To encourage liberalizing tendencies within the Soviet Union and its client states.
4. To resolve peacefully disputes which affect U.S. interests in troubled regions of the world. Regional conflicts which involve allies or friends of the United States may threaten U.S. interests, and frequently pose the risk of escalation to a wider conflagration. Conflicts or attempts to subvert friendly governments, which are instigated or supported by the Soviets and their client states, represent a particularly serious threat to the international system and thereby to U.S. interests. Specifically:
      a. To address, where possible, the root causes of regional instabilities which create the risk of war.
      b. To maintain stable regional military balances vis-à-vis the Soviet Union and states aligned with it.
      c. To neutralize the efforts of the Soviet Union to increase its influence in the world, and to weaken the links between the Soviets and their client states in the Third World.
      d. To aid in combating threats to the stability of friendly governments and institutions from insurgencies, subversion, state-sponsored terrorism and the international trafficking of illicit drugs.
5. To build effective and friendly relationships with all nationals with whom there is a basis of shared concern. In the world today, there are over 150 nations. Not one of them is the equal of the United States in total power or wealth, but each is sovereign, and most, if not all, touch U.S. interests directly or indirectly. Specifically:
      a. To make major international institutions more effective in promoting peace, world order and political, economic and social progress.
      b. To seek opportunities to improve relations with the Soviet Union on a realistic and reciprocal basis.
      c. To improve relations with other nations hostile to us in order to reduce the chance of future conflict.
      d. To strengthen U.S. influence throughout the world.

As the American government's foreign policy actively assumed a global character, however, so did many of the problems traditionally characteristic of American policy within the Western Hemisphere. For example, whereas the U.S. had traditionally been sensitive to Latin American aspirations for independence from the European powers, it had often reflected insensitivity as to the Latin desire to be free from the specter of United States hemispheric hegemony. As a result, over the decades, Latin American nationalists became quite cynical about Washington's statements of American foreign policy principles, such as its commitment to the principle of national self-determination of peoples. Since, the U.S. had never sought to establish hegemony within the Eastern Hemisphere, American policy had always reflected a much greater appreciation for the desires of the peoples of the Middle East, Africa, and Asia for political and economic independence. Hence, nationalists in these areas traditionally took the United States' commitment to such principles as national self-determination much less cynically than their Latin American counterparts. In the Western Hemisphere, American foreign policy often seemed to belie the principles underpinning American foreign policy, whereas, in the Eastern Hemisphere, the United States' words and deeds appeared to coincide more closely.

The post-World War II containment objective, with its emphasis, particularly during the 1950s, upon promoting the establishment of regional alliances designed to contain the Soviet Union and offering to assist Third World governments defend themselves against internal communist subversion, often tended to eclipse this traditional American sensitivity to African, Asian, and Middle Eastern nationalist aspirations. The resultant change in African, Asian, and Middle Eastern perceptions of the Americans, in turn, came at an especially awkward time, since, during the two decades following the conclusion of World War II, most of the peoples of these areas obtained their independence from the European powers. Hence, African, Asian, and Middle Eastern nationalists were particularly vigilant against any possible threats, perceived or actual, to their newly won freedom. To most of the Third World nationalists, the Soviet and communist threat was an abstraction with which they had little or no direct experience. The only threat they were familiar with emanated from the former colonial and mandatory powers. Hence, in their eyes, the American proposed security organizations appeared to be a thinly disguised effort to perpetuate Western domination over their countries. Similarly, the American offers to help combat left-wing internal threats emanating from within these new independent states appeared to many nationalists as merely another Western excuse for interference in the internal affairs of their countries.[43] Clearly, the United States was attempting to impose its perceptions of a bipolar Cold War world upon Third World nationalists who simply did not view the international system in similar terms.

In many respects, at least that element of American Cold War strategy that was directed toward the newly independent states of the Middle East, Africa, and Asia and was designed, in turn, to help secure U.S. objectives served poorly to promote American national interests. The United States failed to recognize aspirations of the indigenous peoples of the Third World and built its policy along lines that were fundamentally incompatible with their aspirations. The efforts to contain the Soviet Union and local communist elements throughout the Third World might well have been more effectively served had the United States confined its efforts to actively promoting its commercial and political interests, rather than by promoting politico-military alliances toward which these nationalist elements were at best indifferent, and at worst hostile. In the words of Egyptian President Nasser, "It is only by a period of complete independence during which mutual trust is built up between Egypt and the Western powers that Egyptians will be able to look without suspicion on any closer ties between this country and other powers". Mr. Nasser went on to note, however, that, "left alone, the Arabs will naturally turn toward the West and ask it for arms and assistance".[44] This observation applied to much of the developing world.

Moreover, the United States' preoccupation with the containment of the Soviet Union and communist subversion often led the U.S. to associate with and, at least implicitly, endorse regimes, which, though anti-communist, failed to conform to the principles of human rights, the democratic process, national self-determination of peoples with the right of autonomous development, and the peaceful resolution of international disputes. Yet, from the American perspective, while often expressing regret for the domestic character and policies of these regimes, most post-World War II administrations felt that the U.S. critical national objective of containing communism took priority over the United States' commitment to pursue objectives designed, in turn, to actively promote its political interests. By identifying itself with non-democratic, anti-communist regimes which often violated the human rights of their citizenry, however, the United States often not only alienated those forces abroad which sought to actively advance the same principles as those traditionally underpinning American foreign policy, the U.S. often tended to drive those elements into the arms of left-wing revolutionaries in a common effort to overthrow the United States' reactionary partner. In short, a strategy of supporting non-democratic regimes that failed to conform to the principles which underpin American foreign policy in order to help secure the priority objective of containment of communism, often only served to reinforce the threat posed by left-wing subversion and, hence, became, in effect, a self-fulfilling prophecy. In a larger sense, however, especially since the early 1970s, many Americans, as well as observers abroad increasingly questioned whether the United States had sufficient resolve and/or power to defend friendly regimes over a prolonged period of time against genuinely popular, indigenous efforts to overturn those regimes.

Finally, in the post-World War II period, the United States was often confronted with additional problems and situations that did not lend themselves to easy solutions. For example, even by the standard of the principles underpinning American political interests, a clear choice was often difficult or impossible between rival non-communist elements contesting over a particular area and justifying their claims on the basis of principles endorsed by the United States. Similarly, even by the standard of American security interests, how was the United States to react to conflict between U.S. allies where the vital interests of both parties were intimately involved and compromise was difficult or impossible? Siding with one would likely alienate the other, but to remain aloof would probably alienate both antagonists. Indeed, could a policy of aloofness be possible for a superpower that claimed to be the leader of the "free world" and was recognized as such?

In short, American policy in the Eastern Hemisphere during the Cold War period was often characterized as both confusing and contradictory. This, in large measure, was caused by the interplay of two factors. The first was the post-World War II expansion of the United States government's national security focus to include the entire "free world," not merely confining it to only those regions immediately contiguous to the U.S. and/or materially necessary for the protection of American military and/or economic security. The second factor was the emphasis on actively protecting American interests from threats from the left, while, simultaneously, often overlooking threats to those interests emanating from the right. These factors, combined, led to the conclusion of "entangling alliances" with powers in regions marginal to the immediate military and/or economic security interests of the United States, often against the will of the indigenous peoples, as well as identification with unpopular and reactionary regimes. Thus, the United States, once viewed by the peoples of the Third World as a new force in international affairs pointing mankind in a more enlightened direction, was now, too often, perceived by them to be merely another state in the international arena, distinct only in the amount of power which it wielded, but playing the same game of power politics as that traditionally played by the European states. Simply put, during the Cold War, the United States allowed its immediate, priority global objective of protecting American security and the security of the "free world" by means of containment of the Soviet Union and communist subversion, to eclipse the United States' longer range, traditional goal of creating a new international order based upon the principles underpinning American foreign policy.

United States National Objectives at the Dawn of the 21st Century

The world of the 21st Century is obviously quite different from the world of the 1790s, or even the world of the 1970s and 1980s. During the final third of the 20th Century, the international system witnessed: the European and Far Eastern recovery from the devastation of the Second World War; decisive movement within Western and Central Europe toward economic and political integration within the framework of the European Union; the political disintegration and economic collapse of the USSR, leading, in turn, to dramatic changes in Russia's political, economic, and societal character; the accompanying collapse of Russia's domination over the USSR's non-Russian republics and the USSR's satellites in Eastern Europe, leading, in turn, to the emergence of politically and economically reoriented older powers and newly independent states throughout Central and Eastern Europe, as well as in Central Asia; the increased role played by the Peoples Republic of China in international affairs; and, finally, the emergence of several of the states in the Middle East, Southwest, Central, and South Asia, and Latin America as significant economic and, often, political powers within the international system. These developments, accompanied by a variety of others, have all contributed to a general, ongoing transformation of the international power configuration from the bipolarity of the immediate post-World War II period to a system which must be characterized as politically, economically, socio-culturally, and, in many respects, militarily multipolar. Moreover, accompanying their growing power and status within the international system, these various states have become increasingly assertive in pressing their individual policy agendas, which are sometimes incompatible with the national objectives sought by the United States. As such, unlike the relatively rigid power alignment patterns that characterized the international power configuration at the height of the Cold War, the multipolar world of the 21st Century will probably see a much greater level of power alignment fluidity. Notwithstanding these often dramatic changes, however, in many respects, the international power configuration at the dawn of the 21st Century remains within the Westphalian construct, based on sovereign states as the principal actors within the international arena.

In other respects, however, globalization and the emergence of powerful transnational actors from a variety of quarters challenge the applicability of the Westphalian construct as the framework for the international order in contemporary times. For example, the dramatic technological breakthroughs which have revolutionized telecommunications have made the instantaneous, global exchange of information and opinion across state boundaries a matter of routine. Indeed, the revolution in information technology has both complemented and facilitated the unprecedented level of interconnected interdependence among the economies of the various states within the international system, leading, in turn, to a truly global economy. Moreover, the information technology revolution has facilitated and encouraged dramatically greater access to information and contact among the peoples of the world than was imaginable even a few decades ago. This, in turn, has increased global momentum toward more open societies. Similarly, the movement toward greater openness of borders, combined with revolutionary technological progress in the capacity to quickly transport both peoples and goods virtually anywhere on the planet have further multiplied this trend toward global social and economic integration. Finally, economic globalization has invited, facilitated, and accelerated the establishment of multinational commercial entities, which, often, are more powerful than many of the states of the international system.

While, in many respects, these trends toward greater global societal and economic integration have resulted in greater freedom, prosperity, and understanding within the global community, in other respects, for many people, globalization has come to represent economic, political, and socio-cultural neo-imperialism which threatens to destroy national, regional, and even individual social, cultural, economic, and political identities. Such factors as: the political disintegration of a number of the states of Central and Eastern Europe; the, often accompanying, rise in religious, national, and ethnic tensions, buttressed by territorial national rivalries and separatist demands; the exploitation of natural resources and cheap labor; environmental pollution and degradation; exponential growth in population; increases in disease and world hunger; yawning gaps between rich and poor both between states, as well as, in many cases, within states; massive foreign debt; and a host of similar factors have created a context for resentment and extremism. It is in this context that militant, extremist organizations have emerged as increasingly powerful actors within the international arena. In some cases these groups are ideologically or religiously inspired, while in other cases they are secularly based. In some cases the focus of their efforts falls exclusively within a particular state, whereas with others groups, the focus transcends state boundaries. Whether nationally based or transnational in character, whether ideologically or religiously motivated, these militant, clandestine, extremist groups present a growing threat to the international order at the dawn of the 21st Century.

Compounding the seriousness of the expanding number of these militant extremist groups and their adherents is their penchant for terrorism, utilizing a variety of weaponry and tactics to implement their strategies. Not only has a wide variety of light weapons become plentifully available to extremists, the threat emanating from these groups is exponentially compounded by the increasingly immediate prospect of the widespread proliferation of chemical, biological, radiological, and nuclear weapons of mass destruction and delivery methods, as well as the vulnerability of the interdependent, global telecommunications, international finance, and transportation networks to cyber attack. In short, all of these factors, joined by a variety of others, combine to create an increasingly high level of vulnerability for our 21st Century globally oriented, integrated and interdependent, urban, industrial, and technologically based societies and economies. Indeed, the dimensions of this transnational vulnerability are unprecedented in human history.

Beyond the threat of terrorism emanating from extremist, militant groups operating across national boundaries, the nature of modern society has given rise to international criminal activity on an unprecedented international level. Transnational crime networks are actively engaged in such activities as: drug trafficking; smuggling of all sorts; money laundering and other fraudulent financial activities; and the theft of intellectual property; to name only a few. The inability or, in some cases, unwillingness of individual states and the international community to eradicate these transnational criminal organizations endangers the security and stability of the entire global community.

Finally, throughout the 20th Century, especially since 1945, state sovereignty has, to a degree, been qualified by the efforts of the entire international community to establish and codify fundamental norms of behavior to which all powers must adhere. The significance of these norms has, in turn, been reinforced by their increasingly vigorous enforcement by international organizations and internationally sanctioned tribunals.

In short, at the dawn of the 21st Century, the international arena is composed not only of the traditional sovereign state actors. Throughout the 20th Century, international organizations and internationally accepted legal constraints have increasingly shaped the international environment and significantly influenced the conduct of relations between states, as well as affairs within states. Furthermore, developments and trends which transcend state boundaries, ranging from: the dramatic expansion of inexpensive, immediate, and readily available global communications and transportation linkages which, in turn, have greatly compounded the momentum toward increased global social and economic integration; the rise of all sorts of transnational organizations, ranging from international corporations to militant, extremists groups and criminal networks; as well as the ever increasing vulnerability of our 21st Century societies and economies to sudden and dramatic disruption, catastrophic devastation, and even complete destruction through the use of weapons of mass destruction and cyber attack, join with other similar developments to alert us to the significance of transnational actors and forces which will increasingly influence the direction of international affairs. The growing significance of all these international actors and forces, in turn, serve to challenge the appropriateness of the pure Westphalian paradigm of sovereign states as the key actors within the contemporary international arena as the analytical construct within which to base analysis of the international system and as the construct within which to formulate policy appropriate for the challenges and opportunities of the 21st Century.

On January 20, 2001, the torch of American presidential leadership was passed from President Clinton to his successor, George W. Bush. As the transition of presidential leadership takes place and as the Bush administration formulates its own interpretation of American national objectives, it is both an opportune and appropriate moment to review and assess the national objectives that underpin contemporary American foreign policy. [45]

Today, as throughout its two and a quarter century history, the United States' national interests may be defined in a manner consistent with the delineation of national interests set forth at the outset of this chapter. Indeed, as President Clinton noted in his administration's final statement defining the parameters of American national security policy, the words of the preamble to the U.S. Constitution state that the people of the United States established their government in order to: "provide for the common defense, promote the general welfare, and secure the blessing of liberty to ourselves and our posterity." Based upon this, President Clinton defined the national interests of the United States as: "enhancing security at home and abroad" through the establishment and maintenance of "a stable, peaceful international security environment, . . . one in which our nation, citizens and interests are not threatened";[46] "promoting prosperity";[47] and promoting "democracy, human rights, and respect for the rule of law".[48] Thus, while citing many of the specific developments and challenges which characterize the contemporary world noted above, the Clinton Administration appropriately maintained that, as the United States enters the 21st Century, the fundamental goals of the United States remain constant.[49]

For purposes of this study, contemporary American national objectives are framed within the parameters of two crosscutting, overarching categories. The first, topically organized, overarching category consists of those broadly defined, globally oriented national objectives that apply throughout the entire contemporary international system. The second, overarching category is geographically organized and crosscuts the first category. It focuses on those U.S. national objectives which are specifically applicable to the challenges and opportunities which are present within particular, contemporary geographic regions: Europe and Eurasia; East Asia and the Pacific; the Western Hemisphere; the Middle East, North Africa,

Southwest, Central, and South Asia; and Sub-Saharan Africa. Given the crosscutting character of these two broad categories of national objectives, they are mutually reinforcing.[50] Finally, the contemporary national objectives of the United States, as specifically delineated within the context of this study, are prioritized into four categories:[51] primary, secondary, tertiary, and quaternary objectives. Primary objectives are goals that are vital to the survival and immediate security of the United States. Secondary objectives are goals that, while not vital to U.S. survival and immediate security, are extremely important to the well-being and prosperity of the United States and the international community. Tertiary objectives are goals that are important for the socio-economic and political development of peoples and states of the international community along lines compatible with the principles underpinning American foreign policy. Finally, quaternary objectives are goals that would enhance the security and prosperity of the international community. While quaternary objectives are not unimportant, their importance does not rise to the level of priority occupied by those goals categorized as primary, secondary, or tertiary objectives.[52] In short, while not claiming to offer a comprehensive list of contemporary U.S. national objectives, and certainly one which should not be interpreted as an authoritative statement of official U.S. policy, the following outline represents a prescriptive overview of what, in the opinion of this author, are some of the key contemporary national objectives which the U.S. ought to pursue, as delineated by priority of importance.

U.S. National Objectives Applicable Throughout the Entire International System:

1. Protect and defend the security interests of the United States against any actual or potential hostile national power(s) or transnational, non-state element(s) that might threaten those interests by threatening to attack or actually attacking the territory of the United States, American citizens and their property, U.S. allies and partners with which the U.S. has specific mutual security guarantees, geographic areas vital to American security interests, and/or unimpeded U.S. access to those geographic areas, irrespective of the form or source of the attack or threatened attack. (PRIMARY OBJECTIVE)
    a. Control and reduce arsenals of weapons of mass destruction and their delivery systems, prevent their further spread, and limit the spread of destabilizing conventional weapons (PRIMARY OBJECTIVE)
        (1) Detect and prevent the spread of materials, technologies and expertise necessary for the development of chemical, biological, nuclear, and radiological weapons of mass destruction and their delivery systems, especially missile delivery systems, to states and transnational elements currently not possessing these weapons and delivery systems[53] (PRIMARY OBJECTIVE)
        (2) Constrain, subject to verification, the further increase of existing national inventories of dangerous, destabilizing weapons of mass destruction, eliminate incentives for their use, and, insofar as possible, reduce the levels of these weapons and delivery systems throughout the international system.[54] (PRIMARY OBJECTIVE)

(a) Reduce the number of nuclear warheads and destabilizing delivery systems, especially missile delivery systems (PRIMARY OBJECTIVE)
(b) Reduce the danger of inadvertent launch of a nuclear strike based upon false warning. (PRIMARY OBJECTIVE)
(c) Eliminate all existing arsenals of chemical and biological weapons (PRIMARY OBJECTIVE)
(d) Ensure the complete safety, strict security, and full accountability of all existing arsenals of chemical, biological, nuclear, and radiological weapons of mass destruction by responsible national authorities (PRIMARY OBJECTIVE)

(3) Limit and provide greater transparency in the transfer, acquisition, and buildup of destabilizing, conventional weapons[55] (SECONDARY OBJECTIVE)
(a) Limit the proliferation of technologically sophisticated conventional weapons and prevent access to sensitive technical information that would be useful in the development of advanced conventional weaponry[56] (SECONDARY OBJECTIVE)
(b) Limit the spread of light weaponry and small arms[57] (QUATERNARY OBJECTIVE)
(c) Reduce the threat to civilians posed by anti-personnel landmines[58] (QUATERNARY OBJECTIVE)
[1] Ban all use of "non-detectable" anti-personnel landmines (QUATERNARY OBJECTIVE)
[2] Limit the deployment of "long-duration" anti-personnel landmines to specifically designated, clearly delineated and "monitored" areas so as to prevent intrusion by civilians (QUATERNARY OBJECTIVE)
[3] Remove "non-detectable" and "long-duration" mines from unmarked areas (QUATERNARY OBJECTIVE)
[4] Ban, permanently and universally, the export of anti-personnel landmines (QUATERNARY OBJECTIVE)

b. Protect the safety and security of the United States, its allies with which the U.S. has specific mutual security guarantees, and areas vital to American national interests (PRIMARY OBJECTIVE)
(1) Protect against, deter, and prevent any acts of coercion or aggression by any potentially hostile national power(s) or transnational, non-state element(s), including terrorists, that might threaten American security interests by attacking the territory of United States, American citizens and their property, its allies and partners with which the U.S. has specific mutual security guarantees,

geographic areas vital to U.S. security interests, and/or unimpeded U.S. access to those geographic areas, irrespective of the form or source of the threatened attack (PRIMARY OBJECTIVE)
- (a) Maintain sufficient survivable, robust, redundant nuclear delivery systems and command, control, and communications infrastructures so as to credibly ensure the delivery of a controlled, effective response, including a nuclear response, to any attack, using any weapons, including chemical, biological, nuclear, and/or radiological weapons of mass destruction, upon the United States or its allies and partners with which the U.S. has specific mutual security guarantees[59] (PRIMARY OBJECTIVE)
- (b) Maintain sufficient conventional forces such as to, alone or together with its allies and partners, credibly deter any regional acts of aggression or coercion directed against the security interests of the United States[60] (PRIMARY OBJECTIVE)
- (c) Prevent acts of terrorism directed against the territory of United States, American citizens and their property, its allies and partners, geographic areas vital to U.S. security interests, and/or unimpeded U.S. access to those geographic areas, irrespective of the form or source of the threatened attack[61] (PRIMARY OBJECTIVE)

(2) Protect the safety and security of the United States, the American citizens, and the international community from a variety of non-traditional security threats (PRIMARY OBJECTIVE)
- (a) Combat international criminal activities (PRIMARY OBJECTIVE)
    - [1] Combat drug trafficking (PRIMARY OBJECTIVE)
        - [a] Dismantle organizations engaged in drug trafficking and prosecute drug traffickers[62] (PRIMARY OBJECTIVE)
        - [b] Eliminate the domestic and overseas cultivation and production of illegal drugs[63] (PRIMARY OBJECTIVE)
        - [c] Interdict the flow of illicit foreign drugs and prevent their entry into the United States[64] (PRIMARY OBJECTIVE)
        - [d] Promote anti-drug programs[65] and prosecute drug abusers within the United States[66] (PRIMARY OBJECTIVE)

[2] Prevent the smuggling of migrants and trafficking in people[67] (QUATERNARY OBJECTIVE)

[3] Prevent illegal financial transactions and economic activities[68] (QUATERNARY OBJECTIVE)

[4] Prevent criminal activities that result in environmental contamination[69] and/or "illegal trafficking in endangered and threatened species"[70] (QUATERNARY OBJECTIVE)

(b) Prevent the spread of dangerous, highly infectious diseases, such as Ebola, tuberculosis, and HIV/AIDS[71] (PRIMARY OBJECTIVE)

(c) Ensure the safety of foods and other goods imported into the U.S. from abroad[72] (PRIMARY OBJECTIVE)

(d) Prevent ecological degradation and preserve natural resources globally[73] (PRIMARY OBJECTIVE)

[1] Protect against the threat of deterioration of the earth's ozone layer (PRIMARY OBJECTIVE)

[2] Protect against the threat of global warming (PRIMARY OBJECTIVE)

[3] Encourage global efforts to preserve the earth's environment and to conserve the natural resources of the planet (PRIMARY OBJECTIVE)

(e) Protect those cultural and natural locations throughout the world which have been designated as World Heritage Sites by UNESCO (SECONDARY OBJECTIVE)

c. Defend against, respond successfully to, defeat, and prevail over any hostile national power(s) or transnational, non-state element(s) that might threaten American security interests by attacking the territory of the United States, American citizens or their property, its allies and partners with which the U.S. has specific mutual security guarantees, geographic areas vital to U.S. security interests, and/or unimpeded U.S. access to those geographic areas, irrespective of the source or form of the attack[74] (PRIMARY OBJECTIVE)

(1) Defend the territory of the United States, preserve the effective functioning of its socio-economic, political, and military institutions, and protect American citizens and their property against any possible type of attack, including an attack utilizing chemical, biological, nuclear, and/or radiological weapons of mass destruction, emanating from any source[75] (PRIMARY OBJECTIVE)

(a) Develop and, when feasible, deploy a limited National Missile Defense system to defend the territory of the United States against a limited missile attack[76] (PRIMARY OBJECTIVE)

(b) Preserve the capacity of the United States government, as well as the capacity of state and local government to continue to function effectively and provide leadership and essential services to the American people following an attack upon the territory of the United States[77] (PRIMARY OBJECTIVE)

(c) Defend American territory, society, its citizens, and their property against any attack of any kind, including attacks which employ chemical, biological, nuclear, and/or radiological weapons of mass destruction, emanating from any national or transnational source[78] (PRIMARY OBJECTIVE)

(d) Protect critical cyber/computer, financial, energy, water, telecommunication, and transportation infrastructure networks from hostile intrusion and disruption[79] (PRIMARY OBJECTIVE)

(2) Retaliate against, defeat, and prevail over any hostile national power(s) or transnational, non-state element(s) that might threaten American security interests by attacking the territory of the United States, American citizens or their property, its allies and partners with which the U.S. has specific mutual security guarantees, geographic areas vital to U.S. security interests, and/or unimpeded U.S. access to those geographic areas, irrespective of the source or form of the attack (PRIMARY OBJECTIVE)

(a) Respond to, retaliate against, defeat, and prevail over any power(s) or element(s) which would launch any attack upon the territory of the United States, American citizens, or their property, irrespective of the source or form of the attack (PRIMARY OBJECTIVE)

(b) Respond to, retaliate against, and destroy any terrorist element(s), as well as any state(s) and/or element(s) within the international system that lend any form of assistance and/or support to terrorists, that attack the territory of the United States, the safety and property of American citizens, and/or threaten U.S. national interests throughout the international arena, emanating from any source and using any type of weapons, including chemical, biological, nuclear, and/or radiological weapons of mass destruction[80] (PRIMARY OBJECTIVE)

(c) Respond to, retaliate against, defeat, and prevail over any power(s) or element(s) which would launch any acts of "large-scale, cross-border aggression", simultaneously within two geographically separate theaters, against U.S. allies and partners with which the U.S. has specific mutual security guarantees, geographic areas vital to U.S. security interests, and/or unimpeded U.S. access to those geographic areas, irrespective of the source or form of the attack[81] (PRIMARY OBJECTIVE)

 (d) Respond to and protect against threats to the U.S.'s vital security interests in situations involving interstate conflicts and/or internal upheavals, including revolutions, civil wars, and other forms of violent domestic unrest[82] (PRIMARY OBJECTIVE)

 (e) Assist "failed states" and prevent vacuums of power in geographic areas and/or in circumstances involving the vital security interests of the United States (PRIMARY OBJECTIVE)

 (f) Prevent the use of chemical, biological, nuclear, or radiological weapons of mass destruction in geographic areas and/or in circumstances involving the vital security interests of the United States (PRIMARY OBJECTIVE)

d. Ensure U.S. self-sufficiency in critical defense industries (PRIMARY OBJECTIVE)

e. Ensure U.S. access to vital raw materials and energy resources[83] (PRIMARY OBJECTIVE)

f. Preserve "freedom of navigation" and "freedom of overflight" over international waters[84] (PRIMARY OBJECTIVE)

g. Maintain "unimpeded access to and use of space"[85] (PRIMARY OBJECTIVE)

 (1) Deter, and if necessary, neutralize any hostile actions by any power that might threaten the United States' free access to space and use of space assets[86] (PRIMARY OBJECTIVE)

 (2) Prevent the deployment of weapons of mass destruction in space (PRIMARY OBJECTIVE)

 (3) Maintain the U.S. use of space assets to retain "information superiority"[87] (PRIMARY OBJECTIVE)

2. Promote regional peace and stability[88] (SECONDARY OBJECTIVE)

a. Prevent the use of chemical, biological, nuclear, or radiological weapons of mass destruction in geographic areas and/or in circumstances not immediately involving the vital security interests of the United States (SECONDARY OBJECTIVE)

b. Stabilize and ameliorate interstate conflicts, and/or internal upheavals, including revolutions, civil wars, and other forms of violent domestic unrest in geographic areas and in circumstances not immediately involving the security interests of the United States [89] (SECONDARY OBJECTIVE)

c. Assist "failed states" and prevent "power vacuums" in geographic areas and in circumstances not immediately involving the security interests of the United States [90] (SECONDARY OBJECTIVE)
d. Mitigate suffering caused by man-made and natural disasters as they may occur anywhere in the international community[91] (QUATERNARY OBJECTIVE)

3. Promote the establishment and maintenance of an international order predicated upon the principles underpinning American foreign policy and compatible with political and economic interests of the United States (SECONDARY OBJECTIVE)
    a. Promote democracy and human rights globally (TERTIARY OBJECTIVE)
        (1) Promote responsible, limited, transparent government, based upon democratic principles, strong democratic institutions and processes, and free, frequent, and fair elections[92] (TERTIARY OBJECTIVE)
        (2) Promote freedom of expression, the free flow of information, and media independence[93] (TERTIARY OBJECTIVE)
        (3) Promote the rule of law, and civilian control of the military and security forces[94] (TERTIARY OBJECTIVE)
        (4) Promote adherence to the principles of human rights and, when necessary, take appropriate sanctions against governments which violate those rights[95] (TERTIARY OBJECTIVE)
            (a) Prevent genocide, "ethnic cleansing", and forced relocation of selected peoples [96] (TERTIARY OBJECTIVE)
            (b) Ensure that the human rights of women, children, refugees and displaced persons, workers, and ethnic, religious, and political minorities are protected[97] (TERTIARY OBJECTIVE)
    b. Expand U.S. foreign trade and investment within the context of a stable international economy based upon the principles of free trade and open markets (SECONDARY OBJECTIVE)
        (1) Promote and maintain a strong, resilient U.S. economy, capable of successfully competing in the global economic market[98] (PRIMARY OBJECTIVE)
        (2) Promote the universal establishment of a stable international economic order based upon the principles of free trade and open markets[99] (SECONDARY OBJECTIVE)
        (3) Encourage all states within the international arena to reduce and eventually totally eliminate of all informal and/or formal barriers to international investment and trade (SECONDARY OBJECTIVE)
        (4) Ensure that trade liberalization strengthens, rather than weakens, worker rights and environmental protection[100] (SECONDARY OBJECTIVE)

(5) Expand American global trade and investment [101] (SECONDARY OBJECTIVE)

    c. Promote international economic stability capable of withstanding financial crises, by promoting sound financial structures and policies among all members of the international community, and sustaining global economic growth and prosperity (PRIMARY OBJECTIVE)

(1) Strengthen the international financial system so that it can better contribute to global financial stability and promote economic strength among the various members of the international economic community individually[102] (PRIMARY OBJECTIVE)

(2) Promote sustainable, socio-economic development on a global scale, in a manner compatible with global ecological quality[103] (SECONDARY OBJECTIVE)

(3) Promote sustainable demographic policies[104] (TERTIARY OBJECTIVE)

U.S. National Objectives Unique to Individual Geographic Regions

4. Europe

    a. Ensure and, if necessary defend the continued political independence and territorial integrity of those European states with which the United States has specific mutual security guarantees (PRIMARY OBJECTIVE)

    b. Ensure that no state hostile to the United States or its interests establishes hegemony over the European continent or portions thereof (PRIMARY OBJECTIVE)

    c. Promote the safety, security, reduction, and nonproliferation of Russia's inventory of weapons of mass destruction, its weapons grade chemical, biological, or nuclear materials, its delivery systems, especially its missile technology, or its supporting expertise in the manufacture of weapons of mass destruction and/or its delivery systems[105] (PRIMARY OBJECTIVE)

(1) Ensure against the launch of nuclear weapons against the United States or its allies from Russia (PRIMARY OBJECTIVE)

(2) Promote reductions in Russia's inventory of deployed nuclear weapons and a shift to more stabilizing nuclear weapons systems within Russia's remaining inventory of nuclear weapons[106] (PRIMARY OBJECTIVE)

(3) Promote the dismantling of the former USSR's inventory of chemical and biological weapons (PRIMARY OBJECTIVE)

(4) Prevent the proliferation of materials, technologies, or expertise necessary for the manufacture of chemical, biological, nuclear, or radiological weapons of mass destruction and/or delivery systems, especially missile delivery systems, from the states of the former Soviet Union[107] (PRIMARY OBJECTIVE)

    d. Promote an end to conflict and promote the peaceful resolution of disputes between the states of post-Soviet Central and East Europe, including Russia and the newly independent states of the former Soviet Union, and the peaceful resolution of domestic conflicts within these states, based upon such principles as mutual respect for sovereignty, political independence, and territorial integrity[108] (SECONDARY OBJECTIVE)

e. Promote an end to conflict and promote the peaceful resolution of disputes between the states of Southeast Europe, especially between those of the former Yugoslavia, as well as between Greece and Turkey, an end to domestic strife within the states of Southeastern Europe, the establishment of peace and stability throughout the sub-region, based upon such principles as mutual respect for sovereignty, political independence, territorial integrity, and the peaceful resolution of disputes, and the apprehension and prosecution of war criminals[109] (SECONDARY OBJECTIVE)

f. Support the establishment and/or maintenance of stable, democratically elected, limited governments, which respect the human rights and freedoms of all their citizen throughout the whole of Europe, especially Central and Eastern Europe, including Russia and the newly independent states of the former Soviet Union, the Balkan states, and Turkey[110] (TERTIARY OBJECTIVE)

g. Support the establishment and/or maintenance of stable, prosperous, privatized, free market oriented economies throughout the whole of Europe, especially Central and Eastern Europe, including Russia and the newly independent states of the former Soviet Union, the Balkan states, and Turkey (SECONDARY OBJECTIVE)

h. Support the European Union's efforts to promote the integration of a peaceful, prosperous, free market oriented, undivided Europe, based upon democratic principles, the rule of law, respect for human rights, and individual freedom[111] (SECONDARY OBJECTIVE)

i. Promote the integration of the peoples and states of Central and Eastern Europe, especially those of the Balkans, Turkey, the newly independent states of the former Soviet Union, and Russia into the whole of the European and trans-Atlantic communities[112] (TERTIARY OBJECTIVE)

j. Promote the expansion of trans-Atlantic trade, investment and economic interaction between the U.S. and the European Union,[113] as well as with newer market economies of Russia, the newly independent states of the former USSR, and those of Eastern Europe, within the context of open, stable free market economic environments which are conducive for trade, investment, and mutual prosperity (SECONDARY OBJECTIVE)

k. Ensure secure U.S. and global access to vital raw materials and natural resources located in Europe, such as Russia's energy resources[114] (PRIMARY OBJECTIVE)

l. Promote trans-Atlantic cooperation between the U.S. and its European partners and allies within the framework of the Atlantic Alliance in addressing various actual or potential national and transnational threats to U.S. interests and the global and regional challenges and opportunities that confront the U.S., the European powers, and the international community[115] (PRIMARY OBJECTIVE)

5. East Asia and the Pacific Basin
    a. Ensure and, if necessary defend the continued political independence and territorial integrity of those East Asian and Pacific Basin states with which the United States has specific mutual security guarantees (PRIMARY OBJECTIVE)
    b. Ensure that no state hostile to the United States or its interests establishes hegemony over East Asia, the Pacific basin, or portions thereof (PRIMARY OBJECTIVE)
        (1) Ensure that no state or elements hostile to the U.S. or its vital interests establishes hegemony over the areas adjacent to the sea lines of communication which pass from the Pacific, through the Strait of Malacca, into the Indian Ocean (PRIMARY OBJECTIVE)
        (2) Ensure that no state hostile to the U.S. or its interests establishes hegemony over the Sea of Japan, the East China Sea, or the Yellow Sea (PRIMARY OBJECTIVE)
    c. Promote a peaceful, non-nuclear, prosperous, economically integrated, democratic, and "reunified" Korean Peninsula[116] (SECONDARY OBJECTIVE)
        (1) Deter any possible threats or acts of aggression emanating from North Korea, the termination of all ties between the North Korean government and international terrorist elements, and the renunciation of all programs designed to develop nuclear, chemical, biological, or radiological weapons of mass destruction by the North Korean government (PRIMARY OBJECTIVE)
        (2) Prevent the proliferation of weapons of mass destruction and/or their delivery systems, especially missile technologies, materials, or expertise from North Korea (PRIMARY OBJECTIVE)
        (3) Promote reconciliation and economic integration of the Korean Peninsula (SECONDARY OBJECTIVE)
    d. Promotion of a stable, prosperous, politically and economically open, and ultimately democratic China that is more fully integrated into the global economic community and which actively contributes to international peace and stability[117] (SECONDARY OBJECTIVE)
        (1) Ensure against the Chinese launch of nuclear weapons against the United States or its allies and partners with which the United States has specific mutual security guarantees (PRIMARY OBJECTIVE)
        (2) Secure Chinese cooperation in preventing the spread of materials, technologies, or expertise necessary for the manufacture of chemical, biological, nuclear, or radiological weapons of mass destruction and/or their delivery systems, especially missile delivery systems (PRIMARY OBJECTIVE)
        (3) Secure Chinese cooperation in counter terrorism, and counter narcotics efforts (PRIMARY OBJECTIVE)
        (4) Encourage a peaceful resolution to disputes between Taiwan and the PRC within the framework of the U.S.'s "one China" policy (SECONDARY OBJECTIVE)

e. Promote the resolution of various territorial disputes which threaten peace and stability within East Asia and the Pacific basin (SECONDARY OBJECTIVE)
f. Promote the establishment/maintenance of stable democracies, based upon the rule of law, and respect for basic norms of human rights and individual freedom among the states of the region, with special emphasis on such troubled states as Burma, Indonesia, and East Timor[118] (TERTIARY OBJECTIVE)
g. Support the establishment and/or maintenance of stable, prosperous, privatized, free market oriented economies throughout East Asia and the Pacific Basin[119] (SECONDARY OBJECTIVE)
h. Promote the expansion of trans-Pacific trade, investment, and economic interaction between the U.S. and the states of the region within the context of open, stable, free market economic environments which are conducive for trade, investment, and mutual prosperity[120] (SECONDARY OBJECTIVE)
i. Ensure secure U.S. and global access to vital raw materials and natural resources located in East Asia and the Pacific Basin (PRIMARY OBJECTIVE)
j. Promote trans-Pacific cooperation between the U.S. and its allies and partners in East Asia and the Pacific basin, especially its traditional partners, such as Japan, South Korea, Australia, New Zealand, the Philippines, Thailand, and Singapore, in addressing the various actual or potential national and/or transnational threats to U.S. interests and the global and regional challenges and opportunities that confront the U.S., the regional states, and the international community[121] (PRIMARY OBJECTIVE)

6. Western Hemisphere
    a. Ensure and, if necessary defend the continued political independence and territorial integrity of those Western Hemispheric states with which the United States has specific mutual security guarantees (PRIMARY OBJECTIVE)
    b. Protect and defend the vital security interests of the United States within the Western Hemisphere (PRIMARY OBJECTIVE)
        (1) Ensure that no state hostile to the United States or its interests or "failed state" establishes itself along the border to the U.S., in the Caribbean sub-region, or in Central America (PRIMARY OBJECTIVE)
        (2) Ensure that no state hostile to the United States or its interests establishes hegemony over the South American continent or portions thereof (PRIMARY OBJECTIVE)
        (3) Ensure the security of the sea lines of communication in the waters around the Western Hemisphere (PRIMARY OBJECTIVE)
            (a) Ensure that no state or elements hostile to the U.S. or its interests establishes hegemony over the Panama Canal or the areas adjacent to the waters which approach the Canal (PRIMARY OBJECTIVE)
            (b) Ensure that no state or elements hostile to the U.S. or its vital interests establishes hegemony in

areas adjacent to the sea lines of communication which pass from the Atlantic, through the Strait of Magellan or around Cape Horn and through the Drake Passage, into the Pacific Ocean (PRIMARY OBJECTIVE)

c. Reinforce the restoration / consolidation / development of democratic norms and processes and respect for the principles of human rights, and individual freedom within the states of the Western Hemisphere[122] (TERTIARY OBJECTIVE)
    (1) Promote the rights of workers and minorities throughout the Hemisphere[123] (TERTIARY OBJECTIVE)
    (2) Promote civilian control over the military[124] (TERTIARY OBJECTIVE)

d. Promote the development of stable, prosperous, privatized, free market oriented economies throughout the Hemisphere and the integration of these economies into a hemispheric free trade area[125] (SECONDARY OBJECTIVE)
    (1) Reduce income disparities, facilitate educational opportunities, and promote the expansion of health services within the states of the Hemisphere[126] (TERTIARY OBJECTIVE)
    (2) Ensure environmentally protected, sustainable economic development[127] (SECONDARY OBJECTIVE)

e. Promote U.S. trade and investment within the Western Hemisphere[128] (SECONDARY OBJECTIVE)

f. Ensure secure U.S. and global access to vital raw materials and natural resources located in the Western Hemisphere (PRIMARY OBJECTIVE)

g. Promote the peaceful establishment of a democratic, free market oriented Cuba which observes the rule of law and respects the human rights of its citizens[129] (SECONDARY OBJECTIVE)
    (1) Promote the eventual political and economic integration of a democratic, free market based, post-communist Cuba into the larger Western Hemispheric community (SECONDARY OBJECTIVE)
    (2) Ensure the safe, orderly, and legal migration of peoples from Cuba[130] (TERTIARY OBJECTIVE)

h. Promote sustained Western Hemispheric and sub-regional (North American, Caribbean, Central American, Andean, and Southern Cone) stability through effective political, economic, and security cooperation between the United States and its hemispheric allies and partners in addressing various actual or potential threats to U.S. interests, as well as global and regional challenges which emanate from the Western Hemisphere[131] (PRIMARY OBJECTIVE)
    (1) Combat transnational hemispheric threats, particularly illicit drug crop production/drug trafficking; corruption; money-laundering; illicit weapons trafficking; illegal migrant trafficking/illegal immigration; terrorism (PRIMARY OBJECTIVE)

(2) Combat insurgent groups that seek to destabilize the states and various sub-regions within the Hemisphere (PRIMARY OBJECTIVE)
(3) Promote the peaceful resolution of disputes throughout the Hemisphere (PRIMARY OBJECTIVE)
(4) Protect the ecology and preserve/conserve the natural resources of the Western Hemisphere from further degradation or destruction (PRIMARY OBJECTIVE)
  (a) Prevent environmental degradation in territories and waters adjacent to the United States (PRIMARY OBJECTIVE)
  (b) Protect the natural resources and ecology of the Amazon basin (SECONDARY OBJECTIVE)

7. Middle East, Southwest, Central, and South Asia
  a. Ensure and, if necessary defend the continued political independence and territorial integrity of those Middle Eastern, Southwest Asian, Central Asian, and/or South Asian states with which the United States has specific mutual security guarantees (PRIMARY OBJECTIVE)
  b. Ensure that no state hostile to the United States or its vital interests establishes hegemony over the Mediterranean, Middle East, Southwest Asia, Central, or South Asia, or portions thereof (PRIMARY OBJECTIVE)
    (1) Ensure that no state or elements hostile to the U.S. or its vital interests establishes hegemony over the Persian Gulf sub-region (PRIMARY OBJECTIVE)
    (2) Ensure that no state or elements hostile to the U.S. or its vital interests establishes hegemony over areas adjacent to the sea lines of communication which pass from the Atlantic, through the Mediterranean Sea, the Suez Canal, the Red Sea, the Bab-el-Mandeb, and the Gulf of Aden into the Indian Ocean (PRIMARY OBJECTIVE)
  c. Promote stability and the peaceful resolution of disputes throughout the Middle East, Southwest, Central, and South Asia, predicated upon the promotion of U.S. interests and the well being of the U.S. regional partners and allies[132] (PRIMARY OBJECTIVE)
    (1) Promote a comprehensive and permanent peace in the Arab-Israeli sub-region, based upon the normalization of political and economic relations between Israel and all of her Arab neighbors (SECONDARY OBJECTIVE)
    (2) Promote the reduction of tensions and the peaceful resolution of conflicts between India and Pakistan (SECONDARY OBJECTIVE)
  d. Deter any threats to stability and/or the security of U.S. interests and the interests of the U.S.'s allies and partners in the Middle East, Southwest, Central, and South Asia (PRIMARY OBJECTIVE)
    (1) Deter Iraq from upsetting regional stability by threatening or engaging in military action directed against neighboring states, such as Kuwait, or its own people, such as the Kurdish, Shiite, or other minorities (PRIMARY OBJECTIVE)

e. Reduce the threat to regional and global stability and security by the threat posed by chemical, biological, nuclear and/or radiological weapons of mass destruction and their delivery systems, especially missile delivery systems [133] (PRIMARY OBJECTIVE)
  (1) Prevent Iraq, Iran, or Libya from acquiring the materials, technologies, or expertise necessary for the manufacture of chemical, biological, nuclear, and/or radiological weapons of mass destruction or their delivery systems, especially missile delivery systems[134] (PRIMARY OBJECTIVE)
  (2) Encourage India and Pakistan to reduce and, optimally, terminate their nuclear weapons programs and to join international nonproliferation efforts as non-nuclear weapons states[135] (PRIMARY OBJECTIVE)
f. Promote mutual cooperation concerning transnational issues collectively affecting many of the regional powers[136] (TERTIARY OBJECTIVE)
  (1) Promote educational expansion throughout the Middle East, Southwest, Central, and South Asia[137] (TERTIARY OBJECTIVE)
  (2) Promote regional cooperation with respect to trans-boundary environmental issues and disputes, such as pollution, water resources, etc., toward sustainable economic development throughout the Middle East, Southwest, Central, and South Asia[138] (TERTIARY OBJECTIVE)
g. Promote the establishment/consolidation of democratic processes and institutions, reinforced by respect for the rule of law and the human rights of all peoples, throughout the Middle East, Southwest, Central, and South Asia[139] (TERTIARY OBJECTIVE)
  (1) Eliminate discrimination and/or persecution directed against women and/or religious, ethnic, national, or other minority elements[140] (TERTIARY OBJECTIVE)
    (a) Promote the rights of workers and end the use of child labor or exploitive working conditions (TERTIARY OBJECTIVE)
    (b) Protect the human rights of refugees (TERTIARY OBJECTIVE)
  (2) Replace the current Iraqi regime with a democratic government that adheres to the rule of law and respects the human rights of its peoples[141] (SECONDARY OBJECTIVE)
  (3) Encourage the Iranian government to accelerate movement toward democracy and to cease violating the human rights of its peoples[142] (SECONDARY OBJECTIVE)
  (4) Encourage the rapid and complete restoration of democracy and civilian rule in Pakistan[143] (TERTIARY OBJECTIVE)
  (5) Encourage the establishment and consolidation of a democratic government which is based upon the rule of

law and respect for the human rights of all its peoples in post-Taliban Afghanistan (SECONDARY OBJECTIVE)
- h. Promote the development of stable, prosperous, privatized, free market oriented economies throughout the Middle East, Southwest, Central, and South Asia (SECONDARY OBJECTIVE)
- i. Promote the integration of the economies of the states of the Middle East, Southwest, Central, and South Asia into the global economic community[144] (SECONDARY OBJECTIVE)
- j. Promote trade between the U.S. and the states of the Middle East, Southwest, Central, and South Asia[145] (SECONDARY OBJECTIVE)
- k. Ensure secure U.S. and global access to Middle Eastern oil at stable prices, as well as access to other raw materials and natural resources located in the Middle East, Southwest Asia, Central Asia, and South Asia[146] (PRIMARY OBJECTIVE)
- l. Promote cooperation between the U.S. and its Middle Eastern, Southwest Asian, Central Asian, and South Asian partners and allies in addressing various actual or potential national and transnational threats to U.S. interests and the global and regional challenges and opportunities that confront the U.S., the regional powers, and the international community (PRIMARY OBJECTIVE)
    - (1) Prevent acts of terrorism both within and emanating from the Middle East, Southwest, Central, and South Asia and eliminate terrorist activities and organizations which are based in these areas[147] (PRIMARY OBJECTIVE)
        - (a) Persuade such states as Iran, Libya, and Iraq to immediately terminate all forms of support for terrorism or terrorist organizations and their activities (PRIMARY OBJECTIVE)
        - (b) Support and encourage efforts by other regional states, such as Afghanistan, Pakistan, Syria, the Palestinian authorities, etc., to prevent terrorist organizations from using their territory as a refuge and base of operations from which to commit acts of terrorism regionally and globally (PRIMARY OBJECTIVE)
    - (2) Stem the flow of illegal drugs from these areas, particularly from South Asia, especially Afghanistan[148] (PRIMARY OBJECTIVE)

8. Sub-Saharan Africa
   - a. Ensure and, if necessary defend the continued political independence and territorial integrity of those Sub-Saharan states with which the United States has specific mutual security guarantees (PRIMARY OBJECTIVE)
   - b. Ensure that no state or elements hostile to the United States or its vital interests establish itself in those areas of Sub-Saharan Africa containing oil or other natural resources or raw materials vital to the United States or threaten the security of the sea lines of communication which pass around the Cape of Good Hope (PRIMARY OBJECTIVE)
   - c. Prevent regional conflict and instability within and among African states[149] (SECONDARY OBJECTIVE)

d. Reduce weapons proliferation throughout Sub-Saharan Africa[150] (PRIMARY OBJECTIVE)
    (1) Reduce the flow of conventional arms into Africa (QUATERNARY OBJECTIVE)
    (2) Prevent African states from acquiring weapons of mass destruction or their delivery systems, especially missile technologies (PRIMARY OBJECTIVE)
e. Prevent human rights violations and acts of genocide in Sub-Saharan Africa[151] (TERTIARY OBJECTIVE)
f. Promote the establishment of stable, democratic governments, based upon the rule of law and respect for the principles of human rights throughout Sub-Saharan Africa[152] (TERTIARY OBJECTIVE)
g. Promote the development of stable, prosperous, privatized, free-market economies throughout Sub-Saharan Africa[153] (SECONDARY OBJECTIVE)
    (1) Promote economic reforms, debt reduction, infrastructure development, and agricultural development throughout much of Africa (SECONDARY OBJECTIVE)
    (2) Promote the integration of Sub-Saharan African economies into the global economic community (TERTIARY OBJECTIVE)
h. Promote the expansion of U.S. trade with the economies of Sub-Saharan Africa[154] (SECONDARY OBJECTIVE)
i. Ensure secure U.S. and global access to raw materials and natural resources located in Sub-Saharan Africa (PRIMARY OBJECTIVE)
j. Promote cooperation between the U.S. and the states of Sub-Saharan Africa in addressing various actual or potential national and transnational threats to U.S. interests and the global and regional challenges and opportunities that confront the U.S., the regional powers, and the international community[155] (PRIMARY OBJECTIVE)
    (1) Prevent acts of terrorism both within and emanating from the Sub-Saharan Africa and eliminate terrorist activities and organizations which are based in this area (PRIMARY OBJECTIVE)
    (2) Slow, halt, and, and optimally reverse the spread to HIV/AIDS and other highly infectious diseases from Sub-Saharan Africa (PRIMARY OBJECTIVE)
    (3) Stop drug trafficking from Sub-Saharan Africa (PRIMARY OBJECTIVE)
    (4) Stop environmental degradation within Sub-Saharan Africa (SECONDARY OBJECTIVE)
    (5) Control, and optimally stop the trafficking of people, and other international criminal activities in Sub-Saharan Africa (QUATERNARY OBJECTIVE)
    (6) Stop threats to endangered species within Sub-Saharan Africa (QUATERNARY OBJECTIVE)

9. Antarctica
    a. Ensure the continued demilitarized, peaceful, international control over Antarctica (PRIMARY OBJECTIVE)

b. Prevent environmental degradation of the Antarctic continent and surrounding areas (PRIMARY OBJECTIVE)

In positing this outline of some of the United States' contemporary national objectives, it is recognized that some analysts and policy makers will, undoubtedly, disagree with the delineation and/or the hierarchical prioritization of the individual national objectives. Indeed, informed discussion geared toward refining and prioritizing U.S. national objectives can only serve to help clarify America's conception of its foreign policy goals. Few, if any, Americans, however, would disagree with the contention that clarity concerning the national objectives is a necessary prerequisite for an effective foreign policy.

Notwithstanding efforts to refine, and optimally arrive at a consensus, concerning the delineation and order of prioritization among the national objectives, however, vexing dilemmas will often emerge as policy makers attempt to develop strategies, using a variety of instruments of policy, in pursuit of these various objectives. For example, central to the implementation of many of the primary national objectives of the United States as outlined above is the imperative that U.S. policy makers clearly delineate the geographic areas considered to be vital to the U.S.'s immediate security interests. As reviewed earlier in this chapter, during the initial century and a quarter following independence, various U.S. administrations defined America's de-facto, primary geographic zone of U.S. foreign policy concern (those areas vital to the security interests of the United States) as the geographic areas contiguous to the United States. Gradually, that primary zone of foreign policy concern was expanded to include the entire Western Hemisphere. Similarly, as the U.S. enters the 21st Century, policy makers must determine which regions are vital to the U.S.'s immediate security interests, and, thus, what constitutes the contemporary, de-facto, primary zone of foreign policy concern. Today, as has been the case throughout most of the 20th Century, America's primary focus must be global, and not just confined to the Western Hemisphere.

While the list of vital geographic areas would obviously be a subject for considerable discussion, it would be based, in part, on the U.S.'s vital needs for certain raw materials and natural resources which emanate from sources abroad, as well as for unimpeded access through strategic waterways which are, in turn, critical for access to these vital overseas assets. Arguably, the United States' contemporary, primary zone of foreign policy concern would include the entire Western Hemisphere, as well as the NATO member states, Russia, the Caucasus Mountain and Caspian Sea region, Morocco, Egypt, Yemen, the Persian Gulf region, the island of Diego Garcia in the Indian Ocean, Australia, Singapore, New Zealand, Japan, South Korea, key islands in the Pacific, and parts of Africa. While perhaps some would argue that other countries and geographic areas should be added to the list, while others might argue for the deletion of some of the countries and areas proposed, certainly the list of areas considered vital to the immediate security interests of the United States would not include all areas of the world.

Once the scope of the contemporary American zone of primary foreign policy concern has been determined, U.S. policy makers must carefully assess the degree to which there is presently or, in the future, likely to be a threat to continued American access to these strategically vital regions and their resources. The threat may be from another state or coalition of states that seek to project influence throughout one or several of these areas. In today's world, however, the threat is equally, if not more likely to emanate from domestic elements within these regions themselves, or from transnational movements and forces based within these regions or in other parts of the globe, and which, for political, ideological, or religious reasons, seek to destabilize areas of primary concern to the United States, as well as, perhaps even directly threaten the United States itself. In any case, it is necessary for policy makers to not only delineate the areas vital to American security interests, but also to assess actual and anticipate potential threats, which may take a variety of forms, to these areas of primary U.S. foreign policy concern.

Once this is accomplished and is subject to periodic review, policy makers can then formulate strategies, utilizing various instruments of policy, to pursue the primary, secondary, tertiary, and quaternary national objectives, usually in that order of priority, within these regions of primary foreign policy concern. For example, in those contexts where hostile national, coalition, or transnational threats have been identified, the United States will undoubtedly, formally or informally, conclude mutual security arrangements and military assistance programs with the U.S.'s interested allies and partners, based upon a community of interest in regional security, in response to the actual or potential threat. Realistically, however, controversies will periodically erupt among allies and partners concerning the most appropriate defense strategy and the relative apportionment of the defense burden to be shared by the various powers. But, if the threat is clear, the disruptive impact of such controversies will probably be temporary and an equitable, effective defense strategy can be formulated and maintained over time. Policy makers, however, must remember that military instruments are only one of the tools of foreign policy and may not always be the most appropriate in response to all threats. For those strategies within which military instruments are primary, however, it is incumbent upon political leaders to ensure that the United States has sufficient military power and national resolve to perform what must be clearly defined missions in pursuit of primary national objectives.

Beyond these considerations, there are other complications which may arise from what are often "entangling alliances". For example, the United States has periodically been confronted with situations in which its allies and partners clash over issues unique to their bilateral relationships. Moreover, U.S. allies and partners may undertake dangerous political initiatives and even military operations that, though perhaps vital to the ally or partner's national interests, are quite marginal to U.S. security interests. Even if the U.S.'s ally or partner does not attempt to pressure the U.S. into supporting these initiatives, the situation may escalate to a point where the U.S. must intervene in order to protect its own security interests. Obviously, there are no simple formulas for dealing with situations such as these and each must be assessed on an individual basis. In general, however, strict neutrality, while counseling in favor of a peaceful resolution of disputes is probably the best way to minimize the costs to American interests in situations involving conflicts between America's allies and partners. In situations involving independent policy initiatives by allies and partners, it is probably best for the United States to clarify the degree to which the U.S. supports the initiative and the limits of that support to its ally or partner. Unfortunately, irrespective of how situations like these are managed, they are, almost inevitably, both dangerous and damaging to U.S. security interests.

Perhaps an even more vexing dilemma for policy makers as they attempt to secure the national objectives in the primary zone of foreign policy concern emanates from those situations in which the threats to stability originate from transnational or indigenous, militant, political, ideological, or religious elements based outside or within the region. While recognizing that each case possesses its own unique characteristics and, consequently, must be treated individually, in these types of situations which capitalize on domestic poverty and discontent, military assistance and cooperation may be important, but perhaps even more important is the application of other instruments of policy, especially socio-economic, educational assistance designed to help, insofar as possible, to provide economic opportunities and lift the local standard of living. It is important to demonstrate to the peoples of these regions of primary concern to the United States, not just to the local elites, that the U.S. is genuinely committed to a mutually beneficial partnership. In return for commercial and political ties aimed at protecting U.S. security interests and/or profitable, but not exploitive economic relations between the U.S. and the states of these areas, the peoples of these regions, not just those associated with U.S. companies operating in the area, can expect a gradual, but increasingly visible improvement in their living standards as a result of their partnership with the United States. Indeed, so that these expectations can be met, the American people must also be made aware of the importance of maintaining these mutually beneficial partnerships and, hence, provide sustained priority to the allocation of foreign assistance resources to those less developed areas deemed vital to U.S. security.

Regimes controlling portions of the zone of primary U.S. foreign policy concern which are clearly anti-democratic and/or which grossly violate the human rights of their citizenry endanger, not only endanger regional stability, they also endanger continued secure U.S. access to these regions and their vital resources. In vexing situations such as these, the U.S. should clearly, though as non-abrasively as possible, indicate that the U.S. government not only deplores such anti-democratic policies and human rights violations, policies and violations such as these can only, at most, provide the offending regime with temporary, immediate security. Lasting stability and security can only come by promoting democratic principles and enforcing, not violating the human rights of peoples. Beyond this, however, within its zone of primary foreign policy concern, the United States should generally avoid involvement in the internal political affairs of its allies and partners. Optimally, dilemmas, such as these, would not present themselves within the primary zone of foreign policy concern for policy makers and the U.S. could pursue and successfully attain its primary, secondary, tertiary, and quaternary objectives simultaneously. But in situations where America's pursuit of its political interests might jeopardize its immediate security interests, in those regions that are vital to the U.S.'s immediate security interests, primary objectives, designed to support the United States' immediate security, must take priority over tertiary objectives, pursued in support of the U.S.'s political interests and designed to promote the long-range security of the entire international community.

Should a genuinely popular uprising challenge a non-democratic partner regime and/or one which is oblivious to, or which violates the human rights of its citizenry, from the outset, the U.S. must make it clear that it regards this as an internal matter and will maintain a strictly neutral stance throughout the crisis. Should the regime be overthrown, the U.S. should immediately move to normalize relations with the new authorities and make it clear to these authorities, as well as the people of the area, that the United States intends to continue its policy of mutually beneficial partnership. American military intervention should be ordered only to directly protect vital U.S. property and investments, as well as access to vital materials, and then only when the local authorities have proven incapable of offering such protection to U.S. security interests. The threat of U.S. military intervention may also have to be used in concert with diplomatic efforts to prevent other external powers from intervening within what is the primary zone of U.S. foreign policy concern. In any case, if at all avoidable, American forces must not be drawn into a local civil war. Such interventions, themselves, often serve as focal points for anti-American expressions that, obviously, are not in the U.S. interest.

Finally, in addition to its efforts to contribute to stability and to diffuse domestic unrest within areas vital to America's immediate security interests, the United States must also respond to increasingly immediate threats to its regionally oriented security interests, access to vital areas and their resources, as well as to the broader stability of these regions, and, indeed, to U.S. security interests generally, emanating from transnational elements often operating from bases within or outside the primary zone of U.S. foreign policy concern. In addressing this type of threat, the United States must, optimally in concert with its allies and partners, but, if necessary, unilaterally, move to effectively neutralize these transnational elements by applying a mix of policy instruments designed to negate the destabilizing activities of these groups and to deny these elements their havens in what are often failed or failing states. Arguably, at the dawn of the 21st Century, threats emanating from extremist, militant, transnational, terrorist elements pose as great a threat to U.S. security interests, as well as the broader security interests of the entire international community, as traditional threats of interstate invasion and traditional forms of warfare.

Throughout much of the international community, however, American security interests will be marginal or even non-existent. In its focus on those areas that lie outside the U.S.'s zone of primary foreign policy concern, the United States has greater opportunities to formulate policies designed to exclusively promote its secondary, tertiary, and quaternary objectives, relatively unencumbered by immediate, vital security concerns. In these areas, there should be no immediate need for the United States to become entangled in binding security partnerships with any particular states or regimes. Hence, the U.S. should feel relatively unconstrained in speaking out boldly against regimes that violate the political ideals underpinning American foreign policy. In addition, insofar as possible, without jeopardizing priority commitments to facilitate priority socio-economic and educational development policies in the primary zone of U.S. foreign policy concern, the United States should respond positively to invitations from local authorities to help promote the welfare of the peoples and economies of the region through U.S. governmental and/or private philanthropic efforts. Indeed, such policies may complement U.S. efforts to advance its non-essential commercial interests by promoting American trade and investment with these areas. But, in pursuing these policies, the U.S. should avoid becoming politically entangled with individual governments in states that are outside the United States' primary zone of concern and where the U.S.'s immediate security interests are marginal or absent altogether.

Conclusion

These, then, are just a few of the dilemmas associated with crafting and implementing effective foreign policy strategies designed to attain national objectives. The world of the 21st Century is one in which the variety of traditional and nontraditional threats to American security interests and those of the other members of the international community appear to be ever-increasing in scope, magnitude, and complexity. These threats emanate from a wide variety of national and transnational sources, and take an equally wide variety of forms. It is imperative that the United States successfully address these various contemporary threats and defend its globally defined security interests. This can only be done by clearly defining the national security interests and adopting realistic, priority, national security oriented objectives which will successfully protect and defend U.S. territory, American citizens and their property, U.S. allies and partners with which the United States has security agreements, geographic regions vital to American security needs, and reliable access to those areas and their resources. In doing so, however, the United States must never lose sight of its political and commercial interests which, while assuming a lesser level of immediate importance than the protection of the U.S.'s vital security interests, are, nonetheless, extremely important in themselves since they reflect some of the most fundamental values and principles that underpin the identity of the American republic. Indeed, the eventual global attainment of America's commercial and political interests is critical to the long-term security and prosperity, not just the of United States, but of the entire international community. Thus, through domestic socio-economic and political strength which will, in turn, serve as an example to all peoples, vigilance in defense of American security requirements, and adherence to principles and ideals which serve as the bedrock of American foreign policy, the United States will remain an ever-brighter beacon for freedom, democracy, and prosperity for all of mankind throughout the future, just as it has over the past two and a quarter centuries.

Notes

[1] The opinions, conclusions, and/or recommendations expressed or implied within this chapter are solely those of the author and do not necessarily represent the views of Air University, the United States Air Force, the Department of Defense, or any other U.S. government agency.

[2] An earlier version of this section, "Principles and National Interests", was printed as "National Purposes and Interests of the United States" by the Air War College in *National Security Policy Studies*, 1987 and 1988, pp. 33-35.

[3] Current, Williams, & Freidel, 1965, pp. 880-883.

[4] Current, Williams, & Freidel, 1965, pp. 883-895.

[5] DeConde, 1963, pp. 664-667; Bailey, 1958, p. 598.

[6] DeConde, 1963, pp. 600; Bailey, 1958, pp. 728-729.

[7] National interests may be seen as relatively permanent goals that a state seeks over a prolonged period to time.

[8] National objectives refers to specific and "fundamental aims, goals, or purposes of a nation – as opposed to the means for seeking these ends – toward which a policy is directed and efforts and resources of the nation are applied". Joint Chiefs of Staff, U.S. Department of Defense, 1989, p. 244. National objectives are designed to support and promote the national interests within the context of challenges and opportunities that prevail within international arena at a given moment in history. Consequently, unlike the relatively permanent national interests, the delineation of national objectives and the priority hierarchy among the various, individual objectives themselves, is constantly subject to modification and revision, depending upon the domestic and international circumstances of the moment.

[9] Gilbert, 1961, pp. 111-114, 130-134; Ekirch, 1966, p. 9.

[10] DeConde, 1963, pp. 49-61; Bemis, 1965, pp. 46-107.

[11] Ekirch, 1966, pp. 14-15; DeConde, 1963, pp. 74-83; Bemis, 1965, pp. 126-137.

[12] Ekirch, 1966, pp. 15-16; DeConde, 1963, pp. 97-113; Bemis, 1965, pp. 159-17; Pratt, 1949; Coles, 1965; Hickey, 1989.

[13] DeConde, 1963, pp. 113-116; Bemis, 1965, pp. 171-176.

[14] Ekirch, 1966, pp. 16-20; DeConde, 1963, pp. 119-143; Bemis, 1965, pp. 180-212, 384-396; Perkins, 1941.

[15] Ekirch, 1966, pp. 20-21, 24-26, 37-38; Gilbert, 1961, pp. 17, 55-56; Field, 1969, pp. 5, 9, 22, 26.

[16] Ekirch 1966, pp. 40-53.

[17] Ekirch, 1966, pp. 40-53.

[18] Ekirch, 1966, pp. 53-60; DeConde, 1963, pp. 162-205; Bemis, 1965, pp. 215-244, 267-283; Singletary, 1960; Bauer, 1974.

[19] Ekirch, 1966, pp. 53-63; DeConde, 1963, pp. 207-213; 219-225; Bemis, 1965, pp. 244-252, 292-298, 313-319.

[20] DeConde, 1963, pp 242-260; Bemis, 1965, pp. 364-383; Ekirch, 1966, pp. 63-65; Jordan and Pratt, 1931; Owsley, 1959; Hattaway and Jones, 1983; Hensel, 1989.

[21] Prucha, 1969; Utley, 1967; Utley, 1973.

[22] DeConde, 1963, pp. 271-274; Bemis, 1965, pp. 396-399.

[23] Ekirch, 1966, pp. 79-80, 98-99; DeConde, 1963, pp. 263-271, 284-288, 292-300, 330-336; Bemis, 1965, pp. 388-397, 400-404, 415-423, 432-441.

[24] Ekirch, 1966, pp. 61-87.

[25] Ekirch, 1966, pp. 92; DeConde, 1963, pp. 317-330, 339-356; Bemis, 1965, pp. 442-462; Trask, 1981.

[26] Ekirch, 1966, pp. 92-99; DeConde, 1963, pp. 376-383; Bemis, 1965, pp. 503-538; McCullough, 1977.
[27] Gilbert, 1961, pp. 36-52, 68, 72, 111-134; Ekirch, 1966, pp. 1-8, 12-14; Field, 1969, pp. 8, 18.
[28] Gilbert, 1961, pp. 36-52, 68, 72, 111-134; Ekirch, 1966, pp. 1-8, 12-14; Field, 1969, pp. 8, 18, 26.
[29] Gilbert, 1961, pp. 51-52, 55-56, 68-69; Ekirch, 1966, pp. 24-26, 37-38; Field, 1969, pp. 9, 18, 22, 26.
[30] Bemis, 1965, pp. 111-125, 138-158, 176-179, 284-308, 320-363, 479-502, 571-589; Ekirch, 1966, p. 14; Field, 1969, pp. 27-68, 104-113, 245-261, 283-284.
[31] Field, 1969, pp. 121-126, 214-245; Ekirch, 1966, pp. 18, 27-31, 33, 35-39.
[32] Field, 1969, pp. 68-103, 176-206, 262-301, 345-373, 389-435, 443.
[33] Bemis, 1965, pp. 590-649; DeConde, 1963, pp. 440-468; Ekirch, 1966, pp. 110-119.
[34] Osgood, 1953, p. 303.
[35] Ekirch, 1966, pp. 119-122; Bemis, 1965, pp. 650-666; DeConde, 1963, pp. 468-487.
[36] DeConde, 1963, pp. 491-565; Bemis, 1965, pp. 666-834; Ekirch, 1966, pp. 124-137.
[37] DeConde, 1963, pp. 565-610; Bemis, 1965, pp. 835-867; Ekirch, 1966, pp. 137-173.
[38] Bemis, 1965, pp. 868-906; DeConde, 1963, pp. 614-650; Ekirch, 1966, pp. 174-197; Feis, 1965; Feis, 1957; Feis, 1960; Feis, 1967.
[39] DeConde, 1963, pp. 653-685; Bemis, 1965, pp. 907-935; Ekirch, 1966, pp. 174-197; Gardner, Schlessinger, & Morgenthau, 1970; Gaddis, 1990; Dunbabin, 1994; Ulam 1971.
[40] DeConde, 1963, pp. 689-887; Bemis, 1965, pp. 907-935; Ekirch, 1966, pp. 174-197; Gaddis, 1990; Dunbabin, 1994; Ulam, 1971.
[41] Reagan, 1988, p. 3.
[42] Reagan, 1988, pp. 3-5.
[43] Lenczowski, 1980, pp. 201, 283-286, 336-340, 343, 367, 370-371, 480-488, 526-536, 593, 797-798.
[44] Lenczowski, 1980, p. 527.
[45] *A National Security Strategy for a Global Age*, published in December 2000, constituted the final, definitive statement of American foreign policy by President Clinton and his administration. The analytical framework utilized in this chapter, however, does not complete coincide with the framework of analysis used by the Clinton administration in its December, 2000 description of American national security policy. For example, while employing the analytical terms "interests" and "objectives", the Clinton administration did not consistently apply them throughout the entire document. Moreover, the document also utilized other terms, such as "values", "goals", "purposes", and "elements", which have not been used in this chapter. Finally, the document often did not clearly differentiate between "objectives" and the component parts of the "national security strategy". Hence, while the Clinton administration's statement provided the basic ingredients for the author's interpretation of what constitutes contemporary American interests and objectives, the material presented in this chapter represents the author's own application of these analytical terms and, as such, does not completely coincide with either the framework of analysis used by the Clinton administration, nor the precise application of that framework as expressed in *A National Security Strategy for a Global Age*. Clinton, 2000.
[46] "Vital interests" were defined by the Clinton administration as "those directly connected to the survival, safety, and vitality of our nation. Among these are the physical security of our territory and that of our allies, the safety of our citizens both at home and abroad, protection against WMD proliferation, the economic wellbeing of our society, and the

protection of our critical infrastructures . . . from disruption intended to cripple their operation". Clinton, 2000, p. 4.

[47] The Clinton administration defined the promotion of "shared prosperity" (Clinton, 2000, p. 31) as "important national interests", consisting of those interests which affect "our national well being or that of the world in which we live. Principally, this may include developments in regions where America holds a significant economic or political stake, issues with significant global environmental impact, infrastructure disruptions that destabilize but do not cripple smooth economic activity, and crises that could cause destabilizing economic turmoil or humanitarian movement". Clinton, 2000, p. 4.

[48] Commenting further on this "third category" of American national interests, the Clinton administration observed, "Since the founding of the republic, our actions as a nation have always been guided by our belief that individuals should control their own destinies: economically, politically, and spiritually. Our core values - - political and economic freedom, respect for human rights, and the rule of law - - support this belief, guiding the conduct of our government at home as well as in its dealing with others outside our borders". Clinton, 2000, pp. 4, 35.

[49] Clinton, 2000, pp. 1, 3-7, 9-12, 22, 24, 26, 31, 35-37, 67.

[50] The organizational divisions used in this study are similar, though not identical to those utilized by the Clinton administration in its December 2000 statement describing the national security policy of the United States. In Chapter I of its statement, entitled, "Fundamentals of the Strategy", the Clinton Administration divided the national security strategy of "engagement" into three "strategic concepts", sub-divided, in turn, into a series of "elements" which "support the three strategic concepts for engagement". These "strategic concepts" and "elements" were defined as: (1) "shaping the international environment", sub-divided, in turn, into (a) "adapting our alliances and encouraging the reorientation of other states, including former adversaries", (b) "encouraging democratization, open markets, free trade, and sustainable development", and (c) "preventing conflict"; (2) "responding to threats and crises", sub-divided, in turn, into (a) "countering potential regional aggressors", (b) "confronting new threats", and "steering international peace and stability operations"; and (3) "preparing for an uncertain future". Clinton, 2000, pp. 1, 2, 3. Chapter II of the document, entitled "Implementing the Strategy" discusses American national security strategy from a global perspective, whereas, Chapter III, entitled "Integrated Regional Approaches" examines U.S. national security strategy from a regional perspective. Clinton, 2000.

[51] The Commission on America's National Interests, co-chaired by Robert Ellsworth, Andrew Goodpaster, and Rita Hauser, attempted a similar prioritization in *America's National Interests*, 2000. The Executive Directors of the commission were Graham Allison, Dimitri Simes, and James Thomson, and the members included Richard Armitage, Robert Blackwell, David Gergen, Bob Graham, Geoffrey Kemp, Paul Krugman, John McCain, Sam Nunn, Condoleezza Rice, Brent Scowcroft, among others. The commission divided the U.S. national interests into four categories: vital, extremely important, important, and less important or secondary. Summarizing its findings, the commission stated that "vital U.S. national interests are to: 1. Prevent, deter, and reduce the threat of nuclear, biological, and chemical attacks on the United States or its military forces abroad; 2. Ensure US allies' survival and their active cooperation with the US in shaping an international systems in which we can thrive; 3. Prevent the emergence of hostile major power or failed states on US borders; 4. Ensure the viability and stability of major global systems (trade, financial markets, supplies of energy, and the environment); and 5. Establish productive relations, consistent with American national interests, with nations that could become strategic

adversaries, China and Russia". "Extremely important US national interests are to: 1. Prevent, deter, and reduce the threat of the use of nuclear, biological, or chemical weapons anywhere; 2. Prevent the regional proliferation of WMD and delivery systems; 3. Promote the acceptance of international rules of law and mechanisms for resolving or managing disputes peacefully; 4. Prevent the emergence of a regional hegemon in important regions, especially the Persian Gulf; 5. Promote the well being of US allies and friends and protect them from external aggression; 6. Promote democracy, prosperity, and stability in the Western Hemisphere; 7. Prevent, manage, and, if possible at reasonable cost, end major conflicts in important geographic regions; 8. Maintain a lead in key military-related and other strategic technologies, particularly information systems; 9. Prevent massive, uncontrolled immigration across US borders; 10. Suppress terrorism (especially state-sponsored terrorism), transnational crime, and drug trafficking; and 11. Prevent genocide." "Important US national interests are to 1. Discourage massive human rights violations in foreign countries; 2. Promote pluralism, freedom, and democracy in strategically important states as much as feasible without destabilization; 3. Prevent and, if possible at low cost, end conflicts in strategically less significant geographic regions; 4. Protect the lives and well being of American citizens who are targeted or taken hostage by terrorist organizations; 5. Reduce the economic gap between rich and poor nations; 6. Prevent the nationalization of US-owned assets abroad; 7. Boost the domestic output of key strategic industries and sectors; 8. Maintain an edge in the international distribution of information to ensure that American values continue to positively influence cultures of foreign nations; 9. Promote international environmental policies consistent with long-term ecological requirements; and 10. Maximize US GNP growth from international trade and investment." Finally, the Commission stated that "less important or secondary US national interests include: 1. Balancing bilateral trade deficits; 2. Enlarging democracy everywhere for its own sake; 3. Preserving the territorial integrity or particular political constitution of other states everywhere; and 4. Enhancing exports of specific economic sectors". Commission on America's National Interests, 2000, pp. 5-9 The commission's specific delineation of its categories of national interests, cited above, roughly coincides to what are defined in this study as "national objectives".

[52] The four prioritization categories utilized in this study roughly coincide with those used by the Commission on America's National Interests, 2000, pp. 5-8.

[53] See Clinton, 2000, pp. 2, 3, 4, 6, 9, 11, 12, 13, 14, 15, 45, 49, 50, 51, 58, 59, 60.

[54] As stated by the Clinton administration in December 2000, "constrain inventories of dangerous weapons, reduce incentives and opportunities to initiate an attack, reduce mutual suspicions that arise from and spur on armaments competition, and help provide the assurance of security necessary to strengthen cooperative relationships and direct resources to safer, more productive endeavors." Clinton, 2000, p. 11. See also, Clinton, 2000, p. 12.

[55] See Clinton, 2000, pp. 14, 34.

[56] In its statement of national security policy, the Clinton administration "seeks to prevent destabilizing buildups of conventional arms and to limit access to sensitive technical information, equipment, and technologies". Clinton, 2000, p. 15. See also Clinton, 2000, p. 14.

[57] Discussing this, the Clinton administration observed that "inexpensive, widely available, and easy to use, these weapons exacerbate regional conflicts, expand casualties, increase crime, and hinder economic development. They can jeopardize the safety of peacekeepers, potentially putting U.S. Forces at risk". Clinton, 2000, p. 15. See also Clinton, 2000, p. 2.

[58] See Clinton, 2000, pp. 11, 16.

[59] Discussing this point, the Clinton administration observed, "Our nuclear deterrent posture is one example of how U.S. military capabilities are used effectively to deter aggression and coercion against U.S. interests. Nuclear weapons serve as a guarantor of our security commitments to allies and a disincentive to those who would contemplate developing or otherwise acquiring their own WMD (weapons of mass destruction) capability. Those who threaten the United States or its allies with WMD should have no doubt that any such attack would meet an overwhelming and devastating response. Our military planning for the possible employment of U.S. strategic weapons is focused on deterring a nuclear war and its emphasizes the survivability of our nuclear systems, infrastructure, and command, control, and communications systems necessary to endure a preemptive attack yet still deliver an overwhelming response. Another key element of the U.S. nuclear deterrent strategy is ensuring the National Command Authorities have a survivable and endurable command, control, and communications capability through which to execute the mission and direct nuclear forces during all phases of a nuclear war. The United States will continue to maintain a robust triad of strategic nuclear forces sufficient to deter any potential adversaries who may have or seek access to nuclear forces – to convince them that seeking a nuclear advantage or resorting to nuclear weapons would be futile". Clinton, 2000, p. 17.
[60] Clinton, 2000, p. 17.
[61] Concerning this point, the Clinton administration stated, "domestically, we seek to stop terrorists before they act, and eliminate their support networks and financing. Overseas, we seek to eliminate terrorist sanctuaries; counter state and non-governmental support for terrorism; help other governments improve their physical and political counter terrorism, and consequence management efforts; tighten embassy and military facility security; and protect U.S. citizens living and traveling abroad". Clinton, 2000, pp. 22, 23.
[62] See Clinton, 2000, pp. 6, 26.
[63] See Clinton, 2000, pp. 16, 25, 26.
[64] See Clinton, 2000, pp. 6, 25, 26.
[65] See Clinton, 2000, pp. 25, 26.
[66] See Clinton, 2000, p. 26.
[67] See Clinton, 2000, pp. 2, 9, 18.
[68] See Clinton, 2000, p. 26.
[69] See Clinton, 2000, pp. 18, 26, 27.
[70] See Clinton, 2000, p. 27.
[71] See Clinton, 2000, p. 19.
[72] See Clinton, 2000, p. 19.
[73] Commenting on this, President Clinton observed, "Our natural security must be seen as part of our national security". Amplifying upon this point, the December 2000 statement regarding U.S. national security policy stated, "Decisions today regarding the environment and natural resources can affect our security for generations. Environmental threats do not heed national borders; environmental perils overseas and environmental crime pose long-term dangers to U.S. security and well-being. Natural resource scarcities can trigger and exacerbate conflict, and phenomena such as climate change, toxic pollution, ocean dumping, and ozone depletion directly threaten the health and well-being of Americans and all other individuals on Earth". Hence, "responding firmly to environmental threats remains a part of mainstream American foreign policy". Clinton, 2000, p. 18.
[74] Commenting on this point, the Clinton administration stated that "the United States must be able to respond at home and abroad to the full spectrum of threats and crises that may arise". Clinton, p. 19. Indeed, the U.S. must "ensure that we can prevail on the battlefield

despite the threatened or actual use of NBC (nuclear, chemical, and/or biological) weapons by adversaries". Clinton, 2000, p. 18.

[75] "Protecting the homeland" was emphasized in the Clinton administration's statement of national security policy. It stated, "Emerging threats to our homeland by both state and non-state actors may be more likely in the future as our potential adversaries strike against vulnerable civilian targets in the United States to avoid direct confrontation with our military forces. Such acts represent a new dimension of asymmetric threats to our national security". Consequently, "the United States has embarked on a comprehensive strategy to prevent, deter, disrupt and when necessary, effectively respond to the myriad of threats to our homeland that we will face". Clinton, 2000, p. 20.

[76] The Clinton administration stated that it was "committed to the development of a limited National Missile Defense (NMD) system designed to counter the emerging ballistic missile threat from states that threaten international peace and security". The Clinton administration further observed that, "missile defense policy must take into account important arms control and nuclear nonproliferation objectives". Hence, it emphasized its "goal of adapting the ABM (Anti-Ballistic Missile) Treaty (with Russia) to permit the deployment of a limited NMD that would not undermine strategic stability". Clinton, 2000, pp. 12, 20, 21.

[77] Discussing this point, the Clinton administration emphasized the need to "preserve the capability to govern, lead, and perform essential functions and services to meet essential defense and civilian needs". It specifically emphasized the requirement to "be prepared to respond effectively at home and abroad to protect lives and property, mobilize personnel, resources, and capabilities necessary to effectively handle the emergency, and ensure the survival or our institutions and infrastructures". Clinton, 2000, p. 25.

[78] "Defending the United States against weapons of mass destruction" was deemed a "top national security priority" by the Clinton administration. In addition, the administration emphasized that "concerted efforts have been undertaken to mitigate the consequences of a WMD attack. The Federal Government, in coordination with state and local authorities, will respond rapidly and decisively to any terrorist incident in the United States involving WMD". Clinton, 2000, p. 23.

[79] See Clinton, 2000, pp. 2, 3, 4, 7, 9, 24.

[80] Elaborating on this point, the Clinton Administration stated that the United States must be able to "accurately attribute the source of attacks against the United States or its citizens, ... respond effectively and decisively to protect our national interests", and bring "its perpetrators to justice". The administration went on to maintain that, "As long as terrorists continue to target American citizens, we reserve the right to act in self-defense by striking at their bases and those who sponsor, assist, or even actively support them". Clinton, 2000, pp. 17, 22, 23. See also Clinton, 2000, pp. 3, 6, 18.

[81] Commenting on this objective, the Clinton administration stated that the United States "must maintain the ability to rapidly defeat initial enemy advances short of the enemy's objectives in two theaters, in close succession. We must maintain this ability to ensure that we can seize the initiative, minimize territory lost before an invasion is halted, and ensure the integrity of our warfighting coalitions". Moreover, "the United States must be prepared to fight and win under conditions where an adversary may use asymmetric means against us – unconventional approaches that avoid or undermine our strengths while exploiting our vulnerabilities ... such as NBC weapons, information operations, attacks on our critical infrastructure, or terrorism". In the final analysis, "the primary mission of our Armed Forces is to deter and, if necessary, to fight and win conflicts in which our vital interests are threatened". Clinton, 2000, pp. 2, 3, 5, 10, 16, 27, 28.

[82] This goal was identified by the Clinton administration as "aimed at checking aggression and addressing local and regional crises before they escalate or spread". As such, while such situations may "involve other than 'vital' national security interests", intervention may serve to "prevent greater and costlier conflicts that night well threaten U.S. vital interests". Clinton, 2000, p. 27.

[83] See Clinton, 2000, pp. 6, 7, 34.

[84] This objective was said by the Clinton administration to be "critical to the future strength of our nation and the maintenance of global stability". It went on the observe, "Freedom of navigation and overflight are essential to our economic security and for the worldwide movement and sustainment of U.S. military forces". Clinton, 2000, p. 18. See also, Clinton, 2000, p. 6.

[85] Clinton, 2000, p. 20.

[86] Discussing this, the Clinton administration stated that "consistent with our international obligations, we will deter threats to our interests in space, counter hostile efforts against U.S. access to and use of space, and maintain the ability to counter space systems and services that could be used for hostile purposes against our military forces, command and control systems, or other critical capabilities". Clinton, 2000, p. 20.

[87] "Information superiority" consists of such capabilities as "the capability to collect, process, and disseminate and uninterrupted flow of information while exploiting and/or denying an adversary's ability to do the same". Clinton, 2000, p. 20.

[88] Commenting on this point, the Clinton administration stated that the U.S. must be prepared to "support international peace and stability operations". Clinton, 2000, p. 67. See also, Clinton, 2000, pp. 3, 16.

[89] See Clinton, 2000, pp. 3, 10, 38, 67.

[90] See Clinton, 2000, pp. 3, 16.

[91] See Clinton, 2000, pp. 10, 11.

[92] See Clinton, p. 36.

[93] Commenting on this, the Clinton administration observed, "The sometimes difficult road for new democracies in the 1990s demonstrates that free elections are not enough". Democratic societies must also institutionalize an "independent media capable of engaging an informed citizenry". Thus the United States seeks to "encourage a free and independent local media" that promotes democratic principles and human rights "without fear of reprisal". Clinton, 2000, pp. 10, 36.

[94] The Clinton administration stressed that democratic societies must also institutionalize "a robust civil society and strong Non-governmental Organizations (NGO) structures; the rule of law and an independent judiciary, open and competitive economic structures". It also requires "civilian control of the military". Thus, the administration stressed that the United States "must help democratizing nations strengthen the pillars of civil society by supporting administration of justice and rule of law programs; promoting the principle of civilian control of the military; and training foreign police and security forces to solve crimes and maintain order without violating the basic human rights of their citizens. And we must seek to improve their market and educational institutions, fight corruption and political discontent by encouraging good government practices". Clinton, 2000, pp. 7,10, 36, 38.

[95] The Clinton administration maintained that "genuine, lasting democracy also requires respect for human rights, including the right to political dissent; freedom of religion and belief; . . . mechanisms to safeguard minorities from oppressive rule by the majority; (and) full respect for women's and worker's rights". The administration especially emphasized the need to "ensure that international human rights principles protect the most vulnerable or traditionally oppressed groups in the world – women, children, indigenous peoples, workers,

refugees, and other persecuted persons". Clinton, 2000, pp. 36, 37. See also Clinton, pp. 7, 11, 36, 38, 67.

[96] The Clinton administration stressed this by noting, "Ethnic conflict represents a great challenge to our values and our security. When it erupts into ethnic cleansing or genocide, ethnic conflict becomes a grave violation of universal human rights. We find it clearly opposed to our national belief that innocent civilians should never be subject to forcible relocation or slaughter because of their religious, ethnic, racial, or tribal heritage". Clinton, 2000, p. 37.

[97] This point was punctuated by the Clinton administration, noting that the United States must lead efforts to combat "violence against, and trafficking in women and children". It strongly opposes "sexual exploitation of minors, child labor, use of child soldiers, and homelessness among children". It supports "efforts to combat violence against women, reform unfair inheritance and property rights, and strengthen women's access to fair employment and economic opportunity". The United States also seeks to "advance religious freedom and to counter religious persecution". Finally, the U.S. seeks to "protect the rights of refugees and displaced persons". Clinton, 2000, pp.. 37, 38.

[98] The Clinton administration noted that "gaining the full benefit of more open markets requires an integrated strategy that maintains our technological advantages, promotes American exports abroad, and ensures that export controls intended to protect our national security do not unnecessarily make U.S. high technology companies less competitive globally". Clinton, 2000, pp. 32, 33. 34.

[99] See Clinton, 2000, pp. 6, 7, 9, 31-34.

[100] See Clinton, p. 32.

[101] See Clinton, pp. 2, 5, 6, 9, 10, 31, 32, 33.

[102] See Clinton, 2000, pp. 6, 10, 31.

[103] Discussing this goal, the Clinton administration stated that the United States supported policies "promoting sound development policies that help build the economic and social framework needed to encourage economic growth and poverty reduction and facilitate the effective use of external assistance. Debt relief to free up developing countries' resources for meeting the basic needs of their people. Public health assistance . . . for the prevention and treatment of epidemics such as AIDS, malaria, and tuberculosis, as well as the training of individuals to continue providing public health services. Human capacity development assistance for basic education and literacy programs, job skills training, and other programs specifically designed to promote women's health, provide educational opportunity, and promote women's empowerment" Summarizing, the Clinton administrations observed, "True and lasting social and economic progress must occur in a sustainable fashion, that meets the human and environmental need for enduring growth". Clinton, 2000, p. 35. See also: Clinton, 2000, pp. 11, 18, 19, 31.

[104] See Clinton, 2000, p. 19.

[105] Clinton, 2000, pp. 11-16, 45.

[106] Clinton, 2000, pp. 11-12, 45.

[107] Clinton, pp. 39, 40, 45.

[108] Clinton, 2000, p. 45.

[109] Buttressing this objective, the Clinton administration noted, "that continued instability, ethnic conflict, and potentially open warfare in Southeastern Europe would adversely affect European security and set back the process of creating a Europe that is truly whole and free". Clinton, 2000, p. 39. In pursuing American objectives toward Southeastern Europe, the administration further articulated the following goals: "A peaceful resolution of the status of Montenegro and Kosovo through arrangements acceptable to all sides,

strengthening regional cooperation as a basis for the region's revitalization and eventual integration with the rest of Europe; Adherence to international agreements such as the Dayton Accords, especially in recognition of international boundaries". Clinton, 2000, p. 39. See also, Clinton, 2000, pp. 42, 43, 47, 48.

[110] Along these lines, with reference to Southeastern Europe, the Clinton administration stated that the U.S. seeks, "Coexistence among ethnic groups and the rebuilding of civic society; Promotion of the return of refugees and displaced persons to their homes to undo the pernicious consequences of ethnic cleansing; Economic reform and revitalization, leading to sustainable economic growth; Democratic government based on the rule of law and full respect for human rights; Support for the nascent democratic government in the Federal Republic of Yugoslavia (FRY) as a means for advancing its return to the international community". Clinton, 2000, p. 39. See also Clinton, 2000, pp. 40-47.

[111] Emphasizing this objective, the Clinton administration stated, "The United States strongly supports the process of European integration embodied in the EU". Clinton, 2000, p. 46.

[112] See Clinton, 2000, pp. 39-47.

[113] See Clinton, 2000, pp. 44-45. Discussing economic relations with the European Union, the Clinton administration stated that the United States sought to "reduce barriers to trade and investment through the creation of an open New Transatlantic Marketplace". Commenting further, the United States wanted to "deepen our economic relations, reinforce our political ties, and reduce trade frictions. The first element . . . is reducing barriers that affect manufacturing, agriculture, and services. In manufacturing, we are focusing on standards and technical barriers that American businesses have identified as the most significant obstacle to expanding trade. In agriculture, we are focusing on regulatory barriers that have inhibited the expansion of agricultural trade, particularly in the biotechnology area. In services, we seek to facilitate trade in specific service sectors, thereby creating new opportunities for the service industries that are already so active in the European market". Clinton, 2000, pp. 45-46.

[114] Discussing economic relations with the newly independent states of the former Soviet Union, the administration commented that the United States focuses "particular attention on promoting the development of Caspian energy resources and their export to world markets, thereby expanding and diversifying world energy supplies and promoting prosperity in the region". Clinton, 2000, pp. 46-47.

[115] Discussing this further, the Clinton administration commented that "this means working together to consolidate this region's historic transition in favor of democracy and free markets; supporting peace efforts in troubled areas both within and outside the region; tackling global threats such as the potential use and continued proliferation of NBC weapons, terrorism, drug trafficking, international organized crime, environmental problems or health crises, mass uncontrolled migration of refugees, and building a more open world economy without barriers to transatlantic trade and investment". Clinton, 2000, p. 40.

[116] See Clinton, 2000, pp. 2, 49-50.

[117] See Clinton, 2000, pp. 50-52.

[118] See Clinton, 2000, pp. 53-54.

[119] Clinton, 2000, pp. 52-53.

[120] Commenting further on this point, the Clinton administration stated, "Our economic objectives in the region include the following: continuing recovery from the financial crisis; further progress within APEC toward liberalizing trade and investment; increasing U.S. exports to Asia/Pacific countries through market-opening measures and leveling the playing

field for U.S. business; and concluding the WTO accession negotiations for the PRC and Taiwan on satisfactory commercial terms". Clinton, 2000, pp. 52-53.

[121] These threats were said by the Clinton Administration to include "the following priorities: deterring aggression and promoting peaceful resolution of crises; promoting access to and the security of sea lines of communications in cooperation with our allies and partners; actively promoting our nonproliferation goals and safeguarding nuclear technology; strengthening both active and passive counter proliferation capabilities of key allies; combating the spread of transnational threats, including drug-trafficking, piracy, terrorism and the spread of AIDS; fostering bilateral and multilateral security cooperation, with a particular emphasis on combating transnational threats and enhancing future cooperation in peacekeeping operations; and promoting regional dialogue through bilateral and multilateral fora". Clinton, 2000, pp. 48-49.

[122] In this context, the Clinton Administration stated, "Latin American nations have made notable advances over the last several years, with the restoration of democratic institutions in old democracies like Chile and Uruguay, the consolidation of democratic practices in countries like Nicaragua and Guatemala, and the move to a competitive democratic system in Mexico... Of particular significance has been the growing hemispheric consensus on the importance of defending democracy when threatened. Through the OAS, the nations of the Hemisphere have stood firm in support of constitutionally-elected governments under stress, as in the cases of Ecuador, Guatemala, Paraguay, Haiti, and the Dominican Republic. In Peru, the OAS is playing a critical role in facilitating democratic reforms..." Clinton, 2000, pp. 56-57.

[123] Clinton, 2000, pp. 56, 57.

[124] Clinton, 2000, pp. 55, 57.

[125] The Clinton administration asserted that the United States seeks "to advance the goal of an integrated hemisphere of free market democracies by building on NAFTA". The proposed "Free trade Area of the Americas" which the administration hoped to establish by 2005 would facilitate common hemispheric policies regarding "market access, investment, services, government procurement, dispute settlement, agriculture, intellectual property rights, competition policy, subsidies, anti-dumping and countervailing duties". Finally, the U.S. "will seek to ensure that the agreement also supports workers' rights, environmental protection and sustainable development". Clinton, 2000, p. 56.

[126] Clinton, 2000, p. 56.

[127] Regarding the issue of environmentally sustainable development, the Clinton administration stated, "We also view it as essential that economic prosperity in our hemisphere be pursued in an environmentally sustainable manner. From our shared seas and freshwater resources to migratory bird species and transboundary air pollution, the environmental policies of our neighbors can have a direct impact on quality of life at home". Along these lines, the administration noted that, "Working with Mexico, we have taken concerted action to monitor air quality, intensify research on environmental health issues, follow the cross-border movement of toxic wasters or illegal migrants, coordinate activities that will benefit nature preserves, and use debt relief to further protect tropical forests. Unites States government assistance to the region recognizes the vital link between sustainable use of natural resources and long-term prosperity a key to developing prosperous trading partners in this hemisphere". Clinton, 2000, p. 56.

[128] Clinton, 2000, pp. 55-56.

[129] Clinton, 2000, p. 57.

[130] Clinton, 2000, p. 57.

[131] See Clinton, 2000, pp. 54, 55.

[132] Clinton, 2000, pp. 2, 58-60.
[133] Clinton, 2000, pp. 58-60.
[134] Clinton, 2000, pp. 15, 58, 59.
[135] Commenting further on this goal, the Clinton administration states that the United States encourages both India and Pakistan "to take steps to prevent further proliferation, reduce the risk of conflict, and exercise restraint in their nuclear and missile programs. The United States does not believe that nuclear weapons have made India or Pakistan more secure. We hope they will abandon their nuclear weapons programs and join the NPT as non-nuclear weapon states. Indian and Pakistani nuclear and long-range missile tests have been dangerously destabilizing and threaten to spark a dangerous arms race in South Asia. Such a race will further undermine the global nonproliferation regime and thus threaten international security". Hence. The U.S. "has called on Indian and Pakistan to take a number of steps that would bring them closer to the international mainstream on nonproliferation". Clinton, 2000, p. 60.
[136] Clinton, 2000, pp. 58, 61.
[137] Clinton, 2000, p. 61.
[138] Clinton, 2000, pp. 58, 61.
[139] Clinton, 2000, p. 61.
[140] Clinton, 2000, pp. 58-61.
[141] Clinton, 2000, p. 59.
[142] Clinton, 2000, pp. 59-60.
[143] Clinton, 2000, p. 60.
[144] Clinton, 2000, p. 61.
[145] Clinton, 2000, p. 61.
[146] Clinton, 2000, pp. 6, 61.
[147] Clinton, 2000, pp. 58-61.
[148] Clinton, 2000, p. 60.
[149] Clinton, 2000, pp. 62-63.
[150] Clinton, 2000, pp. 62-63.
[151] Clinton, 2000, pp. 62, 63, 65.
[152] Clinton, 2000, pp. 62-65.
[153] Clinton, 2000, pp 63-64.
[154] Clinton, 2000, pp. 63-64.
[155] Clinton, 2000, pp. 62-65.

References

Bailey, Thomas A. (1958), *A Diplomatic History of the American People*, New York, NY: Appleton-Century Crofts.
Bauer, K. Jack. (1974), *The Mexican War*, New York, NY: Macmillan Publishing Co.
Bemis, Samuel F. (1965), *A Diplomatic History of the United States*, New York, NY: Holt, Rinehart and Winston.
Clinton, William J. (2000), *A National Security Strategy for a Global Age*, Washington DC: U.S. Government Printing Office.
Coles, Harry L. (1965), *The War of 1812*, Chicago, Illinois: University of Chicago Press.
Current, Richard N., Williams, T. Harry, and Freidel, Frank. (1965), *American History: A Survey*, New York, NY: Alford A. Knopf.
DeConde, Alexander. (1963), *A History of American Foreign Policy*, New York, NY:

Charles Scribner's Sons.
Dunbabin, J.P.D. (1994), *The Cold War: The Great Powers and Their Allies*, London: Longman.
Ekirch, Arthur A. (1966), *Ideas, Ideals, and American Diplomacy*, New York, NY: Appleton-Century Crofts.
Feis, Herbert. (1950), *The Road to Pearl Harbor*, Princeton, NJ: Princeton University Press.
Feis, Herbert. (1957),*Churchill, Roosevelt, Stalin: The War They Waged and the Peace They Sought*, Princeton, NJ: Princeton University Press.
Feis, Herbert. (1960), *Between War and Peace: the Potsdam Conference*, Princeton, NJ: Princeton University Press.
Feis, Herbert. (1966), *The Atomic Bomb and the End of World War II*, Princeton, NJ: Princeton University Press.
Field, James A. (1969), *America and the Mediterranean World*, Princeton, NJ: Princeton University Press.
Gaddis, John L. (1990), *Russia, The Soviet Union, and the United States*, New York,NY: McGraw-Hill Publishing Co.
Gardner, Lloyd, Schlesinger, Arthur Jr, and Morgenthau Hans. (1970), *The Origins of the Cold War*, Waltham, MA: Ginn & Company.
Gilbert, Felix. (1961), *To the Farewell Address*, Princeton, NJ: Princeton University Press.
Hattaway, Herman and Jones, Archer. (1983), *How the North Won*, Urbana, Illinois: University of Illinois Press.
Hensel, Howard M. (1989), *The Sword of the Union*, Washington, DC: U.S. Government Printing Office.
Hickey, Donald. (1989), *The War of 1812*, Urbana, Illinois: University of Illinois Press.
Jordan, Donaldson and Pratt, E. J. (1931), *Europe and the American Civil War*, Boston, MA: Houghton Mifflin.
Lenczowski, George. (1980), *The Middle East in World Affairs*, Ithaca, NY: Cornell University Press.
McCullough, David. (1977), *The Path Between the Seas*, New York, NY: Simon and Schuster.
Osgood, Robert. (1953), *Ideals and Self-Interest in America's Foreign Relations*, Chicago, Illinois: University of Chicago Press.
Owsley, Frank. (1959), *King Cotton Diplomacy*, Chicago, Illinois University of Chicago Press.
Perkins, Dexter. (1941), *Hands Off: A History of the Monroe Doctrine*, Boston, MA: Little Brown & Co.
Pratt, Julius. (1949), *Expansionists of 1812*, New York, NY: Peter Smith.
Prucha, Francis P. (1969), *The Sword of the Republic*, New York, NY: Macmillan Publishing Co.
Reagan, Ronald. (1988), *National Security Strategy of the United States*, Washington, DC: U.S. Government Printing Office.
Singletary, Otis. (1960), *The Mexican War*, Chicago, Illinois: University of Chicago Press.
The Commission on America's National Interests. (2000), *America's National Interests*, Commission on America's National Interests.
Trask, David F. (1981), *The War with Spain in 1898*, New York, NY: Macmillan Publishing Co.
U.S. Joint Chiefs of Staff. (1989), *Department of Defense Dictionary of Military and Associated Terms*, Washington DC: U.S. Government Printing Office.

Ulam, Adam B. (1971), *The Rivals:America and Russia since World War II*, New York, NY: Penguin Books.
Utley, Robert M. (1967), *Frontiersmen in Blue*, New York, NY: Macmillan Publishing Co.
Utley, Robert M. (1973), *Frontier Regulars*, New York, NY: Macmillan Publishing Co.

Chapter 2

Understanding the European Union's Enlargement: The International Society Approach of the English School

Yannis A. Stivachtis

The purpose of this chapter is twofold. First, it seeks to provide an empirical contribution to the existing literature on the EU's enlargement and second, it aims to offer a theoretical contribution to the literature on international society by treating the EU as a regional international society which tends to expand outwards. In so doing, it compares the enlargement process with that of the historical expansion of the European society of states. Similarities between the two processes appear to lead to the conclusion that such a comparative study would help one to explain and understand better the process of the EU's enlargement and the events associated with it.

From a theoretical perspective, investigating the process of the EU's enlargement one may enrich one's existing knowledge about issues; such as why do regional international societies wish to expand? What happens when regional international societies tend to expand? How do candidate states respond to this expansion? Why do states, which are not members of the regional international society, wish to join it and what do they have to do in order to gain their entry into this society? What is the role of culture in this process? What happens when divergent cultures meet? Is it the logic of culture or the logic of anarchy that determines the expansion and membership processes?

With reference to the EU's enlargement, the chapter seeks to answer questions like: why does the EU seek to expand its membership? How does the EU approach each particular candidature and why? Why is there a significant debate within the EU itself regarding its enlargement process as well as which states should be accepted? Why do non-member states wish to join the EU? Is it because of political or economic considerations, or both? Why is there a debate within some candidate states regarding the appropriateness of joining the EU? What do non-member states have to do in order to gain their entry into the EU? What is the role of culture in the admission process? What happens when the culture of the EU differs from that of the candidate states? Finally, does the process of EU's enlargement follow the logic of culture or the logic of anarchy?

Preparing for the New Enlargement

One of the major issues surrounding the last Inter-governmental Conference (IGC) of the EU, the Amsterdam Treaty and the whole future of the EU in the period 1997 to 2005-7 has been that of enlargement. Enlargement is not a new phenomenon for the EEC/EU, but the next enlargements are generally regarded as qualitatively different because of the number of states and the challenge that their entry poses to both of them and the Union.

As the 1995 enlargement (Austria, Finland and Sweden) was being negotiated, Poland and Hungary both applied for membership. They were followed by applications from the other Eastern and Central European states (Romania, Bulgaria, the Czech Republic, Slovenia and Slovakia) and the Baltic states (Estonia, Latvia and Lithuania), applications already having been received from Malta, Cyprus and much later Turkey.

As early as June 1993, in Copenhagen, the EU had declared that it was ready to consider applications if the applicants were able to assume the obligations of membership by satisfying the economic and political conditions required. These conditions included stability of institutions guaranteeing democracy, the rule of law, human rights and respect for protection of minorities, the existence of a functioning market economy as well as the capacity to cope with pressure and market forces within the Union. In addition, it was made clear that the applicants need to be able to meet and fulfil the so-called *acquis*, namely, to accept all the decisions of the EU since their inception, subject to periods of transition. It is worth mentioning that the applicants have to accept conditions that not all current members accept, given the 1990s vogue for flexibility.

If strictly interpreted by the Union and the applicant states, the above criteria constitute a daunting set of requirements especially since the *acquis* includes not only the *acquis communautaire* of the First Pillar (Single Market), but also that of the Second and Third Pillars (Common Foreign and Security Policy and Justice and Home Affairs). In 1998 the British Presidency made that position clear by stating, "Accession implies full acceptance of the actual and potential rights and obligations attaching to the Union system and its institutional framework...The *acquis* has to be applied at the time of accession. Furthermore, accession requires effective implementation of the *acquis*, which implies in particular the establishment of an efficient, reliable public administration. The Union attaches a primordial importance to Justice and Home Affairs and the need for all applicant States to make rapid progress in this area before accession. There is a need for a progressive alignment of the applicants States' policies towards third countries...The acceptance of the rights and obligations resulting from membership may give rise exceptionally to non-permanent transitional measures, to be defined during the accession negotiations. Transitional measures shall be limited in time and scope, and accompanied by a plan with clearly defined stages for application of the *acquis*".[1]

These requirements are perhaps all the more daunting since one of the ironies of contemporary Europe is that countries which struggled to retain their sovereignty and resume control over their own destiny then rushed to share that destiny and their new sovereignty with their Western neighbours.

Subsequent European Council meetings after Copenhagen in June 1993 agreed to help to prepare the applicants for accession by developing the "Europe Agreements" that had already been signed with most of these states. These agreements were designed to provide a framework for political dialogue, to establish free trade between the states concerned and the EU, to help associate states progress towards the economic freedoms of the Union, and to help in the development of market economies. The EU, for example, in December 1994 as its Essen European Council meeting agreed to develop these arrangements into a comprehensive strategy for preparing the Central and East European states for membership. A year later in Madrid, the EU states asked the Commission to prepare a paper on the issues arising out of enlargement, a request that led to the publication of 'Agenda 2000' in July 1997.

Meeting these requirements has not been and will not be at all easy for the applicants. Indeed in mid-July 1997 the Commission gave its view on the ability of the various applicants to meet the criteria set out earlier and it issued independent opinions on each (Turkey, Cyprus and Malta having already been advised upon). The Commission concluded as a result of detailed analysis that accession negotiations should begin with the Czech Republic, Estonia, Hungary, Poland and Slovenia, the Member States having already agreed to open talks with Cyprus six months after the signing of the Amsterdam Treaty in October 1997. These negotiations symbolically opened in April 1998 with no target date being set for their conclusion. The first round-the-table negotiations did not take place until November 1998.

With regard to the other applicants, the Commission declared that the preparation of negotiations will be speeded up, in particular through an analytical examination of the *acquis*. To try to make these states feel less left behind, the Luxembourg Council also agreed to the establishment of a 'European Conference' to bring the EU states and all aspiring members of the EU, regardless of the stage of their application.

The first convocation of this Conference took place in 1998 during the British Presidency. As a sign of potential difficulties ahead, Turkey refused to attend, although the EU has maintained that the Commission would still seek to help Turkey to prepare for membership and that there would be regular reports on its progress towards meeting the Copenhagen criteria. Turkey had taken grave offence at the decision of December 1997 to exclude it from the first wave of negotiations due to its human rights record. It is perhaps indicative for future enlargements that the Amsterdam Treaty introduced for the first time the principle that the Council could "determine the existence of a serious and persistent breach by a Member State of the principles...of liberty, democracy, respect for human rights and fundamental freedoms, and the rule of law...and decide to suspend certain of the rights deriving from the application of this Treaty to the State in question...".[2]

The other five countries, which did not receive a favourable opinion, are continuously invited to an annual 'European Conference' and they remain under continuous review. It has not been excluded that they might be reassessed and join the first group of five, belatedly.

At the same time as it issued its detailed view on each applicant state, the European Commission also issued "Agenda 2000: For a Stronger and Wider Union". The latter sought to identify the challenges facing the Union both in terms of its policies and gave some indication of the size of the adjustments that will be necessary. The Commission in Agenda 2000 made generous assumptions about economic growth in the EU and managed to argue that by the end of the period the EU would have potential additional resources available to help in the new members' adjustments. Most commentators regarded these forecasts with great suspicion.

Since 1997, Cyprus, the Czech Republic, Estonia, Hungary, Poland and Slovenia started preparing by beginning to adjust to the requirements of the Single Market, and by seeking to converge their laws in a whole swathe of areas to make them compatible with the requirements of the EU *acquis*, subject only to traditional derogations. But the task has been large and there have been questions as to the ability of socio-economic, administrative and political systems that have to cope with the traumatic and seismic changes in and since 1989 to cope with another set of upheavals.

Partly, but not exclusively, because of the prospect of enlargement, the EU felt the need to examine a number of its policies and to begin a process of reform. The major areas for reform are: Cohesion and Structural Funds and the Common Agricultural Policy. The agenda is large and difficult since many existing policies reflect the particular vested interests of certain states, indeed even the parochial and domestic electoral interests of governments and political parties. In addition, reform of these policies is ultimately related to arguments about 'winners' and 'losers'; that is, who pays money into the EU budget and who receives the money. By early 1999 progress was slow and problems were multiplying.

Enlargement has a number of implications for the EU. There are a series of questions to the effectiveness of the EU, especially given the greater heterogeneity in experience, socio-economic and political systems and geo-political location on the wider map of Europe. These touch on issues such as the capacity of the EU to make decisions and to ensure that the decisions and the full *acquis* are implemented and respected. It raises the question of whether a wider, in terms of membership, Union must by definition be different in character, identity and nature from a Community of Six or Fifteen. Similarly it raises the question whether a wider Union covering three pillars, plus the European Monetary Union (EMU), must be different from an EEC. This in turn brings forward the question of whether there will be more opt-outs, variable geometry or use of flexibility. As it can be seen from the attitude of many of the current members, especially the small states, there are also large concerns over maintaining the institutional balance, and especially the rights of the smaller members to at least some form of equality of membership. This has arisen in the debate, for example, about the number of Commissioners and the nature and composition of the rotating Presidency. Larger states have become concerned that they might be outvoted by a weight of states that do not form a majority of the EU's population. To this concern one can add the question of finance as well as operational issues such as the provision of translating and interpreting services, staffing, structure and culture.

All these questions and issues have provided the fertile ground for a significant debate not only among the member states but also among the various political forces and pressure groups within each of them concerning whether enlarging the EU would be a wise policy.

On the other hand, there are questions that arise for the applicant states. Can they accept the *acquis* and the full objectives and agenda of the EU? Will seeking to fulfil these requirements destabilise in some cases fragile economies? Do they gain more stability by being in or out? How troublesome is the presumption of functioning marketing economies and the ability to compete in and face competition from the Single Market? Can they cope with and absorb all the changes – social, economic and political – that are required? What will happen if the enlargement is phased? Will some win and others lose? It was decided by the EU that the initial negotiations would be with Estonia, the Czech Republic, Cyprus, Hungary, Poland and Slovenia, but not Bulgaria, Latvia, Lithuania, Romania, Slovakia and Turkey. Will there be a continuous series of enlargement in the near future? Will membership actually deliver on providing them with a sense of security? They all know that there is still no formal defence guarantee in the founding treaties of the European Union, but many of these states seem to take for granted that membership of the EU will automatically increase their security, because they will be identified as members of the Union 'club'.

European Union and the English School of International Relations

Since the publication of *The Anarchical Society*, Hedley Bull has had a significant impact on the discussion of whether there is an international society that is distinguishable from an international system.[3] Focusing on historical examples, Bull observed that the relations among particular political entities were more ordered than the relations between these entities and the other political communities existing in the international environment at the same time. These two different types of relations have been reflected in the concepts of 'international system' and 'international society'.

Nevertheless, the apparently simple idea and framework that Bull employed has been a good deal more complex and problematic than it appears at first sight. Specifically, two main, albeit inconsistent, criticisms of the system/society distinction have been advanced First, that the distinction is invalid;[4] and second, that the distinction is valid and only the boundary line that Bull has drawn between system and society is problematic.[5]

Hedley Bull, Adam Watson and their colleagues have argued that the global international society of today has been the result of the expansion of the European society of states, which brought different regional international societies into contact with one another.[6] Trying to establish a clear boundary between an international system and an international society, Barry Buzan has advocated that international society may develop either according to the *gemeinschaft* or alternatively according to the *gesellschaft* mode of society reflected in the logic of culture and the logic of anarchy respectively.

Examining the process of international society's enlargement from the perspective of the *gesellschaft* mode, Yannis Stivachtis has argued that international society has developed according to the logic of anarchy rather than the logic of culture.[7] Among other things, this implies that the culturally heterogeneous global international society of today encompasses many regional international societies, which are relatively more homogeneous. EU represents an example of such a regional international society.

Moreover, the logic of culture is closely associated with the logic of anarchy in the sense that the power distribution within the global international society may also reflect the existence of divergent cultures. For example, during the Cold War the global international society was divided into two power blocs (communist and non-communist states) each with its own distinctive culture. The end of the Cold War has paved the way for a multi-polar international society. In this new international distribution of power, EU is seen as constituting one of the main poles.

The growing importance of the European Union (EU) and the current international distribution of power has, on the one hand, made several states to ask for EU membership, while on the other hand has pushed the EU to accept its enlargement as a means to achieve its economic, political, and strategic objectives. Many believe that the process of the EU's enlargement represents a new phenomenon in the history of international relations. Nevertheless, this process is not new in the sense that certain patterns of behaviour that the EU members as well as the candidate states display appear to be quite similar to those of the European and extra-European states during the era of the expansion of the European society of states across the globe. Yet, one may observe that even within some of the EU members and the candidate states discussion about membership itself and the direction of the EU has taken the form of a debate, which very often is associated with questions of identity. Similar questions had also confronted the European and non-European states during the era of European society's expansion.

EU's Enlargement: The Need for an Explanatory Theoretical Framework

With the end of the Cold War, many traditional concerns in international relations have been put aside. It has been suggested that the Cold War was an aberration and that, because the study of international relations was so heavily influenced by it, the focus of the discipline has consequently been distorted. During the Cold War, Kenneth Waltz put one of the most notable frameworks for analysing international relations forward.[8] Attempting to develop a systems theory, he offered an alternative conceptualisation of the international system, which did not rely on the notions of Classical Realism. Actually, he sought to place Realism in a secure scientific basis and he thus generated interest in the philosophical foundations of International Relations theory.[9]

Waltz's approach retained the earlier Realist claims as to the primacy of conflict and power in international politics,[10] but shifted the explanation for this on the workings of the anarchical nature of the international system. In other words, he depicted the world as an anarchic arena and sought to examine how the anarchical structure of the international system affects relations among states. According to Waltz, the anarchical structure of the international system encourages states to think and act primarily in terms of a struggle for survival. This, in turn, makes power the principal means by which these relations are conducted. In an anarchic international system, therefore, the possibilities for international co-operation are limited and international order is determined by the distribution of power in the system.

Moreover, Waltz and other Neorealists have depicted the complex history of international relations as taking place within an unchanging and highly competitive anarchic international system. They have acknowledged that although the distribution of power amongst states had constantly shifted and new states had emerged over time, the underlying structural features of the international system had remained unchanged. From this perspective, the Cold War was simply a global extension of an adversarial international system that found its origins in Europe.

But soon it began to be acknowledged that the international system had been extensively rule-governed even during the Cold War.[11] As theorists became interested in the process whereby co-operation takes place and rules are formed, they became frustrated with the restrictive framework of Waltz, according to whom rules and co-operation appear as anomalies.[12] As a result, new conceptions of the world and how it works have risen and challenged the assumptions of Neorealism. Scholars have proposed alternatives for the study of international relations, which are more consistent with contemporary realities. The discipline has, therefore, moved to different directions. Given the increasing power of the U.S., for example, there has been a growing interest in using a Neoliberal framework to show how the loss of hegemony would affect the working of the international system and explain how international co-operation is achieved under anarchy.[13] This led to a 'great debate' between Neorealists and Neoliberals.[14]

In the 1990s, international relations became a subject of dispute, which may in part account for frequent complaints of lack of progress. Many international relations theorists have claimed that the discipline has lost its direction, or it is in a state of disarray.[15] There is, therefore, considerable uncertainty about how to proceed. Although several attempts have been made to compare and contrast the different perspectives, no general agreement has been reached on which is the most powerful theoretically. Since there is not dominant theory, the discipline offers a number of competing views attempting to explain the central events of the international system.

After the Cold War, the long-established assessment of the international system was immediately challenged by two competing meta-narratives. One, most closely associated with Francis Fukuyama,[16] argued that the Cold War was never more than a staging post along a route which is leading inexorably to the universal adoption of liberal beliefs and the emergence of a universal peace. The second, much less benign meta-narrative was advanced by Samuel Huntington who has depicted world history in terms of evolving civilizations. From this perspective, the Cold War is considered to have obscured deep-seated cultural fault-lines, which cut across the globe and make for an inevitable future 'clash of civilizations'.[17]

Both of these meta-narratives have been subjected to searching criticisms but they have managed in the process to overshadow another meta-narrative developed during the Cold War. This meta-narrative has been advanced by the international society scholars associated with the 'English School of International Relations'. The scholars in question have employed a historical approach, comparing and contrasting state systems that have existed at historical stages and have sought to point out how they have evolved over time.[18] In other words, they have sought to compare the historical evidence and see what states systems existing at different points in time have in common and how they differ, as well as examine how a particular state system was replaced by another. In this respect, they attempted to develop a theory of change and continuity.[19]

Under the influence of Arnold Toynbee,[20] Martin Wight, one of the key founding fathers of the English School, recognised that it is not possible to provide a history of the international system from a purely European perspective. He argued that it is necessary to locate the study of international relations on a global canvas that extends back to the origins of civilization. Although the English School has not managed yet to establish a full-blown meta-narrative for the entire history of international relations, its members assume that the study of international relations must be approached from the perspective of the divergent civilizations that have existed throughout history. To assist in this task, a distinction has been drawn between a 'world society of individuals' who share a common culture, an 'international society', which is a collection of states bound together by common rules and underpinned by the common culture of a world society, and an 'international system', which is formed by a set of interacting states which lack common culture.

The meta-narrative of the English School presupposes that Europe evolved as an international society of states existing, initially, within a larger international system of states. Subsequent world history can then be recounted in terms of an expanding international society centred in Europe, following in the wake of an expanding international system. A full world history, however, would require an understanding of how international systems evolved in other parts of the world.

Closer inspection of the approach established by the English School, however, has revealed weaknesses, which make it difficult to generate a coherent meta-narrative. Buzan has observed, for example, that there is now a global international society formed in the absence of a global world society. This assessment undermines the essential role of culture in the English School conceptualisation of international society.[21] Arguing that international society may develop either according to the *gemeinschaft* or according to the *gesellscaft* mode of society, Buzan has developed a very intriguing solution to the problem of culture and has demonstrated that although there are weaknesses in the English School approach, it is sufficiently robust to make it worth while remodelling.[22]

Adopting Buzan's reformulation, the author of the present chapter argues that international society seems to develop more according to the logic of anarchy rather than according to the logic of culture. Moreover, it is claimed that historically the two logics have performed different functions. While the logic of anarchy, operating in the international system, has brought states into international society, once in, the logic of culture has determined the degree of their integration into international society. This accounts for the observed uneven development within international society. The logic of culture, however, has performed an additional function: that of serving as another factor in the calculations of states.

In recent years there has been a growing interest in large-scale historical change, which refers to transformational moments in world history. Scholars have argued that it is not possible to understand large-scale historical change without taking into account the international system, and have recognised that international relations has long relied on a very static conception of the international system, and has therefore lacked the necessary theoretical tools to accommodate processes that precipitate change.[23]

Despite the growing interest in large-scale historical change, international relations has failed to develop a framework that can fully embrace the evolution of history at a global level.[24] The reason for this is that Neorealism has successfully propagated the view that world history has occurred within an unchanging international system and its ahistorical view made it more difficult to develop a view of the world history from a global perspective.[25] An attempt has been made to establish a framework from a structural realist perspective that will make it possible to examine world history from an international perspective.[26] This framework is based on three fundamental assumptions. First, there is a structural differentiation among the units in the international system; second, the units and the international system are mutually constituted, so that as the structure of the units change, so does the nature of the international system; and third, it is necessary to explore the international system from various perspectives.

In the recent years, new interest in the work of the English School has emerged and efforts have been made to relate the approach of this school of thought to the American Neorealist and Neoliberalist modes of theorising, as well as to theoretical attempts aimed at developing a framework that can fully embrace the evolution of history at a global level. Central to these efforts is the concept of 'international society' and special emphasis is given to the process whereby the current global international society has historically evolved.[27]

In fact, already in the 1980s Bull and Watson endeavoured to develop a framework for explaining and understanding the development of international society. This framework was built on the sharp distinction between an international system and an international society, and saw one evolve from the other. Drawing on the expertise of their colleagues, Bull and Watson conducted a study which explored how the European society of states extended across the globe and how the extra-European states were admitted into this society. In essence, they saw European society extending into a broader global society. The present chapter is based on this very framework whose details and application to EU's enlargement will be discussed in the following sections.

EU as a Regional International Society

Bull's contribution to the theory of international relations is 'considerable and nowhere more acute than in the distinction made between the concept of a system of states and that of international society'.[28] The system/society distinction seems an empirical and practical formula which Bull gradually evolved in order to distinguish between groups of states held together by a web of economic and strategic interests and pressures so they are forced to take account of each other, and groups of states which form a conscious contract by instituting rules and mechanisms to make their relations more orderly and predictable and to further shared principles and values.[29]

Actually, Bull sought to distinguish the homogeneous relations among a particular constellation of states from the heterogeneous relations of these states with the remainder of the political entities prevailing in the international system. In this sense, there may exist an international society confined within limited geographical boundaries, which is distinguishable from an international system extended beyond the boundaries of society.

Specifically, Bull defined the international system as being formed 'when two or more states have sufficient contact between them, and have sufficient impact on one another's decisions, to cause them to behave as parts of a whole'.[30] According to this definition, EU is certainly qualified to be an international system since the EU members have sufficient contact between them, and have sufficient impact on one another's decisions, to cause them to behave as parts of a whole.

An international society, on the other hand, exists when 'a group of states, conscious of certain common interests and common values, form a society in the sense that they conceive themselves to be bound by a common set of rules in their relations with one another, and share in the working of common institutions'.[31] This implies that an international society is always an international system (since sufficient contact and impact are necessary conditions for a society to exist), but not *vice versa*. This also implies that there may exist a regional international society confined within limited geographical boundaries which is distinguishable from an international system extended beyond the boundaries of society or from another neighbouring regional international society.

The above definition of international society can easily apply to the international societies of the past, or certain contemporary regional international societies, but it cannot apply to the global international society of today. This does not mean that there is not a global international society. Rather, it means that there is an international society, which has undergone significant change throughout history and which currently, takes a particular form. Such evolution also implies that contemporary global international society may not be the same as the future global international society. Because the term 'society' corresponds to a number of different definitions, the question therefore is not whether international relations correspond to one definition of society, but rather to which definition international relations may most closely correspond. Thus the crucial question is how far particular conceptions of international society are, or are not concerned with co-current international reality.[32]

To deal with the issue of global international society's cultural diversity, in their most recent work, Bull and Watson re-defined international society as 'a group of states which not merely form a system, in the sense that the behaviour of each is necessary factor in the calculations of the others, but also have established by dialogue and consent common rules and institutions for the conduct of their relations, and recognise their common interest in maintaining these arrangements'.[33]

At first sight, the two definitions of international society appear to be similar, but actually, not only are they not similar, but they, in fact, correspond to two different types (*gemeinschaft* and *gesellschaft* modes) and historical forms (post-Westphalian European society of states and contemporary global international society) of international society.

According to the first definition of international society, EU can also be regarded as a regional international society since it represents a group of states that have certain common interests and common values and they are bound by an exclusive common set of rules in their relations with one another, and share in the working of common institutions. Although nobody may disagree that the EU members have certain common interests (for otherwise could not have formed this special association of states), they are bound by a common set of rules and share in the working of common institutions, one may question whether they also have common values. However, their commitment both to the liberal form of government and market economy and their acceptance of sharing common cultural origins (European civilization) reveals that despite certain cultural divergence, such as between the southern and the northern EU members, EU states indeed have certain values in common. Thus, although it is part of a global international society, EU forms a regional international society that is confined within limited geographical boundaries and which is distinguishable from the international system/society that extends beyond its boundaries.

Since the first definition of international society (*gemeinshaft* mode) is stricter than the second one (*gesellschaft* mode), EU can easily be seen as a regional international society if the latter definition is applied. Moreover, the *gesellschaft* mode of international society would allow one to consider the EU as a regional international society that tends to expand itself outwards (enlargement) even if it has to include states, which have divergent cultures, such as Turkey.

The Expansion of Regional International Societies

No aspect of medieval society has been considered as more important than the European expansion that carried European civilization to the rest of the world. Examining the process of the expansion of the post-Westphalian European society of states, the real distinction is not between an international system and an international society, but between a very broad international system and a regional (European) international society which gradually expanded into the former, transforming it gradually into a broader international society. This process ended when the global international system was transformed into a global international society.

When the expansion began, the world was not organised into any single international system or society. Rather it comprised several regional international societies each with its own distinctive rules and institutions reflecting the dominant regional culture. The global international society of today was not a global international system that at some point turned into a global international society. It was the European international society that expanded gradually and brought other regional international systems/societies into contact with one another. It follows that European international society was superimposed on regional international systems/societies, thereby transforming these not only into a global international system but also into a global international society.

What these regional international societies had in common was their tendency to create a hegemonial system where the dominant political community could force its rules and values on the lesser communities. Within each of these suzerain systems, relations among political authorities were regulated by specific treaties as well as by traditional codes of conduct. On the other hand, contacts between regional international societies were much more limited than contacts within them. Thus the emergence of a truly universal international society would not be possible unless one of the regional international societies could expand itself to the degree that it could combine the divergent regional international societies into a single universal society organised around a common body of rules and values. The great contribution of European expansion is that it made the rules and institutions of Europe common to all the regional political communities that existed around the globe.

Thus it was the European expansion that brought the political, economic and technological unification of the world, and it was the rules and institutions of the European international society that were eventually accepted in principle by the non-European states, even if the states sought to modify them to some extent.[34]

The enlargement of the EU constitutes one of the most important issues of the post-Cold War international relations. Examining EU's enlargement, the real question is not whether the EU constitutes a regional international system or a regional international society (for as it has been shown it is both). The real distinction is between a global international society, which is culturally heterogeneous, and a regional international society (EU), which is relatively homogeneous and gradually expands into the former. This does not mean that the EU will expand itself across the globe. It rather means that parts of the global and culturally heterogeneous international society will join a relatively homogeneous regional international society, which will expand its boundaries and at the same time may homogenise an additional part of the globe.

The great contribution of EU's enlargement would be that it would make the rules and institutions of the EU available to states, which are not currently members of the regional international society (EU) although they are members of the global international society. Thus EU's enlargement would bring political, economic and technological unification among an additional number of states, and it will be the rules and institutions of the EU that will be eventually accepted in principle by the candidate states, even if they seek to modify them to some extent.

In examining the nature of contact between European and non-European states, two main questions need to be asked: first, why did the European states seek to integrate non-European states into their society; and second, why did non-European states seek to be integrated into the expanding European society. Likewise, investigating EU's enlargement process, one may ask why does the EU seek to expand its membership? And why do candidate states wish to join the EU?

Answers to these questions point to a process whereby pressures developing from the workings of the anarchic international system, such as political, economic and strategic concerns, not only can transform the international system into an international society, but they can also cause a regional international society to expand. This corresponds to Waltz's argument that in an anarchical international system, the shoving and shaping forces of socialisation and competition pressure the units to adapt to the practices of the most powerful by punishing the weak and insecure.[35]

Reasons behind the Expansion of Regional International Societies

The European society of states was established with the Treaty of Westphalia and was the result of a power struggle between the forces driving towards a hegemonial order and those that succeeded in establishing a new European order based on the principle of anti-hegemonialism. The creation of the European society of states resulted from the pressures of an anarchic European system and not from the existence of a culture common among European states.

The motives behind the expansion of the European society of states were both political and economic. According to Watson, the resolution of medieval Christendom into sovereign states enabled rules and governments to concentrate great powers into their hands. The growing resources and ambitions of princes and merchants, and the new forms of wealth and strength, which were continually being separated by the highly inventive and dynamic European civilization, combined to produce a society of states which increasingly pressed and jostled against one another and competed in the arts of war and peace. Wariness, and an eye for economic and military threats from outside, were important for survival and necessary for success. Europe did not have enough room for the power of all its active thrusting communities.[36]

As the military and economic capacities of the European states increased, and the practice of the balance of power brought them more into equilibrium, it became clear that a given expenditure of effort produced ever less advantage within Europe compared with what could be achieved outside it. European states were therefore encouraged their expansive forces to push outward. Therefore, the quest overseas of governments, and the efforts of subjects sponsored by governments, was for economic and territorial gains, which would enhance the position of their state in the struggle for power and independence in Europe. The European expansion consisted of a number of parallel and competitive enterprises by European states and trading companies in which the main enemy was not an overseas power but a European rival. Each European state wanted the advantage of trade, bases, and settlement to be exclusive extensions of its own domain. The economic development of the European colonies and trading points was designed to cater exclusively to the needs and interests of the individual imperial power. The wealth brought back to Europe, and European military operations against each other overseas became important elements in the European system.

As in the case of the expansion of the European society of states, the reasons behind the EU's enlargement are both political and economic. In fact, in the case of the EU is extremely difficult to separate politics from economics.[37] Because the anarchic structure of the international system makes states insecure, it pushes them to devise different political and economic strategies to assure their survival and welfare. At the same time, it allows states, or groups of states, such as the EU, to increase their overall power in the international system and consequently their weight in international politics. The end of the Cold War has provided the EU with the opportunity to increase its status in international society and the enlargement has been seen as serving the political and economic interests of the EU.

Reasons for Joining Regional International Societies

Investigating the reasons for which states sought to gain entry into international society one may conclude that their will was basically determined by the logic of anarchy. Russia, for example, gained its entry during the reign of Peter the Great, who sought to Westernise Russian society and the state. What made Russia willing to accept Western ideas and models were the pressures of the anarchic European system/society. To increase its power, strength and diplomatic leverage, Russia needed to develop, and the only way to achieve this development was to adopt the more advanced European models and techniques. Likewise, Japan, China and Siam all sought to increase their position in the international arena and were therefore willing to fulfil the 'standard of civilization' imposed by the Europeans. Finally, the Ottoman Empire was admitted to international society as a result of the efforts of the Ottoman Sultans to modernise their society and develop their state in order to avoid the disintegration of their empire.[38] In sum, the reasons behind the willingness of extra-European states to join the expanding European international society were mainly political and highlighted the struggle of those states for survival in a highly competitive anarchic international system as well as their interest in participating in the main international decision-making bodies of the time; a fact that could reflect their growing power and status within the international society.

The reasons for which candidate states have expressed their willingness to join the EU are also primarily political. As it has been argued above, because the anarchic structure of the international system makes states insecure, it pushes them to devise different political and economic strategies to assure their survival and welfare. The end of the Cold War has, therefore, pushed extra-EU states to seek EU membership as a means to deal with the insecurities that the end of the Cold

War brought with it. The case of the Eastern and Central European states is illustrative. Yet, the EU has been seen as a vehicle through which the candidate states attempt to achieve their national interests, whether political or economic. The Republic of Cyprus, for example, has sought EU membership as a way to resolve the Cyprus problem.[39] Moreover, with the end of the Cold War, EU has emerged as a new pole of world power and entry into the EU could therefore provide the candidate states with certain advantages, which would not otherwise enjoy.

Reasons for Regional International Societies for Admitting New Members

Searching for the reasons for which the European states sought to admit extra-European states into international society one may argue that membership of the international society was also determined by the logic of anarchy. For instance, European states were aware of the increasing power of Russia and sought to integrate it into their diplomatic framework as a means of controlling it. European powers were also aware of the growing power of China and Japan, as well as of the economic and commercial importance of Siam and therefore sought to integrate these countries into international society. Working together seemed to be a better policy for controlling them than keeping them in isolation. Yet, the Ottoman admission to international society was the result of the need of the Western European powers to maintain order and stability in Europe threatened by the collapse of the Ottoman Empire. This disintegration could be advantageous to Russia, which sought to extent its influence in the Balkans and the Mediterranean region.[40]

The reasons for which the EU seeks to accept new members are both political and economic. Specifically, the enlargement process would allow the EU to create a greater economy of scale and thus be more competitive at the global level.[41] In return, the improving of its economic position worldwide would allow the EU to increase its weight in world politics. Moreover, by admitting new states EU would add to its political strength in the sense that the pulling together of the political and economic resources of more and more European states could improve the overall power and bargaining position of the EU *vis-à-vis* the other poles of power. Yet, the enlargement process seems to be advantageous to the big states of the EU, such as Germany and France, which compete for leadership and try to achieve their political and economic targets.

Culture and the Creation and Expansion of Regional International Societies

Although the creation of the European society of states resulted from the pressures of an anarchic European system and not from the existence of a culture common among European states, the role of a common European culture was essential in the development of certain aspects of European international society. This common European culture reinforced and distinguished European international society from a broader international system that existed at that time. Order among European states was thus generated not only by their agreements on international rules and institutions but also by their common cultural values which helped to facilitate the creation and working of international institutions.[42]

During the years of the European expansion, the European states became increasingly convinced of the superiority of their institutions and moral values. As the sense of the specifically European character of the society of states increased, so did the sense of its cultural differentiation from what existed beyond itself. International society was then regarded as privileged association of European and civilised states, which had a visible expression in certain institutions and rules.[43] In the eyes of the Europeans modern civilization was synonymous with European ways and European standards, which it was their duty and their interest to spread in order to make the world a better and safer place. Thus European powers became heavily involved in imposing their administration and civilization around the globe.

Despite the importance of culture, the expansion of international society has followed the logic of anarchy. In fact, although both in operation the two logics have performed different functions. While the logic of anarchy, operating in the international system, has brought states into international society, once in, the logic of culture has determined the degree of their integration into international society.

The cultural factor has been very important for the development of the EU.[44] With the exception of Turkey, all other candidate states share a common European cultural heritage. Nevertheless, political culture is considered of great importance and this is the reason for which the EU has set certain standards that the candidate states have to fulfil in order to join the EU. Thus commitment to the liberal form of government and market economy are necessary requirements for a state to join the EU. The only case that could threaten the cultural homogeneity of the EU is that of Turkey and it is for this reason that the Turkish candidature constitutes an important issue for the EU and its future.

In the case of EU's enlargement, the logic of culture plays a very interesting role. While the logic of anarchy makes the enlargement necessary, the logic of culture determines what kind of states would be able to join the EU. It seems that in the case of the EU, culture is important for a state for coming in, while in the case of the European expansion culture was important once in. This does not mean that culture was not important at all in determining membership of international society. It rather implies that cultural diversity at the global level was so great that certain tolerance on the part of the Europeans was necessary for mutual adjustment. The same does seem to apply to the European level today where cultural diversity is not so significant. Thus cultural homogeneity is seen as extremely important for the smooth function of the EU.

Questions of Identity

Closely associated with the issue and function of culture is the identity question. For example, in the process of the European expansion non-European states played a decisive role in the evolution of European identity and in the maintenance of order among European states. This is because the non-Europeans became the 'other' in the European self-definition.[45]

As far as EU's enlargement is concerned, questions of identity have been raised in two directions. First, certain EU members approach very reluctantly the Turkish candidature because they think that the entry of Turkey into the EU would alienate the identity of the Union. Second, the Greek case previously and the Turkish case currently illustrate that within the candidate states themselves there is a significant debate as to whether joining the EU implies alienating national culture.

Mutual Adjustments

Analysing the expansion of the European society of states, it would be wrong to suggest that the Europeans first developed its own rules and institutions and then exported them to the rest of the world. Not only did the European states not have a set of established rules and institutions that they attempted to impose on the rest of the world, but they continually modified the rules and institutions of their developing international system to take account of its wider setting. Thus the evolution of European society and its expansion were simultaneous processes which influenced and affected one another.[46] However, because the European states were convinced of the superiority of their institutions, they thought that it was their duty to spread their institutions and standards around the globe. This meant that for joining the international society, non-European states should be able to fulfil the standards set by the European states.[47]

Like in the case of the European expansion, EU's enlargement process is characterised by the need of the EU members to modify the rules and institutions to take account both of the wider setting and the effects of the enlargement on the working of EU's institutions and policies. Nevertheless, the EU has devised concrete standards that the candidate states have to fulfil to join the Union. But as in the case of the non-European states that sought to join international society, the fulfilling of standards has become an issue of debate within the candidate states. For example, there are political forces that oppose large-scale structural changes with the justification that such changes may jeopardise the societal, political and economic stability of their state. Such an argumentation occurs because EU membership may serve the interests of particular political and economic elites, but it threatens those of other elites whose interests are incompatible with EU membership.

Conclusion

The purpose of this chapter was to explain the process of EU's enlargement by highlighting its similarities with the expansion of the European society of states. Such a comparative study would help one to address questions like: why does the EU seek to expand its membership? How does the EU approach each particular candidature and why? Why is there a significant debate within the EU itself regarding its enlargement process as well as which states should be accepted? Why do non-member states wish to join the EU? Is it because of political or economic considerations, or both? Why is there a debate within some candidate states regarding the appropriateness of joining the EU? What do non-member states have to do in order to gain their entry into the EU? What is the role of culture in the admission process? What happens when the culture of the EU differs from that of the candidate states? Finally, does the process of the EU's enlargement follow the logic of culture or the logic of anarchy?

The chapter has approached the issue of the EU's enlargement from the international society perspective adopted by the English School of International Relations. It has argued that the current global international society, which is taken to be culturally heterogeneous, is composed of a number of regional international societies that are more homogeneous. EU is seen as representing such a homogeneous regional international society.

Because the anarchic structure of the international system makes states insecure, it pushes them to devise different political and economic strategies to assure their survival and welfare. At the same time, the anarchic structure of the international system allows states, or groups of states, such as the EU, to increase their overall power in the international system and consequently their weight in international politics. In this context, it has been argued that the end of the Cold War has pushed extra-EU states to seek EU membership as a means to deal with the insecurities that the end of the Cold War brought with it. Thus, the EU has been seen as a vehicle through which the candidate states attempt to achieve their national interests. Yet, the end of the Cold War has provided the EU with the opportunity to increase its status in international society and the enlargement has been seen as serving the political and economic interests of the EU. Nevertheless, the enlargement process is not without problems and questions of culture and identity, as well as problems related to the undertaking of large-scale structural changes by the candidate states are central features of this process.

Finally, it has been claimed that despite the importance of culture, the expansion of international society has followed the logic of anarchy. While the logic of anarchy, operating in the international system, has brought states into international society, once in, the logic of culture has determined the degree of their integration into international society. In the case of the EU's enlargement, however, the logic of culture plays a very interesting role. While the logic of anarchy makes the enlargement necessary, the logic of culture determines what kind of states would be admitted to the EU. It seems that unlike what happens at the global level, the absence of a significant cultural diversity within Europe makes cultural homogeneity an extremely important and necessary factor for the smooth function of the EU.

Notes

[1] Nicoll William and Salmon Trevor, *Understanding the European Union*, London Longman, 2001, p. 511.
[2] *Ibid.*, p. 512.
[3] Bull Hedley, *The Anarchical Society*, London: Macmillan, 1977.
[4] See Berridge Geoffrey, 'The Political Theory and Institutional History of States Systems', *British Journal of International Studies*, vol. 6, 1980, pp. 82-92 and James Alan, 'System or Society', *Review of International Studies*, vol. 19, 1993, pp. 269-88 and 'International Society', *British Journal of International Studies*, vol. 4, 1978, pp. 91-106.
[5] See Buzan Barry, 'From International System to International Society: Structural Realism and Regime Theory Meet the English School', *International Organization*, vol. 47, 1993, pp. 327-52.
[6] Bull Hedley and Watson Adam (eds.), *The Expansion of International Society*, Oxford: Clarendon Press, 1984.
[7] Stivachtis Yannis, *The Enlargement of International Society: Culture versus Anarchy and Greece's Entry into International Society*, London: Macmillan, 1998.
[8] Waltz Kenneth, *Theory of International Politics*, Cambridge, Mass.: Addison-Wesley, 1979.
[9] Little Richard, 'The Systems Approach', in Smith Steve (ed.), *International Relations: British and American Perspectives*, Oxford: Basil Blackwell, 1985.
[10] See Morgenthau Hans, *Politics Among Nations*, 5th edition, New York: Knopf, 1973.
[11] See Krasner Stephen (ed.), *International Regimes*, Ithaca, NY: Cornell University Press, 1983 and Keohane Robert, *International Institutions and State Power*, Boulder: Westview Press, 1989.
[12] See Kratochwil Friedrich, *Rules, Norms and Decisions*, Cambridge: Cambridge University Press, 1989 and Onuf Nicholas, *World of Our Making*, Columbia, SC: University of South Caroline Press, 1989.
[13] See Keohane Robert, *After Hegemony*, Princeton, NJ: Princeton University Press, 1984.
[14] See Baldwin Richard (ed.), *Neorealism and Neoliberalism: The Contemporary Debate*, New York: Columbia University Press, 1993.
[15] Ferguson Yale and Mansbach Richard, *The Elusive Quest: Theory and International Politics*, Columbia, SC: University of South Caroline Press, 1988 and Holsti Kelevi, *The Dividing Discipline*, London: Allen & Unwin, 1987, p. 1.
[16] Fukuyama Francis, *The End of History and the Last Man*, London: Hamish Hamilton, 1992.
[17] Huntington Samuel, *The Clash of Civilizations and the Remaking of World Order*, New York: Simon & Schuster, 1996; 'The Clash of Civilizations?', *Foreign Affairs*, vol. 72, no. 3, 1993, pp. 186-94 and 'If not Civilizations, What?', *Foreign Affairs*, vol. 72, no. 5, 1993, pp. 162-87.
[18] See Butterfield Herbert and Wight Martin (eds.), *Diplomatic Investigations*, London: Allen & Unwin, 1966; Wight Martin, *Systems of State*, Leicester: Leicester University Press, 1977; *Power Politics*, Leicester: Leicester University Press, 1978; and *International Theory: The Three Traditions*, Leicester: Leicester University Press, 1991.
[19] Vincent John, 'Change in International Relations', *Review of International Studies*, vol. 9, 1983, pp. 63-70.

[20] Toynbee Arnold, *A Study of History*, 12 vols, Oxford: Oxford University Press, 1954.
[21] See Vincent John, 'The Factor of Culture in the Global International Order', *The Yearbook of World Affairs*, 1980, pp. 119-34 and Bozeman Adda, *Politics and Culture in International History*, Princeton NJ: Princeton University Press, 1960 and *The Future of Law in a Multicultural World*, Princeton NJ: Princeton university Press, 1971.
[22] Buzan, 'From International System to International Society: Structural Realism and Regime Theory Meet the English School'.
[23] See Buzan Barry and Jones Barry (eds.), *Change and the Study of International Relations*, London: Pinter, 1981 and Holsti Ole, Siverson Randolph and George Alexander (eds.), *Change in the International System*, Boulder: Westview Press, 1980.
[24] Little Richard, 'International Relations and Large-scale Historical Change' in Light Margot and A.J.R. Groom (eds.), *Contemporary International Relations*, London: Pinter, 1994.
[25] See Keohane Robert (ed.), *Neorealism and Its Critics*, New York: Columbia University Press, 1986.
[26] Buzan Barry, Jones Charles and Little Richard, *The Logic of Anarchy*, New York: Columbia University Press, 1993; Buzan Barry and Little Richard, 'The Idea of International System: Theory Meets History', *International Political Science Review*, vol. 15, 1994, pp. 231-55; and Buzan Barry and Little Richard, *The International System in World History*, Oxford: Oxford University Press, 2000.
[27] See Roberson, B. A. (ed.), *International Society and the Development of International Relations Theory*, London: Pinter, 1998.
[28] Watson Adam, 'Hedley Bull, States Systems and International Societies', *Review of International Studies*, vol. 13, 1987, pp. 147-55, on p. 147.
[29] *Ibid.*, p. 147.
[30] Bull, *The Anarchical Society*, pp. 9-10.
[31] *Ibid.*, p. 13.
[32] Stivachtis, *The Enlargement of International Society*, p. 18.
[33] Bull and Watson (eds.), *The Expansion of International Society*, p. 1.
[34] Cheney, L. J., *A History of the Western World or the Adventure of Europe*, London: Allen & Unwin, 1959, p. 1 and Maclennan Kenneth, *The Cost of A New World*, London: Church Missionary Society, 1926.
[35] Waltz, *Theory of International Politics*, p. 116.
[36] Watson Adam, 'Introduction' in Bull and Watson, *The Expansion of International Society*, p. 16.
[37] See Zysman John and Schaartz Andrew (eds.), *Enlarging Europe: The Industrial Foundations of a New Reality*, San Francisco: University of California at Berkeley, 1998.
[38] See Stivachtis, *The Enlargement of International Society*, chapter 4; Bull and Watson (eds.), *The Expansion of International Society*, chapters 5-13; and Gong Gerritt, *The Standard of Civilization in International Society*, Oxford: Clarendon Press, 1984.
[39] Stivachtis Yannis, 'Greece and the Eastern Mediterranean Region' in Diez Thomas (ed.), *Modern Conflict, Postmodern Union: The EU and the Cyprus Conflict*, Manchester: Manchester University Press, 2002.
[40] See Stivachtis, *The Enlargement of International Society*, chapter 4; Bull and Watson (eds.), *The Expansion of International Society*, chapters 5-13; and Gong, *The Standard of Civilization in International Society*.

[41] See Palan Ronen and Abbott Jason, *State Strategies in the Global Political Economy*, London: Continuum, 1999.

[42] Gulick Edward, *Europe's Classical Balance of Power*, Ithaca, NY: Cornell University Press, 1955, p. 3 and Watson Adam, *The Evolution of International Society*, London: Routledge, 1992, p. 195.

[43] Bull Hedley, Kingsbury Benedict and Roberts Adam (eds.), *Hugo Grotius and International Relations*, Oxford: Clarendon Press, 1990, p. 82.

[44] See Dinan Desmon, *Ever Closer Union*, London: Macmillan 1999, Part I and Nicoll William and Salmon Trevor, *Understanding the European Union*, Part I.

[45] See Neumann Iver and Welsh Jennifer, 'The Other in the European Self-definition', *Review of International Studies*, vol. 17, 1993, pp. 26-44 and Watson, 'Introduction', in Bull and Watson (eds.), *The Expansion of International Soc*iety.

[46] Gong, *The Standard of Civilization in International Society*, p. 6.

[47] See Stivachtis, *The Enlargement of International Society*, chapter 4; Bull and Watson (eds.), *The Expansion of International Society*, chapters 5-13; and Gong, *The Standard of Civilization in International Society*.

References

Baldwin Richard (ed.). (1993), *Neorealism and Neoliberalism: The Contemporary Debate*, New York: Columbia University Press.

Berridge Geoffrey. 'The Political Theory and Institutional History of States Systems', *British Journal of International Studies*, vol. 6, 1980, pp. 82-92.

Bozeman Adda. (1960), *Politics and Culture in International History*, Princeton NJ: Princeton University Press.

Bozeman Adda. (1971), *The Future of Law in a Multicultural World*, Princeton NJ: Princeton University Press.

Bull Hedley. (1977), *The Anarchical Society*, London: Macmillan.

Bull Hedley, Kingsley Benedict and Roberts Adam (eds.). (1990), *Hugo Grotius and International Relations*, Oxford: Clarendon Press.

Bull Hedley and Watson Adam (eds.). (1984), *The Expansion of International Society*, Oxford: Clarendon Press.

Butterfield Herbert and Wight Martin (eds.). (1966), *Diplomatic Investigations*, London: Allen & Unwin.

Buzan Barry. 'From International System to International Society: Structural Realism and Regime Theory Meet the English School', *International Organization*, vol. 47, 1993, pp. 327-352.

Buzan Barry and Jones Barry (eds.). (1981), *Change and the Study of International Relations*, London: Pinter.

Buzan Barry and Little Richard, 'The Idea of International System: Theory Meets History', *International Political Science Review*, vol. 15, 1994, pp. 231-255.

Buzan Barry and Little Richard. (2000), *The International System in World History*, Oxford: Oxford University Press.

Buzan Barry, Jones Charles and Little Richard. (1993), *The Logic of Anarchy*, New York: Columbia University Press.

Cheney. L. J. (1959), *A History of the Western World or the Adventure of Europe*, London: Allen & Unwin.
Diez Thomas (ed.). (2002), *Modern Conflict, Postmodern Union: The EU and the Cyprus Conflict*, Manchester: Manchester University Press.
Dinan Desmon. (1999), *Ever Closer Union*, London: Macmillan.
Ferguson Yale and Mansbach Richard. (1988), *The Elusive Quest: Theory and International Politics*, Columbia, SC: University of South Caroline Press.
Fukuyama Francis. (1992), *The End of History and the Last Man*, London: Hamish Hamilton.
Gong Gerritt. (1984), *The Standard of Civilization in International Society*, Oxford: Clarendon Press.
Gulick Edward. (1955), *Europe's Classical Balance of Power*, Ithaca, NY: Cornell University Press.
Holsti Kalevi. (1987), *The Dividing Discipline*, London: Allen & Unwin.
Holsti Ole, Siverson Randolph and George Alexander (eds.). (1980), *Change in the International System*, Boulder: Westview Press.
Huntington Samuel. (1996), *The Clash of Civilizations and the Remaking of World Order*, New York: Simon & Schuster.
Huntington Samuel. 'If not Civilizations, What?', *Foreign Affairs*, vol. 72, no. 5, 1993, pp. 162-187.
Huntington Samuel. 'The Clash of Civilizations?', *Foreign Affairs*, vol. 72, no. 3, 1993, pp. 186-194.
James Alan. 'System or Society', *Review of International Studies*, vol. 19, 1993, pp. 269-88.
James Alan. 'International Society', *British Journal of International Studies*, vol. 4, 1978, pp. 91-106.
Keohane Robert. (1984), *After Hegemony*, Princeton, NJ: Princeton University Press.
Keohane Robert (ed.). (1986), *Neorealism and Its Critics*, New York: Columbia University Press.
Keohane Robert. (1989), *International Institutions and State Power*, Boulder: Westview Press.
Krasner Stephen. (ed.) (1983), *International Regimes*, Ithaca, NY: Cornell University Press.
Kratochwil Friedrich (1989), *Rules, Norms and Decisions*, Cambridge: Cambridge University Press.
Light Margot and A.J.R. Groom (eds.). (1994), *Contemporary International Relations*, London: Pinter.
Little Richard. 'The Systems Approach', in Smith Steve (ed.) (1985), *International Relations: British and American Perspectives*, Oxford: Basil Blackwell.
Little Richard. 'International Relations and Large-scale Historical Change' in Light Margot and A.J.R. Groom (eds.). (1994), *Contemporary International Relations*, London: Pinter.
Maclennan Kenneth. (1926), *The Cost of A New World*, London: Church Missionary Society.
Morgenthau Hans. (1973), *Politics Among Nations*, 5th edition, New York: Knopf.
Neumann Iver and Welsh Jennifer. 'The Other in the European Self-definition', *Review of International Studies*, vol. 17, 1993, pp. 26-44.
Nicoll William and Salmon Trevor. (2001), *Understanding the European Union*, London: Longman.
Onuf Nicholas. (1989), *World of Our Making*, Columbia, SC: University of South Carolina Press.

Palan Ronen and Abbott Jason. (1999), *State Strategies in the Global Political Economy*, London: Continuum.
Roberson, B.A. (ed.) (1998), *International Society and the Development of International Relations Theory*, London: Pinter.
Smith Steve. (ed.) (1985), *International Relations: British and American Perspectives*, Oxford: Basil Blackwell.
Stivachtis Yannis. (1998), *The Enlargement of International Society: Culture versus Anarchy and Greece's Entry into International Society*, London: Macmillan.
Stivachtis Yannis. 'Greece and the Eastern Mediterranean Region' in Diez Thomas (ed.). (2002), *Modern Conflict, Postmodern Union: The EU and the Cyprus Conflict*, Manchester: Manchester University Press.
Toynbee Arnold. (1954), *A Study of History*, 12 vols, Oxford: Oxford University Press.
Vincent John. 'The Factor of Culture in the Global International Order', *The Yearbook of World Affairs*, 1980, pp. 119-134.
Vincent John. 'Change in International Relations', *Review of International Studies*, vol. 9, 1983, pp. 63-70.
Waltz Kenneth. (1979), *Theory of International Politics*, Cambridge, Mass.: Addison-Wesley.
Watson Adam, 'Hedley Bull. 'States Systems and International Societies', *Review of International Studies*, vol. 13, 1987, pp. 147-155.
Watson Adam (1992). *The Evolution of International Society*, London: Routledge.
Wight Martin (1977). *Systems of State*, Leicester: Leicester University Press.
Wight Martin (1978). *Power Politics*, Leicester: Leicester University Press.
Wight Martin (1991). *International Theory: The Three Traditions*, Leicester: Leicester University Press.
Zysman John and Schaartz Andrew (eds.). (1998), *Enlarging Europe: The Industrial Foundations of a New Reality*, San Francisco: University of California at Berkeley.

Chapter 3

NATO After the Cold War[1]

Joyce P. Kaufman

Introduction

On 7 June 2001 a headline in *The New York Times* read 'Armies of Europe Failing to Meet Goals, Sapping NATO'.[2] Not quite four months later, for the first time in its history NATO invoked Article 5 as a response to the devastating terrorist attacks on New York and Washington. The June article describes clearly the failures of NATO to meet its stated goal to improve its military effectiveness, thereby contributing to a significant gap – political as well as military – between the United States and its European allies. Yet the unambiguous allied response to the events of 11 September suggests a NATO that, if not resurgent, is at least willing to take action when one of the member states is attacked directly. What remains uncertain, however, is what the attacks and the unified response will mean for NATO in the longer-term.

The September attacks and unified NATO response came at a time when NATO's role and usefulness were being questioned. Prior to 11 September, NATO was facing serious questions about its relevance as a collective defense alliance. In fact, its primary role seemed to have evolved into one of peacekeeping in the Balkans, albeit without any clear decision that NATO *should* focus on that role. Since then, the Alliance's actions indicate that it has the will to take military action against an aggressor in response to a direct attack, as originally envisioned in the NATO treaty. But what remains unclear is what the continuing role of the Alliance will be, especially since the United States has chosen to operate militarily largely outside the NATO framework in response to 11 September. Does this suggest that despite the initial message sent by invoking Article 5, the primary mission of NATO will remain peacekeeping? What does Article 5 really mean when the attack was by a non-state actor, (e.g., a terrorist group), rather than a nation-state against whom a military response could easily be defined? And, most important, questions remain about what role NATO really does and should play in the world today, i.e., what is the future of NATO after the Cold War?

Clearly questions confront the Alliance as it looks to its future. I will argue here that in order to think about its future, NATO first must examine the lessons of its recent past, especially Bosnia and Kosovo, for the answers they can provide. But what does the future hold for NATO, given those lessons? With the 'war on terrorism' underway as this paper is being revised, how the Alliance chooses to answer those questions will determine its success and endurance in the future.

In this piece, I will review two of the major challenges to Alliance unity after the Cold War ended: the conflicts in the Balkans (specifically, Bosnia and Kosovo) and the decision to enlarge, and will draw some conclusions from those cases about the lessons that NATO learned. Although the focus is on the period 1989 through 1999, I will conclude by speculating on NATO's prospects for the future, given the Balkans and the events of 11 September 2001.

NATO: 1989-1999

The decade from 1989 to 1999 was a time of change and even crisis for the Atlantic Alliance as it confronted the fall of the Berlin Wall and German unification, the end of the communist regimes in Eastern and Central Europe, and the disintegration of the Soviet Union, all things that the West had hoped for but never imagined would become reality. Suddenly NATO no longer had to face a single threat emanating from the Soviet Union but rather confronted new challenges tied to ethnic and civil unrest on the borders of Western Europe. Rather than facing a military attack through the Fulda Gap, the classic NATO conflict/crisis scenario, NATO was facing human rights abuses and questions about out-of-area intervention. Coming at a time when the Alliance was trying to look forward and to incorporate new members, the growing conflicts in the Balkans served to remind NATO members that they had a responsibility to ensure peace and stability in Europe, even at great political cost. And the Alliance members were confronted with trying to make policy decisions in these new areas while simultaneously balancing different domestic political priorities. With the end of the Cold War it was incumbent upon NATO to redefine itself and its mission in light of these changing global political, military and strategic realities.

This decade was also noteworthy for NATO because it was characterized by the confluence of a number of critical events and changes in Alliance policy. While it can be argued that dealing with the wars in former Yugoslavia represented a policy strand separate from other issues that NATO was dealing with during this period such as enlargement and the Partnership for Peace (PfP), the reality is that the issues converged and in that intersection, influenced the direction that each strand would take. While addressing the enlargement issue in 1993 and 1994, which was contentious enough, NATO preferred to defer decisions regarding military action in the Balkans, lest the latter derail the former. Similarly, the formal admission of new members at the 50th anniversary summit in April 1999 was overshadowed by the bombing campaign against Serbia and Montenegro, which also made dramatically clear what NATO membership would now involve. (As a new NATO member Hungary, for example, became a forward base for the air operations, which is not necessarily what that country envisioned as part of NATO membership.) Ultimately the decisions that NATO made on these various issues were influenced or even guided by the domestic political considerations of each of the member states and not solely Alliance priorities.

The NATO policy-making process, too, brought with it certain challenges that were affected by domestic as well as Alliance politics. While the individual nations ultimately might have agreed to support the consensus position on a range of issues, individually some clearly continued to have reservations that inevitably affected the public position(s) taken by representatives of that nation or policies made by its legislative bodies. In other words, speaking of a single 'NATO position,' disguises the fact that the Alliance had, and continues to have, differences among member nations that will affect the Alliance into the future.

NATO today, early in the 21st century, is an Alliance of 19 nations, some of whom had been adversaries in the past.[3] Further, the organization is planning to enlarge still further at some point in the not-too-distant future. These new members, recently admitted and future, bring with them a different perspective on membership as well as on their relationship to the Alliance, both of which will change the character of the organization still further. Their reasons for joining NATO are far different from those that brought in the original members, as are their expectations of Alliance membership. Some of the countries of Central and Eastern Europe see Alliance membership as an important stepping-stone to joining the European Union and a way of gaining recognition as a 'western' nation, in other words, political and economic rather than or in addition to security reasons.

Given the fact that it is no longer solely a defensive alliance premised on the need to deter an aggressive adversary, if NATO is to continue and to remain credible the 'new NATO' must be prepared and able to meet the changing nature of the threats it is likely to encounter in the future. The conflicts in the former Yugoslavia bear witness to some of the types of threats challenges that the Alliance is likely to confront on its borders. The continuing possibility of conflict in Macedonia, for example, serves as another stark reminder that peace in the Balkans is far from assured and that NATO's work there is not yet done. And 11 September is a clear warning that no NATO nation is immune to direct attack, thereby underscoring the ongoing relevance of Article 5.

The conflicts in the former Yugoslavia that started in 1991 served as a challenge to NATO at a time when the Alliance was dealing with a number of issues. There is little doubt that NATO after June 1999, and the ending of the conflict with Yugoslavia, is a different Alliance than NATO of 1989. These changes are reflected in the Strategic Concept that the Alliance adopted in1999, compared with the Strategic Concept of 1991, as well as the ways in which NATO now operates, for example. The Balkans was a test of NATO and its Partnership for Peace in a way that it had not been tested before. While the lessons were painful and difficult, if learned they will ensure that the Alliance will be stronger and more enduring.

The Balkans and Enlargement Issues

It would be impossible to determine what lessons NATO learned since 1991 and the end of the Cold War that would help guide the Alliance into the next century without considering the two major issues that NATO had to, or chose to, confront: the conflicts in the Balkans, and the decision to enlarge the Alliance eastward to include new members from Central and Eastern Europe. This is not to suggest that these are the only issues that NATO has confronted, e.g., the need to modernize militarily and restructure organizationally. However, these two areas are instructive because they represent instances where domestic political priorities clashed directly with Alliance needs, contributing to uncertainty and dissension among NATO members.

In trying to determine how some of the decisions were made within NATO on each of these issues, I interviewed decision makers at NATO headquarters, but also in London and Berlin as well as Washington. Most of the policy makers with whom I spoke claimed that the decisions regarding NATO enlargement and the PfP were separate from the decisions made regarding military action in the Balkans, or, at the least, that they were 'different sides of the same policy' which, when taken together, were designed to help build a more stable Europe. However, the reality is that they were not nor could they remain distinct from one another. The lesson here is that the Alliance needs to recognize that there will inevitably be a confluence among policy issues and, further, that dissension in one area will overlap into and influence decisions made regarding another area.

NATO and the Conflicts in the Balkans

In 1990 and 1991, as Yugoslavia was beginning to disintegrate, the governments of Western Europe as well as the United States had other concerns. In addition to the impact of the end of the Cold War, bringing with it German unification among other significant changes, Western Europe was dealing with the prospect of political union as outlined in the Maastricht Treaty of December 1991. Further, the U.S. and Europe had just come through the Persian Gulf War and were not eager to get engaged in another conflict with so many political issues still outstanding.

The US and European allies were not unaware of the conflicts that were escalating in the former Yugoslavia, but each of the allied countries had other priorities. As a result of the domestic political and economic issues that the alliance members were facing, and despite the European countries' desire to take more responsibility for their own security, the reality was that no country wanted to or emerged to take a leadership role within NATO to address the growing conflict. In effect, then, as an alliance NATO did little to address the crisis growing on its borders at that time. Rather, the burden fell first on the EC/EU nations and then the United Nations. It was only after their inability to control the conflict(s) became apparent and the tide of public opinion shifted that NATO started to take an aggressive role.

The notion of the impact of domestic politics and the need to respond to internal priorities at the expense of Alliance action, is made by Michael Mandelbaum as a way to explain NATO's reluctance to enter the conflict and the deep divisions that were growing within the Alliance because of the former Yugoslavia. 'NATO's members came to the conflicts in Yugoslavia with different sympathies which had their roots in history and domestic politics.... These different sympathies led inevitably to different interpretations of the conflict.'[4] The result of these differences in interpretations, policies, and priorities was that both NATO, which was founded to protect the countries of Western Europe, and the European

Community, the organization then-working toward political and economic union in Europe, proved unwilling to intervene militarily in any way to limit or control the conflict growing in Yugoslavia. As the situation continued to escalate, the inability to act raised fundamental questions for both these organizations. For the EC, Yugoslavia was the first major test of an organization seeking to create unified political and defense policies for Western European and, as history shows, the EC failed that test. For NATO, determining how to deal with the conflicts escalating first in Croatia and then in Bosnia proved to be a challenge to Alliance unity, but also regarding the role that NATO should – and could – play in the post-Cold War world.

By early in 1993, the war in Bosnia was escalating and the United States had a new president who had campaigned for a more assertive US role in Bosnia. The European countries were moving toward integration and, in response to the desire to take some responsibility regarding the situation in Bosnia, had begun to deploy troops in support of the UN (UNPROFOR) mission. And although NATO was starting to take some action, it was limited in scope.[5] In retrospect, one of the lessons of Bosnia for NATO is the realization that as an Alliance of sovereign nations, NATO cannot take action unless or until there is pressure to do so and the member states perceive that it is in their political interest.

That confluence did not take place until two years later, when NATO faced increased political pressure to take action following a mortar attack on the market in Sarajevo on 28 August 1995, that killed 37 civilians and wounded 88. The boldness of that attack against the civilians in the city who had already suffered so much was the focus of a great deal of media attention in the United States and Europe, and provoked an outcry against the human rights abuses that had been inflicted during the war. Although these abuses had been going on for a number of years at that point, the August Sarajevo market massacre proved to be the proverbial straw that broke the camel's back, resulting in public outcry and concomitant political pressure on political leaders to take action. This provided the political push that the leaders of the Alliance nations needed, and opened the way for the initiation of a three-week campaign of NATO air strikes against Bosnian Serb targets, 'Operation Deliberate Force', which was ordered following the mortar attack.

This is not to suggest that nothing had been done between the outbreak of the conflicts in 1991 and NATO's decision to mount a major campaign in August 1995. However, the actions that were taken were neither decisive nor did they convey a sense that NATO had the political will to follow through with any of its threats. For example, under EC auspices, attempts were made to negotiate a settlement in 1992 and 1993. When those attempts failed for any number of reasons (including U.S. reticence to support the agreement),[6] the then-newly-created Contact Group tried unsuccessfully to revive the negotiations. During this period from 1991 through 1995, the United Nations became the primary organization with responsibility for Bosnia, and the attempts that this organization made to control the situation was ineffectual as well. NATO did mount a number of military actions during this period, but they, too, were limited in scope and were tied specifically to supporting existing UN resolutions. In short, despite pressure at various points on NATO to take decisive action, it was not until the Sarajevo massacre that the Alliance agreed to do so.

It is now clear that a number of factors converged so that by the end of August 1995, NATO was finally in a position to initiate the air strikes that it had only threatened in the past. Reviewing these is instructive for the lessons that they can teach. First, changing domestic factors within the NATO nations cannot be underestimated in understanding the reasons for the subsequent and rather dramatic shift in policy leading to decisive military action. For example, an article entitled 'Enter the Americans', published in *The Economist* in August 1995, notes somewhat cynically that 'Bill Clinton seems to have decided, rather suddenly, that the Bosnian war should be settled before next year's American presidential election'.[7] Nonetheless, the change in U.S. policy, contributing directly to its apparent willingness to take the lead regarding Bosnia, was what NATO needed in order to become more aggressive militarily which changed the course of the conflict. Second, this assertion of U.S. leadership altered further the dynamics within NATO, which resulted finally in a clear policy direction for the Alliance. Third, the last of the British troops which had been on the ground in support of UNPROFOR had been withdrawn, and the 'dual-key' arrangement that required NATO to go through the UN prior to authorizing air strikes had been lifted so that NATO had more direct authority over its military decisions in Bosnia.

After three years of war in Bosnia that had contributed directly to dissension within the Alliance regarding policy and procedures, domestic and international political factors converged resulting, finally, in a push for NATO action. As a result, the NATO nations agreed upon what they should do, and they had both the political will and military forces available to ensure that they would be successful. Operation Deliberate Force, coupled with a shift in the dynamics on the ground, contributed directly to the willingness of all the belligerents to negotiate an end to the conflict. On November 1, 1995, formal talks began at Wright-Patterson Air Force Base in Ohio, with the formal peace agreement signed in Paris in December 1995. The war in Bosnia was finally over.

NATO and Kosovo

In 1999, NATO was moving toward enlargement while simultaneously heading toward war with Serbia over the situation in Kosovo. By January 1999, it was apparent that the cease-fire imposed in October 1998 in the hope of avoiding conflict was barely holding, as fighting broke out between Serb police and ethnic-Albanian rebels in the province. Once again, though, initially the hope was that the situation could be addressed through negotiation. With the threat of NATO air strikes as a backdrop, and facing increasing international pressure to take action, the various sides came to the negotiating table in February, meeting at Rambouillet, a chateau outside Paris. Called under European leadership, the meeting was to be co-chaired by the British and French assisted by American envoy Chris Hill, a Russian representative, and Wolfgang Petrisch, Austrian Ambassador to Belgrade and designated EU special envoy.

From the beginning, this negotiation was surrounded by political drama not only for the obvious reason of taking place under the ongoing threat of NATO military action, but for the political subtext, specifically, the relationships among the allies. Rambouillet represented a chance for the Europeans to redeem themselves following their early failure to successfully halt the conflict in Bosnia and the secondary role that they played in the Dayton negotiations, which, under U.S. leadership, did bring an end to that war. And, if the Rambouillet talks were successful, France and Britain were prepared to take the lead in providing troops for a peacekeeping force. In addition, the central role played by the Europeans at Rambouillet was seen as an important step forward in the creation of a common European foreign and security policy.

Even given the alternative, which was assurance of NATO bombing, the talks failed. Despite the ongoing threats of NATO action, the decision to move forward with military action against Yugoslavia (i.e., Serbia and Montenegro) at the end of March was divisive for the Alliance which had not yet agreed upon the force that would be deployed or what authority such a force would have. This was in spite of the fact that the delegates to the talks were told that they had a two-week window in which to reach an agreement or NATO force would be used.

It is here that the divisions within NATO become even more apparent. France, which continued to remain outside the formal NATO military command structure, demanded that any NATO force deployed would have to report to the Contact Group. However, the divergent views of those six nations regarding the use of force inevitably diluted NATO's authority as well as undermined its will to act. Ultimately, although the Contact Group members did agree that NATO could authorize air strikes against Yugoslavia if Milosevic did not accept a peace agreement, other divisions remained. For example, going into the negotiations France and Britain were committed to sending ground troops to Kosovo if that should become necessary, but other NATO nations, especially the United States, were unwilling to make that commitment at that time. And even when the use of force appeared to be inevitable, the prospect raised important sovereignty questions as well as confronting Article 5 head-on. NATO forces had never been used in a direct confrontation such as the mission required here. Further, there was no direct attack on any NATO partner, and the territory in question was, theoretically, out of the NATO guidelines area, *per se*. Hence, if agreed to, the bombing of Yugoslavia would not only be a new mission but an out-of-area one for the Alliance, thereby setting a precedent for future NATO actions.

The failure of the negotiations at Rambouillet made NATO military action necessary if the Alliance was to appear credible. But the decision surrounding that next step put pressure on an already fractured alliance. NATO was facing two sets of decisions: first, when and how to respond to the failure of the talks and, second, once a decision to use air strikes was made, how long should NATO continue before taking additional measures such as sending in ground troops? At one end, Britain was taking the lead in asserting the need for a forceful response while, at the other extreme, Greece and Italy resisted the use of force at all and continued to press for a diplomatic solution. In Germany, the recently elected government of Chancellor Gerhard Schroeder had to balance a tenuous political coalition and therefore found itself in a delicate position that only grew worse once the use of ground forces was raised as a possibility. And the United States' position was that the bombing was necessary to demonstrate NATO's opposition to aggression, to deter further attacks on civilians, and to damage Serbia's capacity to wage war. But it remained steadfast in its opposition to the deployment of ground forces, further illustrating the range of opinions – and disagreement – among the members of the Alliance.[8]

Finally, on March 24 with a negotiated settlement apparently impossible, NATO initiated a military attack against Yugoslavia. Although getting an agreement had not been easy and, in fact, further split an already divided Alliance, escalating violence by the Serbs in Kosovo during the period from mid-February through mid-March while the talks were underway finally convinced even the most recalcitrant allies, such as France, that action needed to be taken. Further, the prevailing belief that the bombing would last only a few days and that Serbia would back down quickly in the face of NATO military force helped make the decision more palatable. However, the NATO air bombing lasted eleven weeks until finally, early in June, a peace agreement was signed that brought an end to the military action.

With the signing of the agreement, NATO deployed more than 30,000 (KFOR) troops to Kosovo under British command to maintain the peace that was agreed upon. In addition, civilian experts were sent to help facilitate the transition to civilian control. But the lessons and legacies of Kosovo remain. On the one hand, despite many differences initially, the Alliance was able to pull together and take action far more rapidly than it was able to in Bosnia. On the other hand, miscalculations about Serb intentions and mistakes that were made from the initial negotiation and throughout the campaign in Kosovo led to questions about NATO's credibility and raised some serious questions about its place and roles after the Cold War. Perhaps most damning have been the accusations that from the beginning NATO miscalculated what Milosevic would do, thereby leading the Alliance into a war that it was reluctant to begin.

NATO Enlargement

In March 1999, as NATO was grappling with the situation in Kosovo, the failure of the talks at Rambouillet and discussing what actions to take next, it was also preparing for a summit in celebration of its 50th anniversary as well as the admission of three new members. The decision to admit new members was the result of six years of discussion within the Alliance tied, in part, to questions about NATO after the Cold War. Hence, in 1993 as NATO was dealing with the situation escalating in Bosnia, it was also attempting to bring about another major change in policy, that is, the inclusion of new members. The decision to enlarge the Alliance eastward brought with it a separate set of political issues that threatened Alliance unity. Despite the goals outlined in the Strategic Concept of 1991, the discussions surrounding NATO enlargement illustrate clearly the lack of agreement about the future of the Alliance.

The impetus for enlarging the Alliance came from the United States as early as 1993. In January 1994, in the first European trip of his presidency, Bill Clinton met with other NATO leaders in Brussels and reaffirmed the notion that Alliance membership should be open to new members.[9] In the final communique of that meeting, an invitation was issued by NATO for countries to join a new Partnership for Peace (PfP) program, the next step toward NATO enlargement. Hence, in 1993 and 1994, as the war in Bosnia was escalating, the attention of the U.S. regarding NATO policy was directed primarily at ways to enlarge the Alliance, rather than on ways to work within it to address the escalating conflict.

The road to enlargement was a politically difficult one for NATO. Many of the European allies felt that the U.S. had not consulted with them before moving forward to push this idea, conjuring up images of past events when the U.S. took the lead in policy decisions leaving the European allies to trail behind, often having to justify those decisions to an uncertain legislature and wary public.[10] One of the major questions raised on both sides of the Atlantic was regarding the costs associated with an enlarged Alliance that included members of the former Soviet bloc which had outdated and obsolete equipment that was not compatible with other NATO forces. And, within Europe especially, there was growing concern about how NATO enlargement would affect Russia.

The sense of unease about the cost issue increased over time as information was released from a Clinton administration study that suggested that Western Europe, not the United States, should shoulder the financial burden for NATO expansion, and the estimated costs varied wildly. A 1995 Rand study estimated that the total costs would be between $10 and $50 billion, assessed at the rate of anywhere between $1 and $5 billion a year for ten years. The Congressional Budget Office, the accounting arm of the U.S. Congress, estimated the costs at $125 billion over 15 years. And the Defense Department, in its own report, estimated that the amount would be between $25 and $37 billion over 10 to 12 years.[11] And these still did not answer the question of who would pay.

However money was not the only consideration, especially for the European allies. An article in *Survival* on the costs of NATO enlargement notes that this 'is not just a financial calculation but also a political and strategic one'. The article explains that cost estimates will depend on a number of factors including 'who joins the Alliance, how new Article 5 commitments are implemented in terms of military strategy, how defense postures in both old and new members are adjusted, and how the financial burdens are distributed among NATO members'.[12] In short, estimating 'costs' had to take into account a number of factors, not all of them tangible, which the Alliance had not yet addressed.

Nonetheless, the plan to enlarge the Alliance moved forward. But the more it was discussed, the more divisive it became. Russia was especially threatened by the prospect, fearing that NATO enlargement would push Russia out of Europe at a time when, for a number of reasons, it needed and wanted to be included the most. Boris Yeltsin was also directly threatened by the move that gave credibility to right-wing elements within Russia, undermining his leadership directly. As the discussions continued, Germany remained supportive of the idea, while Britain and France resisted in part due to the belief that expanded membership would alter the delicate decision making balance that existed within the Alliance. Where Britain eventually did reverse its position and supported enlargement, France did not, thereby creating further strains between the United States and France and, by implication, within the Alliance as a whole. When France did finally support the idea of opening NATO to new members, it also believed that the invitation must be extended to Romania and Slovenia, as well as the Czech Republic, Hungary and Poland, which were the three countries supported by the United States. These internal disagreements further politicized the enlargement issue and precluded the possibility that France would return to the NATO military command structure, a possibility that had been under discussion.

Despite the internal disagreements, a formal invitation was issued to Hungary, Poland and the Czech Republic in May 1997 at a NATO summit meeting in Madrid. The invitation was made possible only after then-NATO Secretary General Solana was able to negotiate an agreement with Russia, the 'Founding Act on Mutual Relations, Cooperation and Security,' that laid out the terms for a formal relationship between NATO and Russia, including the mechanisms for, and areas of consultation and cooperation.

The three newest members joined the Alliance as of the Washington Summit of April 1999, as NATO was in the midst of its bombing campaign against Serbia over Kosovo. It is important to note that the three members who joined the Alliance in 1999, Hungary, Poland and the Czech Republic, inherited the situation that was unfolding rather than being directly involved with the decision making, and they were clearly ambivalent. The three had planned to join what had been the longest-lived peaceful alliance, only to find themselves in the midst of a war. The Czech government was divided on its support of this action, with President Havel supporting it and Prime Minister Zeman against it; only 35 per cent of the Czech public indicated support for the air strikes. By contrast, the Polish government supported the war, as did 60 per cent of the Polish public.[13] Hungary, even with a large ethnic population in the Vojvodina province of Serbia, agreed to open its airspace, military bases, and transportation routes to NATO.

Kosovo served as a quick and clear reminder of what Alliance membership would mean in the post-Cold War world as NATO had to face new challenges and threats. Further, these three newest members came to the Alliance with different goals, perspectives and expectations as well as different reasons for joining than the countries of Western Europe, the United States and Canada did. And those attitudes and perspectives most likely will be shared by additional countries, such as Romania, Slovenia and the Baltic states which might be invited to join in the future. The experiences of Kosovo, and the fact that the three members admitted in April 1999 had to become part of that military action, will also mean that any nation invited to join will now look at Alliance membership in a different way. Hence, despite 'official' NATO attempts to keep these issues separate, the reality is that the linkage between Alliance membership and the conflict over Kosovo cannot be minimized. Whether deliberately or not, the differences in the character of the membership of the Alliance cannot help but change the perspective and outlook of NATO as a whole.

According to the chronology outlined for enlargement, it is likely that the next round of discussions will take place within the next few years (i.e., by 2005). The new members will be entering a different NATO, however, than the Alliance that existed in 1999 when the first round of enlargement occurred. The decisions to take military action, first in Bosnia and then regarding Kosovo, were made by the "core" members of the Alliance, (i.e., the United States, Britain, Germany and France). Although decisions continue to be made by consensus it is clear that especially in the case of Kosovo, the Alliance was far from united on what, if any, action should be taken and when. Although agreement finally was reached, for no decision can go forward unless there is consensus, which is, in effect, unanimity, it is clear that ultimately consensus was achieved because those four countries pushed for it.

As NATO looks to further enlargement, it must be cognizant of the fact that in the future, as in the past, enlargement is and will remain a political issue as well as a security one. The three newest members were not admitted based on decisions tied solely to military or security needs, nor is there any reason to assume that that will be the case in the future. Rather, the decisions surrounding which nations to invite and which to defer were, and will continue to be driven in part by domestic as well as Alliance politics, and for that reason will be divisive. There is a great danger that those divisions of the past, which temporarily were minimized in light of larger issues, will again surface and might, in fact be exacerbated when the three newest members weigh into the decision making process and as the next round of enlargement discussions begins.

Another challenge that NATO will have to face as it does admit more members will simply be the decision making process. Consensus, as opposed to voting, requires all participants to agree or in effect stand aside. However, if one participant feels strongly enough about an issue it can block any decision from going forward, in effect, imposing a veto. As the situation regarding Bosnia and then Kosovo illustrated, in the future the Alliance will be facing crisis situations in which it will have to respond relatively quickly. To be prepared for that contingency, the Alliance must come to terms with how it can effectively make decisions, especially those that could be contentious but will also need to be made in a timely fashion, in light of a larger NATO whose character is quite different. As we have seen, differences within the Alliance have made consensus decision making difficult enough with 16 member states; enlarging to 19 and more than that will make the process even more unwieldy. It will be incumbent upon NATO to anticipate and consider these issues before it is put into a position of having to respond quickly to the next crisis.

The Lessons of Bosnia and Kosovo: The Strategic Concepts of 1991 and 1999

Nowhere can the lessons of the former Yugoslavia be seen more dramatically than in a comparison of the Strategic Concept documents of 1991 and 1999. The 1991 document was approved by the NATO heads of state and government in November 1991 at the end of the Cold War and just as the conflicts in the former Yugoslavia were starting to escalate; the 1999 documents was approved at the 50th anniversary summit in April as the NATO bombing campaign against Yugoslavia was underway.

The Strategic Concept of 1991 was prescient in raising the possibility that the greatest threat to the stability of Europe would come from the ethnic rivalries and territorial disputes faced by many countries in Central and Eastern Europe. But while the document identified the new likely threats to European stability and Alliance solidarity, it did not prescribe ways to address them beyond the need for 'dialogue, cooperation, and the maintenance of a collective defense capability'.[14] One of the weaknesses of this document was the assumption that the use of military force could be avoided by negotiating a solution to a conflict. While negotiation can be an effective and important means of avoiding or resolving conflicts, some cases, such as those in Bosnia and Kosovo, cannot be resolved just with 'dialogue and cooperation'. Rather, they ultimately require the use of force, albeit in a very different way and setting than that which was initially envisioned when the Alliance was created in 1949.

In contrast to the 1991 document, the realities of the changing environment and some of the lessons learned by NATO are reflected in the 1999 Strategic Concept. One example is the acknowledgment that 'The last ten years have also seen, however, the appearance of complex new risks to Euro-Atlantic peace and stability, including oppression, ethnic conflict, economic distress, the collapse of political order, and the proliferation of weapons of mass destruction'. Reflecting these changes, the document addresses the agenda for the future, which includes, above all, the necessity to 'maintain the political will and the military means required by the entire range of its missions'.[15] In other words, this document, which was approved in the midst of NATO's bombing campaign against Yugoslavia, reflects the lessons of the Balkans that 'dialogue and cooperation' are not enough, but that the Alliance must also have the military might and political will to use those weapons if it is to remain successful and credible in achieving its goal of ensuring stability in Europe.

The 1999 document makes another important point reflecting the changes in perspective as a result of NATO's experiences in the Balkans. The section entitled 'Conflict Prevention and Crisis Management' addresses explicitly the need for NATO 'to prevent conflict, or, should a conflict arise, to contribute to its effective management, consistent with international law, including through the possibility of conducting *non-Article 5 crisis response operations'*. (Emphasis added.) This section then notes the need to support 'on a case-by-case basis... peacekeeping and other operations under the authority of the UN Security Council or the responsibility of the OSCE...' and refers explicitly to 'its subsequent decisions with respect to crisis operations in the Balkans'. Again drawing on the lessons of the conflicts in the former Yugoslavia, the document also stresses the need for NATO to 'make full use of partnership, cooperation and dialogue and its links to other organizations to contribute to preventing crises and, should they arise, defusing them at an early stage'.[16]

This suggests a number of important lessons learned as a result of NATO's experiences subsequent to 1991; primary among these is the necessity for NATO to broaden its outlook regarding what constitutes the need for non-Article 5 intervention. Also, given the importance and political necessity of working with the United Nations, NATO must anticipate that likelihood and be prepared to either get the support of the UN, or, if necessary, take whatever military action is necessary in spite of the UN. It seems clear that the points made in the 1999 document, the importance of partnership and coordination with other organizations, the need to address and defuse crises 'at an early stage', the possibility of non-Article 5 operations, all reflect NATO's experiences in the Balkans as well as the changing realities that will guide NATO operations in the future. Further, the 1999 Strategic Concept strongly suggests that NATO is willing to consider other such operations should circumstances arise in the future that could threaten European peace and stability.

Changing geopolitical as well as military realities reinforce the lessons of the Balkans that NATO must be prepared to take the initiative again in the future in other out-of-area missions. Or, more important, it must be prepared to outline clearly *and to reach agreement on* what the criteria are for intervention in the future, just as Article 5 defined NATO's role from 1949 until Bosnia. What set of circumstances would NATO consider both relevant and important enough to the member states and the Alliance as a whole to require military intervention? Clearly the conflicts in the Balkans were one case where the human rights violations were so egregious and the dangers of escalation into the territory of Greece, (a NATO ally), seen as possible enough to warrant NATO action. What remains unclear is where the lines for NATO action are now drawn beyond the Balkans. Further, should NATO peacekeeping troops should be brought in to augment any UN contingent posted in any part of Europe, broadly defined? If the Alliance is really committed to the terms of the 1999 Strategic Concept and the goal of promoting Euro-Atlantic values throughout Europe, then it must be prepared to intervene in future out-of-area conflicts assuming all relevant criteria are met, or risk further undermining of its credibility.

What we see then as we look to the future of NATO into the 21st century is an Alliance that acknowledges the need to move away from a Cold War force posture and policies and toward the type of flexible force structure that will better enable it to meet the challenges it is likely to face. Concomitant with that must be NATO's willingness to use those forces in support of its newly defined mission. As one high level official in the British government noted in an interview reflecting upon this point, 'Despite all the talk about the need to change and meet new challenges, nothing really did change until NATO was forced to do so'.[17]

NATO After the Cold War: Lessons Learned

Given the brief synopsis of critical events presented above, the question remains: what lessons did NATO learn that would help direct it in the future?

Political/Diplomatic versus Military Action

As NATO begins to look to its future, as an Alliance it also must reflect upon the recent past. The Strategic Concept of 1999 reflects the lessons of the Balkans with the acknowledgment that if it is to be successful at avoiding or resolving conflict, dialogue and cooperation must be supported by military force and the political will to use those forces. But, I contend, the lesson is more fundamental than that. When the conflicts started to emerge in the former Yugoslavia, first in Slovenia and then Croatia, the countries of the West opted to do nothing militarily, at least initially, in the belief that these conflicts were not directly related to 'national interest'. When they did choose to act, their first reaction was to use diplomacy, which, as it turns out, was successful in helping to draw those two conflicts to a quick conclusion. But that taught the wrong lesson; while resorting to diplomacy and negotiation initially to end the escalating conflict in Bosnia, that approach allowed the conflicts to grow and fester for another three years, until NATO finally agreed to take decisive action in 1995. And once the Alliance did agree to take action, to remain credible it could not fail. When NATO force was used aggressively, it did not take long for the belligerents to agree to come to the negotiating table and to reach an agreement that would be enforced by the presence of NATO peacekeeping troops.

As the crisis escalated in Kosovo in 1998 and into 1999, once again the initial tendency was to try to address the situation using diplomatic means. But here, too, the Western powers took the wrong lesson from Bosnia. Because it had been possible to negotiate and reach an agreement with Milosevic in Dayton, thereby ending the war in Bosnia, the Western countries engaged in the discussions at Rambouillet assumed that the past would be repeated here as well. But it is now clear that that assumption proved to be incorrect. Rather than driving Milosevic to an agreement using the threat of NATO bombings as a 'stick', the West in effect gave up control of the situation to him, a pattern that had started earlier in the growing conflict. The negotiations at Rambouillet were fraught with misunderstandings and misperceptions on both sides; the West underestimated Milosevic and he, in turn, misinterpreted the signals regarding divisions within the Alliance. The result was that the negotiations failed, and NATO, taking the lesson of Bosnia regarding the decisive use of force and with its credibility at stake, ultimately agreed to military action.

But reviewing the history of the negotiations regarding both Bosnia and Kosovo underscores another lesson for NATO – the importance of bringing both the political and military tracks together when addressing a conflict situation. In effect, the diplomatic track and the use of military force are different approaches to achieving the same policy goals and one must reinforce and support the other. But this means there must be close coordination between the two tracks. NATO cannot threaten the use of force, the introduction of the proverbial 'stick', into the negotiations unless it has the forces ready and is prepared to use them.

This also suggests that NATO be ready to adapt its forces and command structure in order to be more consistent with the possible roles they will have to play in the future. The NATO forces used to support the operations in Bosnia and Kosovo are very different from those, which were envisioned during the Cold War. A clear lesson of these two campaigns is that NATO must continue to evolve away from a Cold War force posture and move toward the creation of more flexible forces that will be appropriate for likely post-Cold War missions. This might include the limited but aggressive use of air strikes, as we saw in both Bosnia and

Kosovo, but also the need to be prepared to accept a peacekeeping function on the ground, such as the IFOR/SFOR and KFOR forces currently in place. And the Alliance needs to look forward and anticipate those needs, rather than being put into a position of having to react and then creating the appropriate force structure.

As NATO looks to the future and the complementary or even conflicting roles of diplomacy and military force, it also must realize that the situation it faced in Bosnia was, in many ways, unique. Rather than two belligerent sides fighting with one another, the reality was that there were three sets of actors involved, Serbs, Croats and Bosnian Muslims, which meant that alliances kept shifting. This, in turn, made the negotiation process far more difficult as the balance of power was unstable and uncertain. And, when the negotiations failed, it made it more difficult to go to war, as 'the enemy' was less clear cut. The reality, though, is that this type of situation is one that NATO is more likely to confront in the future as ethnic and religious rivalries within a given state erupt into armed conflict. This has implications for how, and with whom, NATO chooses to negotiate and against which side it might ultimately take up arms.

The Transatlantic Relationship

One of the lessons of the Balkans is that the Alliance was able to make tough decisions and remain intact, even when there were problems and disagreements. However, it is also clear that some of the policy decisions regarding the Balkans were among the most difficult and divisive that the Alliance has faced in its history to date. This was due, in part, to the impact of domestic politics, but also because of the fact that the perspectives of the various member nations, especially on both sides of the Atlantic, were very different.

I do not mean to suggest that the European allies acted as a monolithic entity who spoke with one voice. That, in fact, definitely is *not* the case. In reviewing NATO decisions during this period (1991 through 1999), whether on enlargement, Bosnia, Kosovo, etc., there was no single internal 'European' position. However, what complicated the situation was the juxtaposition of EU policy, where there was apparently one European position, as opposed to the policy positions taken by the United States, which sometimes appeared to diverge from or even be in competition with that of the EU.

Nonetheless, one of the most interesting, and potentially most important, lessons for NATO that came out of the conflicts in the Balkans is that of the importance of the transatlantic relationship, i.e., the relationship between the United States and its Western European allies. A slightly different point was made by a high-level official in the British government who noted in an interview with me that Europe could not meet a major crisis without the United States, but that the need was psychological as well as military.[18] His point, and it is a valid one, is that the transatlantic linkage has more than a political and military dimension but, virtually since it was created, one of the major advantages of NATO was ensuring ties between the United States and the countries of Europe, which, as 11 September show, clearly remain important. In fact, another official in the British government made the point even more strongly when he told me that, in his opinion, the Alliance only works if there is strong U.S. leadership. He went on to note that recent history has shown that if the United States leads and is supported by Britain and Germany, than the rest of NATO will generally support the decision.[19]

It is also apparent that another lesson to emerge that can help guide the Alliance into the future is that domestic politics cannot be ignored and that the perspectives regarding the use of force are quite different on both sides of the Atlantic. Nonetheless, and despite their differences, when they had to, the 16 member states of NATO were able to reach consensus on any number of important issues and in so doing Alliance cohesion appeared to be maintained, at least temporarily.

Lessons of Bosnia and Kosovo

One of the most important lessons of Bosnia and Kosovo is that, despite differences and disagreement, the Alliance was able to hold together and to succeed. But there are other lessons that the Alliance should draw from these experiences as well. On the one hand, in reviewing the ways in which NATO responded first to Bosnia and then to Kosovo, it is clear that the Alliance was able to act more rapidly and decisively in the latter case than in the former. To confirm this, one only has to note that it took three years for NATO to agree to act militarily in Bosnia and three months regarding Kosovo, at least from the time when the Alliance decided that action was necessary. It can be argued that at least part of the reason for the change can be attributed to the lessons of Bosnia. However, in some ways, that assessment is deceptive. The reality is that the situation in Kosovo was festering for two years before NATO decided to take action, with the delay, attributable to both domestic and Alliance politics. Nonetheless, the point that cannot be ignored is that once NATO did decide to take action it did so far more quickly than it did in Bosnia. It is possible to extrapolate still further and argue that one of the lessons of Bosnia and Kosovo is that, should similar situations arise in the future, NATO will be ready and able to act even more quickly. Or, even more optimistically, as a result of the lessons of Bosnia and Kosovo, it is possible that other such situations will be even less likely to arise in the future.

To ensure a more peaceful future in Europe will mean that NATO must continue to remain aware of and concerned about crises or potential crisis areas on its borders. It must be able to anticipate problems and have a policy and long-term strategy in place that will allow it to address problems as they arise, rather than waiting and then having to react to situations, as was the case in the Balkans. It must transform itself in order to continue to address non-Article 5 situations, which realistically, are those that the Alliance is most likely in the future. And it must be cognizant of the fact that it is likely that the situations that will arise will be even more complex and difficult to address than any anticipated during the Cold War, or perhaps even than those which the Alliance had to deal with in the Balkans to date.

NATO: The Future

When NATO invoked Article 5 as a response to the terrorist attacks on the United States it sent an unambiguous message that the Alliance members take their responsibility of mutual security and defense seriously. Since that time, under the leadership of Prime Minister Tony Blair, Britain has become a strong supporter of the United States' 'war on terrorism'. In addition to sending troops to Afghanistan to fight with the United States and then accepting the responsibility of leading the peace-keeping force, Prime Minister Tony Blair has traveled widely with his message of support. Canada has sent warships, aircraft and servicemen to Afghanistan. German Chancellor Gerhard Schroeder forced a no-confidence vote in the *Bundestag* over the issue of sending German forces in support of this mission. And even Turkey, which as the only Muslim country in NATO is in an especially precarious position, has allowed US aircraft to overfly its airspace on route to Afghanistan, as well as being the home of Incirlik air base which is being used to supply and refuel those aircraft. In short, NATO appears to be unified once again.

However, as the war on terrorism continues, so do questions about NATO's longer-term role. In reality, the United States has chosen *not* to use the NATO framework for its mission, preferring instead to work with individual countries bilaterally in support of its global coalition. Individual NATO nations, despite their initial support for the United States, have shown and are continuing to show signs that that support cannot continue, especially if the United States chooses to expand the war beyond the borders of Afghanistan. France, already an uncertain ally, has had to confront its own domestic realities as the government tries to balance a left-wing coalition led by Prime Minister Lionel Jospin, which is already divided regarding its responses to the attack. While Schroeder in Germany was able to win the support he needed, the margin was slim and it is not clear that he will be able to sustain this in the longer-term, especially given the uncertain outcome of the German elections scheduled for September 2002. And polls are already suggesting that many in Turkey are opposed to military involvement in Afghanistan and certainly would not support an extension of the war to any of Turkey's Muslim neighbors, including Iraq.[20] And while the United States and many of its NATO allies are fighting the war on terrorism, they continue to have troops in the Balkans, necessary to preserve the delicate peace there.

The events of 11 September serve as a stark reminder that ensuring peace is by no means a certainty. Successfully confronting the probable challenges of the future will require the Alliance to remain focused and cohesive, even with the admission of new members. It will require ongoing strong U.S. leadership, but also acknowledgment by the United States of the role and support of its European. It will also require European acknowledgment that a European force cannot and will not replace the Atlantic Alliance. It will require serious review and restructuring of NATO forces and command structure appropriate to meet the circumstances that the Alliance is likely to face in the future. And, politically, it will mean that all members of the Alliance must acknowledge that NATO decisions will be affected by domestic political priorities, and be prepared to balance those often competing demands.

But underlying all this means looking carefully, clearly and objectively at the lessons of the past, and asking some new and serious questions about NATO's role in the future.

Notes

[1] This chapter is a revision of a paper prepared for presentation at the Comparative Interdisciplinary Studies Section/International Studies Association Millennium Series conference, Heidelberg, Germany, June 2001. Special thanks to Andrew Dorman of Kings College, London, for his extensive comments on that draft. The material included here is drawn from a book by the author entitled *NATO and the Former Yugoslavia: Crisis, Conflict and the Atlantic Alliance* (Boulder: Rowman & Littlefield, Publishers, Inc., 2002). This research has been funded in part by a NATO Research Fellowship for the period June 2000 through June 2002. I am indebted to NATO and to CIES for this award. I am also grateful to the Professional Interests Committee of Whittier College for awarding me a faculty research grant which also helped fund my travel. Special appreciation goes to all those individuals in Washington, London, Berlin and Brussels who were willing to take the time to meet with me during research trips to Europe in 1999 and 2000. Since all spoke only 'off the record' and not for attribution, their comments are noted in the text by the place and time of the interview. The insights that I gained from those interviews have been invaluable. Any errors of fact or interpretation rest solely with me.

[2] 'Armies of Europe Failing to Meet Goals, Sapping NATO', by Michael R. Gorden, *The New York Times*, June 7, 2001, p. A6.

[3] In addition to Poland, Hungary and the Czech Republics, all of which were members of the former Warsaw Pact, Greece and Turkey have had a difficult relationship which, in turn, threatened Alliance unity at various points, for example, over Cyprus. In addition, the unification of Germany meant that the former (Communist-bloc) German Democratic Republic became part of the Alliance.

[4] Michael Mandelbaum, *The Dawn of Peace in Europe* (New York: Twentieth Century Fund, 1996), 30-31.

[5] In July 1992, the North Atlantic Council (NAC) agreed to mount a NATO operation in the Adriatic to monitor the UN-imposed arms embargo and economic sanctions. 'Operation Maritime Monitor' was the first attempt by NATO to address the situation in Bosnia and it became the Alliance's first out-of-area operation. In November 1992, this operation was expanded to become 'Operation Maritime Guard', which authorized NATO to use force to enforce UN Security Council Resolution 787, reaffirming the territorial integrity of Bosnia-Herzegovina. However, these actions were accompanied by the statement that 'Further implementation decisions by the Alliance will be taken...on the recommendations by the Military Committee,' thereby suggesting that future actions would be taken if and/or when they were seen as necessary. NAC Statement of 19 November 1992, in *NATO Communiques, Volume V, 1991-1995* (Brussels: NATO Office of Information and Press,1995), 81.

[6] In his memoir about the negotiation, Lord David Owen suggests that lack of US support for the agreement is one of the primary reasons for the failure. See David Owen, *Balkan Odyssey* (New York; Harcourt Brace & Company, 1995).

[7] 'Enter the Americans', *The Economist*, August 9, 1994, 41.

[8] According to a summary in *The New York Times*, a memoir by then-NATO commander

General Wesley Clark, also illustrates the degree of division within the United States policy-making apparatus regarding Kosovo and what position the US should take. Michael R. Gorden, 'General in Balkan War Says Pentagon Hampered NATO', *The New York Times*, *May 21, 2001*, 1.

[9] Germany, especially Defence Minister Volker Ruhe, was an early supporter of the idea of NATO enlargement in general, and for membership in NATO for the Visegrad states in particular, and argued this point before the NAC in May 1993. His argument was that 'political instability and economic dislocation in central Europe were a threat to German security...'. In addition, both Lech Walesa and Vaclav Havel, with whom Clinton met in March 1993, had been pushing since 1991 for full membership in NATO for each of their countries. Both saw NATO membership not only as a first step to joining the EU, but also as an important hedge against nationalist resurgence in Russia. Christoph Bluth, *Germany and the Future of European Security* (New York: St. Martin's Press, 2000).

[10] There are a number of such examples over NATO's history. Most notable among these are the initial nuclear decisions of the early-to-mid-1950s, Suez in 1956, the Thor-Jupiter decisions of 1957-1960 followed by the multilateral force discussion, DeGaulle's decision to withdraw France from the unified military command structure in 1966, the Enhanced Radiation Warhead (ERW) decision of 1977, and the dual-track decision of 1979. For more detail on these and other specific cases, see David N. Schwartz, *NATO's Nuclear Dilemmas* (Washington, D.C.: The Brookings Institution, 1983), and Leon V. Sigal, *Nuclear Forces in Europe: Enduring Dilemmas, Present Prospects* (Washington, D.C.: The Brookings Institution, 1984).

[11] Figures are from Margaret Warner, 'NATO Expansion: The Domestic Political Debate', in Kenneth Thompson (ed.), *NATO Expansion*, (Lanham, MD: University Press of America, 1998), 137.

[12] Ronald D. Asmus, Richard L. Kugler, and F. Stephen Larrabee, 'What Will NATO Enlargement Cost', in *Survival*, 38, no. 3 (Autumn 1996), 5.

[13] Ivo H. Daalder and Michael E. O'Hanlon, *Winning Ugly: NATO's War to Save Kosovo* (Washington, D.C.: The Brookings Institution Press, 2000), 129.

[14] 'The Alliance's Strategic Concept', in *NATO Handbook, Documentation* (Brussels: NATO Office of Information and Press, 1999), 288.

[15] "The Alliance's Strategic Concept Approved by the Heads of State and Government Participating in the Meeting of the North Atlantic Council, Washington, D.C. 23-24 April 1999", in *NATO Handbook, Documentation* (1999), 407.

[16] "The Alliance's Strategic Concept", in *NATO Handbook, Documentation* (1999), 415-6.

[17] Interview in London, December 2000.

[18] Interview in London, December 2000.

[19] Interview in London, September 2000.

[20] "Western Outpost", in *The Economist*, October 13, 2001, 50-51.

References

Asmus, Ronald D., Kugler, Richard L., and Larrabee, F. Stephen. (1996), 'What Will NATO Enlargement Cost,' *Survival*, 38, No. 3, Autumn, pp. 28-40.

Bluth, Christoph. (2000), Germany and the Future of European Security, New York: St. Martin's Press.

Daalder, Ivo H. and O'Hanlon, Michael E. (2000), *Winning Ugly: NATO's War to Save Kosovo*, Washington, D.C.: The Brookings Institution.

The Economist (1994), *Enter the Americans*, August 9, p.41.

Gordon, Michael R. (2001), 'Armies of Europe Failing to Meet Goals, Sapping NATO,' *The New York Times*, June 7, p. A6.

Gordon, Michael R. (2001), 'General in Balkan War Says Pentagon Hampered NATO,' *The New York Times*, May 21, p. 1.

Kaufman, Joyce P. (2002) *NATO and the Former Yugoslavia: Crisis, Conflict and the Atlantic Alliance*, Boulder, CO: Rowman & Littlefield, Publishers, Inc.

Mandelbaum, Michael. (1996), *The Dawn of Peace in Europe*, New York: Twentieth Century Fund.

NATO Communiques, Vol. V, 1991-1995 (1995), Brussels: NATO Office of Information and Press.

NATO Handbook, Documentation (1999), Brussels: NATO Office of Information and Press.

Owen, Lord David. (1995), *Balkan Odyssey*, New York: Harcourt Brace & Company.

Schwartz, David N. (1983), *NATO's Nuclear Dilemmas*, Washington, D.C.: The Brookings Institution.

Sigal, Leon V. (1984), Nuclear Forces in Europe: Enduring Dilemmas, Present Prospects, Washington, D.C.: The Brookings Institution.

Warner, Margaret. (1998), 'NATO Expansion: The Domestic Political Debate,' in Kenneth Thompson. (ed.), *NATO Expansion*, Lanham, MD: University Press of America, pp. 115-135.

'Western Outpost,' (2001), *The Economist*, October 13, pp. 50-51.

Chapter 4

NATO, the European Union, and European Security

Roger E. Kanet
and
Nouray V. Ibryamova

Introduction

The end of the Cold War concluded a period of clear division of Europe into east and west, each closely tied for security and other purposes to the Soviet Union or the United States.[1] With the collapse of the Warsaw Pact in 1991 and the scramble of its former members to enter into what until then had been Western organizational structures, the definition of 'Europe' became blurry. For most of the prior half century the term was usually associated with the European Community/Union or with the broader group of Western European democratic countries. As the European Union moves ahead with its plans to absorb an unprecedented number of entrants from the east and the south, its geographic center will shift even more toward Germany, adding to that country's already increased political and economic weight on the continent, as Mayhew (1998) and Kaufman (2001) have noted. In the meantime, the questions concerning where political and economic Europe ends and what shape it is likely to take in the future continue to be debated by observers and politicians alike.

Enlargement has become the major new undertaking of the European Union, as well as of NATO. With more than a dozen countries lining up to enter over the next decade, the Union is facing an historic opportunity to end the division of the continent, thereby creating the foundations for durable peace, stability, and prosperity on a pan-European basis. This turn in the European integration project will likely change the global stature of the EU and require substantial geopolitical as well as economic and political readjustments within the organization (Lund and Kanet, 1999; Mayhew, 1998).

Europe's New Security Environment

The end of the global confrontation between the Soviet Union and the United States marked the beginning of the reconfiguration of the security environment in

Europe. It brought to an end security arrangements, based in large part on a military standoff in Europe that had lasted for close to half a century and had sustained the bipolar world dominated by the superpowers.[2] With the dissolution of the Warsaw Pact in spring 1991 and the implosion of the Soviet Union later in the year, the primary external threat for the West disappeared; almost immediately calls were heard for the dismantling of NATO as an unnecessary anachronism. However, the West was faced with a new set of security dilemmas, some of which were related to the rise of ethnically based conflict in portions of former communist Europe and the concern that the new disorder might spill over into the West. Within a very brief period, as Aybet (2000) and Yost (1998) have demonstrated, the conclusion was reached – in Washington and more broadly within NATO -- that the new situation required the reconfiguration of the existing security arrangements, including specifically an expanded and active peacekeeping role for NATO outside its historic borders.[3] The process occurred in several stages between 1990 and 1995. After the redefinition of European security, including NATO's mission and relevance to the new situation in Europe, the process of gaining acceptance for these views ensued. Both the Gulf War and the conflicts in former Yugoslavia helped to solidify the view that the existing Western security community and its institutions should be expanded to incorporate other parts of the continent.

A decade later NATO remains the lynchpin of Euro-Atlantic security. After the initial calls for its dismantling, the organization has undergone much adaptation, including both a redefinition of its mission and the addition of three former adversaries as new members, with close to three dozen other countries involved in the Partnership for Peace program, widely accepted as the waiting room for possible future NATO membership.[4] At the same time the European Union is in the process of establishing a Common European Security and Defense Policy. The creation of a European defense force is intended to complement NATO's ability to act and to enable the Europeans to engage in operations that the United States would not join, but for which it would permit the use of NATO military capabilities.[5]

The present essay will examine the importance of U.S. and Russian policy, including the enlargement of NATO (plus the initiation of the European Union's Security and Defense Policy) and their implications for future security throughout East-Central Europe. We argue that, although a new round of NATO enlargement would enhance European security, increase regional stability, and strengthen democracy within the newly admitted member states. Russian concerns must be addressed, as well as those of other states left out of the process, if enlargement is not to create new problems. Absorbing the Central and Eastern European countries into NATO and the European Union is seen in the West as an extension of the multilateral frameworks that made peace and prosperity possible for Western Europe. But, ignoring Russia's continued reservations about NATO expansion, even after the recent policy shifts in Moscow, and excluding it from European security and economic integration could lead to renewed confrontation reminiscent of that which characterized the Cold War era. Moreover, it would place those

East-Central and Southeast European countries not admitted to European security institutions in a very difficult situation - a sort of security limbo.

Despite assurances from Europe and the United States that the dual NATO and EU expansion eastward is not targeted against Russia and should not be construed as a threat to Russian security, expansion has in fact until now reinforced the feeling of exclusion in Russia, since it challenges directly Russia's place within its self-proclaimed sphere of influence (Black, 2000; Facon, 1997; Kobrinskaya, 1997).[6] NATO's actions in Kosovo also fueled the perception among some in Russia of a direct threat from the alliance to Russia's interests, including the concern that in the future the West might be willing to put military pressure on Russia in a confrontation between the federal government in Moscow and a recalcitrant minority region, such as Chechnya. In sum, to understand the emerging security environment of Europe, one must take into account a complex set of factors that include the enlargement of NATO, as well as of the European Union, and the EU's initiative in developing its own defense capabilities as part of the establishment of a common foreign and security policy capability. While these steps indicate a movement toward the development of security arrangements with pan-European features, the continued dependence of Europe on the United States and the positive engagement of Russia, of the type that has been under way since the terrorist attacks on the United States, are essential for any viable security arrangement.[7]

NATO Enlargement

During the past decade Russian relations with NATO have at times been marked by acrimony and have marred other aspects of Russia's interactions with the West, particularly the United States (Kanet, 2001; Kanet and Ibryamova (2001). Although NATO has been evolving in parallel with the European Union as the centerpiece of the new political organization of Europe, it has nonetheless effectively excluded Russia from its decision-making - thus contributing to the perception of Russia's being left at the sidelines of Europe without a voice in the critical issues of the continent. The collapse of the Warsaw Pact in 1991 and NATO's expansion has meant for Russia a loss of old allies. Perhaps worse still, this course of events led Moscow to look elsewhere for friends and allies who shared its concerns about U.S. global dominance, thus drawing it farther from Europe geopolitically and ideologically and sending an alarming signal that the country's development may progress in a direction opposite to the one taken by Europe (Baranovsky, 2000, p. 446; Black, 2000, p. 119 ff.). The enlargement of NATO faces the fundamental challenge of treading the fine line between the inclusion of some former communist states and the exclusion of others, the most important of which is Russia. Yet, since the terror attacks on the United States on 11 September 2001 President Putin has reoriented Russian foreign policy in a pro-Western direction and indicated a willingness to discuss security issues related to both NATO and to national missile defense that have concerned the Russians, despite vocal opposition among various groups in Moscow (McFaul, 2001; Rogov, 2001; McFaul and Zlobin, 2001; Daniszewski, 2001).

The classic rationale for NATO's existence was to keep the Americans in, the Russians out, and the Germans down. At the end of the Cold War the calls for the dissolution of the alliance did not succeed in their objective, as NATO adapted to the new international dynamics and even expanded to include three Central European states of the former Soviet bloc and become a central element of the new security environment in East-Central Europe. Enlargement was primarily a U.S. project. The role of its European allies, although essential, was overshadowed by Washington's decisions concerning who would become members, and when (Goldgeier, 1999; Michta, 1999). Hungary, Poland, and the Czech Republic had argued that they should be relieved from their position as a buffer between Western Europe and Russia. Entry into NATO would supposedly remove them from the Russian sphere of influence and eliminate the possibility that they would ever again fall under domination from the east. Moreover, the leaders of the candidate states argued, they still required the benefits of collective security and the consolidation of the processes of democratization and market development of the region that would result from membership ('Official Perspectives from Eastern Europe,' 1997).[8] In the United States the process of enlargement generated support from groups with three distinct sets of concerns, each of which was seeking guarantees against different, historically based, threats to security. One factor that drove enlargement was the concern about the containment of unified Germany and the desire to enmesh it in multilateral institutions anchored in the West, and to move NATO's boundary from the eastern border of Germany to that of Poland. The second factor was the goal of preventing in East-Central Europe conflict situations like those in former Yugoslavia – although, in fact, the potential for such conflict in that region was never significant. For Poland, the Czech Republic and Hungary membership in NATO was actually a reward for their efforts at democratization and marketization. It was believed that encouraging the development of these institutions would lead to peace and prosperity that could be consolidated by NATO. Lastly, the concern that Russian imperial aspirations might reemerge was yet another reason to proceed with expansion. Hence, the traditional Cold War justifications for NATO's existence still remained in the background of its decision to incorporate members from Central Europe after the end of the Cold War (Kennedy-Pipe, 2000, p. 51, and Goldgeier, 1999, pp. 170-171).

The overall objective of the new security arrangements created in the mid-1990s was to provide stability and security without creating new dividing lines. The concept of security was expanded to include political and economic, as well as military, components; the new security architecture would, therefore, be built using gradual processes of integration and cooperation through organizations such as NATO, the WEU, the European Union, and the Organization of Security and Cooperation in Europe. NATO enlargement, therefore, was intended to extend the benefits of common defense and integration to the countries of the former eastern bloc and, thereby, contribute to the overall integration of these countries into Europe (NATO, 1995; Michta, 1999, pp. 198-203; Aybet, 2000, p. 230).

Almost from the outset the Russians opposed NATO enlargement, not just because of the changed strategic orientation of its former allies, but also because of the direction in which the European security organization was headed. Moscow argued that enlargement created new dividing lines in Europe, betrayed the terms on which the Cold War had ended and Germany had been reunified, and affected its domestic politics. Consequently, Russia argued in favor of strengthening pan-European organizations such as the CSCE as the primary security organizations on the continent, an argument that along with providing Russia a major voice in major security issues in Europe carried implications for a diminished U.S. role and a rebuff to its efforts to continue to operate in a unipolar world.[9]

The expansion of NATO affected Russian domestic politics, as well. The pro-Western leanings of Foreign Minister Kozyrev and the liberal Westernizers in the early 1990s provided fodder for nationalists and communists alike. The issue of NATO enlargement was one area where Kozyrev and his allies could agree with their political opponents, allowing for unanimous condemnation of the Western alliance's actions across the spectrum of Russian politics. Nonetheless, early discussions and plans for NATO enlargement contributed to the decline of the liberal Westernizers in Moscow. Even if Russian policy makers and analysts eventually realized that, despite their strongest opposition, Russia could not prevent the expansion, some in Russia continued to see it as a threat. This trend was further reinforced by NATO's actions in Kosovo and its new strategic concept adopted at the anniversary Washington Summit in May 1999, confirming the alliance's open door admission policy. Nationalists interpreted the war in Kosovo as a training ground for attacks that would be repeated elsewhere, thus presenting a direct threat to Russia.[10]

The instruments of participation that NATO had offered to Russia were the Partnership for Peace and the Russia-NATO Founding Act, signed in 1994 and 1997 respectively, with the latter establishing the Russia-NATO Permanent Joint Council (PJC) (Delpech, 1997; Umbach, 2001). The Partnership for Peace Program, although initially regarded by Russia as a success in having its concerns taken into consideration by the West, in effect was clear evidence that Russia was unable to prevent NATO enlargement. Russian participation in the Partnership for Peace may have been driven more by a desire to retain some influence on the decisions of a body over which it was unable to obtain a veto and which was going to expand to include the Central European countries regardless of Russian approval. As Russia continued to argue for a pan-European organization to handle the security issues of Europe, the Permanent Joint Council was set up as the primary mechanism for consultation between the two sides. Russia, however, neither obtained a veto over NATO decisions, nor had any hopes at the time of becoming a member itself, considering its inability to fulfill NATO's political and economic criteria for admission (Carr and Flenley, 1999).

Until very recently the Russian view of further NATO expansion to the east has remained negative. Despite this the Baltic republics have reiterated their strong desire to join NATO and, along with several Central European countries, have come closest to achieving that goal (Heurlin, 1998). Moreover, at a meeting in Bratislava in early May 200_ thirteen Central and East European countries reminded the West of its commitment to admit the former communist states into full membership in the Western community, including NATO (Kempre, 2001; Hutchings, 2001). The outcry among Russian political circles against the prospect of a Baltic presence in NATO has been quite strong. In early 2001, for example, Sergei Ivanov, head of the Russian Security Council, voiced the position long taken by Russian nationalists who have warned of the possibilities of increased military spending, a renewed arms race, and the search for new allies, should NATO proceed with its plans for further expansion (Socor, 2001). Tony Lake (2000, pp. 230-233), former National Security Advisor to President Clinton, has written that it was disingenuous to pretend that Russia is a partner of the United States or that Russia could exercise a veto on NATO membership:

> It is very important that we made clear to Russia from the start of the process that NATO enlargement was on track and would happen, with or without Russia's blessing. To the degree that Russian leaders made opposition to NATO enlargement a test case of their international power, to that degree they would appear all the weaker. This would hurt them at home as well as abroad. It is essential that Russian leaders understand now they cannot force NATO to deny the Baltic states entry into the alliance, if they meet the criteria for membership....Any European nation that meets the criteria for membership, including the Baltic states and Russia itself, must sooner or later be allowed entry.[11]

This kind of realism has been present in Russian perceptions as well, as most members of the political elite understand that Russia's response to U.S. security initiatives must be curbed by its limited economic and political capabilities. In addition to its inability to prevent NATO expansion in the Baltic region, at present Russia can do little to stop NATO from taking a more active role elsewhere. As an example, the air strikes over Serbia during the Kosovo war -- against the strong vocal opposition of Moscow -- arguably made a mockery of the NATO-Russia Founding Act, which supposedly provided Russia with the ability to influence NATO decisions. However, Moscow's countermeasures were largely symbolic and it very soon resumed its participation in the activities of the PJC. As one Russian analyst noted, although Russian concern about the welfare of fellow Slavs in Serbia was praiseworthy, it was important to recognize that NATO jets represented a market for Russian oil (Druzenki, 1999). Even prior to the terror attacks in the United States, Russian relations with NATO and with the United States had begun to improve (Zagorski, 2001; Umbach, 2001).

The events in Kosovo appear to have had a two-pronged effect on Russia. They justified Russian hostility toward a NATO-centered Europe, consolidating the anti-NATO and related anti-American attitudes; but, they also drew Russia's attention to Europe. The war in Kosovo also showcased the marginalization of Russia, underscored by the circumscribing of the role of the PJC, and the adaptation of the alliance itself to its newly expanded security roles.

This adaptation and the evolution of NATO during the 1990s as a military alliance are indicative of the multiple factors that have shaped its character and role. Although there have been fluctuations over the future role, shape, and functions of the alliance, the member states have demonstrated the ability to build consensus, as in the case of Kosovo.[12] Along with its traditional functions, NATO has a new role to play, defined by the new post-Cold War European reality. Specifically, it has been instrumental in drawing the Central and Eastern European countries toward a Western-centered focus. It has served as a major driving force in bringing the end of open hostilities to the Balkans and in mediating tensions between Greece and Turkey -- two issues that the Europeans alone have been unable to tackle successfully. Moreover, there exists the possibility, enhanced since September 2002, that NATO will have a role in further developing relations with Russia (Nye, 2000; Colton and McFaul, 2001). In the words of Javier Solana (1999), former Secretary General of NATO and now responsible for the development of EU security policy, 'there can be no security in Europe without a stable Russia', and the NATO-Russian Founding Act and the Permanent Joint Council have set the stage for cooperation with Russia on issues of proliferation, environmental damages, nuclear safety, and terrorism.

In some ways NATO's approach has become more incremental and conditional following the first wave of enlargement, and reinvigorating the ties with Russia remains a priority. Enlargement is consistent with NATO's current strategic objectives, while at the same time it takes advantage of the inclusiveness and partnerships with the countries from Central and Eastern Europe. Poland, Hungary, and the Czech Republic are unlikely to remain the only new members of the alliance, but relations with Russia are too important for European security not be given careful consideration in NATO decision-making. Some analysts have advocated the pursuit of policies that give primacy to the concerns of Russia, explicitly limiting further enlargement and providing special types of support for those countries of the region that remain excluded from membership (Croft, et al., 2000, p. 517; Arbatov, 1998).[13] Engagement with Moscow seems to be the leading and most obvious answer with regards to managing the post-Cold War international relations through NATO as well as the European Union. Until very recently, however, this approach was not likely to gather support with the current Bush Administration in Washington, which at the beginning of 2001 had adopted a unilateralist approach to the pursuit of virtually all of its foreign and security policy objectives (Kanet and Ibryanova, 2001). Moreover, the primary factor determining whether successful engagement will be possible will depend on the development of Russian policy itself more than on specific Western policies. Whether or not NATO absorbs other members over the next few years will likely be less important in determining Russian policy toward the West than political and economic developments in Russia itself – although they will surely have some influence on that policy.

However, the terrorist attacks on the United States of 11 September 2001 have provided the stimulus for precisely such a shift in Russian policy – as well as in that of the United States. President Putin has taken the opportunity presented to begin to craft a new relationship with the United States – despite concern, even opposition, from various groups within Russia. Soon after the attacks Putin opted to support U.S. efforts to track down and root out terrorism and has provided unprecedented assistance – from its support in the U.N. Security Council to the use of former Soviet military facilities in Central Asia. On the U.S., as the Bush Administration has sought support for its campaign against terrorism, it has been forced to reconsider its earlier unilateralist approach to international politics and to collaborate more closely with both formal allies and with other states, such as the Russian Federation. These shifts have meant that U.S.-Russian relations have been reinvigorated and that the possibility exists that the major issues that have strained relations – NATO expansion, the creation of a U.S. national missile defense system, and Russian policy in Chechnya – may be resolved (McFaul, 2001; Colton and McFaul, 2001). The meeting of presidents Putin and Bush in Washington and Crawford, Texas, in mid-November 2001 highlighted the changes in both Russian and U.S. policy and in relations between the two countries that would have been almost impossible to predict two months earlier. Putin, for example, has indicated his willingness to work out a rapprochement with NATO, while Bush has muted criticism of Russian policy in Chechnya and committed the United States to massive reductions in nuclear weapons. Immediately following the summit meeting, Prime Minister Blair of the United Kingdom followed up with a public proposal for a new security partnership between Russia and the NATO alliance (Gornostayev, 2001: Evans, 2001).

The Enlargement of the European Union

EU officials, who have often reiterated the fact that they do not want to create new dividing lines, nonetheless seem to face that very prospect, if enlargement stops at the borders of Russia, Ukraine and Belarus.[14] The first two countries are both strategically important, with Russia still possessing the status of a nuclear power with its due share of influence on international affairs. The main frameworks within which their engagement with the EU occurs are the Partnership and Cooperation Agreements, the TACIS program [Technical Assistance to the Commonwealth of Independent States], and the European Council's Common Strategy on Russia adopted in 1999 (Gianaris, 1994, pp. 147-186; Zagorski, 1997; Wettig, 1998; Crawford, 90-127; Wedel, 1998). Despite these and a number of other, more specific, cooperative arrangements, Russia has largely been excluded from the process of European integration, at least for the foreseeable future.

Having defined themselves as European in their identity and orientation, the Ukrainians have given serious consideration to possible future membership in the Union (D'Anieri, Kravchuk, and Kuzio, 1999, pp. 229-232; Bukkvoll, 1997, p. 61 ff; Lieven, 1999, pp. 153-161); in contrast, Russia, while generally not openly opposed to the EU's eastern enlargement, has no such aspirations for membership. The perception of Ukraine's future, especially among nationalists in the western part of the country, seems to be one of little choice but to be an integral part of European integration. The lack of any indication from the EU of the desirability of Ukraine's membership has been a source of frustration, despite Brussels' criticism of its slow economic reforms, protectionist measures, and refusal to abandon plans for constructing new nuclear reactors. There is also the awareness of the problems EU enlargement would pose for Ukraine itself, including visa restrictions for

Ukrainian citizens in the accession countries with which they had enjoyed largely unobstructed travel for the past decade. Enlargement that does not include Ukraine is likely to have negative economic consequences for that country because of Central Europe's continuing reorientation of trade toward the Union.[15] It is also likely to have an impact on bilateral Ukrainian-Russian relations, since, many analysts believe, it will result in Russia's putting increasing pressure on Ukraine for the coordination of policies. In sum, it will most likely deepen the already existing sense of exclusion in a country that sees its European orientation as only way it can become a 'normal' country (Light, White, and Lowenhardt, 2000).[16]

The implications of exclusion will probably be even more acute in the case of Russia, which has always had an ambivalent relationship with Europe. Geographical considerations aside, Russia has long exemplified – along with the Ottoman Empire and later Turkey – Europe's 'other.' Iver Neumann (1998, p. 67) maintains that its status has been that of a 'learner,' a country always seen in some stage of Europeanization, without ever quite reaching the goal of full integration. This image has sometimes been difficult to reconcile with the conviction of most Russians that theirs is country of great power – a claim now supported almost solely by its nuclear arsenal. Although, historically 'Europe' has been equated with the West, as the embodiment of enlightenment, rationalism, liberalism, secularism, and materialism (MacFarlane, 1994, p. 237), perceptions of Europe and the United States have changed considerably during the 1990s. In contrast to the rising anti-Americanism in the second part of the decade, Russian attitudes about Europe remained positive.[17] They regard themselves as Europeans, and more than two-thirds of them consider Russia to be a natural part of Europe and think that it will develop closer ties with the rest of the continent in the future. The Eurasian cultural and historical orientation is also widespread, but not dominant – less than one third of Russians support the actively popularized version of Eurasianism (Working Group of the Russian Independent Institute of Social and National Problems, 2000; Chulos and Piirainen, 2000; Allensworth, 1998). This is reflected in the attitudes toward the EU and NATO, as well; whereas the latter is seen as an instrument of the United States and as a threat to Russia despite assurances to the contrary, the former has enjoyed a far more favorable image. NATO's eastward expansion has raised grave concerns in Russia and continues to have a negative influence on Russian-U.S. relations. Conversely, the overtures of the Central and Eastern European countries toward the EU were looked upon more favorably, even as a substitute for NATO membership (Zagorski, 1997). As we have already noted, however, Foreign Minister Ivanov (1998) has pointed to the potential negative economic implications for Russia of continued EU expansion.

The reason for the divergent attitudes toward the two main Euro-Atlantic organizations lies also in their different natures. NATO has been seen as the main political and security organization for the continent, but one that remains strongly influenced by the United States, while the European Union, with its emphasis to date on economic integration represents a less direct challenge to Russian political and security interests. Not surprisingly Russia has continually insisted on the increased role of the Organization of Security and Cooperation in Europe [OSCE], in which it is a member, to replace NATO as the pivotal organization in European security matters.

An important part of Russia's policy toward Europe has focused on limiting the role of NATO – and, hence, that of the United States. In this respect, initially Moscow saw the nascent European Security and Defense Policy of the European Union as an opportunity to move Europe in this direction, but also as a means for Russian participation in European military operations and above all as an instrument for driving a wedge between the United States and its European allies.[18] Since it has become clear, however, that the ESDP is likely to be implemented only in a manner that will complement, rather than compete with, NATO, Russia's position has taken on a more critical tone (Light, White, and Lowenhardt, 2000, pp. 77-83). Russia does not share the EU's perceptions of itself as the emerging other great power on the continent. It still prefers to emphasize its bilateral relations with the other European states, particularly with Germany. The *Foreign Policy Concept* of Russia (Ministry of Foreign Affairs of the Russian Federation, 1993; Ministry of Foreign Affairs of the Russian Federation, 2000; Knabe, 2000; Kassianova, Alla, 2001, esp. p. 829 ff.) points to the traditionally high importance given to European affairs, with the EU as a key player. Moscow states that the Partnership and Cooperation Agreement (PCA) of 1994 has not yet achieved its full promise. Moreover, President Putin has positioned himself as a 'Europeanist,' further underscoring the importance of relations with Europe for the course of Russia's development, as well as its influence in international relations (Timmermann, 2000; Diligenskij and Tschugnow, 2000). Since the terrorist attacks on the United States the Western orientation of his policy has become even more visible. Problematic areas between the two exist, but there has also been the attempt on both sides to develop political and security cooperation, the exact nature and parameters of which are yet to be determined.

Yet, making Europe the focus of its foreign policy would help to reinforce Russia's claim to the status of a great power; hence, it is in Russia's fundamental interest to pursue such a policy approach. Only by establishing and nurturing close economic and political ties with the West will Moscow be able to obtain the technological and financial resources necessary to effect the country's transformation.

Reciprocally, an indication of Russia's importance to the EU was provided by the fact that first Common Strategy to be adopted by the European Council (1999) following the Treaty of Amsterdam dealt with the Russian Federation. Building on the experience of the 1994 cooperation agreement and the technical assistance agreement (TACIS), the document aims at reinforcing the 'strategic relationship' between the Union and Russia. Its principal objectives are the consolidation of democracy and the rule of law in Russia; its economic and social integration with Europe, and cooperation in security challenges in Europe and beyond.[19] Along with TACIS, the core legal instrument of EU-Russian relations is the Partnership and Cooperation Agreement signed in 1994, but not ratified by the former until the end of 1997, partly because of the Western concern about human rights issues in Chechnya. The PCA covers mainly economic and commercial issues, such as the potential move toward the establishment of a free trade area, and sets up the institutional framework for regular political dialogue. Among its objectives are also the consolidation of democracy, the establishment of a functioning market economy, and a framework for the 'gradual integration between Russia and a wider area of cooperation in Europe', (European Communities, 1998; Zagorski, 1997 pp. 527-530). Within the TACIS framework, the EU provides technical assistance and support for a number of specific projects, thereby allowing Brussels some influence, albeit limited, on the development of stable democratic institutions and a functioning market economy.

Although often driven by the perceived need to support liberal reforms in Russia, in recent years the EU's long-term strategy has become clearer and communication more regular. The EU remains committed to the development of channels of cooperation with Russia that cover a wide gamut of issues, in the hope of anchoring it in the broader security, political, and economic map of Europe. Problems do exist, though; some of them quite serious. The future eastern enlargement of the EU, including the Baltic states, is not seen in Russia as a threat, so long as it does not include countries that Russia perceives to be in its direct sphere of influence, such as Ukraine. Russia has demanded that its concerns and sensitivities be given serious consideration; this Brussels has attempted to do in an ongoing dialogue. Officials in Moscow, nonetheless, recognize enlargement's potentially negative consequences, which are similar to those to be faced by Ukraine. Since the Union has not granted Russia the status of a market economy, it regularly initiates anti-dumping measures against Russian exports. As the countries from Central and Eastern Europe adopt the *acquis communitaire* and their trade volume with the Union increases, there is the potential for adverse effects on the trade relations with Russia – an outcome that Russia is determined to avoid (Höhmann and Meier, 1999; Ivanov, 1998). The EU is already Russia's main trading partner and enlargement will likely expand this dependence. In addition, as the accession negotiations progress, the CEECs are increasingly working to tighten their border controls, thereby making it more difficult for Russian citizens to travel. Kaliningrad, the Russian exclave between Poland and Lithuania, is also a matter of concern; as an economic free zone, it has the potential to contribute to trade relations or to be a locus of tensions because of its role as an important Russian military and naval base. Ultimately, however, the cooperation with Europe will depend on Russia's domestic political stability. Both the PCA and the Common Strategy on Russia contain provisional clauses that reinforce the crucial importance of continuous reform and stability in Russia. The ability to move forward with reform toward completing the transition to a full-scale market economy and consolidating its fledgling democracy will be the deciding factors in Russia's further integration in or exclusion from European structures.

Paul-Henry Spaak (1971, p. 141) once noted that the title 'father of European unity' belonged to Stalin because, without his aggressive policies and the threat the Soviet Union posed to the West, the movement for European unity would not have been as successful as it was. At present, despite occasional references in the Russian press to eventual Russian membership, the prospect is not pursued seriously.[20] In Europe there exists the understanding that security and stability on the continent cannot be achieved unless Russia is firmly anchored in the new

European order; economic interdependence could be the way to achieve that objective. The goal with regards to Russia seems to be a model of integration without membership; the challenge – how to keep Russia from disengaging, without actually letting it into the organization (Baranovsky, 2000, p. 446; Gower, 2000, p. 68).

NATO and the Common European Security and Defense Policy

As we have already noted, the European Union has taken steps toward the Europeanization of some security arrangements on the continent. The Treaty on the European Union of 1993 allowed for the possible common foreign policy of the member states, which would lead to common defense policy, thereby strengthening the European pillar of the NATO alliance (Dinan, 1999, pp. 515-516; Gärtner, 2001; Schmidt, 2001). As a consequence of the Bosnian debacle, even the most ardent Europeanists came to support NATO's supremacy in European security, thereby justifying the necessity for a continued strong U.S. military presence. These two factors contributed to bridging the divide between Europeanists and Atlanticists within the EU that had become evident at the 1996 Intergovernmental Conference. Moreover, in the 1990s the initial U.S. suspicion of the Common Foreign and Security Policy gradually turned into support for European security and defense cooperation, which in effect meant that the United States encouraged the strengthening of European military forces capable of dealing with militarized conflicts on the continent – although differences remained about the relationship between NATO and the new EU security force (Hay and Sicherman, 2001). In 1994 NATO had agreed to the establishment of Combined Joint Task Forces to make available to the alliance's European members NATO's capabilities for operations outside the NATO area in which the US chose not to participate. In 1997, the NATO summit in Madrid endorsed the enlargement of NATO and asserted its primacy over the attempts of the EU to create its own defense mechanisms (Dinan, 1999, p. 526; Yost, pp. 1998, 199-217). NATO's expansion had been a contentious subject since the early 1990s, but it was the final decision made by the United States concerning which countries would be included in the first wave of entrants that drew the most criticism from EU officials. Nonetheless, the support for NATO remained strong among all the member states, and there appeared to be a consensus on the approach to establishing post-Cold War European security (Mattox and Rachwald, 2001; Aybet, 2000).

Despite the commitment to develop a common foreign and security policy, the members states of the European Union have made little practical headway in establishing the mechanisms necessary to accomplish this goal. The divergence of the foreign policies of the EU member states, as well as the deficiencies of the European military capabilities came to the fore once again during the crisis in Kosovo and the subsequent postwar efforts.[21] In fact, some have criticized the United States for taking the lead in Kosovo and for its proneness toward unilateralism, citing the location of the problem in Europe's "backyard". Critics have argued that by taking the leadership role, subsidizing European defense, and moderating European conflicts the United States in fact ensures continued European passivity and provides disincentives for the development of independent defense capabilities.

In contrast to his predecessor's policy of specific emphasis on a NATO-focused approach to security in Europe, President Bill Clinton was more sympathetic toward European efforts to develop a common defense policy that diverged from the NATO collectivity. This support for the creation of a unified European defense force, however, was contingent upon its operating as a complementary mechanism to the central role of NATO in transatlantic defense cooperation. From the beginning the creation of a stronger and more autonomous European security capability has been a EU political project and a NATO military project (Bandow, 1999; p. 82). Proponents argued that "separable but not separate" forces would give NATO a flexibility it did not possess before and would also head off any effort by the French to turn the Western European Union into a competitor to NATO in the European security environment (Goldgeier, 1999). The existing doubts regarding the project are still related to these concerns: namely, how far can the CESDP go and especially what the nature of relations with the U.S. and with NATO will be, and how the non-EU members of NATO will be accommodated. While the United States has been urging increased burden sharing, Washington has tied the development of European capacity and autonomy to alliance enhancement (Croft, et al., 2000). Relations were complicated almost immediately by the reduced support of the Bush Administration for European initiatives and by its willingness – at least until September 2001 -- to push ahead on security matters regardless of the views of its European allies – as on the issue of the establishment of a national missile defense system.[22]

Indeed, there have been voices in the United States that have argued that the European plan may be riskier than it appeared earlier, leading to a waste of European military assets, the alienation of NATO members outside the EU, and the creation of rival military structures that might make it difficult for the United States and the EU to respond coherently to future crises (Drozdiak, 2000). The most serious objection has been the perception of the Europeanization of the alliance as a step toward the eventual decoupling of the alliance. From a more practical point of view, the leadership in Washington could scarcely imagine security crises that would not involve NATO and the United States. Hence, behind Former Secretary of State Madeleine Albright's argument (2000, p. 4) of "no duplication, no decoupling, no discrimination," the United States seems to have been able to impose on the EU the perspective that its new force is not to be seen as a European army distinct from NATO, that it can be used only for peacekeeping purposes, and that its use will almost always involve NATO in one way or another. Thus, the U.S. position has combined an attempt to accommodate the European endeavor, while keeping NATO intact – and the United States in a leadership position in the continent's security (Croft, et al., 2000, p. 510; Pond, 2000, p. 11).

The latest developments, however, show that the European Union still expects to implement the military goals upon which the members agreed in December 1999, goals that were at least partially prompted by the shortcomings that appeared during the air campaign against Yugoslavia. Despite the fact that many EU countries are downsizing their Cold War military structures, the plans for the formation of a new defense force are set to be realized by 2003. The United States remains skeptical of the success of this project in view of the shrinking military budgets of the large EU member states, but nonetheless supportive, provided that the primacy of NATO remains unchallenged. [23]

At the beginning of the new century the security challenges for NATO are shifting from Europe's center to its periphery and beyond. [24] The response to the terrorist attacks of September 2001 is clear evidence of this fact. The United States remains the dominant security actor in Europe. At the same time U.S. and NATO security concerns extend increasingly to areas outside the traditional geographical focus of the alliance in Europe, the Middle East, and Eurasia. At the same time the reorientation of security priorities to the south and east increases the risks of confrontation with Russia. If Russia continues to conduct a more assertive foreign policy, underscored by a rising sense of nationalism, it may challenge Western[25] interests in areas such as the Balkans, the eastern Mediterranean, the Caspian and Gulf regions – something it can no longer do in Central Europe (Lesser, 1999, pp, iii, 2; Lynch, 2001). Yet, as we have seen, since the terrorist attacks on the United States President Putin has opted for an approach to relations with the United States and the West that is based much more on cooperation. What is not clear is the durability of this approach, which will depend both on domestic politics in Russia and on the willingness of the Bush Administration to work out policy differences with the Russians.

In view of these developments, Russia has continued to express its support for a pan-European security organization in which its role would be granted. Partnership with the newly emerging common European Security and Defense initiative appears desirable, especially in view of the possibility of its diminishing Washington's influence. In fact, the major U.S. European allies, led by the UK and Germany, have not intended to pursue a policy of decoupling from NATO; rather, the CESDP is to complement NATO, focusing on humanitarian and peacekeeping operations, in which the United States did not wish to participate.

Following a decade that saw the countries of the former Soviet bloc striving to achieve membership in Western institutions, especially the two most demanding clubs, the European Union and NATO, and the first steps toward the possible resolution of the last Balkan hotbed in ex-Yugoslavia, the prospects for incorporating East-Central Europe into a single Europe-wide security community are becoming more plausible. However, the parameters of this community remain unclear and undetermined and, in fact, they may not be incorporated within one single institution. What the leaders of the West will have to do is to clarify Russia's role in the new European security environment. Stephen Hadley (2000, p. 3) has argued that, while 'the primary interest of Europe lies in building a regional system conducive to economic and political integration without compromising national sovereignty, Russia is stuck in a 19th century realist calculus without the ability to influence outcomes'. But Russia's perception of its own economic weakness and the limitations on its ability to wield power is shared among some Western analysts and politicians. Nonetheless, there exists a general consensus that Europe cannot be 'whole and free' without a stable Russia that is part of that Europe. Toward that goal many advocate expanded consultations with Russia to try to keep the rising anti-Western character of its national security strategy from becoming the new reality of Russian policy. The new agenda should include new forms of engagement between the European Union and the United States, as well as the establishment of new 'rules of the road' to order relations with Russia in the post-Kosovo world (Hadley, 2000, p. 3; Solovev, 2001). Integration and cooperation within well-defined political, economic, and security parameters on a pan-European basis can be a safeguard for the security, peace, stability, and democracy within member states, obliterating the dividing lines of ideology and making war unthinkable.

Notes

[1] An earlier version of this article was presented at The CISS 2001 Millennium Series Conference, Heidelberg, Germany, 24-26 June 2001. The authors are grateful for critical comments made on that draft by Joyce Kaufman. A related article, by Roger Kanet and Nouray V. Ibryamova entitled 'La Sécurité en Europe Centrale et Orientale: un Systeme en Cours de Changement' is forthcoming in *Revue Comparatives des Études Est-Ouest*, no. 1 (2002).

[2] Kolodziej (1991) and Kremenyuk (1991) argue that after the mid-1950s U.S.-Soviet relations represented a form of 'cooperation' in managing global conflict.

[3] See, also, the examination of the various national debates that preceded the expansion of NATO membership in Mattox and Rachwald (2001).

[4] On NATO expansion see Clemens (1997) and David and Lévesque (1999. On the further expansion of NATO membership to include other former communist states see Kempre. (2001) and Hutchings (2001).

[5] On the development of a Common European Security and Defense Policy see Hay and Sicherman (2001), Croft, *et. al.* (2000), Roper (2000), and Hoffmann (2000).

[6] Although Russian concerns have focused on NATO, current Russian Foreign Minister Igor Ivanov (1998) has warned that Russia has underestimated the negative implications of EU expansion, as well.

[7] The authors are well aware of the potential role of other European states, such as Ukraine and Serbia/Yugoslavia that are not short-term candidates for entry into European institutions. However, the current analysis will focus only on the reactions and importance of the Russian Federation for the creation of a new security system centered on Western and Central Europe.

[8] On international support for democratization in the region see Sharman and Kanet, 2000, and Mattox and Rachwald, 2001.

[9] In early 2001 President Putin and Sergei Ivanov, head of the Security Council, restated in very assertive and harsh terms the Russian opposition to NATO expansion and to the U.S. development of a missile defense system. 'We consider the policy of NATO enlargement to be a mistake and we say that it is unacceptable to us,' Putin (2001) noted in a public statement on 26 January 2001. 'The normalization of our relations with NATO is advancing with difficulty and our relations have moved backwards since the events in the Balkans,' he added. Less than two weeks later a security conference in Munich organized by NATO Ivanov, in terms reminiscent of the Cold War, charged NATO with creating a 'Chernobyl-like nuclear disaster' in Kosovo and virtually demanded that the West write off part of

Russia's debt or run the risk of Russia's expanding its dealings with what the U.S. calls 'rogue' states. (Socor, 20001).

[10] Shiraev and Zubok (2000, pp. 122-126) discuss in some detail the internal debates in Russia concerning the meaning of U.S. policy in Kosovo and the most fruitful Russian response, while Lynch (2001) notes the relative stability of policy over time. The noted Russian foreign policy analyst Alexei Arbatov (1993, 1997) provides perceptive analyses of Russian policy.

[11] In a speech in Aachen, Germany, on 2 June 2000 President Bill Clinton (2000) reiterated the point about possible eventual Russian membership in NATO: 'No doors can be sealed shut to Russia, not NATO's, not the EU's. The alternative would be a future of harmful competition between Russia and the continent'.

[12] For a detailed analysis of the complexities of group decision making in NATO see Daalder and O'Hanlon (2000); Both (2000).

[13] For an important set of articles that provide arguments on both sides of the issue of NATO expansion see David and Lévesque (1999).

[14] For an assessment of the status of the applicant countries see Richter *et al.* (2000) and Solovev (2001).

[15] An illustration of the dramatic shift in trade patterns can be seen in the following data:

Central and East European Exports and Imports by Region
Shares in the total, in %

Country	Trading Partner	1990 exports	imports	1999 exports	imports
Bulgaria	EU (15)	5.6	11.5	52.4	48.6
	Russia	64.0	56.5	5.5 (98)	20.0 (98)
Czech Republic	EU (15)	38.4	40.5	69.2	64.0
	Russia	25.1	24.3	1.4	4.8
Slovak Republic	EU (15)	40.8	44.8	59.5	51.7
	Russia	25.1	16.6	1.7	12.0
Hungary	EU (15)	42.1	43.1	76.2	64.4
	Russia	20.2	19.1	29.2	5.0
Poland	EU (15)	52.7	51.1	70.5	64.9
	Russia	14.5	17.0	2.6	5.9
Romania	EU (15)	33.9	21.8	65.5	60.4
	Russia	25.6	23.2	0.6	6.8
Slovenia	EU (15)	64.8	69.0	66.1	68.6
	Russia	13.3	6.4	1.5	1.6

Source: Havlik et al. (2000), pp. 17-18.

[16] For an assessment of the likely economic impact of EU enlargement on those countries not accepted see Gligorov (2000).

[17] On growing anti-American attitudes see Shiraev and Zubok (1998); on recent shifts in Russian attitudes see Colton and McFaul (2001). Recent poll data in Russia support Colton and McFaul's argument ('Rossiiane vyskazyvaiutsia za sushchestvennoe sblizhenie c SShA,' 2001).

[18] It is most interesting to note that events in former Yugoslavia, especially in Kosovo, have played an important role in influencing the West European commitment to building up its own foreign and security policy capabilities that will enable it to act independently of the

United States. See, for example, Van Oudenaren. (2000), pp. 296-303. For a discussion of Russia's policy toward the EU see Timmermann, (1999).

[19] Then Prime Minister Putin personally turned over the Russian policy response (Russian Federation, 1999) at a Russia-EU meeting in October 1999 that lays out Russia's positive response to the EU initiative. Other statements of Russia's official foreign policy orientation under Putin can be found in Russian Federation (2000a) and Russian Federation (2000b).

[20] As late as 1997 Premier Chernomyrdin said that Russia's aim was eventual membership. (Mannin, 1999, p. 1).

[21] For an excellent discussion of the issues involved in reaching foreign policy agreement within the EU see Both (1999).

[22] Some in the U.S. political establishment, including President Bush, have argued that the ABM treaty is dead and invalid, and that instead of amending the United States should simply scrap it altogether, clearing the way for building a national missile defense system. The Bush Administration has been strongly committed since its very inception to the deployment of a far more comprehensive NMD than that under consideration by President Clinton until his decision in summer 2000 to delay a deployment decision. For early statements of the Republican position see the comments of Senator Jesse Helms, the former powerful chair of the Senate Foreign Relations Committee (Helms, 1999; U.S. Senate Committee on Foreign Relations, 2000). In introductory remarks before the Committee on Foreign Relations, Senator Helms stated that the hearings would proceed from the presumption that the ABM Treaty has ceased to exist and that will be defeated (U.S. Senate Committee on Foreign Relations, 1999).

Given the largely unilateral approach to foreign and security policy exhibited by the Administration of George W. Bush in its first six months in office, as well as the dramatic changes occurring the relationship between the United States and its European allies, there is little likelihood in the near future of U.S. support for an autonomous European security capability. The commitment of individual West European countries to the continued reduction of military spending also makes the development of an independent security capability in the near future highly problematic.

[23] For recent discussions of European efforts to develop a coordinated defense and security policy and compatibility see Roper, 2000; Hoffmann, 2000; Gärtner, 2000). Recently former Defense Secretary Cohen warned that NATO could become "a relic of history" if the European members of the alliance did not closely coordinate with NATO (Cited in Black, 2000).

[24] A study commissioned by the U.S. Air Force poses the question of NATO's potential role in the Caspian region (Sokolsky and Charlick-Paley, 1999).

References

Albright, Madeleine. (2000), Cited in Georg Wiessala and Geoffrey Edwards, 'Editorial: Revolution Beyond Reform?' *Journal of Common Market Studies*, vol. 38.

Allensworth, Wayne. (1998), *The Russian Question: Nationalism, Modernization, and Post-Communist Russia*. Lanham, MD: Rowman & Littlefield.

Arbatov, Alexei. (1993), 'Russia's Foreign Policy Alternatives,' *International Security*, vol. 18, no. 4, pp. 5-43.

Arbatov, Alexei. (1997), 'Russian Foreign Policy Thinking in Transition', in Vladimir Baranovsky, ed., *Russia and Europe: The Emerging Security Agenda.* Oxford/New York: Oxford University Press, pp. 135-159.

Arbatov, Alexei. (1998), 'Pora nachat' perenaladku otnoshenii', *Nezavisimaia gazeta,* 21 July.

Aybet, Gülnur. (2000), *A European Security Architecture after the Cold War: Questions of Legitimacy* Houndmills, ENG: Macmillan Press; New York, St. Martin's Press.

Bandow, Doug. (1999), 'NATO's Balkan Disaster: Wilsonian Warmongering Gone Mad', *Mediterranean Quarterly* vol. 10, no. 3.

Baranovsky, Vladimir. (2000), 'Russia: A Part of Europe or Apart from Europe?' *International Affairs*. vol. 76, no. 3.

Black, Ian. (2000), 'US Warns of NATO Risk in EU Rapid Reaction Force', *The Guardian* 6 December 2000. http://www.guardianunlimited.co.uk

Black, J.L. (2000), Russia Faces NATO Expansion: Bearing Gifts or Bearing Arms? Lanham, MD: Rowman & Littlefield.

Both, Norbert. (2000), *From Indifference to Entrapment: The Netherlands and the Yugoslav Crisis, 1990-1995.* Amsterdam: Amsterdam University Press; distributed in North America by The University of Michigan Press.

Bukkvoll, Tor. (1997), *Ukraine and European Security*. London: Royal Institute of International Affairs.

Carr, Fergus, and Flenley, Paul. (1999), 'NATO and the Russian Federation in the New Europe: The Founding Act on Mutual Relations', *Journal of Communist Studies and Transition Politics,* vol. 15, no. 2, pp. 88-110.

Chulos, Chris J., and Timo Piirainen, eds. (2000), *The Fall of an Empire, the Birth of a Nation: National Identities in Russia.* Aldershot, UK/Burlington, VT: Ashgate.

Clemens, Clay, ed. (1997), *NATO and the Quest for Post-Cold War Security.* Houndmills: Macmillan; New York: St. Martin's.

Clinton, President William J. (2000), 'Clinton Calls for Inclusion of Russia by Europe,'*CNN.com* .http://www.cnn.com/2000/WORLD/Europe/06/02/Clinton.europe.02/

Colton, Timothy, and McFaul, Michael. (2001), 'America's Real Russian Allies', *Foreign Affairs,* vol. 80 , no. 3, pp. 46-59.

Crawford, Gordon. (2000), 'European Union Development Co-operation and the Promotion of Democracy', in *Democracy Assistance: International Co-operation for Democratization,* edited by Peter Burnell. London: Frank Cass, pp. 90-127.

Croft, Stuart, Howorth, Jolyon, Terriff, Terry, and Webber Mark. (2000), 'NATO's Triple Challenge', *International Affairs*, vol. 76, no. 3.

D'Anieri, Paul, Robert Kravchuk, and Taras Kuzio. (1999), *Politics and Society in Ukraine.* Boulder, CO: Westview Press.

Daalder, Ivo H. and O'Hanlon, Michael E. (2000), *Winning Ugly: NATO's War to Save Kosovo.* Washington: Brookings Institution Press.

Daniszewski, John. (2001), 'Russians Demand Substance Over Style Diplomacy: Criticism of Putin's Budding Relationship with the U.S. is Growing", *Los Angeles Times,* 16 November; in *Johnson's Russia List,* no. 5550, item 1, 16 November 2001. http://www.cdi.org/russia/johnson

David, Charles-Philippe, and Lévesque, Jacques, eds. (1999), *The Future of NATO: Enlargement, Russia, and European Security.* Montreal-Kingston-London: McGill-Queen's University Press.

Delpech, Thérèse. (1997), 'La question russe après l'accord avec l'OTAN', *Politique Étrangère,*, vol. 62, no. 3, pp. 279-89.

Diligenskij, German, and Tschugrow, Sergej. (2000), 'Der "Westen" in russischen Bewußtsein', *Berichte des Bundesinstituts für ostwissenschaftliche und internationale Studien*, no. 22

Dinan, Desmond. (1999), *Ever Closer Union: An Introduction to European Integration*. Boulder and London: Lynne Rienner Publishers, Inc.

Drozdiak, William. (2000), 'US Tepid on European Defense Plan', *The New York Times*, 7 March, p. A01.

Druzenki, Egor. (1999), 'Ne dai Bog! Zashchishchaia Jugoslafiiu, Rossiia ne mozhet riskovat' svoim budushchim', *Neft' I Kapital*, no. 2, pp. 78-81.

European Communities. (1998), *Agreement on Partnership and Co-operation between the European Communities and their Member States and Russia*. http://europa.eu.int/comm/external relations/ceeca/bilateral_rel/pca_russia.pdf

European Council. (1999), *Common Strategy of the European Union of 4 June 1999 on Russia1999/414/CFSP)*. http://europa.eu.int/comm/external_relations/russia/common_strategy/index.htm.

Evans, Michael. (2001), 'Blair Plans Wider Role for Russia with NATO', *The Times*, 17 November 2001; in *Johnson's Russia List*, no. 5551, item 7, 17 November. http://www.cdi.org/russia/johnson

Facon, Isabelle. (1997), 'La Russie, l'OTAN et l'avenir de la sécurité en Europe', *Politique Étrangère*, vol. 62, no. 3, pp. 291-305,

Gärtner, Heinz. (2000), 'European Security, the Transatlantic Link, and Crisis Management', in *Europe's New Security Challenges*, edited by Heinz Gärtner, Adrian Hyde-Price, and Erich Reiter. Boulder, CO/London: Lynne Rienner Publisher, pp. 125-147.

Gianaris, Nicholas V. (1994), *The European Community, Eastern Europe, and Russia*. Westport, CT/London: Praeger.

Gligorov, Vladimir. (2000), *Delaying Integration: The Impact of EU Eastern Enlargement on Individual CEECs Not Acceding or Acceding Only Later*. Research Reports. The Vienna Institute for International Economic Studies, no. 267 (July).

Goldgeier, James M. (1999), *Not Whether But When: The US Decision to Enlarge NATO*. Washington, DC: Brookings Institution Press.

Gornostayev, Dmitry. (2001), "Vladimir Putin: Russia is Ready to Accept Rapprochement with NATO with Regard to Its Own Interests", *Russian Observer.com*, 15 November. http://www.russianobserver.com

Gower, Jackie. (2000), 'Russia and the European Union', *Russia and Europe: Conflict or Cooperation?* edited by Mark Webber. New York: St. Martin's Press.

Hadley, Stephen. 2000), *Defining the Path to a Peaceful, Undivided, and Democratic Europe*. Washington, DC: United States Institute of Peace.

Havlik, Peter, et al. (2000), *The Transition Countries in Early 2000: Improved Outlook for Growth, But Unemployment Still Rising*. Research Reports. The Vienna Institute for International Economic Studies, no. 266 (June), pp. 17-18.

Hay, William Anthony, and Sicherman, Harvey. (2001), 'Europe's Rapid Reaction Force: What, Why, and How?' *Watch on the West*, Foreign Policy Research Institute, vol. 2, no. 2 (February). http://www.fpri.org.

Helms, Jesse, Senator. (1999), 'Amend the ABM Treaty? No, Scrap it.' Editorial. *The Wall Street Journal*, 22 January.

Heurlin, Bertel. (1998), 'NATO, Security, and the Baltic States: A New World, A New Security, a New NATO', in *The Baltic States in World Politics*, edited by Birthe Hansen and Bertel Heurlin. New York: St. Martin's Press, pp. 65-85.

Hoffmann, Stanley (2000), 'Towards a Common European Foreign and Security Policy', *Journal of Common Market Studies*, vol. 38, no. 2, pp. 189-198.

Höhmann, Hans-Hermann, and Christian Meier. (1999), 'Conceptual, Internal and International Aspects of Russia's Economic Security', in *Russia and the West: The 21*st *Century Security Environment*, edited by Alexei Arbatov, Karl Kaiser, and Robert Legvold. Armonk, NY: M.E. Sharpe, pp. 77-97.

Hutchings, Robert L., rapporteur. (2001), *Permanent Alliance? NATO's Prague Summit and Beyond*. Policy Paper, The Atlantic Council of the United States. April.

Ivanov, Igor. (1998), 'Razshirenie Evrosoiuza: scenarii, problemy, psledstviia', *Mirovaia ekonomiki I mezhdunarodnie otnosheniia*, no. 8.

Kanet, Roger E. (2001), 'Zwischen Konsens und Konfrontation: Rußland und die Vereinigten Staaten', *Osteuropa*, vol. 51, no. 4/5, pp. 509-521.

Kanet, Roger E., and Ibryamova, Nuray V. (2001), 'Verpaßte Gelegenheiten? Americanisch-Russische Beziehungen in den 90er Jahren', *Osteuropa*, vol. 51, no. 8, pp. 985-1001.

Kassianova, Alla. (2001), Russia: Still Open to the West? Evolution of the State Identity in the Foreign Policy and Security Discourse', *Europe-Asia Studies*, vol. 53, no. 6, pp. 821-839.

Kaufman, Joyce P. (2001), 'NATO After the Cold War', unpublished paper presented at the Comparative Interdisciplinary Studies Section/International Studies Association Millennium Series conference, Heidelberg, Germany, 24-26 June.

Kempre, Frederick. (2001), 'Get Ready for the Vilnius Ten', *Wall Street Journal Europe*, 2 May.

Kennedy-Pipe, Caroline. (2000), 'Russia and the North Atlantic Treaty Organization', in *Russia and Europe: Conflict or Cooperation*, edited by Mark Webber. New York: St. Martin's Press.

Knabe, Bernd. (2000), 'Rußlands neue 'Konzeption der nationalen Sicherheit''. *Aktuelle Analysen*, Bundesinstitut für ostwissenschaftliche und internationale Studien, no. 11.

Kobrinskaya, Irina. (2001), 'Russia: Facing the Facts', in Mattox, Gale A., and Rachwald, Arthur R., eds., *Enlarging NATO: The National Debates*. Boulder, CO/London: Lynne Rienner Publishers, pp.169-186.

Kolodziej, Edward A. (1991), 'The Cold War as Cooperation', in Roger E. Kanet and Edward A. Kolodziej, eds., *The Cold War as Cooperation: Superpower Cooperation in Regional Conflict Management*. Houndmills, ENGL.: Macmillan Press, and Baltimore: The Johns Hopkins University Press, pp. 1-30.

Kremenyuk, Viktor A. (1991), 'The Cold War As Cooperation: A Soviet Perspective', in Roger E. Kanet and Edward A. Kolodziej, eds., *The Cold War as Cooperation: Superpower Cooperation in Regional Conflict Management*. Houndmills, ENGL.: Macmillan Press, and Baltimore: The Johns Hopkins University Press, pp. 31-61.

Lake, Anthony. (2000), *Six Nightmares: Real Threats in a Dangerous World and How America Can Meet Them*. Boston, New York, and London: Little, Brown, and Company.

Lesser, Ian O. (1999), *NATO Looks South: New Challenges and New Strategies in the Mediterranean*. Santa Monica: RAND.

Lieven, Anatol. (1999), *Ukraine and Russia: A Fraternal Rivalry*. Washington: United States Institute of Peace Press.

Light, Margot, Stephen White, and John Löwenhardt. (2000), 'A Wider Europe: The View from Moscow and Kyiv', *International Affairs*, vol. 76, no. 1, pp. 77-88.

Lund, Julie A., and Kanet, Roger E. (1999), 'The Russian Federation and Central Europe's Entry into European Institutions', in *Russia After the Cold War* edited by Mike Bowker and Cameron Ross. Harlow/London: Longman, pp. 280-298.

Lynch, Allan C. (2001), 'The Realism of Russia's Foreign Policy', *Europe-Asia Studies*, vol. 53, no. 1, pp. 7-32.

MacFarlane, S. Neil. (1994), 'Russian Conceptions of Europe', *Post-Soviet Affairs*. vol. 10, no. 3.

Mannin, Mike. (1999), 'EU-CEE Relations: An Overview', *Pushing Back the Boundaries: The European Union and Central and Eastern Europe*, edited by Mike Mannin. Manchester: Manchester University Press.

Mattox, Gale A., and Rachwald, Arthur R., eds. (2001), *Enlarging NATO: The National Debates*. Boulder, CO/London: Lynne Rienner Publishers.

Mayhew, Alan. (1998), *Recreating Europe: The European Union's Policy towards Central and Eastern Europe*. Cambridge/New York: Cambridge University Press.

McFaul, Michael. (2001), 'U.S.-Russian Relations after September 11, 2001', Testimony prepared for Hearings of the U.S. House of Representatives Committee on International Relations, 24 October 2001 [hearings postponed] Available in *Johnson's Russia List*, no. 5507, 25 October. http://www.cdi.org/russia/johnson

McFaul, Michael, and Zlobin, Nikolai. (2001), "A Half-Democratic Russia will Always be a Half-Ally to the U.S.", *Obshchaya Gazeta*, no. 46, 14-21 November 2001; translated in *Johnson's Russia List*, no. 5549, item 4, 16 November. http://www.cdi.org/russia/johnson

Michta, Andrew A., ed., (1999), *America's New Allies: Poland, Hungary, and the Czech Republic in NATO*. Seattle-London: University of Washington Press.

Ministry of Foreign Affairs of the Russian Federation. (1993), '*Kontseptsiia venshnei politiki Rossiiskoi Federatsi,*', *Vestnik Ministerstva inostrannyck del*, no. 1, pp. 3-23.

Ministry of Foreign Affairs of the Russian Federation. (2000), *Foreign Policy Concept of the Russian Federation.* http://www.mid.ru/mid/eng/econcept.htm; 12 January 2001; translated in *Johnson's Russia List*, no. 4403, item 3, 14 July. http://www.cdi.org/russia/johnson

NATO. (1995), *Study on NATO Enlargement.* Purposes and Principles of Enlargement. September. http://www.nato.int.docu.basictxt/enl-9502.htm.

Neumann, Iver B. (1998), 'Russia as Europe's Other', *Journal of Area Studies*. no. 12.

Nye, Jr., Joseph S. (2000), 'The US and Europe: Continental Drift?' *International Affairs*. vol. 76, no. 1.

'Official Perspectives from Eastern Europe.' (1997), in *NATO and the Quest for Post-Cold War Security,* edited by Clay Clemens. London: New York: St. Martin's, Press, pp. 102-122.

Pond, Elizabeth. (2000), 'Come Together: Europe's Unexpected New Architecture', *Foreign Affairs* vol. 79, no. 2, p. 11.

Putin, Vladimir. (2001), Moscow, Jan 26 (AFP). Cited in *Johnson's Russia List*, no. 5052, item 1, 26 January.

Richter, Sándor, et al.. (2000), *EU Eastern Enlargement: The Case of the Former 'Second-Wave' Applicant Countries.* Research Reports. The Vienna Institute for International Economic Studies, no. 270 (September).

Rogov, Sergei. (2001), 'Window of Opportunity for Russia, U.S.', *The Russian Journal,* 19-25 October. Translated in *Johnson's Russia List,* no. 5499, 19 October 2001. http://www.cdi.org/russia/johnson

Roper, John. (2000), 'Two Cheers for Mr Blair? The Political Realities of European Defence Co-operation', *Journal of Common Market Studies*, vol. 38, (September), pp. 7-23.
'Rossiiane vyskazyvaiutsia za sushchestvennoe sblizhenie c SshA'. (2001), Interfax, *Nezavisiamya gazeta*, (internet version), 3 November 2, no. 207. http://ng.ru/politics/2001-11-03/1_moscow.html
Russian Federation. (1999), 'Strategiia razvitiia otnosheniia Rossiiskoî Federatsii s Evropeiskim Soiuzom na srednosrochnuiu perspektivu (2000-2010 gg)', *Diplomaticheskii Vestnik*, no. 11, pp. 20-28.
Russian Federation. (2000a), 'Doktrina informatsionnoi bezopasnosti Rossiiskoi Federatsii.' *Rossiiskaia gazeta*, 28 September, pp. 3-4. http://www.scrf.gov.ru/Documents/Degree/2000/09-09.html
Russian Federation. (2000b), 'Kontseptsiia natsional'noi bezopasnosti Rossiiskoi Federatsii'. *Nezavisimoe voennoe obozrenie* (Internet Version), 11 July. http://nvo.ng.ru/concepts/2000-01-14/6_concept.html
Schmidt, Peter. (2001), 'The Compatibility of Security Organizations and Policies in Europe', in *Europe's New Security Challenges*, edited by Heinz Gärtner, Adrian Hyde-Price, and Erich Reiter. Boulder, CO/London: Lynne Rienner Publisher, pp. 148-163.
Sharman, J.C. and Kanet, Roger E. (2000), 'International Influences on Democratization in Postcommunist Europe', in *Pathways to Democracy: The Political Economy of Democratic Transitions*, edited by James F. Hollifield and Calvin Jillson. New York/London: Routledge, pp. 226-241.
Shiraev, Eric, and Zubok, Vladislav. (2000), *Anti-Americanism in Russia: From Stalin to Putin*. New York Palgrave, St. Martin's Press.
Socor, Vladimir. (2001), 'Sergei Ivanov Shatters Credibility at Munich Security Policy Conference', *Jamestown Monitor*, vol. 7, no. 24, 5 February; reprinted in *Johnson's Russia List*, no. 5075, item 4, 6 February 2001. http://www.cdi.org/russia/johnson
Sokolsky Richard and Charlick-Paley Tanya. (1999), *NATO and Caspian Security: A Mission Too Far?* Santa Monica, CA: The RAND Corporation..
Solana, Javier. (1999), 'NATO in the 21st Century: An Agenda for the Washington Summit' *Congressional Digest Quarterly*. Vol. 7, no. 4.
Solovev, Vadim. (2001), 'Moskva ustupila Vashingtonu', *Nezavisimaya gazeta* ,(Internet version), 3 November, no. 207. http://ng.ru/politics/2001-11-03/1_moscow.html
Spaak, Paul-Henri. (1971), *The Continuing Battle: Memoirs of a European 1936-1966*. Boston and Toronto: Little, Brown and Company.
Timmermann, Heinz. (1999), 'Rußland und die internationalen europäischen Strukturen', *Berichte des Bundesinstituts für ostwissenschaftliche und internationale Studien*, no. 29.
Timmermann, Heinz. (2000), 'Rußlands Strategie für die Europäische Union: Aktuelle Tendenzen, Konzeptionen und Perspektiven', *Berichte des Bundesinstituts für ostwissenschaftliche und internationale Studien*, no. 5.
Umbach, Frank. (2001), ' Rußland und NATO-Osterweiterung – Integration, Kooperation oder Isolation?' *Osteuropa*, vol. 51, no. 4, pp. 423-440.
U.S. Senate, Committee on Foreign Relations. (1999), *Ballistic Missiles: Threat and Response: Hearings Before the Committee on Foreign Relations United States Senate One Hundred Sixth Congress First Session April 15 and 20, May 4, 5, 25, 26, and September 16, 1999*. Washington: Government Printing Office.
U.S. Senate Committee on Foreign Relations. (2000), *Helms Says Any Clinton ABM Deal With Russia 'Dead-on-Arrival'*. Press Release. 26 April.
Van Oudenaren, John. (2000), Uniting Europe: European Integration and the Post-Cold War

World. Lanham, MD: Rowman & Littlefield.

Wedel, Janine R. (1998), Collision and Collusion: The Strange Case of Western Aid to Eastern Europe, 1989-1998. New York: St. Martin's Press.

Wettig, Gerhard. (1998), 'NATO, Russia and European Security after the Cold War', *Aktuelle Analysen*, Bundesinstitut für ostwissenschaftliche und internationale Studien, no. 3.

Working Group of the Russian Independent Institute of Social and National Problems RNISiNP). (2000), 'Russian Society At the Turn of the Century'. *Nezavisimaya Gazeta*., 20 July; translated in *Johnson's Russia List*, no. 4416, item 8, 21 July 2000. http://www.cdi.org/russia/johnson

Yost, David S. (1998), *NATO Transformed: The Alliance's New Roles in International Security*. Washington: United States Institute of Peace Press.

Zagorski, Andrei. (1997), 'Russia and European Institutions', in *Russia and Europe: The Emerging Security Agenda*, edited by Vladimir Baranovsky. Oxford: Oxford University Press, for SIPRI, pp. 519-540.

Zagorski, Andrei. (2001), 'Great Expectations', *NATO Review*, vol. 49 (Spring), pp. 24-27.

Chapter 5

Squaring the Circle? British Defence Policy in a Changing World

Andrew Dorman[1]

Introduction

For many time stopped still on 11th September 2001. The devastating attacks on the World Trade Center, the subsequent use of anthrax by an as yet unidentified foe and the war in Afghanistan has caused some to call for a rethink of western security policy. The end of the Cold War led to similar calls and the resulting peace dividend led to a significant reduction in the west's military forces. It is within this context of a rapidly changing world that British defence policy, like that of its western counterparts, has attempted to adapt.

Britain's focus has, historically, been on two areas: firstly, on Europe and maintaining some form of balance of power; and secondly, on the world beyond Europe. The reasoning has been relatively simple. As a small island nation unable to feed itself and with insufficient raw materials to sustain it there has long been a requirement to trade. Thus the requirements of trade have frequently determined defence policy. A peaceful Europe allows trade to occur with Europe and also beyond Europe. Europe has therefore been and continues to be at the very heart of British defence policy.

But Europe has changed. Since 1989 Europe the Soviet Union has collapsed and the Warsaw Pact has come to an end. At the same time the North Atlantic Treaty Organization (NATO) has found itself involved for the first time in the actual application of force in Yugoslavia with forces committed to Bosnia and Kosovo whilst the Western European Union (WEU) is being absorbed into the European Union (EU) in order to help provide the latter with a military capability. Not surprisingly Britain has been deeply involved in all this and, in particular, in the mechanics of institutional adaptation as both NATO and the European Union (EU) have sought to expand in both the size and their respective remits. Despite the European emphasis Britain has continued to be an active participant on the world stage with its leadership of the International Security and Assistance Force being only the latest manifestation of this.[2]

The end of the Cold War has brought little respite; in fact, the tempo of operations has increased dramatically. The increasingly reticent attitude of the British government to the deployment of their military forces outside the NATO region in the latter half of the Cold War has given way to the commitment of significant military forces in a variety of operations outside Europe. These have included the Gulf War and the subsequent operation to relieve the Kurds in Northern Iraq, peace support operations in Cambodia, humanitarian operations in Mozambique, support for the government of Sierra Leone and now Afghanistan.[3]

Whilst all this has been going on there has been significant change to Britain's armed forces.[4] Since 1989 they have generally had to reduce themselves in size and have slowly begun to re-orientate themselves towards an expeditionary warfare capability-based approach and away from the Cold War threat-based one. However, the progress has generally been slow with the result that Britain, like the rest of its European allies, found itself totally dependent upon an American decision to use force and for the conduct of the majority of the air campaign.[5] When the Americans subsequently put a limit on their own ground deployment the Europeans struggled to put sufficient land forces together in time to implement the peace agreement.[6] This led to a Franco-British call for a European corps level intervention capability.[7] The Joint Declaration of the British and French Governments gave a renewed impetus to the Saint Malo Declaration and put concrete proposals forward, which were subsequently endorsed at the EU's Helsinki Summit.[8] More recently in Afghanistan Britain has been severely restricted in its ability to project air power into the region. Instead it has been left to contribute support aircraft, Special Forces and a few Tomahawk Land Attack Missiles (TLAMs).[9]

This chapter therefore seeks to examine the reality behind Britain's moves towards managing the changing nature of conflict. It has been divided into three parts. Firstly, it sets out the reasoning behind the government's decision to adopt an expeditionary capability. Secondly, it assesses the reality behind these goals – to what extent have the armed forces actually been able to re-orientate themselves? Finally, it draws some conclusions about British defence policy and the implications this has for the future.

Reasons for Sending the Cavalry or why an Expeditionary Capability is Needed

Seven reasons can be identified for a British government, either acting alone or as part of a coalition, resorting to the deployment and/or use of its expeditionary forces. Firstly, Britain is a former colonial power, which still retains some vestiges of its empire. Some dependent territories continue to require protection whilst in others an interest still remains. A recent example of this was the deployment of forces to Sierra Leone, initially as part of a Services led evacuation but later in support of the fledgling democratic government.[10] Also worthy of note is the ongoing concern expressed by the British government about events in Zimbabwe.[11]

Secondly, Europe remains dependent upon other states for the supply of essential raw materials including oil. Britain's *Strategic Defence Review* (SDR) expressed this most forcibly:

> 18. We are a major European state and a leading member of the European Union. Our economic and political future is as part of Europe. Our security is indivisible from that of

our European partners and Allies. We therefore have a fundamental interest in the security and stability of the continent ...

19. But our vital interests are not confined to Europe. Our economy is founded on international trade. Exports form a higher proportion of Gross Domestic Product than for the US, Japan, Germany or France. We invest more of our income abroad than any other major economy. Our closest economic partners are the European Union and the US but our investment in the developing world amounts to the combined total of France, Germany and Italy. Foreign investment into the UK also provides nearly 20% of manufacturing jobs. We depend on foreign countries for supplies of raw materials, above all oil.[12]

Britain's dependence upon trade means it has to protect not only its own access to raw materials but also that of its main trading partners. Any failure to do so could have significant domestic repercussions.

Thirdly, there will continue to be external political pressure for the use of military intervention. The United States has historically called upon Britain for joint action when its own interests have been involved.[13] It was noticeable that the initial strikes against Afghanistan included the use of US and British TLAMs. Whilst the number of the latter was not militarily significant their use was politically vital. Britain has also been a firm supporter of United Nations (UN) operations. As one of the five permanent members of the Security Council, the continued presence of Britain on the Security Council has been linked to their support to UN operations.

Fourthly, the threat posed by the proliferation of ballistic missiles and weapons of mass destruction has long been a cause for concern but not to the extent felt by the US. The events of 11 September may change this but current policy places less emphasis upon national missile defence and more on force protection and the option of pre-emptive action.[14]

Fifthly, there is a growing fear from the ramifications of ethnic unrest in the states bordering Europe. Since the end of the Cold War turmoil in the Balkans has led the various states of Europe to deploy a significant number of troops to Bosnia and Kosovo. Europe's experience of World War I has left its leaders with a particular fear of conflict escalation within the region and the area remains a source of deep-seated rivalry. The present UK government places greater emphasis upon preventive diplomacy and deployment than past administrations and this has increased the frequency of operational deployments. A recent example of this was the deployment of British troops to the Former Yugoslav Republic of Macedonia to lead a NATO force overseeing the disarmament of Albanians.[15]

Sixthly, internal politics have increasing had an important influence as foreign and domestic policy become more entwined. In particular, domestic public opinion influenced by the media has an important role to play *vis-à-vis* the humanitarian intervention element within military intervention.[16]

Lastly, and perhaps most importantly, has been the present administration's own emphasis on 'forces for good'. Prime Minister Blair has made a number of important speeches in this area such as that made in Chicago in 1999 entitled ' The Doctrine of the International Community'.[17] More recently the MOD's annual performance report set out the two purposes of the MOD and the mission of the armed forces:

- Defend the United Kingdom, and Overseas Territories, our people and interests;

- Act as a force for good by strengthening international peace and security[18]

Whilst the first one is unsurprising and links into the traditional realist view of the national interest the second reflects this internationalist agenda. This moral dimension has been demonstrated further in the Prime Minister's recent visit to India and Pakistan.

Reality behind the Rhetoric: Force Adaptation Since the End of the Cold War

Officially no security policy was ever articulated during the period from 1945 to 1989. Nevertheless Europe, rather than the Empire, became the principal focus for British defence policy as Britain slowly withdrew from much of its empire.[19] Within this transformation four inter-linked assumptions remained consistent throughout the period and revolved around maintaining the balance of power in Europe. These were the hostility of the Soviet Union, the maintenance of the 'special relationship' with the United States to offset the Soviet Union, the preservation of NATO in order to keep the United States committed to the defence of Europe and the creation and maintenance of an independent strategic nuclear deterrent as a final means of deterring the Soviet Union. In the background a diminishing ability to influence decisions on the world stage remained. These four assumptions, which underpinned Britain's defence policy, were perhaps inevitable, given the position with which Britain was confronted in 1945. At the time, Britain was the only major European power to survive the war relatively intact, with the exception of the Soviet Union. Germany, a defeated and disarmed nation, was physically occupied, whilst France and Italy were economically crippled and politically divided. It was Britain, therefore, which had to confront the situation of a Central and Eastern Europe dominated by a Soviet military and political presence.[20]

The Soviet Union had been a consistent and enigmatic problem for successive British Governments from the time of its inception. Concern with the Soviet Union began to increase even before the Second World War had ended as the Allies sought to agree a peace.[21] Subsequent events only reinforced these fears and led the former Prime Minister, Winston Churchill, to refer in 1946 to an 'Iron Curtain' dividing Europe in two.[22] Throughout the late 1940s the perception of the Soviet threat increased. From a defence point of view, Russia was a Euro-Asiatic continental land power. It had relied upon its immense reserves of manpower and vast geographical scale to provide for its defence. Its historical experience of invasion and the resulting devastation of its own lands and large civilian casualties contributed to its commitment to the maintenance of significant land and air forces in Central an Eastern Europe. In contrast, Britain's defence had traditionally relied on its control of the seas around its shores. If the Soviet Union were the most likely enemy, then the Royal Navy would be of limited direct use against a power that could only be confronted on land.

The situation was complicated further by the changing nature of conflict. During the First World War German airship and bomber raids had demonstrated that Britain was no longer immune from direct attack whilst U-boat operations against merchant shipping had got close to starving Britain out of the War.[23] This experience was repeated in the German aerial offensive on Britain during the Second World War, particularly between 1940 and 1941, and in the U-boat offensive from 1939 until 1945.[24] Moreover, the development of the atomic bomb finally demonstrated the potential for a single bomber to destroy a city and fulfil the claims of the early air power theorists.[25] As a result, Britain's defence planners found themselves confronted with the unenviable situation in which they were not only aware of Britain's vulnerabilities but also of its inability to deter the Soviet Union.

There was a further problem. The world wars had virtually bankrupted Britain and from 1945 onwards Britain's management of the problem was continuously undermined by its financial insecurity.[26] As a result, the support of the United States was paramount. It alone was capable of matching the might of the Soviet Union. This led successive British Government's to seek to foster their relations with the United States. The post-war Labour government adopted a twin-track policy. The first track was to organize the rest of Western Europe into a number of alliances nominally against a resurgent Germany, but also with a potential Soviet threat in mind.[27] The first step was the 1947 Dunkirk Treaty between Britain and France. The following year, the Benelux countries joined the Dunkirk Treaty arrangement under the Brussels Treaty. In the short term, these measures were of little military significance. They did, however, send an important political signal to the United States in that they indicated Western Europe's determination to contribute to its own defence. It also reinforced the second track of British strategy, which was to encourage the US to commit itself formally to the defence of Europe.

Since that time, US involvement in the defence of Europe has remained a fundamental part of British Cold War security policy. The twin-track approach reached fruition with the creation of the North Atlantic Treaty Organization (NATO). However, this was not without cost. First, Britain was forced to commit troops to the defence of Germany from 1950 to show solidarity with the United States.[28] This ultimately forced it to accept that a world role would have to assume a lower priority in British defence policy. Second, Britain's involvement in NATO provided a potential forum for undermining Britain's relationship with the United States and also for isolating it from its European allies. In other words Britain would frequently be caught between the two and suffer the resulting fallout in both relationships.

The fourth assumption in British Cold War defence policy lay in the creation and subsequent deployment of an independent strategic nuclear deterrent. The reasoning behind this was threefold. First, Britain had been forced to abandon its French ally and withdraw its forces from the Battle of France at Dunkirk in 1940. This had caused much ill feeling between the two allies and both drew a similar conclusion from the experience - namely, that one state could not be expected to sacrifice itself for another.[29] Ultimately Britain could not rely on a US nuclear guarantee and should therefore develop and maintain its own independent nuclear deterrent. Second, the ownership of nuclear weapons was an important part of maintaining Britain's place in the world and, in particular, retaining its seat on the UN Security Council. Finally, there was Britain's active participation in the development of the first atomic bomb. Its exclusion from the US nuclear weapons programme after the end of the war clearly rankled with those involved. As a result, one of the first significant post-war defence decisions was made by a subcommittee of the British Cabinet, GEN 75, in 1946 to order the construction of fissile production facilities with a view to producing a British atomic weapon. As the Chiefs of Staff argued, 'the best method of defence against the atomic bomb is likely to be the deterrent effect that the possession of the means of retaliation would have on a potential aggressor'.[30] At the same time, the first British strategic jet bomber specification was drawn up and issued as an operational requirement.[31] These programmes fitted neatly into early post-war defence planning that emphasised strategic bombing as the only effective counter-weight to the Soviet Union's massive superiority on land.

The other dimension to defence policy was Britain's wider world role. In 1945, Britain was one of the three leading world powers and considered itself as such. This was made clear from the 1948 Statement on the Defence Estimates, "The United Kingdom, as a member of the British Commonwealth and a Great Power, must be prepared at all times to fulfil her responsibility not only to the United Nations but also to herself".[32] Whilst not a superpower in its own right, its military and civilian presence throughout the world, particularly within the British Commonwealth and Empire, led many to assume that its world role would continue, particularly given the US relative inexperience and lack of interest in many regions.[33] The government hoped that with the European balance of power established through NATO, Britain could once again look beyond Europe to promote and preserve its out-of-area, global interests. This shift in emphasis was attempted in the 1957 Defence Review, which made significant reductions in Britain's conventional forces deployed in support of Europe in favour of their deployment East of Suez.[34] Changing patterns in trade, de-colonization, fear of the Soviet Union and continuing financial pressures resulted in Europe, in 1964, becoming once again, after the election of a Labour administration, the focus of British foreign and defence policies, coupled with the large-scale withdrawals of British forces from the Empire.[35] Even under the leadership of Margaret Thatcher from 1979 this policy remained largely unaltered. British defence policy, epitomized by the Nott Defence Review of 1981, which focused almost entirely on Europe, with only token gestures to the world role.[36]

The end of the Cold War almost inevitably meant that this position would be challenged as those elements became less important and NATO's security agenda broadened. However, British defence policy took far longer to adapt to the changed environment as British foreign policy floundered. This position was partly due to internal conflicts within the Government but it also reflected the innate conservatism of the armed forced and MOD. A new foreign policy slowly began to emerge but a new defence one did not, as successive defence reviews merely reduced the overall size of the armed forces. The 'Options for Change' exercise[37] and 'Frontline First: the Defence Cost Studies process (DCS)' were merely cost cutting exercises with little strategic redefinition.[38] The Services and the MOD maintained their traditional force priorities and there was no significant redistribution of finance between account headings. Instead what eventually emerged was a defence policy officially based on three defence roles:[39]

- Defence Role One was largely about home defence and the defence of Britain's dependent territories. In reality it was almost entirely about the preservation of an independent nuclear deterrent, support for the civilian authorities in Northern Ireland and the defence of the Dependent Territories – where feasible. Other areas, such as the air defence of the United Kingdom were effectively abandoned;
- Defence Role Two was the defence of Europe. NATO was viewed as the key defence role and the majority of resources were earmarked towards it. Finally, and of least priority; and
- Defence Role Three swept up the remaining missions, in particular the out-of-area role and support for UN peacekeeping missions. In reality this was simply a repackaging of existing Cold War defence policy with some reference made to increasing mobility.

As a result of these roles, perceived importance of the strategic nuclear deterrent remained and successive reviews left the Trident programme virtually untouched.[40] The reason was threefold, not only has Trident been viewed by the Conservative Party as its sacred cow,[41] but it has also traditionally been used as one of Britain's justifications for her permanent seat on the UN Security Council. Moreover, the political and financial cost of acquiring the Trident system meant that the Conservative administration was loathed to admit that it was no longer needed. Nevertheless, all Britain's other nuclear capabilities were ultimately cutback with the Trident system given the sub-strategic role in place of the cancelled tactical air-to-surface missile.[42]

The majority of defence cuts therefore fell on the conventional forces. However, like the earlier Nott and Healey reviews[43] the issue of retaining influence within NATO remained key. With the advent of NATO's new Strategic Concept, a major reorganisation of NATO's command structure was undertaken.[44] This resulted in Britain's loss of its one major command[45] and led the British Government to successfully pursue command of the new Allied Command Europe Rapid Reaction Corps (ARRC) at Germany's expense. However, there was a significant cost to this - the commitment of two divisions and a headquarters staff.[45] Support for Europe's other institutions, in particular the WEU, remained more sanguine. Britain's position within NATO allowed it to have more influence and use its relationship with the US to its advantage. However, the Conservative's support for Bush in the 1992 Presidential election soured Anglo-American relations. Moreover, support for the WEU rose as the EU expanded. This led to Britain frequently finding itself increasingly isolated within Western Europe.

To cover the high cost of the ARRC commitment defence cutbacks fell on other conventional areas. Officially, the aim was to have 'smaller forces, better equipped, properly trained and housed, and well motivated. They will need to be flexible and mobile and able to contribute both in NATO and, if necessary, elsewhere'.[47] However, although 'Options for Change' allowed the services to get rid of a lot of their older kit, the goal of making the remaining forces more flexible and mobile was sacrificed. In practice the Services continued to purchase their Cold War legacy systems such as the Type 23 anti-submarine warfare frigate, the Challenger 2 main battle tank and Eurofighter whilst other decisions were delayed, such as the order for new amphibious ships. The situation was subsequently made worse with the 'Defence Costs Study' review, which made further reductions. These principally focused on the support units with the result that deploying and sustaining forces abroad became increasingly problematic. This reflected the need for the government to emphasise its defence credentials at minimum cost. This trend towards political tokenism was most evident in the announcement of the purchase of 65 Tomahawk Land Attack Missiles in 1995.[48] This decision was announced in Parliament to the surprise of the Services, whilst ministers quietly ignored the navy's subsequent argument for a second, more substantial buy, to give it a sustainable capability.

With smaller forces the Ministry of Defence was initially loathed to undertake further overseas commitments. Amongst its West European allies Britain was noticeable in failing to send ground troops to Somalia when the United States called for assistance.[49] It was also was one of only two EU states to vote against the EU sending military forces as peacekeepers during the initial break-up of the Yugoslav Federation. However, circumstances subsequently forced the British government to take a more pro-active role, especially once the issue of Britain's retention of its permanent seat on the UN Security Council again became an issue in the mid-1990s.[50] In Bosnia it subsequently pulled together an infantry force for the escort of humanitarian aid in Bosnia and when a Serb mortar attack in February 1994 led to wide-scale casualties the British deployment was increased with elements of 24 Airmobile Brigade. After Dayton Britain was involved not only heavily as part of the ARRC commitment but also took responsibility for one of the three sectors deploying a divisional headquarters and supporting units.

For defence policy the early years of the post-Cold War era were traumatic. Institutional conflict and the jockeying for position within the various organizations dominated defence policy. Major cutbacks in defence left Britain, like many of its European counterparts, with smaller, poorly equipped forces. At the same time, the operational tempo for these forces had increased significantly and the various services found themselves over-stretched and in reality unable to support their traditional military tasks. The situation was exacerbated by the Service's own emphasis upon their traditional core war-fighting areas rather than addressing the changing environment.

Not surprisingly the Labour front-bench team were very critical of the Conservative government's handling of defence policy. In part this was an attempt to usurp the traditional Conservative stronghold on defence as an election issue. They argued for a defence review based on foreign policy, highlighting the hollowness of Britain's defence capabilities and Britain's isolation within Europe.

However, the criticism also reflected the internationalist agenda within Labour and their concern about the role Britain should play in the world. As a consequence, once in office they began the SDR process in 1997. Their aim was to 'maintain and reinforce the present favourable external security situation'.[51] SDR was officially based on the requirement:

> To move from stability based on fear to stability based on the active management of these risks, seeking to prevent conflicts rather than suppress them. This requires an integrated external policy through which we can pursue our interests using all the instruments at our disposal, including diplomatic, developmental and military. We must make sure that the Armed Forces can play as full and effective a part in dealing with these new risks as the old.[52]

The first obvious change to defence policy within SDR was the creation of an eighth defence mission - defence diplomacy. The previous three defence roles had been repackaged in 1996 into seven defence missions.[53] In part this drew together a number of existing tasks under a new heading. However, it also reflected the government's internationalist agenda and the desire that Britain should be a force for good in the world. Although defence diplomacy initially had a European focus, continuing the pro-European bias of defence policy this soon broadened to stretch beyond Europe, with the government's contribution to the peacekeeping mission to East Timor being only a recent example of this.[54]

SDR also drew attention to Britain's position as a leading member of the EU and this was linked into Britain's membership of NATO and the importance of the United States. On first appearances this was an apparent reversal of previous policy reflecting a European, rather than transatlantic, focus. However, the change is subtler. It represented an attempt to sit on both the US and European stools. The latter encouraged by the 'EU first' language of the document and the subsequent British-led initiatives on defence. The former placated by the preservation of the close links of a EU led force with NATO with the latter (i.e. US) retaining a veto on the release of NATO assets. Moreover, any initiative that seeks to shift the defence burden from the United States to Europe inevitably has the support of the incumbent US President.[55]

This emphasis on giving the European's their own capability as a means of reinforcing the Atlantic Alliance received a boost when the British and French agreed that the EU 'must have the capacity for autonomous action, backed up by credible military forces, the means to decide to use them, and a readiness to do so, in order to respond to international crises'.[56] This was a significant change in previous policy and this initiative was followed through at the EU's Amsterdam summit, which sought to provide a crisis management mechanism for the EU partners.[57] The key to preserving American goodwill had been NATO's retention of a veto over dual-hatted units, which British negotiators have been willing to concede.

However, the process seemed set for slow progress until the Kosovo experience provided the British government with further grounds for a renewed impetus. When the Americans subsequently put a limit on their own ground deployment the Europeans struggled to put sufficient land forces together in time to implement the peace agreement. On the first day of the KFOR deployment Lieutenant-General Mike Jackson the ARRC commander only had nine battalions available (four of these were British) with a total of forty tanks. By day 2 of the operation a further two battalions had deployed (1 British) giving him forces inferior in number to the withdrawing Yugoslav Army.[58] This led to a Franco-British call for a European corps level intervention capability.[59] The Joint Declaration by the British and French Governments in London in November 1999 gave a renewed impetus to the Saint Malo Declaration and proposed the creation of a corps level capability. These were subsequently endorsed at the EU's Helsinki Summit[60] Linked into this was the British decision to assign troops to the headquarters of the Eurocorps. Politically this was also very symbolic for the previous British administration had been one of the corps principle critics had sought to block its evolution at every opportunity. This quiet reversal of policy, therefore, represents a shift of the UK from a confrontational position with the Franco-German founded Eurocorps to an acceptance of its importance. Conversely the French government agreed to English becoming the sole working language within the corps. Following on from this it was agreed that the Eurocorps would take over from the ARRC in Kosovo[61] with the Eurocorps reporting directly to NATO's SACEUR. This marked the first significant step post-Helsinki to the creation second rapid reaction force within NATO run by the Europeans. Subsequently NATO's military staff has set the requirement for three high-level readiness headquarters and Eurocorps is one of the six bidders for inclusion.[62] If successful, it will significantly enhance NATO's expeditionary capability and by implication the Eurocorps will serve as the basis of a European capability to match NATO's ARRC. However, in reality it is likely that a political compromise will ensue at the expense of true capability with units double-hatted between Eurocorps and ARRC. Britain has accepted that it will not have the European lead of this corps and, as a result, it has seen off any challenge to its control of the ARRC, which will allow it to remain closely aligned to the US, without it appearing at all disloyal to the Eurocorps.

By way of contrast SDR also placed a considerable amount of emphasis on joint capabilities and the ability to unilaterally project military force.[63] To manage the re-modelled expeditionary forces a new Permanent Joint Task Force Headquarters (PJHQ) has been created, which is capable of overseeing simultaneous operations. This marks a significant advance over the previous situation and, if fully implemented, will mean that more than one operation can be undertaken outside the United Kingdom without recourse to the callout of a significant number of reserve personnel. This will, therefore, give the government a greater degree of flexibility than it has had to-date and ensure that it is not forced to choose between NATO and EU-led operations.

To support this SDR also contained a number of structural changes. The navy's doctrine and programme remain essentially unchanged with emphasis centred upon the three core capabilities:

- Aircraft carriers;
- Attack submarines; and
- Amphibious warfare.

In the short term the navy's force of three *Invincible*-class aircraft carriers remains unchanged from the Cold War.[64] These vessels can support an air group of Sea Harrier FA2s, RAF Harrier GR7s and Sea King AEW2 and HAS6 helicopters. Their major weakness lies in the small size of their air group. Thus when HMS *Invincible* was deployed to support NATO strikes on Kosovo in April 1999 she carried a mere seven Sea Harriers FA2s and no Harrier GR7s. 'Senior staff are keenly aware that the ships were not specifically designed for the operational role they are being called upon to fulfil ...'[65] and a number of measures have been taken to increase the capability.[66] In the longer-term the government has announced plans for two larger and far more capable vessels capable of carrying an air group of 50 aircraft, but these will not be available until after 2010. Thus with a reduction from three to two aircraft carriers the navy will only be able to guarantee support for one of the two near simultaneous deployments planned for within SDR.

Of the navy's three core capabilities the amphibious capability is currently the most developed. The Royal Navy is scheduled to receive a number of new and capable ships in service over the next ten years and the SDR has agreed to retain a brigade lift capability.[67] 3 Commando Brigade had already been given a central role within the JRDF and as one of only two light brigades its future is assured.[68] However, the current state of the amphibious fleet is the subject of some concern and a 'window of vulnerability' looks likely to remain until the first of the new LPDs enters service 2002. *HMS Ocean*, the new helicopter carrier commissioned last year, has resurrected a capability that was lost with the paying off and subsequent sale *of HMS Hermes* in 1984. Her standard air group will comprise 12 Support Helicopters and six Light Helicopters, although Apache attack helicopters and Chinooks can be embarked. Limited C4I facilities have been accepted and *HMS Ocean* will only be able to support a single commando group rather than a larger brigade size amphibious assault force, this being the role of the LPDs or aircraft carriers.[69] The other weakness lies in *HMS Ocean* being a single unit. *RFA Argus* could act as a limited helicopter carrier, and plans to purchase two hospital ships will release her from these duties, but her capability will remain very limited. The current generation of Landing Ship Logistics (LSLs) are also getting old and an order has been placed for four new ships based on a variant of the Dutch *Rotterdam* LPD. These are much larger more capable ships and represent a significant capability improvement.[70] The navy has also ordered six roll-on/roll-off ships under a Private Finance Initiative contract (PFI).[71] The role of these ships is primarily heavy lift in support of the Joint Rapid Reaction Force (JRRF). Consequently, if all these plans go ahead then by 2010, the specialized amphibious force will comprise two groups each comprising a new LPD, *Ocean or Argus*, two-three LSLs and three roll-on/roll-off vessels. This is far more impressive than that maintained over the last decade but, like the aircraft carrier force, this can only guarantee to support one operation at any one time.

The third core capability currently comprises twelve nuclear-powered attack submarines (SSNs), which SDR plans to reduce to 10. Before the 'Options for Change' and 'Defence Cost Study' reviews the force had 16 SSNs and 11 SSKs (Conventionally-powered attack submarines).[72] The loss of the SSKs, in particular, has caused considerable disquiet in the navy, especially given the move towards littoral rather than blue water operations. Questions about the force's future credibility have already been raised, especially when it is remembered that the Falklands War utilised five SSNs and one SSK.[73] This confirms the view that the navy will only be able to perform one significant operation at any one time especially. Nevertheless, the capability of this force will be significantly increased as all the existing and new boats are equipped with the Tomahawk Land Attack Missile (TLAM). This will give the navy the capacity to strike deep in land, a capability lost with the demise of the conventional aircraft carriers equipped with the Buccaneer. However, there are only 65 missiles on order, which raises questions about the sustainability of the TLAM force in any conflict.[74] The Kosovo experience has already highlighted this as an issue with a request made to the US for the sale of a further 30 missiles.[75] However, unless a further significant purchase is made then this weapon will remain a political symbol with very few ever being launched in any single conflict.

The army has used SDR to undertake a significant re-organisation of its deployment cycles by the decision to convert 5 Airborne Brigade into a mechanized brigade. This means both the army's divisions will now have three mechanized/armoured brigades with each brigade in a different part of the training cycle.[76] As a result both divisions will be able to rapid deploy a single brigade utilising the navy's expanded roll-on/roll-off fleet in the first instance. This represents a significant improvement on the British Army's current ability to deploy large formations at short notice. The delays in the deployment of 24 Airmobile Brigade in 1995 to Bosnia highlighted the need to have on-call large formations with the appropriate support to get them into the field.

The battalion parachute capability will be transferred to the new Air Cavalry Brigade formed out of the existing 24 Airmobile Brigade and the new Apache attack helicopters.[77] This means that only one battalion rather than the existing two battalions will remain parachute qualified at any point in time with the result that the one battalion air drop will be a one shot option for future governments.[78] Similarly, by creating only one Air Cavalry Brigade the deployment of such a force can only occur once and this may make politicians reluctant to use this particular unit because of its uniqueness. As a result of these moves the army has become more armoured focused at the brigade level of deployment than was the case previously. With only a single army brigade earmarked for non-armoured warfare outside the United Kingdom the British government may well find itself constrained in the type of operations it undertakes and even more dependent upon the Royal Marines to supplement the British Army's light forces. In marked contrast the US has retained four out of ten divisions in the light role. We may therefore find Britain with the infrastructure to support two simultaneous operations, but with inappropriate front-line units to mount two operations. Thus whilst the shift from the JRDF to the JRRF is an attempt to ensure that heavy units are available and capable of rapid deployment the reorganisation could backfire in the future if the wrong type of conflicts break out. This is particularly disturbing given the emphasis placed upon support for UN peacekeeping as a means of preserving Britain's permanent seat on the Security Council.

The air force remains the Service least affected by the SDR. It has accepted a cut of 36 aircraft from its front-line strength but has managed to preserve the Eurofighter programme in full. Moreover, this cutback looks as though it will only be a temporary measure as 87 Tornado F3s and 40 Jaguars are scheduled for replacement by 140 Eurofighters in the front-line squadrons.[79] Its command structure remains unchanged based on the three operational groups within Strike Command and this leaves it vulnerable to criticism from outside the air force. The Joint Force 2000 concept and the US moves towards Air Expeditionary Forces would seem to indicate that the RAF needs to rethink its deployment structure, especially since the underlying assumption of the whole of SDR is the requirement to deploy and control force over long distances. The deployment of sizeable air assets without an enormous logistic tail remains a problem that the RAF has failed to address and the other two Services are critical of this weakness.

Some improvements have been promised; most noticeably the ability to rapidly deploy forces to a crisis has re-emphasized the need for strategic airlift. As a result, four C-17 aircraft have been leased for the short-term whilst the government looks set to order Airbus A400M in the long-term. The introduction of the Eurofighter into service will provide the Royal Air Force with the air superiority aircraft it so noticeably lacked during the Gulf War. However, other decisions remain undecided. The need to replace the ageing VC-10 and TriStar tanker and transport force is currently awaiting a decision about which consortium will provide the capability under a PFI contract. All these programmes will have a significant impact on the future role the RAF will play in expeditionary warfare. However, as Kosovo has shown, in any coalition conflict the availability of air defence aircraft is generally not the problem. What coalition commanders generally lack is the ability to use precision guided munitions in all weathers in any quantity. This not only requires advanced weaponry but also a significant level of supporting aircraft to protect the strike package and assess the results achieved.

However, the reality behind policy remains dependent upon the provision of the requisite capabilities. This is where the continuity of these policies begins to become questionable. In the future Britain is increasingly likely to be presented with the choice of purchasing limited amounts of equipment in order to allow its armed forces to remain compatible with the United States or to build equipment in conjunction with its European partners. This situation is further confused by the industrial implications of such decisions. For example, there was much prevarication over strategic lift aircraft and the new air-to-air missile for the Royal Air Force. Each decision was viewed as an indication of the MOD's bias towards either the European or transatlantic stool. For example, the decision over airlift emphasized the government's commitment to Europe and European defence industry by deciding to buy the Airbus A400M. This ran contrary to the air force's preferred option, the C-17.[80] The BVRAAM decision had similar implications with France and Germany putting pressure on Tony Blair to intervene and ensure that the Matra BAe Dynamics missile was ordered rather than the rival US product.[81] This time the RAF's preference was for the European option and it got its way. To placate the US an interim purchase of AMRAAMs was announced.[82] Moreover, SDR highlighted the importance of technology in the changing strategic context, particularly the ability to gather information about an opponent and use it to maximum advantage. ISTAR and improved command and control are stressed within the SDR document and one of the first announcements after the SDR document was released was the decision to go ahead with the next generation of military communications satellites. However, the concept of information warfare has only five lines on it.[83] Partly this reflects the innate conservatism that still persists within the MoD to anything that is radically different to that which has gone on before. Moreover, it also represents the desire to see what emerges from the United States before making any financial commitments. Nevertheless, as the United States continues to push further ahead in command and control, communications and intelligence, and long-range interdiction systems the widening gap between America and her allies can only serve to undermine NATO. The Kosovo experience reinforced this conclusion and it is worth noting the limited air contribution made by even Britain and France - Europe's leading military powers. To experience to-date in Afghanistan merely reinforces this.

Conclusion

The Labour government has clearly taken a number of important steps. It has tried to re-establish Britain at the centre of Europe whilst remaining a close ally of the United States. British defence policy has pursued this twin-track approach with some success and Britain has currently managed to restore its level of influence in Europe and with the United States to that achieved during the bleakest days of the Cold War. This is quite an achievement given the state of Britain's relations with both Europe and America that the government inherited. At the same time the government has taken a number of steps in the development of an expeditionary capability. In capability terms SDR has sought to give the British government three options. Firstly, one involving the use of force in conjunction with its European partners as mentioned above. Secondly, to undertake independent action - presumably in support of dependent territories or as lead nation for a Commonwealth type operation. Thirdly, to act in co-operation with the United States outside NATO such as Operation Desert Fox. They therefore fit neatly into the requirements to placate both the Europeans and Americans whilst giving the option to do its own thing in order to preserve Britain's wider interests - such as its retention of its Permanent Seat on the UN Security Council.

However, the ability of Britain to continue this policy remains questionable in the longer term especially if the nature of conflict is itself changing. SDR was a very conventional review after all. Moreover, there are a number of difficult choices ahead, which could easily send this particular train off the rails. Firstly, reference has already been made to the diversity in technological capabilities between the various members of NATO. In essence there are three tiers at present. The United States on its own at the top (tier 1). The next tier down includes the leading military states of Western Europe of which Britain is the leading member (tier 2). Below this lie the smaller West European states and some of the new NATO members (tier 3). The Kosovo experience has indicated the problems of tiers 1 and 2 remaining compatible. There is a significant danger of Britain being forced to choose between tier 1 and 3. Secondly, the defence industrial dimension looks as though it will force the government to choose in favour of Europe. This is probably the area in which the first crack will appear. Moves towards a greater European defence capability will reinforce the trend towards a deepening of the European political relationship and Britain's divisions with its European partners on other issues, such as the single currency, may sour its defence relationship with Europe whilst the trend towards European defence industrial consolidation may drive a schism between the UK and USA. The level of success in maintaining the twin stools policy will therefore revolve around the government's ability to paper over the cracks in the wall as they appear but the ultimate success of such a policy seems doomed to start with. As a result Britain is likely to be left with a fudged expeditionary capability, which is half myth and half reality.

Notes

[1] The analysis, opinions and conclusions expressed or implied in this chapter are those of the author and do not necessarily represent the views of the JSCSC, the UK MOD or any other government agency.

[2] Geoffrey Hoon, 'International Security Assistance Force for Kabul', Statement to the House of Commons, 10 January 2002, *news.mod.uk/news/press/news_press_notice.asp?news Item_id=1336.*

[3] See 'Recent Operations', *www.mod.uk/aboutus/factfiles/operations.htm.*

[4] Colin McInnes, 'Labour's Strategic Defence Review', *International Affairs*, vol. 74, no.4, October 2001, pp. 823-46.

[5] See House of Commons Defence Committee, 'Fourteenth Report: Lessons of Kosovo, Report and Proceedings', *HC.347*, session 1999-2000 (London: Stationery Office, 2000).

[6] Lord Robertson, 'European Defence: the Way Ahead', Speech to Royal Institute of International Affairs, 7 October 1999.

[7] *Joint Declaration of the British and French Governments on European Defence*, Anglo-French Summit, London, 25 November 1999; 'Moving Forward European Defence', MoD Press Release, no. 421/99, 25 November 1999.

[8] Statement on the Estimates, 1999 (*www.mod.uk/policy/wp99*), para.17.

[9] See the MOD homepage on this *news.mod.uk/veritas/vindex.htm*

[10] M. Evans, 'British Officer Takes Over in Sierra Leone', *The Times*, 2 November 2000, p. 20.

[11] Baroness Amos, 'Zimbabwe's Electoral and Public Order Legislation', 10 January 2002, *www.fco.gov.uk/news/newstext.asp?5791.*

12. The Strategic Defence Review, *Cm.3,999*, (London: HMSO, 1998), p. 7.
13. In the deployment to the Gulf and Somalia the West European countries were the first to follow the US in announcing the deployment of their forces.
14. See 'Defending Against the Threat: From Biological and Chemical Weapons', (London: MOD, 1999).
15. 'British Troops Lead NATO Deployment in Macedonia', *MOD Press Release*, 15 August 2001.
16. The role of the media in influencing public opinion has been clearly evident in Britain with the recent airlift of wounded from Bosnia. Operation Irma, the British aerial evacuation of a number of seriously wounded individuals from Bosnia was due largely to the media focus on the plight of one child.
17. Tony Blair, 'Doctrine of the International Community', speech made at the Economic Club of Chicago, Chicago, 22 April 1999, *www.fco.gov.uk/news/speechtext.asp? 2316*
18. 'Ministry of Defence Performance Report 2000/1' (London: The Stationery Office, 2001), p. 57.
19. Lord Carrington, *Reflect on Things Past: The Memoirs of Lord Carrington* (Glasgow: William Collins, 1988), p. 218.
20. See Paul Cornish, *British Military Planning for the Defence of Germany, 1945-50*, London, Macmillan 1996; Christopher Bluth, *Britain, Germany and Western Nuclear Strategy*, Oxford. Oxford University Press, 1995, pp. 10-30.
21. See Winston S. Churchill, *The Second World War Volume VI: Triumph and Tragedy*, London, Penguin Books 1974, pp. 495-507.
22. John Baylis, *op. cit*, p. 34.
23. C.M. White, *The Gotha Summer: The German Daytime Air Raids on England; May-August 1917*, London, Robert Hale, 1986; John Terraine, *Business in Great Waters: The U-boat Wars, 1916-45*, London, Leo Cooper, 1989; Douglas Robinson, *The Zeppelin in Combat: A History of the Naval Airship Division, 1912-18*, Henley-on-Thames, G.T. Foulis (third edition) 1971, pp. 95-138, 204-233, 262-283.
24. E.R. Hooton, *Eagle in Flames: The Fall of the Luftwaffe*, London, Arms and Armour Press, pp. 13-76; John Terraine, *op. cit.*
25. Phillip S. Meilinger, "Proselytiser and Prophet: Alexander P. de Seversky and American Airpower", in John Gooch (ed) *Airpower: Theory and Practice*, London, Frank Cass, 1995, pp. 22-23; Andrew Vallance, *The Air Weapon: Doctrines of Air Power Strategy and Operational Art*, Basingstoke, Macmillan Press, 1995, p. 16.
26. See Malcolm Chalmers, *Paying for Defence: Military Spending and British Decline*, London, Pluto Press, 1985.
27. Michael Dockrill, *British Defence since 1945*, Oxford, Basil Blackwell Ltd., 1988, p. 32.
28. Note the change in emphasis between the 1950 and 1952 'Defence Policy and Global Strategy Papers', *CAB 131/9, DO (50)45*, PRO; *PREM 11/49, COS (52)362*, PRO.
29. See Winston S. Churchill, *The Second World War Book III: Their Finest Hour, The Fall of France, May - August 1940*, London, Cassell, 1949.
30. Quoted in Humphrey Wynn, *RAF Nuclear Deterrent Forces*, London, HMSO, 1994, p.13.
31. *Ibid.*, p. 44.
32. Ministry of Defence, "Statement Relating to Defence, 1948", Cm 7327, London, HMSO, 1948, reprinted in Rear Admiral H.G. Thursfield (ed) *Brassey's Naval Annual*, London, William Clowes, 1948, p. 528.

[33] Clive Ponting, *Breach of power: Labour in Power, 1964-70*, London, Hamish Hamilton, 1989, pp. 41-2.
[34] See, "Defence: Outline of Future Policy", *op.cit.*
[35] Jeffrey Pickering, *Britain's Withdrawal from East of Suez: the Politics of Retrenchment*, London, Macmillan Press, 1998.
[36] "The United Kingdom Defence Programme: The Way Forward", *Cm.8,288*, London, HMSO, 1981, p. 6; Alex Brummer & Ian Aiten, "Thatcher Heading For Battles Over Gulf Force", *The Guardian*, 2 March 1981; Margaret Thatcher, *The Downing Street Years*, London, Harper Collins, 1993 p. 162.
[37] T. King, *House of Commons Parliamentary Debates*, vol.177, sixth series, session 1989-90, 23 July - 19 October 1990. Statement to the House, 25 July 1990, cols. 468-86.
[38] *Front Line First: The Defence Cost Study* (London: HMSO, 1994). See also D. White, 'Strategy Outlined for Blitz on Defence Costs', *Financial Times*, 6 July 1993; and, C. Bellamy and C. Brown, 'Rifkind Squeezes Budget as Peace Dividend Falls Short', *Independent*, 8 July 1994.
[39] *Defending Our Future: Statement on the Defence Estimates, 1993*, Cmnd.2,270 (London: HMSO, 1993), p. 7.
[40] The recent announcement of cuts in Trident warhead numbers appear to have more to do with the problems at the Aldermaston plant than a desire for arms control. Fairhall, David, 'Aldermaston plant delay a factor in decision to scale down warheads'. in *The Guardian*, 16 November 1993, p. 2.
[41] Calvocoressi, Peter, 'Deterrence, the Costs, the Issues, the Choices'. in *The Sunday Times*, 6 April 1980.
[42] Barrie, Douglas, 'Nuclear Conflicts', in *Flight International*, vol. 144, no. 4, 393, 27 October- 2 November 1993, p. 18.
[43] 'The United Kingdom Defence Programme: The Way Forward', *op.cit.*; 'Statement on the Defence Estimates, 1968', *Cmnd.3,540*, London, HMSO, 1968.
[44] Agreed at the NATO Heads of State and Government meeting in Rome, 7-8 November 1991, *NATO Press Communique S-1 (91) 85*, 7 November 1991.
[45] 'Statement on the Defence Estimates 1993 - Defending our Future', op.cit., p. 10.
[46] George, Bruce, & Ryan, Nick, 'Options for Change: a political critique', in *Brassey's Defence Yearbook*, 1993, edited by the Centre for Defence Studies, op.cit., p. 44.
[47] 'Statement on the Defence Estimates, 1991: Britain's Defence for the 1990s', *Cmnd.1,559*, London, HMSO, 1991, p. 6.
[48] ' Statement on the Defence Estimates, 1996', *Cmnd.3,223*, London, The Stationery Office, 1996, p. 57.
[49] House of Commons Select Committee on Defence, 'Fourth Report: United Kingdom Peacekeeping and Intervention Forces: Report together with the Proceedings of the Committee relating to the report, Minutes of Evidence and Memoranda', *House of Commons Paper No.188*, Session 1992-93, London, HMSO, 1993, p. xxiii.
[50] *Ibid.*, p. v.
[51] 'The Strategic Defence Review', op.cit., p. 8.
[52] Ibid., p. 5
[53] Ibid., pp. 14-5; 'Statement on the Defence Estimates 1996', *Cm.3,223*, (London: The Stationery Office, 1996), p. 18.
[54] 'Defence Diplomacy: Good Things Come in Threes', *MOD Press Release No.367/99*, 18 October 1999.
[55] T. Blair, Speech at the Lord Mayor's Banquet, London, 22 November 1999.

[56] Joint Declaration issued at the British-French Summit, Saint Malo, France, 3-4 December 1998. See www.fco.gov.uk
[57] J. Lodge and V. Flynn, 'The CFSP after Amsterdam: The Policy Planning and Early Warning Unit', *International Relations*, vol. 14, no.1 (April 1998), pp. 7-21.
[58] Lieutenant-General Sir Mike Jackson, 'KFOR – The Inside Story', *The RUSI Journal*, vol. 145, no. 1, February 2001, p.15.
[59] 'Joint Declaration of the British and French Governments on European Defence', Anglo-French Summit, London, 25 November 1999. See www.fco.gov.uk
[60] Statement on the Estimates, 1999, para.17.
[61] L. Hill, 'New European Task Force Takes on First Task in Kosovo', *Defence News*, vol. 15, no. 7, 21 February 2000, p. 4.
[62] L. Hill, 'NATO offer for high-alert HQs is oversubscribed', *Jane's Defence Weekly*, vol. 34, no. 17, 25 October 2000, p. 12.
[63] See paragraph 4 of Secretary of State for Defence's introduction to the SDR. 'The Strategic Defence Review', op.cit., p. 2. For a list of the enhancements to joint capabilities see G. Robertson, 'Robertson's Review: Modern Forces for the World', *MOD Press Release 172/98*, 8 July 1998, pp. 2-3.
[64] Joris Janssen Lok, 'New Challenges Force Change on Royal Navy', *Jane's Defence Weekly*, 3 September 1997, p. 42.
[65] Anton Hanney, October 1997, 'Sizing-up the New Carriers', in *Navy* News, October 1997, p. 1.
[66] 'UK navy SAMs to make way for more aircraft', *Jane's Defence Weekly*, 17 September 1997, p. 5.
[67] Vincent Grimes, Richard Scott and Mike Wells, 'Amphibious Advancement', *Jane's Navy International*, September 1998, p. 28.
[68] With the transformation of 5 Airborne brigade into a sixth heavy brigade the only other light brigade will be the air assault brigade.
[69] 'Amphibious Ships', *The Globe and Laurel*, July/August 1997, p. 208.
[70] 'Outcome of the strategic sealift (roro) and Alternative Landing Ships Logistics (ALSLs) Competitions,' 26 October 2000, www.mod.uk/indexphp3?page=2&nid=1059&view=776&cat=0.
[71] Idem.
[72] IISS, *The Military Balance, 1989-90*, (London, IISS), 1989, p. 79.
[73] David Brown, *Royal Navy and the Falklands War*, London, Leo Cooper, 1987, p. 360.
[74] 'Statement on the Defence Estimates, 1996', *op. cit.*, p. 58.
[75] 'Memorandum for Correspondents', *M.065-M*, US Defence Department, 30 April 1999.
[76] Kemp, Ian, 'British Army Packs Double Punch', in *Jane's Defence Weekly*, 28 October 1998, p. 24.
[77] 'Apache Uprising', *Air Forces Monthly*, no.148, July 2000, pp. 50-4.
[78] 'The Strategic Defence Review: Supporting Essays', *op.cit.*, p. 6-8.
[79] *Ibid.*, p. 6-10.
[80] P. Beaver, 'UK MoD Instructed to Re-examine RAF's Future Airlift Requirement', *Jane's Defence Weekly*, 22 December 1999, p. 3; and N. Cook, 'Endgame Nears for UK RAF's New Transporter', *Jane's Defence Weekly*, 26 January 2000, p. 29.
[81] M. Oliver, 'Blair in £900m Missile Row', *Observer*, 27 February 2000, Business Section, p. 1.

[82] 'Major RAF Equipment Order Announced', *www.raf.mod.uk/history/00arch.htmll #eqpt*, 16 May 2000.
[83] The Strategic Defence Review, op. cit., p. 21.

Chapter 6

The Core and the Periphery of European Security Policy

Glen M. Segell

Introduction

This chapter would focus on European security policy to question which institution, the European Union (EU) or North Atlantic Treaty Organisation (NATO), can provide the best security environment for Europe. This is because the EU has limited border controls opened; no external military threat on its common borders and has embraced a singularity in security of states and individuals. Such singularity would be hard to achieve in a single institution disjointed from the economic and social base of trans-national communities with multiple identities which is a problem that NATO faces in operational duties nor by alienating a superpower by excluding its membership which any proposed European military union would have to come to terms with. It would, however, also be foolhardy to have duplication of effort with divided limited resources in two separate institutions. The question that this chapter poses is thus a prime focus for debate in the member states of both NATO and the EU, in seeking enlargement in 2002.

The Dependency School of Core and Periphery (Evans, 1989 and Hagelin, 1988) has traditionally questioned the relations between the developed and the developing world, (Kay, 1975, Sengaas, 1981; Szentes, 1973). This is significant in the EU/NATO enlargement 2002 debate where applicant states have fledgling democracies and free market economies giving cause for considering the shifting focus of the rights of individuals from that of states. (Amin, 1977; Galtung, 1971; Wallerstein 1971) Such issues will affect the decision-making process of civil-military and defence-industrial relations in the enlargement debate as they are pre-requisites for EU and NATO membership. In this debate there will be a diplomatic tendency towards simplifying for a comparative approach to decision-making between domestic and trans-national institutions and the linkages between domestic political science and international relations.

In this approach the core of European security will equate to the formulation of defence policy by the domestic institutions and organizations of states since there is no doubt that it would be naïve to believe that the first and primary consideration of any member state of the EU and NATO is not domestic biased. The periphery of European security will equate to the implementation of defence policy within trans-national and international institutions and organizations such as NATO as noted by the neo-realist and neo-liberalist scholars, (Gilpin, 1981; Keohane and Nye, 1977; Kindleberger, 1970, Leonard, 1980), who since the 1970s have taken trans-national agents into more serious consideration.

The Core

The core of European security equates to the formulation of defence policy by the domestic institutions and organizations of states of the European Union. Such a European military union is fast becoming the successor to monetary union as the next big idea of Europe. (Medley 1999) This idea of a military union, through the Common Foreign and Security Policy (CFSP) and the Common European Security and Defence Policy (CESDP), would translate the EU's financial muscle into geopolitical clout thereby validating the view that the wealth would breed armed might, and armed might would breed wealth. It is hoped that the issue of such a European military union would give the EU stronger bargaining tool to deal with the members of the international community particularly the United States in NATO burden sharing. A Brussels Press Release (1999) from the EU also explains that the idea of a European military union is attractive to new crop of European leaders because it assures European leaders of the kind of personal historical legacy that European heads of state still crave. It is argued that constructing a EU defence pillar would put them at the centre of history in way that tucking in the corners of monetary union never could. Moreover the idea of military union moves Europe one giant step closer to political parallelism with the United States while building a military union means building European-based weapons, aircraft, ships, and satellites.

Such a military union would be a logical move financially. Within the member states of the Europe Union there is insufficient funding and manpower to maintain separate civil organizations to parallel the separate military entities of the armed forces, such as exists in the U.S. Unified Ministries of Defence with a single Secretariat of State oversee the annual procurement and manpower decisions of the entire armed forces. Each section of the armed force vies for a share of a defence budget determined by a democratically elected and accountable legislature. Defence policy is thus formulated based upon domestic societal and fiscal criteria within tight margins. Each member state of the European Union maintains its own fiscal policy though the European Union is approaching a single monetary policy with the creation of the Eurozone on 1 January 2002 where 12 EU states all adopt a single currency – the EURO.

Given these financial circumstances it is not surprising that neighbor states within the EU seek to find the cheapest cost-effective solution to defence needs. The ensuing security policy is more often that not a continuation of fiscal policy and societal needs rather than broad foreign policy considerations. Trans-national collaboration between EU states is increasing in issues of sharing military manpower, since equipment procurement has since the 1950s now reached a stage of the creation of a single European Defence Industrial base.

Whither NATO at the Core

The intent of a common defence, foreign and security policy in Europe is not totally new though North American participation is historically unique. The idea of a common security and defence in Europe was first articulated in the 17th century when Duke Maximilian de Bethune of Sully proposed the setting up of a common European army. The Duke regarded the creation of a common European army as very vital in the promotion of peace and prosperity in Europe, which at that time was marked by intra-European wars. (Salmon, 1993) The idea of the Duke was not realized as European nation-states regarded the idea of a common army as an assault against their sovereignty. Three centuries after, some European states revived the idea of building a common European defence, when in 1952, France proposed the formation of the European Defence Community (EDC) to complement the European Economic Communities (EEC). The proposed community envisioned the creation of a common European defence with a common European army. (Gummett, 1997) The change of leadership in France resulted in the rejection of the EDC by the French parliament while the United Kingdom also refused to join the EDC leading to its stillborn demise in 1954. Instead of the EDC, some European states formed the Western European Union (WEU) that aimed to control stocks of certain armaments of all member states. The United States, on the other hand, led the formation of NATO by including West Germany and Italy, which provided a security umbrella for Western Europe against the former Soviet Union. During this period it was also clear that Europe did not have the capability to defend itself without U.S. assistance.

The concept of a European wide common security next entered the public debate in Europe when the Palme Commission published the 1982 Report of the Independent Commission on Disarmament and Security Issues. (Palme Commission 1982) Common security, was defined to means security with rather than security against the adversary. Common security in the EU adopts the idea of *non-provocative defence* and *non-offensive defence* (Wiseman, 1989). Crucial to the understanding of common security is the concept of common interests - the building blocks of cooperation between and among adversaries. In contrast to the competitive model of collective security of NATO, common security offers a cooperative model of security. The new security landscape in the post Cold War 1990s, where there appeared to be no external military threat to the EU, gave European states an opportunity to re-examine their foreign and security policy towards a common security that would also be a reflection on the future of NATO.

Little change took place initially since a ten nation proposal to merge the EU with WEU was vetoed by Britain at Amsterdam in June 1997. By 1998 it therefore seemed that the primary project of the 1994 Brussels North Atlantic Council appeared to have been overtaken by the secondary project from that same meeting which was NATO Partnership for Peace (PfP). The Albania crises of spring 1997 and the Kosovo campaign 1998-1999 highlighted that Europeans still lacked the mechanism to handle policy formulation and that they were reliant upon the U.S. via NATO for any such military operations that were essential to restore stability. Thus greater responsibility to European countries was forfeited for reinforced U.S.

involvement in European security matters. Hence it was clear that increased European defence capability and common policy was not a threat to the existence of NATO but the very condition for the survival of NATO as a viable alliance.

The Irish Referendum

There are still however areas where European society intervenes on an ethnic and national level. This was all too apparent during the NATO Kosovo campaign in 1999. Denmark for example found that 40% of the forces called up for duty, decided that this did not meet their contractual obligations. They did not report for duty and subsequently a few soldiers won legal cases in civil courts of law. It was fortuitous that NATO ground forces were not needed since the same situation may well have been replicated in other European member states of NATO where such democracy has flourished. Notwithstanding such a crises in times of conflict, the core must also be considered in times of peace. One such instance came about on 9 June 2001. European Union leaders were facing an escalating political crisis following a referendum in the Republic of Ireland that decided to reject the Nice Treaty. This Treaty inter alia detailed institutions for two additional Pillars in the European Union: Home Affairs and Foreign Affairs and Defence. The Nice proposals are also designed to pave the way for EU expansion into Eastern Europe, extend majority voting in a number of policy areas, give more voting power to larger Union countries and lay the groundwork for a European army.

Following Ireland's decision anti-federalist groups in the rest of Europe are now demanding a similar right of veto to the Irish. The first responses came from the institutions of the European Union. In a desperate attempt to keep enlargement on track, the commission has initially downplayed the importance of the Irish vote though Romano Prodi, the President of the European Commission, expressed honesty when noting that he felt "profound disappointment" at the Irish referendum result. Despite this public bravado it was clear that Brussels fears that the Irish vote is already triggering a domino effect of protest elsewhere in Europe, calling into question the democratic legitimacy of EU policy-making and thereby indefinitely delaying enlargement that would endanger European security.

The first part of the domino effect was the response in France. In France, the leader of the centrist UDF party, François Bayrou, who is likely to stand for the presidency next year, said: "I hope the Irish vote means that this treaty is dead even before it had the chance to live. President [Jacques] Chirac should now have the courage and the political honesty to call a referendum in France". The Spanish government may now also face internal pressure to challenge the Union's enlargement plans. As in Ireland, many Spanish people fear that EU expansion would lead to the transfer of regional aid and subsidies from the poorer regions of the Europe Union eastward to the members that would join from Central and East Europe from the Enlargement 2002 debate. The Dutch Prime Minister, Wim Kok, also admitted that the Irish vote was a "serious complication". The impact of this on the periphery is clear. The Irish may be offered the chance to opt out of any future European army, thus preserving their historical neutrality. The question of neutrality was one of the main concerns for Irish "no" voters. A similar "carrot" strategy was used by the commission in 1992, when Denmark rejected the Maastricht Treaty. The Danes eventually obtained an opt-out from European Monetary Union. This would create a many-track approach to European security by the European Union

Common European Security and Defence Policy

Such domestic actions at the core have direct impact on the adoption of the CFSP and the launching of the CESDP that combined equate to the periphery of a single European security or it's implementation of defence policy as security policy. The manner in which this impact is manifest is dependant upon the evolving process of the EU civil-military relations institutions that formulate defence policy.[1] These civil-military relations initiated when the EU Presidency responded as a matter of priority to the mandate given by the Cologne European Council to strengthen the common European policy on security and defence by taking the work forward in military and non-military aspects of crisis management. This Common European Security and Defence Policy (CESDP) was launched at the European Council meeting in Helsinki in December 1999.[2] It was designed to signify an EU politico-military project as distinct from ESDI (European Security and Defence Identity), a NATO military restructuring arrangement. ESDP was turned into CESDP at Helsinki in part to help avoid the confusion between ESDP and ESDI. CESDP was designed to signify the determination, on the part of the EU member states, to develop a distinct European politic-military project, with its own institutional infrastructure and a significant military capacity. CESDP was always intended to develop a close and carefully structured relationship with NATO. Different EU states view the nature of such a relationship in significantly different ways though all agree that it should exist. The work has been based on the provisions of the Treaty on European Union and the guiding principles agreed at Cologne, which had been reaffirmed by the Member States.

To assume their responsibilities across the full range of conflict prevention and crisis management tasks defined in the EU Treaty, more commonly known as the Petersburg tasks, the Member States decided to develop more effective domestic military capabilities and establish new political and military structures for these tasks. In this connection, the objective was for the EU to have an autonomous capacity to take decisions and, where NATO as a whole was not engaged, to launch and then to conduct EU-led military operations in response to international crises. Also in order to assume these responsibilities, the EU intended to improve and make more effective use of resources in civilian crisis management in which the EU as a whole and it's Members States already have considerable experience. Special attention would be given to a rapid reaction capability. It was expected that NATO would remain the foundation of the collective defence of its members, and would continue to have an important role in crisis management.

The development of the common European policy on security and defence would take place without prejudice to the commitments under Article 5 of the Washington Treaty and Article V of the Brussels Treaty, which would be preserved for the Member States party to these Treaties.[3] Nor would the development of the common European policy on security and defence prejudice the specific character of the security and defence policy of certain Member States, such as the neutrality of the Republic of Ireland already mentioned. The EU would thus also be able to contribute to international peace and security in accordance with the principles of the United Nations Charter. The EU recognized the primary responsibility of the United Nations Security Council for the maintenance of international peace and security. Following up the principles and objectives of the OSCE Charter for European Security, the EU would co-operate with the UN, the OSCE, the Council of Europe and other international organizations in a mutually reinforcing manner in stability promotion, early warning, conflict prevention, crisis management and post-conflict reconstruction.

For this purpose, the following was agreed: A common European headline goal would be adopted for readily deployable military capabilities and collective capability goals in the fields of command and control, intelligence and strategic transport would be developed rapidly, to be achieved through voluntary co-ordinated national and multinational efforts, for carrying out the full range of Petersburg tasks. New political and military bodies would be established within the Council to enable the Union to take decisions on EU-led Petersburg operations and to ensure, under the authority of the Council, the necessary political control and strategic direction of such operations. Principles for cooperation with non-EU European NATO members and other European partners in EU-led military crisis management would be agreed, without prejudice to the EU's decision-making autonomy. The General Affairs Council of the EU, with the participation of Defence Ministers of Member States, would elaborate the headline and capability goals. It would develop a method of consultation through which these goals could be met and maintained, and through which national contributions reflecting Member States' political will and commitment towards these goals could be defined by each Member State, with a regular review of progress made. In addition, Member States would use existing defence planning procedures, including, as appropriate, those available in NATO and the Planning and Review Process (PARP) of the NATO Partnership for Peace Program (PfP).[4] These objectives and those arising, for those countries concerned, from NATO's Defence Capabilities Initiative (DCI) would be mutually reinforcing. The Council would decide upon policy relevant to Union involvement in all phases and aspects of crisis management, including decisions to carry out Petersburg tasks in accordance with Article 23 of the EU Treaty. Taken within the single institutional framework, decisions would respect European Community competences and ensure inter-pillar coherence in conformity with Article 3 of the EU Treaty. All Member States would be entitled to participate fully and on an equal footing in all decisions and deliberations of the Council and Council bodies on EU-led operations. The commitment of national assets by Member States to such operations would be based on their sovereign decision.

Member States would participate in the ad hoc committee of contributors in accordance with the conditions provided for by paragraph 24. On closer scrutiny such intentions clearly amounted to the formation of a civil-military institution closely resembling that which exists with sovereign states for the management of manpower and resources for defence of the sovereign state. It must be stressed in developing this capability that the EU does not face a common external military threat though drug trafficking, terrorism and money laundering could eventually lead towards collective action in a single EU security agenda. Such capability would thus have no significance without a clearly defined agenda for its usage nor without the collective intent of the EU member states more commonly associated with a Common Foreign and Security Policy.

Common Foreign and Security Policy

Institutionally things have moved ahead steadily and reasonably smoothly since Europe's Common Foreign and Security Policy (CSFP) took the major qualitative step forward represented by the entry into force of the provisions of the Amsterdam Treaty. It has not however been tested although it will be during 2002 since the most important of foreign policy events of which the EU is the largest player, is its own enlargement. In this enlargement the core of European security policy formulation and its institutions will in 2002 face the tug that exists between the uni-lateralism and the multi-laterism as the guiding star of U.S. foreign policy. This distinguishes the CESDP from the CFSP.

CFSP originated in 1970 called Political Cooperation and has since been a Presidency-driven system. The appointment of the High representative indicates a move away from such a system that also encompasses the Commissioners for External relations, for Trade Policy, for Development and for Enlargement. The European Parliament (EP) has no more than a modest role to play where the need for greater democracy may result in a Foreign Relations Committee of the EU, drawing its members from both the EP and from national parliaments. CFSP's greatest under-utilized resource is the world-wide diplomatic network of its member states.

The development of the institutions to ensure a genuine foreign and security policy for a hybrid body like the EU is always going to be a slow and incremental process. Work included is the attempt by the European Union to bolster the rules of international law through organizations such as the International Court of Justice and the International Criminal Court; the spread of democracy and respect for human rights through multinational organizations such as the UN and OSCE and the British Commonwealth. The CFSP is not yet well equipped to tackle such an agenda that fall to its address. Clearly the way forward is to adopt the Anglo-French Sant-Malo initiative of December 1998 which would be a major challenge to reach decisions that ensure that NATO is strengthened and not weakened in the process of European consolidation including the building of a capacity of a substantial military force of 60 000 men.

In the important advances achieved in CFSP in the last decade, the Member States have not given the Commission a sole right of initiative; nor, in general, have they agreed to abide by majority votes; nor do they accept that Europe has 'occupied the space' reducing national freedom of action. It is important to understand this. Foreign policy remains primarily a matter for democratically elected Member State governments.

Both CEDP and CFSP are works in progress. The important point is that – however awkward they may be - the new structures, procedures and instruments of CFSP recognize the need to harness the strengths of the European Community in the service of each member states foreign policy. That is why the Treaty 'fully associates' the European Commission with CFSP. The Commission participates fully in the decision-making process in the Council, with a shared right of initiative. The role of the Commission could not be reduced to one of 'painting by numbers' – simply filling in the blanks on a canvas drawn by others. Nor should it be. It would be absurd to divorce European foreign policy or the periphery from the institutions of the core that have been given responsibility for most of the instruments for its accomplishment: for external trade questions, including sanctions; for European external assistance; and for many of the external aspects of Justice and Home Affairs.

Towards an Organisation

As is the case with all matters in the European Union, the policy agreement is just a starting point. The organizational structures and institutions that have to be formed to implement the policy present a more difficult negotiation process. The first steps towards a common European Security organization has seen EU states agree that Defence Ministers would be involved in the common European security and defence policy (CESDP); when the General Affairs Council discusses matters related to the CESDP, Defence Ministers as appropriate would participate to provide guidance on defence matters. The following new *permanent* political and military bodies would be established within the Council:

a) A standing Political and Security Committee (PSC) in Brussels would be composed of national representatives of senior/ambassadorial level. The PSC would deal with all aspects of the CFSP, including the CESDP, in accordance with the provisions of the EU Treaty and without prejudice to Community competence. In the case of a military crisis management operation, the PSC would exercise, under the authority of the Council, the political control and strategic direction of the operation. For that purpose, appropriate procedures would be adopted in order to allow effective and urgent decision taking. The PSC would also forward guidelines to the Military Committee.

b) The Military Committee (MC) would be composed of the Chiefs of Defence, represented by their military delegates. The MC would meet at the level of the Chiefs of Defence as and when necessary. This committee would give military advice and make recommendations to the PSC, as well as provide military direction to the Military Staff. The Chairman of the MC would attend meetings of the Council when decisions with defence implications are to be taken.

c) The Military Staff (MS) within the Council structures would provide military expertise and support to the CESDP, including the conduct of EU-led military crisis management operations. The Military Staff would perform early warning, situation assessment and strategic planning for the Petersburg tasks including identification of European national and multinational forces.

As an *interim* measure, the following bodies were set up within the Council as of March 2000:

a) A standing interim political and security committee at senior/ambassadorial level tasked to take forward under the guidance of the Political Committee the follow up of the Helsinki European Council by preparing recommendations on the future functioning of the CESDP and to deal with CFSP affairs on a day-to-day basis in close contacts with the Secretary General/High Representative (SG/HR).
b) An interim body of military representatives of Member States' Chiefs of Defence to give military advice as required to the interim political and security committee.
c) The Council Secretariat would also be strengthened by military experts seconded from Member States in order to assist in the work on the CESDP and to form the nucleus of the future Military Staff.

The Secretary General/High Representative, in assisting the Council, would have a key contribution to make to the efficiency and consistency of the CFSP and the development of the common security and defence policy. In conformity with the EU Treaty, the SG/HR would contribute to the formulation, preparation and implementation of policy decisions. In the case of an EU-led operation, an ad-hoc committee of contributors would be set up for the day-to-day conduct of the operation. All EU Member States would be entitled to attend the ad-hoc committee, whether or not they are participating in the operation, while only contributing States would take part in the day-to-day conduct of the operation. For the coordination of civilian crisis management tools, the co-ordinating mechanism for a civilian crisis management would be established. This mechanism, which would be of inter-pillar nature, would provide expert advice in support of the management of crises. Decision-making and implementation of non-military crisis management tools under the first pillar would remain subject to institutions and procedures of the EC Treaty. A High Representative in the form of Javier Solana, the former Spanish Foreign Minister, former Secretary-General of NATO and former Secretary-General of WEU has also been appointed. The Policy Planning and Early Warning Unit of Solana are far beyond that of the purely secretariat resources hitherto allocated to CFSP. A new Political and Security Committee has been established in Brussels giving him a sounding board and a means by which member states could be directly involve don a day-to-day basis in the handling of business, especially in a crises. CFSP has managed to get through its first year without falling flat on its face.

Ultimately, however, in establishing this new identity Europe and its allies need to ask the questions for the core and the periphery: What is Europe actually trying to do together? What do the Member States want to do with their new structures? And how should it measure its success? Only time will tell whether these new structures are in fact a European Department of Defence and a European Armed Force and if they are viable to support any common European foreign policy!

The Periphery

When considering the periphery of European security policy or those matters pertaining to the implementation of defence policy within trans-national and international institutions and organizations such as NATO then there are three major issues on the table in relations between the European Union (EU) and the United States of America (U.S.). These are further NATO enlargement considerations to be debated in 2002, a European Security and Defence Identity (ESDI) that will be included in the European Union enlargement debate in 2002 and the American National Missile Defence (NMD) proposals. Within these issues falls the discussions of the Balkan situation, Mediterranean security including the Middle East, and the future of arms control measures including Russia, relations between Russia and the EU and Russia and the U.S. and such matters as international drugs trafficking and terrorism. It is recognized that enlargement of NATO, ESDI and NMD would all require a new type of institutional structure different from that currently exists. There will be new institutions at the core. This is not a new issue. Previous NATO enlargements, the formation of the WEU and the IEPG, and the various arms control/disarmament treaties such as INF, SALT and START all brought about changes in the domestic institutional structures of participating states as well as the international organizations that enacted the agreements. The new type of structure that is emerging is however different from previously. It is a structure within the European Union noted in the above discussion on the Core. This structure requires a NATO restructuring. The debate is as important as the results where both would take many years before being resolved.

NATO and the U.S.

NATO is increasingly at the periphery of defence needs of European Union states. NATO however continues to provide an overall security umbrella to Europe through the American nuclear umbrella. There has been no immediate external military threat to EU member states since the demise of the Warsaw Pact and the end of the Cold War in 1989. For example, on a daily basis the security of the English Channel between Great Britain and France is best suited for combined Royal Navy and French Navy patrols. Similarly the security needs of the North Sea are best suited by Anglo-Dutch amphibious forces. The ability of the European Union states to implement defence policy by themselves or with neighbors is far greater than the ability to implement security policy within NATO. This situation was also clearly highlighted when the Danish government was unsuccessful in mobilizing 40% of reserves called up for duty in Kosovo with NATO. This situation was also highlighted when Britain successfully deployed forces to Sierra Leone. These examples clearly indicate the primacy of the domestic politics of each state in its overall contribution to European security.

It is therefore prudent to argue that the proposed CESDP would pose some questions on the future role of NATO in the management of European security.

One crucial issue is the so-called "duplication dilemma". It has been contended that the CESDP would create "unnecessary duplication" of capabilities and infrastructure of NATO. Each member state of the European Union and NATO has a limited quota of resources available to contribute outside of its sovereign boundaries. It would be pointless to split these resources to NATO and a European military union. Since the main objective of the CESDP is to provide EU with stronger military capabilities to secure Europe, it has been argued that this would duplicate what NATO has already made available to secure Europe. Will the CESDP then seek to take over such NATO capabilities and functions and disband NATO? The fear of duplication really conceals the concerns in the United States about the appearance of a new political partner: a single European Union. At present, however, NATO's military infrastructure remains much bigger than EU's military infrastructure.

Despite this reality the U.S., as noted in the International Herald Tribune (2000), regard the EUs seriousness to develop a CESDP as a reflection of EUs desire to lessen Europe"s military dependency on America and hence weaken NATO. In this the proposed CESDP is also said to be challenging the role of the WEU in European security management. It is argued that the CESDP would further facilitate the planned transfer of WEU security functions to the EU by the end of 2002 and in the Enlargement 2002 processes. If this happens, the WEU would be eradicated in virtually all-European security affairs. There is question, however, on whether the actual planning capacity of the EU military staff would go beyond the present rather limited capacities of the WEU military staff. To date, the WEU remains dependent on the NATO"s intelligence planning and gathering system.

Ultimately the EU envisions an eventual capability of fighting "a Kosovo-like war" without the consent and support of the U.S. The consequence of this is that the U.S. might leave the management and maintenance of European peace to the EU and eventually withdraw American troops in Europe. Another possibility is that the U.S. may continue its support to manage peace and security in Europe within the framework of NATO if the Europeans are serious defence partners. The challenge to the EU is how it would balance EU-U.S.-NATO relations within the context of the CFSP and CESDP.

This is just one side of the coin. The other side of the coin is the implication of the CESDP for the American defence industry. The United States welcomes the EU's effort to establish a European defence identity as long as Europe continues to equip itself with American defence technology. Europeans, however, have realized that in their efforts to have their own defence identity, they may buy fewer U.S. defence weapons in the future. There is a contention that EU's CESDP is now likely to be built upon a solid, European industrial-industrial base in which the United States only plays a marginal role. This scenario would greatly affect EU-U.S. relations especially with the consolidation and restructuring of European industrial industry. This is also the case for ESDI. In establishing this new identity Europe and its allies ask the questions for the core and the periphery: What is Europe actually trying to do together? What do the Member States want to do with their new structures? And how should it measure its success?

The Balkans and Russia

In turning from the general to the particular. What should be the ambition of CFSP in key areas of policy such as ESDI - and how should the European Commission be making its contribution? Europe's first responsibility is internal (the core) rather than external (the periphery): to help create a dynamic European economy that could fuel a serious foreign policy. In Enlargement 2002 the Commission's external trade policy is also a crucial part of European foreign policy in addition to its military considerations. The first priority area for this is in the Western Balkans on the borders of the EU. This region poses a tremendous challenge for Europe and for CFSP. The EU's overall approach is clear: the gradual integration of these countries into the EU by way of Stabilization and Association Agreements; that would involve the regeneration of these economies through intra-regional trade, as well as through asymmetric trade concessions by the EU to encourage the transition towards free trade; but in the first instance it means the most rapid possible reconstruction of shattered lives, shattered societies and shattered infrastructure through the establishment of a Reconstruction Agency to oversee this work in Kosovo and a proposed new Regulation to draw the work together within a single legal instrument. This would entail close work with the UN and with the Stability Pact.

The Balkans symbolizes a further danger on the horizon: namely Russia. Russia, whose transformation has been one of the most significant features of the last 50 years. Russia's future relationship with the EU is an issue of profound importance for the EU – and it remains a conundrum. For Russia is undoubtedly European. Russia is also a great power. Yet her enfeebled economy is only 8% the size of the EU's while depending on the EU for 40% of its external trade. Where does this leave any long-term relationship? And where does it leave countries from Central Asia to the Caucasus to Ukraine which lie between the great continental poles? This is a question which could provoke passionate theoretical debate about the geographical limits of EU Enlargement 2002; and about religious and cultural divides. The approach should be pragmatic. The EU's interest and obligation is to engage with all these countries, and with Russia above all, to help them develop the structures they need for sound economic and political development.

The Russians have always placed greater faith in strong leaders than in strong institutions. But if they are now to attract investment; if they are to overcome their huge problems of nuclear safety; if they are to defeat their corruption and fraud; if they are to re-emerge, in short, as the great power they should be – they need strong and effective institutions to underpin the rule of law. No amount of good laws would make any difference if they could not be applied in practice, and if the courts are too weak to enforce them.

NATO is already working with Russia through PfP. The EU is keen to work in partnership with Russia. The future of Russia has a profound bearing on the EU's own enlargement, which is going to transform the EU over the coming years. The full implications of taking in so many new members are impossible to predict. It would require radical changes in the present institutions of the EU. There is concern that powers should be vested upwards from the separate nations in the central structure that is created – not downwards from that structure. Nation states are the basic political unit and would remain the main focus of public loyalty. Enlargement of the EU would also require radical changes in EU policies.

Whatever its structural and policy consequences, EU Enlargement 2002 constitutes the single greatest contribution the EU could make to European – even to global – stability and security. The projection of stability is the EU's essential mission, and the central objective of CFSP. The enlargement of the EU itself is the greatest example of that policy. Previous EU enlargement to include Greece, Spain and Portugal, have shown how membership of the EU has helped to stabilize countries emerging from dictatorship.

Conclusion

The Dependency School that debates the philosophy of the core and the periphery could further consider whether: EU/NATO Enlargement 2002 is offering membership to join the Core of existing European security while non-members will remain as the Periphery; will Enlargement 2002 be selective in choosing only a few new members or will it include all Central and East European states, except Russia; if NATO and the EU are the Core in the international system and if the U.S. is the Core of NATO, then is the U.S. exploiting applicant and new members to NATO and similarly for EU enlargement by existing EU member states. If it did then it would be clear that EU/NATO Enlargement 2002 is taking the concept of "Western" out of the Europe of the Cold War. During the Cold War "Eastern" referred to East of the Iron Curtain and hence the Warsaw Pact. Today the connotation of "Eastern" refers more to the Far East with China and North Korea predominating. There is a singularity in Europe and in European security.

The core of this European security is the formulation of industrial policy by the domestic institutions and organizations by states of the European Union At the core of this security is the individual as much as that of the state. The periphery is the foreign policy of states in the implementation of industrial policy sometimes within trans-national and international institutions and organizations such as NATO and EUROPOL. The nexus of decision-making where industrial and foreign policy meet is in civil-military relations of the institutions and organizations of the EU, NATO and their member states. This results in the formulation of a common industrial and security policy where industrial policy is showing the nature, intent and capability of security policy. Security policy is the foreign policy of a state in its international relations with other states, or the periphery. In this it would be naïve to believe that the first and primary consideration of any state is not domestic biased. The core is thus primary.

Reductio ad absurdum, the core is the management of human and equipment resources. In this management, the EU has resolved the singular management of resources over the last 50 years through collaborative research, development and procurement of weapon systems such as the Jaguar, Tornado, Eurofighter/Typhoon and Airbus A400M aircraft. This has been through a process of corporate mergers and acquisitions with nominal government guidance. This however continues to endanger relations with the U.S. and fractionises NATO in its purpose of Rationalization, Standardization and Interoperability (RSI). The European Union is currently evolving core policies for the singular management of manpower, or that of the armed forces, that is generating further friction in NATO. In this EU Heads of Government have stated their immediate goal very clearly. By the year 2003 they want to be able to deploy 50 – 60 000 troops capable of the full range of what are known as the Petersburg tasks: humanitarian and rescue work, crisis management, peace-keeping, and even peace-making. Until this task is accomplished, the mainstay of European security will be provided by NATO. Once it has been accomplished the mainstay of European industrial will be provided by the European Union and the mainstay of European security will be provided by a combination of NATO and a European military union where there may only be two members of NATO: The European Union and NAFTA.

Notes

[1] Civil-Military Relations is the study of domestic politics in the interactions between politicians, the military and industrialists. Civil-military relations inter-alia entails the study of the management of the human resources and equipment procurement of the armed forces, the sociology of the individual citizen and soldier and the encompassing society,the political systems of the state and its elite, the diplomatic and international public law activitiesthat are prelude and postscript to any conflict and the history that has lead the situation to come into being.
[2] Another acronym had been used prior to June 1999 and had simply been ESDP.
[3] These treaties are the basic treaties of the North Atlantic Treaty Organisation (NATO) where it was intended that futher steps would be taken to ensure full mutual consultation, cooperation and transparency between the EU and NATO.
[4] Switzerland also participates in PfP that is aimed at promoting peaceful relations and the development of democratic practises in former Warsaw Pact countries.

References

Amin, Samir (1977), *Imperialism and Unequal Development*, Sussex: Sussex University Press.
Evans, Peter B., (1989), Declining Hegemony and Assertive Industrialization: US-Brazil Conflicts in Computer Industry, *International Organization*, Vol 43 No 2 pp. 207-38.
Galtung, Johan (1971), A Structural Theory of Imperialism, *Journal of Peace Research*, Vol 8 No 2 pp. 81-117.
Gilpin, Robert (1981), *War and Change in World Politics*, Canbridge MA: Harvard University Press.
Gummett, Philip (1997), Foreign, Defence and Security Policy, in Martin Rhodes, Paul Heywood and Vincent Wright (eds), *Developments in West European Politics*, London: MacMillan Press.
Hagelin, Bjorn (1988), Military Dependency: Thailand and Phillipines, *Journal of*

Peace Research Vol 25 No. 4.

International Herald Tribune (6 March 2000).

Kay, Geoffrey, (1975), *Development and Underdevelopment: A Marxist Analysis*. London: Macmillan.

Keohane Robert O. and Joseph S. Nye (1977), *Power and Interdependence: World Politics in Transition*, Boston MA: Beacon Books.

Kindleberger Charles ed (1970), *The International Corporation*, Cambridge MA: Harvard University Press.

Leonard, Jeffrey H. (1980), Multinational Corporations and Politics in Developing Countries, *World Politics* Vol 32 No 3 pp. 454-83.

Medley, Richard (199) Europe's Next Big Idea: Strategy and Economics to a European Military, *Foreign Affairs*, Vol 78, No 5. p. 18.

Milios, Janos (2000), Social Classes in Classical and Marxist Political Economy. *American Journal of Economics and Sociology* Vol 59 No 2 pp. 283-302.

Modelski George ed (1972), *Multinational Corporations and World Order*. Beverly Hills CA: Sage.

New York Times (13 December 1999).

Palme Commission, (1982), *Common Security: A Programme for Disarmament*, London: Pan Books.

Salmon, Trevor C. (1993), The Union, CFSP and the European Security Debate in Juliet Lodge (ed), *The European Community and the Challenges of the Future*, 2nd edition London: Pinter Publishers.

Senghaas, Dieter, (1981), Self-Reliance and Autocentric Development. *Bulletin of Peace Proposals* Vol 12 No 1 pp. 44-51.

Szentes, Tamas (1973), *The Political Economy of Underdevelopment*. Budapest: Akademini Kiado.

Wallerstein, Immanuel (1979), *Capitalist World Economy*, Cambridge MA: Harvard University Press.

Chapter 7

The Multi-Dimensional Approach of the OSCE in Estonia: Assessing the Organization's Preventive Diplomacy Role

Maria Raquel Sousa Freire

Introduction

The formal end of the Cold War was stated at the 1990 Paris Summit of the Conference on Security and Cooperation in Europe (CSCE), convened by its participating states to address the new issues facing the Conference. In the wording of the 'Charter of Paris' the meeting was a symbol of the beginning of a new era built on democratic principles. The 'Charter of Paris' constituted a turning point in the CSCE history. While Helsinki in 1975 was dealing with division, Paris was based on a sense of unity. Forty years of bipolar rivalry were over and Europe could finally become a united, peaceful and democratic continent.[1] However, events since 1990 have taken a different course from the peaceful one that was expected. Structural adjustments had to take place at different levels. New states have emerged following the collapse of the Soviet empire and Yugoslavia. New conceptions of security have taken shape, adding to politico-military security a socio-economic and cultural dimension. International organizations dealing with security issues in Europe have had to face up to demands to reformulate and adapt to the new conditions.

In this context, the Organization for Security and Cooperation in Europe (OSCE) has gone through fundamental changes. The development of permanent decision-making and operational organisms in the various dimensions of OSCE activity has allowed the incorporation of its new tasks of preventive diplomacy, crisis management and post-conflict rehabilitation. Specialized institutions such as the High Commissioner on National Minorities (HCNM), the Representative on Freedom of the Media or the Office for Democratic Institutions and Human Rights (ODIHR), for example, have been established. Regular meetings and assessment implementation reviews allow the co-ordination of activities and an evaluation of the level of implementation of OSCE commitments by participating states. As regards the organization's innovative character, the intrusive approach in human dimension and military-related affairs of the participating states have been particularly relevant. It complements the OSCE's approaches by monitoring compliance and contributing to the building of stability in its area. Moreover, the all-encompassing nature of the OSCE in both membership and mandate constitutes an asset in the organization's approach to the issues, permitting an enlarged reach of its principles and decisions.

The OSCE's activity is based on common shared principles. Elaborating a common reading of democratic principles and the rule of law, economic freedom, and socio-political development, the OSCE envisages the development of common ground among its participating states to enhance stability in its area. The organization places its activity on the inter-relation of all dimensions it deals with, ranging from political, military and humanitarian aspects to the economy, environment, and scientific and technological issues. The close linkage among all dimensions of OSCE activity has contributed to the raising of awareness and confidence-building and to the development of broad and integrated approaches to the issues it deals with, reflecting the organization's innovative character. Nevertheless, the ideals for which the OSCE stands, a united and peaceful Europe built on common values and shared principles, are still far from achieved.

The OSCE in the European Security Architecture

The OSCE is not alone in the fight for a peaceful and stable Europe where values of cooperation prevail. Other international organizations such as the United Nations (UN), the European Union (EU), the Council of Europe and the North Atlantic Treaty Organization (NATO) work for the same purpose. In the midst of all these organizations working for the building of stability in Europe, where does the OSCE fit? Which are the unique characteristics of the OSCE which differentiate it from the other organizations and confer on it relevance and meaning in the new security framework? The network of relations among these organizations is very complex. In a few words, it could be argued that all are working for the same general goal, though following separate and at times crosscutting paths.

The OSCE distinguishes itself from the other organizations in an institutional and operational manner. It has a broad pan-European membership. While including the United States, Russia and all the former Soviet republics as participating members, the OSCE's all-inclusiveness permits the debate of a broad range of issues, making the OSCE particularly well suited to discuss the current problems in the former Soviet area.

As a norm-setting forum the OSCE has proven its relevance. The adoption of the 'Charter for European Security' in November 1999 by the OSCE participating states, recalling not only previous OSCE commitments but also other agreements between OSCE participating states outside the OSCE framework, is a good example of the broad reach of the OSCE, which ranges from politico-military aspects to economic, scientific, environmental and humanitarian ones.

At the operational level, in post-Cold War Europe the OSCE has added to its activity an ensemble of new tools. The HCNM or the Representative on Freedom of the Media are examples. Moreover, through the deployment of fact-finding, assessment and long-term Field Missions, the OSCE has extended its principles to a wide area. The Russian Federation's acceptance of the OSCE's presence, not without constraints, is positive for the organization's involvement. Nevertheless, the OSCE alone does not have the capability to answer all needs of the former Soviet area. It is through the combination of the OSCE and the other organizations' efforts, through the particular contributions each can make, that an ample strategy can be applied. This will have the benefit of providing a more structured and well-supported approach, fundamental to the new republics' development. Nevertheless, besides the OSCE only the UN has Missions deployed in the former Soviet Union, restricted to the Caucasus. The Council of Europe organizes regular short-term assessment visits to the republics, but has no permanent Field Missions deployed in the area. As such, the OSCE's role in the former Soviet space is strengthened, becoming an important source of stabilization.

The OSCE's relevance in the former Soviet Union is in part derived from the other organizations' weaknesses in the area. Nevertheless, the analysis of OSCE activity in the former Soviet space should not be confined to a negativist approach in the sense of doing what the others are not willing or are unable to do. The OSCE has several assets at its disposal which contribute to its relevance in the former Soviet area. In short, the OSCE's broad membership and all-encompassing concept of security are fundamental aspects of its involvement in the former Soviet space. Its new tools, such as the HCNM, the Representative on Freedom of the Media, the ODIHR and the Field Missions are valuable assets for the organization's pursuit of preventive diplomacy and crisis management efforts. Moreover, the OSCE's permanent decision-making and executive bodies confer permanence and reliability on the organization's activities. The OSCE's flexibility allied to the low-cost character of the organization, and its politically-binding and non-enforcing nature, are also assets in its favor with regard to the other organizations. However, this does not mean the OSCE has not been encountering difficulties, as suggested by the Estonian case where the organization is playing mainly a preventive role.

Preventive Diplomacy

The practice of preventive diplomacy is a gradual process, flexible and adjustable to the problems. One of the major areas of activity of the OSCE, preventive efforts aim the avoidance of the escalation of tensions into armed conflict. As a permanent forum for consultation and dialogue, the OSCE allows regular implementation debates where signs of non-compliance may send the alert. Protests and demonstrations, repressive actions by governments to eliminate opponents, claims for separatism or unification with another state, or guerrilla action against state institutions or their representatives, are some alerting examples. In order that preventive diplomacy may become effective, prompt consultations and early responses to any of these signs are demanded. The political will to act is also requested. Action must encompass a comprehensive approach to the problem, and must seek the underlying causes of tension, in order that preventive diplomacy can be focused and efficient in the addressing of tensions.

The OSCE documents do not explicitly define early warning and preventive diplomacy, but by OSCE practice it is possible to delineate the principal features of each of these concepts. Early warning envisages providing the relevant OSCE bodies with information about escalating developments in time for the OSCE to react and employ preventive diplomacy or other non-coercive measures. Early warning has thus the function of providing the information on the basis of which preventive diplomacy can take place.

The OSCE has developed several conflict prevention mechanisms, which entail preventive diplomacy efforts and early warning actions translated into the promotion of dialogue and exchange of information, advice on new legislation and constitutional matters, and the activities of the Chairman-In-Office, the HCNM, the ODIHR, and the OSCE Representative on Freedom of the Media. Efforts include also the organization of seminars and sessions for the clarification of particular issues, and support to the non-governmental organizations (NGO) sector. At the military level, preventive efforts and early warning signs are translated into the work of the Forum for Security Cooperation, which regularly assesses and exchanges information on military movements and arms-control agreements, as well as on the level of implementation of the Code of Conduct on Politico-Military Aspects of Security's provisions or of agreed confidence and security-building measures (CSBMs). The intrusive character added to the human dimension and as regards certain military aspects, has also been an asset of the organization, conferring a new perspective on preventive diplomacy as practiced by the OSCE. All these new instruments have implications in the Field Missions' activities.

In Estonia the OSCE is playing a preventive diplomacy role. There has been no armed conflict, but the unstable climate and/or the potential for conflict were the underlying motives for the Mission's deployment. The mix of the OSCE instruments allied to the specificity of events in the field form the core strategy of the organization in preventive diplomacy. The case of Estonia envisages clarifying the OSCE's possibilities and limitations as a preventive diplomacy forum, highlighting the organization's new approaches and contribution to the building of a cooperative and peaceful Europe.

The Estonian Case: Background

On 20 August 1991, the Supreme Council of Estonia adopted the resolution on the country's national independence. The immediate post-Soviet independence years were marked by the political strengthening of institutions and procedures, and by the implementation of reforms based on democratic principles and a market-economy system. The adoption of new legislative acts, particularly regulating citizenship and electoral procedures, generated much controversy, intensifying anxiety among non-Estonians.[2]

In February 1992, Estonia reinstated the Citizenship Law of 1938 with the adoption of a resolution 'On the Application of the Law on Citizenship'.[3] According to the Law, all citizens on 16 June 1940 and their descendants received Estonian citizenship, regardless of ethnicity. All others who had taken Estonian citizenship after Soviet annexation were not entitled to automatic citizenship. Those excluded were regarded as foreign nationals or stateless persons. It was, nevertheless, possible to gain citizenship by naturalization. This required residency within the republic for two years starting from 30 March 1990 (plus one year to process the application), the signing of an Oath of Loyalty to the Estonian state and its laws, and knowledge of the Estonian language.

Although individuals who were citizens and their descendants of the pre-war Republic of Estonia were able to acquire citizenship regardless of their ethnicity, the result of the law has been to disproportionately and negatively affect Russian speakers. The vast majority of people to receive citizenship were Estonian. Despite not being discriminatory in ethnic terms, the Citizenship Law left many Russian-speakers with uncertain status, causing dissatisfaction both within the Russophone community and from the Russian Federation. The negative reactions included accusations of the 'Estonian drive along the road to apartheid by declaring a third of its population aliens'[4] and of 'ethnic cleansing'.[5]

The Estonian authorities understand Russian accusations as attempts to influence world public opinion and international organizations in order to isolate Estonia from other democratic nations, diverting foreign investment and hindering the country's socio-economic and political development. The Russian Federation argues the Estonian amendments to legislation have contributed to the deterioration of the situation of many Russian speakers in Estonia. Despite the international evaluation of the conformity of the Estonian legislation to international standards, the Russian Federation maintained criticisms of ethnic discrimination and human rights violations. However, the Russian criticisms and accusations have not been accompanied by concrete actions. The lack of interest of the Russian Federation in contributing to the language training programs is noticeable, which might be interpreted as disinterest in the promotion of non-Estonian integration. Moreover, many Russian residents recognize Estonia offers better living conditions and opportunities than the Russian Federation or other former Soviet republics.[6]

The OSCE's Involvement

The CSCE's involvement in Estonia happened at a time of much instability and tension, both at the internal level (among the Russophone community) and at the international level (difficult Estonian-Russian relations). Estonia became a CSCE participating member on September 17, 1991, after it regained independence. Its expectations on joining the CSCE included international recognition of its statehood and the country's affirmation as a new democracy. The CSCE was the vehicle for the internationalization of the problems between Estonia and the Russian Federation. As a consequence of its geo-strategic location and Westward-looking commitment, Estonia became a privileged region enjoying Western states' concern. After consultations with the HCNM, in September 1992 the Estonian Government invited a CSCE Expert Mission to the country with the aim of evaluating the conformity of the Estonian national laws with those internationally recognized on human rights (within the Moscow Document framework).[7] The

Mission found no evidence of deliberate discrimination, concluding the Estonian Constitution and other laws met the international standards on human rights. Nevertheless, the Mission acknowledged the presence of a large number of non-citizens and recommended the launching of a large-scale program of effective language teaching and the adoption of a detailed Law on the Language Requirements for Acquiring Citizenship.[8]

Post-independence instability in Estonia, translated in uncertainty among non-citizens with regard to their future in the country, and in difficult relations between Estonia and the Russian Federation, defined the background for the deployment of a long-term CSCE Field Mission. In November 1992, the Personal Representative of the CSCE Chairman-in-Office, Gunnar Klinga, visited Estonia with the mandate to explore the modalities for the possible deployment of a CSCE Mission to the country.[9] Klinga classified citizenship procedures and in particular language requirements as the main issues of concern, given the numerous non-Estonians residing in Estonia. The situation was aggravated by the lack of qualified language teachers, materials and financial resources. Gunnar Klinga recommended that the main goal of CSCE activity in Estonia should be to encourage interaction and mutual understanding between the Estonian and Russian communities, avoid tensions and misunderstandings and promote civic society.

The OSCE Mission to Estonia

Following Gunnar Klinga's visit, the CSCE decided in December 1992 on the establishment of a Field Mission in Estonia.[10] The Mission was deployed on 15 February 1993 with the task of fostering dialogue and understanding among the inter-ethnic communities, envisaging the integration of the Russian-speaking population into the life of the country. Its mandate included the establishment and maintenance of contacts with the competent authorities on both the national and local level and in particular with those responsible for citizenship, migration, language questions, social services and employment, as well as with relevant non-governmental organizations (NGOs).[11] In the pursuit of its activity the Mission should engage in the collection of information and serve as a clearing-house for information, technical assistance and advice on matters relating to the status of the communities in Estonia, and the rights and duties of their members. As a contributor to the efforts to recreate a civic society, the Mission should promote local mechanisms to facilitate dialogue and understanding, and prepare local representative institutions for the future transfer of the Mission's responsibilities.

The Mission is composed of six members and operates at its main office in Tallinn and two branch offices in northeastern Estonia. The opening of the Narva and Johvi offices reflected the particularly difficult situation of the mostly Russian population inhabiting the region, and the Mission's concern for the area.[12] The Mission works under the supervision of the OSCE Conflict Prevention Center (CPC) in Vienna, implementing Vienna-made decisions. Nevertheless, given the broadness of its mandate, the Mission enjoys some flexibility with regard to the rendering operational of the tasks it was entrusted of. The field-Vienna link includes daily contact between the Secretariat in Vienna and the Mission in the field through the Liaison Officer, complemented by the regular submission of field reports to the CPC and Head of Mission communications at Permanent Council meetings. High-level visits from OSCE representatives to Estonia confer more legitimacy on the Mission and demonstrate the institutional support of the organization for the Mission's activities in the field.

The Mission follows a bottom-up strategy, promoting understanding and stability between the Estonian and Russian-speaking communities, by fostering civil society through the stimulation of dialogue, human rights and democracy-building. Nevertheless, the Mission also pursues an important confidence-building role at the inter-state level, encouraging dialogue between Estonia and the Russian Federation. Thus, the activity of the Mission in Estonia is broad in vertical and horizontal terms, addressing the various socio-political categories and a vast range of issues, falling not only within the human dimension, but also of a legislative, cultural or social nature. The Mission also co-operates with other international organizations in the field, in particular the UN, NATO, the EU and the Council of Europe. Nevertheless, only the OSCE has a Field Mission deployed in the country.

Although the Mission has been central to the OSCE activity in Estonia, for its presence and continuity in the field, the organization combines different efforts in the promotion of its preventive diplomacy goals in the country. In this regard, the HCNM is a central, high-profile institution of the OSCE concerning preventive diplomacy. The ODIHR has also been assisting the Mission in human-related projects and election monitoring.

The High Commissioner on National Minorities

Max van der Stoel, the OSCE High Commissioner on National Minorities, initiated consultations with the Estonian authorities in 1993 and has ever since been playing an active role in the resolution of citizenship problems in Estonia. Besides the legislative accommodation implied in the High Commissioner's activity, his involvement also encompasses a democratic institution-building dimension. Van der Stoel works in close cooperation with the Mission, particularly as regards the formulation of recommendations on legislation regulating naturalization and citizenship procedures. The Mission supports Ambassador Stoel by providing him with updated and detailed information about the problems in the country, allowing the formulation of more accurate and goal-oriented recommendations. Simultaneously, the Mission benefits from the High Commissioner's involvement and guidelines for future activities, including dissemination of information and clarification of procedures as confidence-building measures.

Unlike the Mission, the HCNM applies a top-down approach focused on contacts at the highest level as regards improvements to legislation which directly affects the Russophone communities in the country. By formulating concrete recommendations as regards legislation adaptation, the HCNM has contributed to the building of an increasingly tension-free scenario in Estonia, mostly by clarifying and simplifying citizenship requirements and related issues. These have been particularly related to the adoption on 21 June 1993 of the Law on Aliens to regularize the status of non-Estonian citizens; the new Law on Citizenship passed by the Estonian Parliament on 19 January 1995; and the new amendments approved on 15 December 1998, by the Estonian *Riigikogu* to the Laws on Elections and the State Language.[13]

The adoption of most of the HCNM's recommendations by the Estonian authorities is the best example of their pertinence. They allowed more transparency and the simplification of procedures, diminishing for example bureaucratic practices. The High Commissioner's recommendations also included suggestions to enlarge the reach of language-training programs, make public language exam results and accelerate the processing of citizenship applications. The extension of deadlines and the addressing of cases where the ambiguous wording of new legislation would suggest tensions are also part of the High Commissioner's recommendations.

The Estonian authorities have fully supported the recommendations of the High Commissioner to take early action to improve a visible policy of dialogue between the Government of Estonia and the non-citizen population, and recognize the importance of drafting and implementing policies and legislation which will aid in the reduction of the number of stateless persons permanently residing on its territory. However, not without controversy. The High Commissioner has been criticized for applying double-standards in the pursuit of his competencies and for his Russian-sided opinions when insisting that the Estonian authorities must come to terms with the Russian minority in the country.[14] The Estonian authorities question not so much the validity of the High Commissioner's recommendations, but his attitude, defined as incoherent. 'Why is not the HCNM recommending improvements to minorities in Western countries or the Russian Federation? Estonia considers it would confer more validity and respect to the HCNM mandate'. The standards applied to one must be valid for all OSCE states; in other words, there can be no 'rubber rulers'.[15]

The Office for Democratic Institutions and Human Rights

The Mission has also been closely co-operating with the ODIHR as regards language training, democracy-building and election monitoring. For example, within the ODIHR's Grassroots Program, the Office provided assistance to the Estonian Law Center in establishing a Center for the Study of Constitutional Law, highlighting cooperation between the Office and the Field Mission as well as local actors. Moreover, the ODIHR has promoted language training in collaboration with the Mission, provided assistance to the Mission as regards the organization of seminars falling within the human dimension, assisted in the monitoring of electoral processes, and provided support as regards NGO training.[16]

The NGO sector has been much valued by the OSCE as a means of promoting democratic structures and civic principles on a solid basis, formed by locals engaged in the promotion of stability and democracy. The OSCE support to NGOs has focused on the training of personnel, legal advice and assistance in requests for funding. The sharing of information and expertise, and participation of representatives from these organizations in OSCE meetings is also current practice.[17]

The OSCE innovative procedures, embedded in these institutions' approaches, combine to offer a multi-dimensional response to the problems. In this integrated environment, how does the Mission, in combination with other OSCE institutions, in particular the HCNM and the ODIHR, render operational its mandate?

Translation of Words into Action: Implementing the Mission's Mandate

The Mission pursues a multi-dimensional approach, addressing the various levels and all sectors of Estonian society and reports on the country's situation and implementation of policies. Monitoring whether implementation of political, legal, social and cultural policies is properly carried out, and preventing distorted results because of inadequate implementation, are at the core of the Mission's activity. Implementation assessments are made through visits to the relevant institutions, such as hospitals, workplaces, and the observation of the level of knowledge and competence of workers and administrators, as well as the evaluation of the population's receptivity to the new integration-related initiatives. Therefore, the Mission is not just a human-rights watcher, but also an instrument to contribute to the smoothness of the integration process.

In the autumn of 1997, the Estonian Government launched the 'Integration Strategy', with the aim of reducing the number of stateless persons through the active participation of non-Estonians in society, diminishing regional isolation and promoting social and political integration of these populations in the legislative and executive branches of Government.[18] Many of the problems in Estonia stem from political and social tension rather than legal discrimination. For this reason, the integration of the Russian-speaking populations is closely tied to the efforts of the Estonian Government to introduce more inclusive policies and to the receptivity of the non-Estonians to the Estonian Government initiatives.

True integration is not limited to the naturalization of aliens. Integration is a two-way and long-term process. All actors must be involved and committed, which has not always been the case, due either to the uncooperative nature of local Estonian authorities or to the passivity of some members of the non-Estonian communities. The activities of the Governmental Citizenship and Migration Boards, state offices which deal with naturalization procedures through the definition of new development and operational programs directed to citizenship issues,[19] have been source of criticism. Problems of mismanagement, corruption, including the issuing of illegal passports, excessive bureaucracy, long lines and insufficient information have been reported.[20] According to Viktor Andreyev, Head of the Russophone United People's Party, the program is based on 'the wrong assumption that integration is only a one-way process, in which the ethnically non-Estonian part of society would adopt the Estonian language'.[21] His arguments run against the Estonian authorities' understanding of the integration process as a two-way process, showing once more the problematic relationship between the Estonian authorities and the Russian-speakers.

Moreover, difficulties with the language and lack of information about language training and citizenship procedures affect particularly old, illiterate or poor people who cannot or do not want for cultural or economic reasons to learn the language, hindering the integration process. 'In regions like Ida-Virumaa, where unemployment is high and the first thing on most people's mind is how to put dinner on the table, there is little time for language classes'.[22]

It remains to be seen, on the one hand, whether the Estonian authorities will fully comply with their commitments to the integration process. And on the other hand, whether the Russophones will reply positively to the opportunities offered, particularly as regards the learning of the language and naturalization procedures, and if they will consider the government's initiatives within the integration program sufficient and adequate.

The OSCE Mission provides assistance to the Estonian authorities in the implementation of the integration strategy through a multi-faceted approach, encompassing language and education, cultural affairs, out-of-school activities, and regional development. The Mission has been developing concrete projects directed to the fostering of integration and inter-community dialogue, many of them with the support of other OSCE institutions, international organizations, NGOs and/or national institutions. Language training projects have been a clear example of the combination of these different efforts, including programs for adults or specific sectors of society, like courses in Ida-Virumaa for nurses, or in Narva for teachers. The aim is to promote improvements in educational and cultural terms which might contribute to new opportunities, particularly in employment, and possibly assist in the fulfillment of the naturalization requirements.

The Mission has also promoted special summer programs, which gave the opportunity to Russian-speaking children of spending their vacation with Estonian families, and organized summer camps for school-children by the Peipsi Lake. Other initiatives include the promotion of civic education through the organization of seminars, mainly on integration and multi-cultural education, such as the cultural lectures on Estonian culture in the city of Narva, where knowledge of Estonian history and language was scarce.[23] Moreover, initiatives directed towards the education of Russian-speaking students in public administration, joint computer and language training for residents of children's homes, and the integration of widows and divorcees of ex-Soviet military officers into Estonian society have also contributed to consolidating the integration process.

Projects involving the Estonian and Russian communities on issues of common concern, such as water supplies[24] or the establishment of a Youth Center in Narva, and of the Narva Resource Center for Teachers of Second (i.e. Estonian) and Foreign Languages, vital for re-training teachers, are practical examples of the integration efforts, demonstrating how the Mission in collaboration with other OSCE institutions in the field, renders its mandate operational. The Mission also addresses requests for advice and clarification as regards citizenship requirements from people contacting the OSCE field offices.[25]

Besides these activities directed at the promotion of inter-ethnic dialogue and cooperation within Estonia, the Mission has also been addressing the inter-state Estonian-Russian relationship. Estonian-Russian dissension has marked the

Estonian post-independence agenda. Besides Estonia's continuous rejection of the Russian Federation's charges of discrimination against the Russian-speaking population inhabiting the country, other problems have been hindering the establishment of good neighborly relations between the two countries. The withdrawal of Russian troops from Estonian soil, the border demarcation, and the Estonian Westward orientation and the desire to integrate into Western structures such as NATO and the EU, which did not please the Russian Federation, define the complex web in which the two countries' relationship has been developing.

Addressing the Estonian-Russian Relationship

The exchange of accusations and the linkage of different issues have been common in the Estonian-Russian relationship. Different views over the same problem and its possible resolution have been the cause of disagreement and poor dialogue. From the mixing of problems and the exchange of mutual accusations, the increase in tensions between the two countries was inevitable. In order to diffuse tensions and promote an environment conducive to dialogue between the two countries, the OSCE has offered a forum where difficult and even delicate issues such as the granting of Estonian citizenship to Russian speakers, the border demarcation[26] or the withdrawal of Russian troops from Estonian soil could be discussed.

At the time of the Estonian declaration of independence, Soviet troops were stationed on Estonian territory. The presence and later maintenance of these troops was understood in Estonia as an attempt by the Russian Federation to keep Estonia within its sphere of influence and as a justification for Russia's involvement in Estonian affairs. Therefore, Estonia urged the withdrawal of foreign troops from its territory. For the Russian Federation, the stationing of troops in Estonia meant continuity for its influence in the region and dissuasion of foreign economic investment in Estonia, thereby maintaining its status as main trading partner of the country. As such, Russia formulated a series of conditions to delay the withdrawal of troops, demanding social guarantees for Russian military pensioners and arguing it faced technical and economic constraints on withdrawal. The withdrawal process was closely tied to other matters, particularly respect for human rights in Estonia through the adoption of appropriate legislative measures and the signing of economic inter-state agreements.[27]

The OSCE, in the field and in Vienna, persuaded the parties to conduct a dialogue according to the agreements reached, and pressured Russia at the decision-making level causing discomfort in Moscow for the persistence of criticisms and the continuous reminders of the Russian failure to assume its international commitments.[28] After many difficulties, Russia completed the troop withdrawal in August 1994.[29]

According to the Agreement on 'Matters Related to Social Guarantees for Military Pensioners of the Russian Federation on the Territory of the Republic of Estonia' of 26 July 1994,[30] residence permits would be issued to military pensioners and their close relatives in accordance with Estonian law. An officer retired before 20 August 1991 was eligible for a residence permit if he was born before 1 January 1930, if his spouse or underage child was an Estonian citizen residing in Estonia or if his permanence in the country was necessary for the Republic of Estonia.[31] However, Estonia safeguarded the right not to confer citizenship on anyone considered a threat to the country's national security. Established in September 1994, the Estonian Government Commission on Military Pensioners deals with the processes of former Russian Military Officials, deciding about the issuing or not of residence permits to the around one thousand officials concerned. It was agreed that a CSCE representative would participate in the work of the Government Commission to assure impartiality and transparency in the evaluation process.[32] Captain Mahrenholtz was appointed the CSCE representative to the Commission and took up his functions on 16 November 1994.[33]

The OSCE's representation in the Commission added a new dimension to OSCE activity in Estonia. Praised by Estonia and the Russian Federation for pursuing an independent role and promoting transparency,[34] it demonstrates the OSCE's availability and versatility to assist in finding a solution to the problems. However, many who thought all applicants would be granted a residence permit misunderstood the OSCE Representative's role in the Commission. Severe criticisms of the OSCE Representative for sanctioning the Estonian Government emerged in Russian newspapers when the Estonian authorities refused residence permits to some applicants. The OSCE Representative regrets the misinterpretation of his mandate within the Commission, as limiting the reach of its activity in Estonia and reflecting a distorted perception of the nature of the organization's involvement.[35]

In the field, the HCNM and the Mission together with other OSCE institutions have also contributed to inter-state dialogue and a reduction of tensions. The support conferred on the establishment of the Presidential Roundtable, headed by the President of Estonia with the participation of representatives from the Association on National-Cultural Minorities, the Representative Assembly and Members of Parliament, is an example.[36] The Roundtable discussions address issues affecting non-citizens and ethnic minorities, contributing to improvement in Estonian-Russian relations, and within Estonia between the two communities. Moreover, the establishment in March 1998 of the Estonian-Russian Intergovernmental Commission to develop cooperation between Estonia and Russia at three different levels, including trade, economy, science and technology; social and humanitarian affairs; and cultural matters aims at reinforcing inter-state ties.[37] The working groups' activity has proved positive in building better understanding, and the discussion and signing of agreements in these areas of cooperation demonstrate flexibility and willingness to co-operate.[38] Nevertheless, the two countries still have a long way to go to the normalization of relations, which must include the building of trust and confidence along with the implementation of the agreed measures.

The OSCE has contributed to the lessening of tensions through counter-arguing Russian accusations of 'ethnic cleansing' with investigations by experts, including Council of Europe legal expertise, while simultaneously pressuring the Estonian authorities to regularize the status of non-citizens living in Estonia. Moreover, the organization offered a forum where difficult issues, such as the troop withdrawal were discussed, continuously pressuring Russia at the decision-making level and causing discomfort in Moscow for the persistence of criticisms and reminders of the Russian failure to comply with international commitments.

Simultaneously, the troop withdrawal problematic demonstrated the OSCE limitations in the face of particular national interests. In general, Russia welcomes the OSCE in Estonia, however, when its interests collide with those of the organization, Russia downgrades it. This Russian 'interest game' is, nevertheless, limited by OSCE agreements over which Russia has not veto power. Allied to this, the continuous violation of agreed commitments by Russia might not only widen international criticism, but lead to the suspension of economic aid, thus Moscow carefully balances its interests in the area with the commitments it has assumed.

A complex 'give and take away' process has always ruled Estonian-Russian relations. Russia has withdrawn its troops from Estonia and Estonia has so far complied with most of the international recommendations and obligations, particularly those of the HCNM. However, political, social, cultural and economic problems remain which need to be solved in the spirit of good neighborliness. Sharing concerns and discussing possible solutions would be an enormous step towards the normalization of relations and towards ending the constant political uncertainty in Estonian-Russian relations: partners or adversaries?

The OSCE in Estonia: Possibilities and Limitations

The OSCE Mission's activity in Estonia, together with other OSCE institutions, particularly the HCNM and the ODIHR, with the support of the decision-making process in Vienna and the OSCE agreed principles, have substantially contributed to the reduction of tensions. The Mission's mandate in Estonia must be understood in its all-encompassing reach, including socio-political, humanitarian, cultural and economic aspects. Through diplomatic moves for the promotion of dialogue, judicial and legal advice and the raising of funds for integration-directed projects, the Mission made its mandate operational.

The High Commissioner, through the issuing of recommendations on legislation adaptation, has been playing a fundamental tension-diffusing role. Addressing the concerns of the Russian-speaking population in the country and promoting a legal environment favorable to integration, van der Stoel's involvement has been complementary to the Mission's activities. The ODIHR has also contributed to the implementation of the Mission's mandate through rendering operational activities falling within the human dimension, particularly directed at integration and democracy-building. The Office's specialized role has strengthened the Mission's activities in Estonia by the complementary nature of the efforts developed.

However, from words to action there are fundamental aspects that escape the control of the Mission. National interests often rise above nicely-worded principles, obstructing the OSCE's activity both in the field and at the decision-making level. Decisions in Vienna are politically-binding and the OSCE has no enforcement mechanisms. It can use diplomatic pressure, causing discomfort and stressing non-compliance, though with limited reach. This is why Russia delayed at its convenience the withdrawal of Russian troops from Estonia, using different arguments to sustain its interests. The successful development of the OSCE Mission's activity in the country is, therefore, shared by the parties' willingness to implement and follow field and headquarters recommendations as beneficial policy options. The OSCE consensus decision-making procedure has also been used by Russia to pursue its interests in the Baltic region, blocking any Estonian attempts to close the Mission. The Mission has, thus, faced a lack of trust between the Estonian authorities and the Russophone community, and at a wider level between Estonia and Russia. Local problems, such as the passivity of many Russian-speakers, scarce financial and human resources and misunderstanding over the Mission's competencies[39] have limited its activity.

The Estonian authorities praise the OSCE Mission, as a forum for dialogue and in the aftermath of the country's independence, for diffusing tensions and promoting negotiations between Estonia and the Russian Federation. According to Estonian sources the OSCE was instrumental in helping Estonia overcome the legacy of its past, particularly at a time when Estonia was preparing to apply for membership of the EU and other European structures.[40] However, not long after the Mission's deployment, Estonia adopted a critical tone over the OSCE Mission's activity in the country. The inauspicious side-effects of the OSCE's presence in Estonia, downgrading human rights in the country and spreading a wrong image of Estonia to the world, have been stressed.[41] Estonia justifies its claims on the improvements made in legislative terms in order to comply with international standards. These acts have reflected the concern for integration through the creation of common interests. The evolution into a new stage, where the government's initiatives are in place and Estonia enjoys an almost tension-free atmosphere, renders, in the Estonian authorities' view, the Mission's presence irrelevant.

Despite the Estonian authorities position, a collaborative approach with the OSCE institutions in the country has been pursued. Nevertheless, the call for the OSCE Mission's withdrawal has intensified, particularly after a public statement by President Meri of Estonia, suggesting the reorganization of the OSCE presence into a Scientific Research Center.[42] Other Estonian representatives share this opinion. Foreign Minister Ilves argued the Research Center could play a more constructive role by raising awareness of human rights and international law, further reinforcing the President's suggestion.[43] Speaker of Parliament Toomas Savi argued 'Estonia has fulfilled the amendments requested by the OSCE, thus it is now time for the Mission to withdraw'.[44] The Estonian authorities argue the OSCE Mission's initial tasks have either been fulfilled or overtaken by NGOs or governmental institutions. As a result, Estonia is working with its partners on an exit strategy for the successful conclusion of the Mission's activity in Estonia.[45]

The OSCE's Preventive Diplomacy Role: An Assessment

The OSCE has been considerably successful in Estonia, though not without controversy. Making operational the goals entrusted by its mandate, the Mission has undergone a learning process, which to a certain extent was a test case of the organization's ability to empower well-worded commitments and procedures. The Mission managed to foster dialogue between Estonia and Russia, easing their relationship, and to promote better understanding between the Russian-speaking and the Estonian communities, through the offering of non-confrontational options. The issuance of several recommendations by the HCNM managed to persuade the Estonian Government to amend controversial legislation, diminishing anxieties. The consequent openness generated confidence among non-citizens, an important factor for integration

Despite difficulties, the conditions for the establishment of harmonious relations between all parties in Estonia have been established. The Russian-speaking population is accommodating to the favorable standard of living in Estonia, learning the Estonian language, and getting acquainted with Estonian history and culture. Moreover, political, economic and cultural organizations have flourished in Estonia,[46] allowing a Russian identity to form within Estonian society. These initiatives have contributed to improvements in inter-community understanding. For their part, the Estonian authorities have adopted several measures to facilitate the accommodation of ethnic differences, particularly within the integration strategy. The current situation in Estonia does not correspond yet to full integration, though it reveals an almost tension-free coexistence between Estonians and non-Estonians. Moreover, at the inter-state level the Estonian-Russian relationship has been eased. Despite the remaining problems and the continuous exchange of accusations, dialogue is on and the resolution of several problems of a cultural, social or economic nature has been positive. The agreements signed in the framework of the Estonian-Russian Intergovernmental Commission are an example.

The OSCE innovative procedures, translated in particular in the activities of the Field Mission, the HCNM and the ODIHR, together with the support of the decision-making process in Vienna and the OSCE agreed principles, have demonstrated how a multi-dimensional and integrated approach might reveal efficacy. By focusing efforts both at the governmental and the local levels, the OSCE activities have contributed to the consolidation and development of democratic political institutions and processes in Estonia, thus responding to the post-Soviet policy imperatives thrust upon the Estonian authorities after the regaining of independence. The OSCE approach to the problems in Estonia must be understood in the broad context where it develops. Here, the role of the Estonian authorities, international organizations, NGOs, and other relevant international actors, such as the Russian Federation, are fundamental.

The OSCE managed to build a triangular relationship where the political institutions of the country, NGOs and international organizations, and the OSCE itself play inter-connected roles, contributing to stability and the consolidation of democracy. In general, the different organizations have proved their mutually-verifying role in the pursuit of their tasks, such as the monitoring of compliance with international norms. The OSCE receives financial support from the UN or the EU, for example for the carrying out of joint projects. Moreover, the Estonian desire to integrate in the EU strengthens the OSCE's activities in the country, particularly the Mission's initiatives and the HCNM's recommendations. The contacts developed by Ambassador van der Stoel with EU authorities about the situation in Estonia were used by the HCNM as a form of pressure over Estonian authorities for compliance. At the same time, by fulfilling the criteria demanded, Estonia was praised by the EU. The same reasoning applies to the Mission-Council of Europe relationship. The division of tasks between organizations as regards language-training initiatives, for example, was positive and a sign of the possible inter-institutional synergies; however, there the OSCE's role is limited. Its real contribution comes from the nature of its commitments and its norm-setting strength as a source of legitimacy for the organization's involvement in certain delicate areas, such as the status of the Russian-speaking community inhabiting Estonia. The Mission's strength derives, therefore, from the development of the concept of mutually-reinforcing institutions and from the particular areas where the OSCE's uniqueness becomes relevant.

Addressing the various levels, including local, national and regional aspects, the OSCE tried to bridge the different dimensions, i.e. political, cultural, social and economic issues. By addressing the concerns of the populations, the OSCE contributed to bridging the Estonian and non-Estonian communities through the promotion of integration policies, in co-ordination with both national and local authorities. These policies, translated in language training courses, seminars or cultural lectures, for example, have also made a contribution to dilute the cultural and economic divides within the Republic of Estonia, by allowing the development of local cultural associations and the promotion of similar job opportunities for the different groups. The general aims of the OSCE in Estonia had, therefore, reflection at the local, national and regional levels, constituting an example of the organization's possibilities in preventive diplomacy.

The OSCE presence in Estonia has contributed to the setting of favorable conditions for progress, although the fundamental changes taking place in the country are part of a long-term process. The small size of Estonia, its commitment to democracy and the country's moderation and reasonableness in addressing difficulties, particularly those related to non-citizens, have greatly contributed to its development. Estonia is advancing with success after almost fifty years of Soviet occupation. A long and painful route that will certainly be crowned with success in the years to come. Undoubtedly, ensuring the satisfactory implementation of legislation, financial, social and political commitments at the nation-wide level, such as the integration strategy commitments, is fundamental.

Conclusion

The OSCE has developed a complex decision-making and operational structure to support its activities. The new institutions of the HCNM, the Representative on Freedom of the Media and the ODIHR are examples of the innovative ways found by the OSCE to address the challenges in its area. The deployment of long-term Field Missions has proved to be a fundamental tool of the OSCE through their flexible nature, monitoring role and non-forceful broad mandates, which have allowed a new type of involvement, as analyzed in the case of Estonia. The international presence embodied by these Missions, along with the multi-faceted goals and approaches they pursue, have made the OSCE's Missions an asset and a relevant contribution to stability in Europe. The combination of the Field Missions' activities with those of other more specialized OSCE institutions have been of most relevance for the overall performance of the organization.

OSCE activity in Estonia has proved positive in many aspects. The combination of different OSCE tools and reliance on the organization's normative strength have been relevant. Its presence has contributed to a reduction in tensions and has had a restraining effect on conflicting parties, providing a forum for dialogue between disputants. Moreover, the multi-dimensional approach contained in its mandate, including the human dimension, democratization and socio-political and economic factors has contributed to its enlarged reach, and to the building of stability and confidence.

However, OSCE field activities are constrained by the level of receptivity and collaboration of the receiving country, and by the context in which they operate. The Estonian authorities will to close the OSCE Mission, possibly reorganizing its presence in the country in a Research Center, is an example. Moreover, the organization's broad membership and its consensus decision-making have proved to be an asset in addressing a vast range of issues and in finding a strong support basis for the OSCE's decisions. Nevertheless, they have had the negative effect of not allowing the adoption of clearly-formulated and goal-oriented resolutions. The vagueness, and in some instances ambiguous decisions, have raised the issue of non-implementation or distorted implementation. At times signaling a lack of understanding in Vienna of events in the field, and at others demonstrating the reluctance of the participating states to allow closer scrutiny of their actions, consensus decision-making has been a controversial aspect within the organization with repercussions at the field level. The withdrawal of Russian troops from Estonia is an example. This issue reveals the fundamental aspect of the political commitment of participating states to implement agreed commitments, without which the OSCE's decisions will have a limited value.

Moreover, the lack of a profound knowledge by the general public and, in many instances, the local populations, also does not contribute to a positive assessment of the Mission's reach. The publicity for the OSCE's preventive diplomacy activities is limited, restricting the understanding of its scope in the former Soviet space. "[T]he OSCE suffers from the unrewarding lot of preventive diplomacy: the test of its success is a non-event, i.e., the non-occurrence of conflicts" (Chilworth, 1994).

Despite criticism and praise, the OSCE remains a privileged forum for addressing problems in the new independent republics of the former Soviet Union, here in particular in the case of Estonia. It cannot be perceived as a threat by its own nature, nor can it be regarded as irrelevant for its contributions to stability-building in the area. The OSCE's role in the transition efforts of Estonia and of other new independent republics in the former Soviet space is relevant, but it does not exhaust the organization's possibilities in the area. OSCE activity includes a broad range of issues, from the human dimension to military, political and economic aspects. It also carries the weight of fundamental agreements between its participating members, which because of their consensus character and ample reach are of the utmost relevance for security in Europe. The Missions currently deployed may be closed, others opened and the dynamics of international politics will dictate the different needs of the OSCE's participating states. Nevertheless, the OSCE's presence may be translated in a different functioning of the long-term Missions, as exemplified by the President of Estonia's suggestion to convert the Mission to the country into a research project addressing human dimension issues.

The development of the CSCE into the OSCE and the process the organization has been following, characterized by the adoption of a series of new mechanisms and procedures, is not complete. The OSCE has shown flexibility and a capacity to adapt to new challenges, within limits and with restraints. Given the course run so far it is not to be expected that the OSCE will reach a point where no other alternatives or tools may be suggested. It will be international conditions and the participating states' will that will determine the evolution of the OSCE at all levels, including membership, administrative and executive functioning, and the geographical and operational reach of the organization's activities. The OSCE has demonstrated its relevance in the midst of various international organizations dealing with security in Europe, has affirmed its usefulness in addressing the problems in the former Soviet Union, as in the case of Estonia, and has shown its flexibility and capacity to adapt. Now, only time will tell what the OSCE may become in the future.

Notes

[1] Charter of Paris for a New Europe, 'A New Era of Democracy, Peace and Unity', 1990. The CSCE was established by the Helsinki Final Act, signed on August 1, 1975 and became the Organization for Security and Cooperation in Europe (OSCE) after the November 1994 Budapest Summit, with effect from 1 January 1995.

[2] The terms 'non-Estonians' and 'Russian-speakers' are here used as convenient forms of shorthand to describe not only ethnic Russians, but also other non-Baltic and non-Russian nationalities, such as Belarussians, Ukrainians or others.

[3] 'Supreme Council of Estonia adopted a resolution to implement the Law on Citizenship as it was on June 16, 1940', Estonian Review, no. 17, 24-28 February 1992. See also 'Overview of the reporting from the CSCE Mission to Estonia', 17 December 1993.

[4] Russian Foreign Minister Kozyrev cited in 'The Estonian Law on Aliens', Radio Free Europe/Radio Liberty (RFE/RL) Research Report, vol. 2, no. 38, 24 September 1993, p. 9.

[5] Kozyrev cited by the Ministry of Foreign Affairs of the Republic of Estonia, Press Release, 'Estonia officially protests slander campaign by Russian officials', 9 February 1994.

[6] See 'Integrating Estonia's Non-Citizen Minority', Helsinki Watch, vol. 5, issue 20, October 1993; 'Emigration: Statistics and Attitudes', Estonia Today, 9 May 1996; 'Special Article: Putin's Russia, The Chaos at the Door', *The Economist*, 31 March 2000, pp. 23-26.

[7] 'Human dimension commitments are of legitimate concern to all participating states and do not belong exclusively to the internal affairs of the state concerned', Preamble of the Moscow Document 1991, Moscow Meeting of the CSCE, October 1991.

[8] Report of the CSCE-ODIHR Mission on the Study of Estonian Legislation, December 1992. A new Law on the Language Requirements for Acquiring Citizenship was soon

drafted by the Estonian Government and adopted by the *Riigikogu* on 10 February 1993. Response to the Report of the CSCE-ODIHR Mission on the Study of Estonian Legislation, 15 January 1993; Estonian Review, no. 89, 8-14 February 1993.

[9] 17th Committee of Senior Officials (CSO) Meeting, Prague, 17CSO/J2, 5-6 November 1992. Gunnar Klinga visited Estonia from 23 to 28 November 1992.

[10] 18th CSO Meeting, Stockholm, 18CSO/J3, Annex 2, 13 December 1992; 'CSCE representation to open in Estonia', Estonian Review, no. 77, 9-15 November 1992.

[11] 19th CSO Meeting, Prague, 19CSO/J2, Annex 1, 2-4 February 1993.

[12] The population in the northeastern regions of Estonia is mostly Russian speaking. For example, in early 1998 there were in Narva 2,901 Estonians against 64,819 Russian inhabitants, and in Sillamae, 598 Estonians against 16,465 Russian-speakers. Data from the Statistical Office of Estonia, 1 January 1998, http://www.vm.ee/eng/index.html

[13] For further detail see Uibopuu (1998), pp. 1-69.

[14] For example 'Strange bedfellows', *Baltic Independent*, 4-11 March 1994; Letter from the HCNM to Foreign Minister Luik, REF.HC/1/97, no.1/19028, 14 February 1997.

[15] 'The President addresses the CSCE Summit', Estonian Review, vol. 4, no. 49.1, 5-7 December 1994. Interviews with representatives from the Estonian authorities, May 1999.

[16] ODIHR Annual Report 2000, Warsaw, pp. 36 and 54; Annual Report 2000 on OSCE Activities, The Secretary General, SEC.DOC/5/00, p. 27.

[17] Charter of Paris for a New Europe, 'Non-governmental Organizations', 1990; Helsinki Document 1992, Helsinki Decisions, chapter IV, parags. 12-17; Budapest Document 1994, Budapest Decisions, chapter VIII, parags. 3 and 17; Istanbul Document 1999, Istanbul Declaration, parag. 3; Charter for European Security, 1999, parag. 27. See also 'OSCE contacts with non-governmental organizations (NGOs)', http://www.osce.org, and Gutlove P. and Thompson, G. (1995), pp. 57-8.

[18] 'The Integration of Non-Estonians into Estonian Society, The Bases of the Estonian State Integration Policy', adopted by the *Riigikogu* on 10 June 1998, unofficial translation, pp. 1-5.

[19] Activities include issuing identity documents, residence and work permits for aliens, visas, applications for asylum and refugee-related issues; the prevention of illegal immigration; the integration of aliens; and the storing of data files. 'Citizenship and Migration Boards', Estonian Official Information, http://www.mig.ee/eng_index.html.

[20] 'Steps to improve citizenship authority's work in north-Eastern Estonia', Estonian Review, vol. 10, no. 3, 16-22 January 2000; 'Estonian Citizenship/Migration Head Dismissed', RFE/RL Baltic States Report, vol. 1, no. 1, 24 January 2000; 'Estonian Citizenship Migration Head Sacked', RFE/RL, 17 January 2000; 'Three arrested suspected of selling 40 Estonian passports', Estonian Review, vol. 5, no. 27, 2-8 July 1995.

[21] RFE/RL Baltic States Report, vol.1, no. 3, 7 February 2000.

[22] Unsigned article of opinion, 'Undemocratic behaviour', *The Baltic Times*, vol. 37, no. 176, 23-29 September 1999.

[23] Other examples include Seminar on 'Training Teachers for Integration', Narva, August 2000; Training workshop on 'Women's Leadership and Participation in Public Life', 25-26 March 2000; 'Integration, Education and Language: On the Brink of the New Millennium', Tallinn, June 1999; Seminar on 'Multi-national Education', Ida-Virumaa, November 1998.

[24] The Mission developed a project discussion on a small northeastern town where local representatives gathered to discuss water supplies. All participants were provided with the same information and translation means, when necessary, to allow similar conditions for active participation in the meetings. The result was a constructive discussion, the sharing of concerns and the suggestion of solutions.

²⁵ Moreover, throughout the year 2000, the Mission and the ODIHR have promoted integration through free legal counselling and advice to the population of Ida-Virumaa on human rights issues. ODIHR Annual Report 2000, Warsaw, p. 54.

²⁶ As regards the negotiations on the border definition, a technical agreement was finally achieved in March 1999, although it lacks ratification. According to the Estonian authorities, its ratification will make no practical difference to Estonian-Russian relations since it deals only with procedural matters. Interviews with Estonian authorities, May 1999; 'Expert in Political Science doubts improvement of Estonian-Russian relations', Estonian Review, vol. 9, no. 50, 5-11 December 1999; Merritt, M. (2000), pp. 244-46.

²⁷ For example, 'Oil supplies from Russia suspended', Estonian Review, no. 58, 29 June-5 July 1992; 'Russian President halts troop withdrawal from Baltics', Estonian Review, no. 75, 26 October-1 November 1992; 'Russia once again declares suspension of troop withdrawal from Baltics', Estonian Review, no. 96, 29 March-4 April 1993; 'Estonia responds to Russian allegations', Estonian Review, no. 107, 14-20 June 1993.

²⁸ For example, Helsinki Document 1992, Helsinki Declaration, parag.15; 4th Council Meeting, 4C/Dec.1, Rome, 30 November-1 December 1993, chapter 1, parag. 5; 28th CSO Meeting, Prague, 28CSO/J2 and J3, 14-16 September 1994.

²⁹ Praised by the CSCE as 'a tremendous accomplishment' positive for the resolution of the remaining difficulties between Russia and Estonia, CSCE Chairman-in-Office Antonio Martino, cited in CSCE Newsletter, vol. 1, no. 8, 7 September 1994, pp. 1-2; 28th CSO Meeting, 28CSO/J2, 15 September 1994; Budapest Document 1994, 'Declaration on Baltic Issues'. However, the expected positive outcomes were limited.

³⁰ For the text of the agreement see 'Russian-Estonian Agreement on Military Pensioners' Rights', BBC Summary of World Broadcasts (SWB), SU/2064 E/1, 3 August 1994.

³¹ Mission Report on the situation in Estonia in accordance with point 5.d) of the draft agenda of the 25th CSO Meeting, 17 February 1994.

³² 28th CSO Meeting, Journal 3, decision (g) under agenda item 6 (e), Prague, 28CSO/J3, 16 September 1994.

³³ Permanent Committee, Journal 40, item 6, Vienna, PC/J40, Ann, 7 November 1994 and CSCE DOC.1024/94, 4 November 1994.

³⁴ The Russian Federation values the OSCE's presence as conferring legitimacy and as a guarantee against the arbitrary rule of bureaucracy. Statement by the Representative of the Russian Federation Deputy Director of the Second European Department of the Russian Minister for Foreign Affairs Vdaltsov, CSCE DOC.862/94, 5 October 1994.

³⁵ Between 1995 and 1999 there were 53 refusals of residence permits, 32 of which to voucher receivers, the others due to criminal records or provision of false information. By mid-1997 the United States was promoting an assistance program consisting of the emission of housing vouchers for the repatriation of ex-military officials to Russia or other former Soviet republics. According to the contract, those opting for the voucher had three months to leave Estonia. However, the lack of tight supervision allowed some officials to apply both for the voucher and for a residence permit to stay in Estonia, illegitimately accumulating benefits. This problem involves around 500 ex-officials who sold or rented their apartments in Russia and remained in Estonia. Interview with Tiina Ilsen, OSCE Representative to the Estonian Government Commission on Military Pensioners, Tallinn, 13 May 1999.

³⁶ CSCE Communication 192/93, 2 July 1993; 22nd CSO Meeting, Prague, 22CSO/J2, Annex 2, 19 June-1 July 1993; 'Estonian President's first Roundtable talks with national minorities', Estonian Review, no. 110, 5-11 July 1993.

³⁷ 'Estonian-Russian Intergovernmental Commission launched', Estonian Review, vol. 8, no. 12, 15-21 March 1998.

[38] For example RFE/RL Baltic States Report, vol. 1, no. 20, 7 June 2000; 'Estonia and Russia sign aviation and motor transport agreements', Estonian Review, vol. 10, no. 27, 3-9 July 2000; 'Estonian-Russian Committee discusses return of cultural property', Estonian Review, vol. 8, no. 24, 7-13 June 1998.

[39] The legal or social complaints addressed to the Mission, often mistaken for human rights violations, are an example.

[40] 'Estonia and the OSCE', Estonia Today, 3 July 2000.

[41] 'It is impossible to measure how much foreign investment Estonia has foregone due to news magazines which print maps which place little symbols indicating a crisis on both the Balkans and the Baltic simply because of the presence of OSCE Missions', Foreign Minister Ilves, 'Estonia: integration of Russian speakers proceeds successfully', RFE/RL, 14 April 1997.

[42] Article of opinion published in an Estonian newspaper in May 1999.

[43] Estonian Ministry for Foreign Affairs, 'Press Releases and News', vol. 1, no. 38, 14 June 1999; 'OSCE Commission meets with Government Officials', Estonian Review, vol. 9, no. 24, 6-12 June 1999.

[44] 'Speaker of Parliament sees OSCE Mission in Estonia concluded', Estonian Review, vol. 10, no. 24, 12-18 June 2000 RFE/RL Baltic States Report, vol.1, no. 22, 27 June 2000.

[45] 'Estonia and the OSCE', Estonia Today, 3 July 2000.

[46] Such as the Estonian Ethnic Minorities Association, the Russian Representative Assembly, the Union of Russian Citizens, the Council of the Russian Community, and the Russian Citizens Union. See Hopf, T. (1996), p. 165.

References

Abadjan, V. (2000), 'OSCE Long-term Missions: Exit Strategy and Related Problems', *Helsinki Monitor*, vol. 11, no. 1, pp. 22-36.

Bedjaoui, M. (2000), 'The Fundamentals of Preventive Diplomacy', in Cahill, K. (ed.), *Preventive Diplomacy, Stopping Wars before They Start*, Routledge and the Center for International Health and Cooperation, New York, pp. 29-50.

'Bibliography on the OSCE High Commissioner on National Minorities: Documents, Speeches and Related Publications', The Foundation on Inter-Ethnic Relations, The Hague, 1997.

Booth, K. and Wheeler, N. (1992), 'Contending Philosophies about Security in Europe' in McInnes, C. (ed), *Security and Strategy in the New Europe*, Routledge, New York.

Estébanez, M. (1997), 'The High Commissioner on National Minorities: Development of the Mandate', in Bothe, M.; Ronzitti, N. and Rosas, A. (eds), *The OSCE in the Maintenance of Peace and Security: Conflict Prevention, Crisis Management and Peaceful Settlement of Disputes*, Kluwer Law International, The Hague, pp. 123-165.

Ghébali, V. (1996), *L'OSCE dans l'Europe Post-Communiste, 1990-1996. Vers une Identité Paneuropéenne de Sécurité*, Étaɔlissements Émile Bruylant, Bruxelles.

Ghébali, V. (1998), 'Preventive Diplomacy as Visited by the OSCE', 3rd International Security Forum and 1st Conference of the PfP Consortium of Defence Academies and Security Studies Institutes, On-line Publications, Zurich, October 19-21.

Holoboff, E. (1995), 'National Security in the Baltic States: Rolling Back the Bridgehead', in Dawisha, K. and Parrott, B. (eds), *State Building and Military Power in Russia and the New States of Eurasia*, M. E. Sharp, New York and London, pp. 111-133.

Hopf, T. (1996), 'Russian Identity and Foreign Policy in Estonia and Uzbekistan', in C. Wallander (ed), *The Sources of Russian Foreign Policy after the Cold War*, The John M. Olin Critical Issues Series, Westview Press, pp. 147-172.

Huber, K. (1994), 'Averting Inter-Ethnic Conflict: An Analysis of the CSCE High Commissioner on National Minorities in Estonia, January-July 1993', The Carter Center of Emory University, Conflict Resolution Program Working Paper Series, vol. 1, no. 2, Atlanta.

Kionka, R. and Vetik, R. (1996), 'Estonia and the Estonians', in Smith, G. (ed), *The Nationalities Question in the Post-Soviet States*, 2nd Ed, Longman, London, pp. 129-146.

Kirch, M. and Kirch, A. (1995), 'Ethnic Relations: Estonians and non-Estonians', *Nationalities Papers*, vol. 23, no. 1, pp. 43-56.

Lahelma, T. (1999), 'The OSCE's Role in Conflict Prevention: The Case of Estonia', *Helsinki Monitor*, vol. 10, no.2, pp. 19-38.

Merritt, M. (2000), 'A Geopolitics of Identity: Drawing the Line between Russia and Estonia', *Nationalities Papers*, vol. 28, no. 2, pp. 243-262.

Pentikainen, M. (1997), 'The Role of the Human Dimension of the OSCE in Conflict Prevention and Crisis Management' in Bothe, M.; Ronzitti, N. and Rosas, A. (eds), *The OSCE in the Maintenance of Peace and Security: Conflict Prevention, Crisis Management and Peaceful Settlement of Disputes*, Kluwer Law International, The Hague, pp. 83-122.

Schlager, E. (1997), 'The Right to Have Rights: Citizenship in Newly Independent OSCE Countries', *Helsinki Monitor*, vol. 8, no.1, pp. 19-37.

The Foundation on Inter-Ethnic Relations (1997), 'The Role of the High Commissioner on National Minorities in OSCE Conflict Prevention, An Introduction', The Hague.

Uibopuu, H. (1998), *Minorities in Estonia, Their Legal Status under Estonian Law and Estonia's International Commitments*, Euroopa Noukogu Tallinna Info-Ja Dokumendikeskus, Salzburg, pp. 1-69.

Van Ham, P. (1998), 'The Baltic States and *Zwischeneuropa*: 'Geography is Destiny?', *International Relations*, vol. xiv, no. 2, pp. 47-59.

Vasilev, S. (1999), 'The HCNM Approach to Conflict Prevention', *Helsinki Monitor*, vol. 10, no. 3, pp. 45-58.

Zaagman, R. (1999), 'Conflict Prevention in the Baltic Area: The OSCE HCNM in Estonia, 1993-1999', *Helsinki Monitor*, vol. 10, no. 3, pp. 30-44.

Zellner, W. (1998), 'The OSCE's High Commissioner on National Minorities - His Own Conception of His Work, Content and Tendency of His Recommendations, Effectiveness, Recommendations for Strengthening the HCNM as an Institution', 3rd Pan-European International Relations Conference and Joint Meeting with the International Studies Association, Vienna, September 16-19.

CSCE/OSCE Documents

Annual reports on CSCE/OSCE activity, the Secretary General of the CSCE/OSCE from 1993. OSCE Seminars and Conferences' Reports.

Chilworth (1994), 'The CSCE Human Dimension: Principles, Mechanisms and Implementation', CC/CSCE 94(4).

CSCE/OSCE Permanent Council, Senior Council, Forum for Security Cooperation, Economic Forum documents; 'OSCE Decisions Reference Manuals', annual compilations from 1993; 'OSCE Documents 1973-1997', CD-ROM compiled and produced by the OSCE, 1998.

'CSCE/OSCE Newsletter', from vol. 1 (1994).
High Commissioner on National Minorities (HCNM): documents, including letters and recommendations.
Office for Democratic Institutions and Human Rights (ODIHR): reports and documents related to human dimension activities of the Office.
OSCE (2000), 'Survey of OSCE Long-term Missions and other OSCE Field Activities', Vienna Secretariat.

Chapter 8

Non-Governmental Organizations and the Liberalization of Global Trade Policy Under GATT/WTO

Zdzislaw W. Puslecki

Introduction

General Agreement on Tariffs and Trade (GATT) had played a special role in the process of liberalization of the contemporary international trade. Nowadays that role has been taken over by the World Trade Organisation (WTO). The strength of GATT could be seen in a record number of international negotiation rounds organised under its auspices. As early as in the initial period of GATT activity, that is, in the years 1947 - 1957, four tariff conferences were held (in Geneva - 1947; in Annecy - 1949; in Torquay - 1951; and once more in Geneva - 1956), where the problems of international trade liberalization were discussed. The chief initiator of these talks were the United States of America. The initial talks did not bring about any significant changes to the existing tariff order. They also did not cause any significant decrease of customs duties. However, the governments of a number of countries, having in mind strengthening their own position in tariff talks, started to modernise and change the tariffs and the customs laws. In the years 1950 - 1959, a number of West European countries, as well as the United States and Japan, adjusted them to their own needs.

During the following decades, the next four rounds of trade negotiations were held (Dillon Round, Kennedy Round, Tokyo Round and Uruguay Round). So far, altogether eight such rounds have been held. Due to a big number of mutual arrangements during the four consecutive and most important rounds, significant areas of the world trade have been liberalised, and the means for the expansion of further liberalization have been worked out. The Uruguay Round itself was completed, after seven years of negotiations, on December 15th 1993. Eight years after the Uruguay Round it can be stated that this round prevented several potentially destructive conflicts in the field of trade and also made possible further liberalization of international trade in agricultural products and in services.

Unlike GATT, WTO is an organisation formed on the principles similar to those of International Monetary Fund or World Bank (Cohn, 2000). First of all, it is a legal entity. Most decisions are reached unanimously, and the rest by the majority rule. The main task of the WTO is supervising the implementation of the Uruguay Round decisions by the particular countries. The organisation is also a forum for the negotiations on further liberalization of the international exchange of goods and services, on foreign investments related to the exchange of goods and on the laws pertaining to the intellectual property rights. The basic principle of the organisation is non-discrimination of member states, manifesting itself through the application of the most favoured nation clause. This is accompanied by the rule of mutual benefits, free access to national markets and the rule of honest competition. Governments may intervene only when there is a necessity to protect the balance of payments, national production, health of citizens and safety of the state. The WTO provides also for the procedure of conflict solving, far more effective than the previous ones and, at the same time, the procedure that is uniform for all the areas under regulations. The competence of WTO is much broader than that of GATT.

All WTO agreements are obligatory for its members. This means that the countries joining WTO are obliged to accept those agreements in the form worked out during the Uruguay Round, without any choice in that matter (as it was possible in case of so-called codices during the Tokyo Round) and without the possibility of introducing any changes. Proper national authorities accept the access in the form reserved for such cases in the state law (in most cases this means the ratification procedure carried out by national parliaments). Besides, each WTO member is obliged to ensure the compatibility of its own administrative regulations and procedures with the obligations resulting from the Uruguay Round agreements.

The creation of WTO resulted in a uniform system of rules in the international economic exchange. The organisation forms the institutional framework for broadly understood trade exchange between its members. This way a uniform system of principles and procedures was established, along with the supervision over the already reached agreements, the employment of protecting means in case of rules violation, methods of solving possible conflicts, and allowing to promote further liberalization. The acceptance of all the Uruguay Round agreements (written down on over 500 pages), or otherwise their rejection, is a necessary condition to be met by those who want to participate in WTO. At the same time, it forms a system encompassing a significantly bigger number of areas of co-operation than GATT, together with the new agreements negotiated in the course of the Uruguay Round. It is obliged to adapt the trade rules of particular member countries to the rules of WTO, as well to publish them, that is, to make them publicly known. The purpose of this is gaining the optimum transparency of the national laws.

As a result of the Uruguay Round three new areas of the international trade were covered with multilateral regulations, namely: trade in services, intellectual property rights protection and the trade related aspects of the investment policy. The purpose of the agreement in the field of services, that is, of the General Agreement on Trade in Services (GATS) is seen in establishing multilateral rules for conducting that type of trade, and in reducing the trade barriers. In the two remaining areas the agreements prepared grounds for the reduction of intellectual property rights abuses (forging of goods, illegal reproduction of computer programs, video cassettes, etc.), and for the reduction, by the member states, of those policy instruments, which make foreign investments more difficult. Similarly, the uniform rules were also established for the trade in agricultural products and textile-clothing goods. Until then, these areas were not covered by the GATT regulations. In addition, many GATT regulations were more precisely defined, among others, those related to fighting the ill effects of dumping, subsidies, some non-tariff measures of trade protection, and the regulations concerned with conflict solving, etc. The new agreements included also the state-related aspects of those agreements that had been signed in the Final Act of the Uruguay Round. They were concerned with the international trade in goods as well as trade in services.

Functioning of the international trade depends now, to a significant degree, on the Agreement on Safeguards, signed in the course of the Uruguay Round, and regulated by Article XIX of WTO, which defines more precisely the conditions of gaining the Most Favoured Nation Clause (MFN) and prohibits the application of the Voluntary Export Restraint Arrangements (VERA) and their varieties. Another agreement introducing restraints is the Agreement on Textiles and Clothing which gradually incorporates the trade regulated by the Multi-Fibre Arrangement (MFA) into the GATT rules, which means that ten years after the WTO agreement has been implemented, the largest forum for introducing the agreements of voluntary export restraints (VERA) will stop functioning (Cohn, 2000).

Non-governmental organizations (NGO) play a very important role in decision making within the World Trade Organization (WTO). The decisions taken by the representatives of the governments participating in the WTO are, to a significant degree, influenced by various lobbies, such as organizations and unions of food producers or other non-governmental organizations, including trade unions. The problems of mutual relations between the representatives of governments and those non-governmental organizations which influence on multilateral trade negotiations conducted on the forum of WTO are the subject of the analysis in the undertaken research program, while special attention has been paid to the trade conflicts between the European Union and the United States of America.

The biggest confrontations within GATT/WTO involved agricultural problems. They could also be observed in other areas, such as steel industry, textile industry or in an environmental protection. There are serious conflicts existing between the idea of international trade liberalization and environmental protection since one has to consider what is more profitable - environmental protection or international trade liberalization.

Different positions of the U.S. and the European Community representatives could be observed during the next round of trade negotiations. In recent years (Uruguay Round) the governments of those two economic powers found themselves under a significant pressure of food producers who had serious difficulties with the sale of agricultural products surplus in the situation of the limited world market and lower prices. The problems of agriculture protection in the European Union, the protection resulting from the Common Agriculture Policy (CAP) of member countries, were becoming a serious obstacle on the way to the final compromise. However, at the same time, like in previous negotiations, global solutions prevailed.

These solutions had to take into consideration the propositions coming from different regions and different interest groups.

Pressures Exerted by Urbanized Labor Force (Trade Unions) in Different Political Systems

The role of trade unions in different political systems may be, to a high degree, different. In authoritarian systems it is, as a rule, smaller than in democratic systems. It would seem that if protectionist pressure on the part of trade unions is weaker, the situation for economic growth is much better. Following that line of reasoning we could come to the conclusion that the authoritarian system is better for the effectiveness of the labor market. The examples of Chile, South Korea, Singapore and Turkey from the seventies and early eighties could confirm that point of view. In many cases during those two decades the authoritarian regimes persecuted trade unions and put restrictions on basic labor rights. During that period of oppression, South Korea, Singapore and Turkey experienced a spectacular growth in the sector of processing industry and in the growth of demand for labor. Growing profits and the demand for labor in a processing industry, caused a general growth of prosperity of the employed. Although similar results were not noted immediately during the authoritarian phase of development in Chile, a number of observers express the opinion that the reforms introduced at that time helped to reorganize Chilean economy in the nineties. The application of democratic rules, on the other hand, may lead to lower productivity of labor force. In a number of years different democracies had to use significant financial resources for the employment of those who belonged to trade unions.

A different point of view says that government legislation concerning the labor market may be applied more effectively in an authoritarian system than in a democratic one. The authoritarian regimes often make use of individual interests of given circles. In most democratic countries there is no broad enough basis that would allow using labor market policy for gaining the support from pressure groups, the urbanized labor marked elite included. The major difference between authoritarian and democratic regimes lies in the level of the outside influence. In a well functioning democracy, the outside opinions are also taken into account and there occur some limitations that come from the outside, which restricts the achievements of given groups of interest. In a dictatorship, a government cares only that those groups are not too strong.

There are, however, a number of democracies among the industrialized countries where an effective labor market exists. There are also a number of democracies with effective labor market policy among the developing countries. Similarly, in the countries in which the transformation from the authoritarian regime towards a democracy is taking place, avoiding unfavorable phenomena on a labor market is often a priority. For example, the Chilean government moved towards democracy and to free trade unions without home income growth. The end of oppression in South Korea, in 1987, started the partnership relations in full of conflicts industry. (Banerji and Ghanem, 1997).

Analytical Construct

It is worth considering which of the two points of view presented above should be given support, that is, which of them is the proper one. The analysis of that problem may be based on the Grossman and Helpman model (Grossman and Helpman, 1994). This model describes economic development on the basis of two sectors - urbanized, regulated processing sector, and rural, unregulated agricultural sector. The protection of the labor market, especially of minimum wages, is usually applied in order to bring the benefits for the employees of the regulated sector, since the sector of unregulated employees does not come under the legislation concerning the labor market.

The sectors of regulated employees, and also the owners, demand from the government that it leads an economic policy that is favorable to them. The employed demand high minimum wages, while capitalists demand high profits. Both groups demand the restrictions on the degree of economy openness. In a closed economy, higher market minimum wages and higher profits are usually connected with higher prices for home consumers, and this is not easy when those consumers are free to buy the substitutes in form of imported goods. Thus, incomes in an economy may be created by protection and later divided among the employees of the regulated sector and the capitalists, although sometimes the government itself takes a part of those incomes (Banerji and Ghanem, 1997).

A government conducting an economic policy takes into account a number of factors. Firstly, it has to decide the degree of obtaining the resources, that is, how much from those resources it wants to obtain. Hence the importance of investments and of future economic growth, and also of defining the possibilities for keeping the power it is currently holding. Secondly, the government should define the scale of support from each of the pressure groups that can influence the situation. The position and importance of each group for the development of political processes should be considered. For example, in the country where the regulated labor market is divided, and politically weak, only the capitalists may have a deciding voice in political processes. And the contrary also happens - in the societies where the labor market is organized; it may play the important role in mobilizing voters.

How can we recognize the type of power, the type of rule? First of all, we should investigate what level of resources a given government is going to achieve. If an authoritarian government is more or less corrupted than a democratic one, it will be creating the income, to a bigger or lesser degree, through protectionism. It will also appropriate some part of that income. Secondly, a given type of government may remain under the influence of different pressure groups. If an authoritarian government is trying, to some extent, to subordinate special pressure groups. including the regulated labor sector, it will be, to some extent, generating incomes through protection and it will be turning over some part of them to those special pressure groups.

The above arguments show that the policy is defined by political factors (including the type of the government and the burdens resulting from obligations towards employees and capitalists), and by economical factors (wages, prices, the structure of production and consumption). On the basis of the present discussion, we can present two equations, one pertaining to the level of protection, and the second pertaining to the national economy and deformation of wages.

1) $\quad = f(e, l, k, R)$
2) $\varphi = f_1(\ldots, e, l, k, R)$,

The level of protection (depends on the economic parameters (e), a relative political importance of urbanized employees and capitalists (l and k, respectively), and on the type of the government (R). Deformation of wages is, on the other hand, the function of and of e, l, k and R. In case of a small economy, economic parameters that can influence and φinclude flexible consumer and producer prices, demand flexibility, wages and the demand for labor force, and also the price of goods on an international market.

One can expect, a priori, that the growth of is dependant on l and k. If interest groups become stronger, the pressure to form incomes based on protectionism may become stronger. The influence of R, that is, the influence of a political authoritarianism on the level of protectionism, that is, , depends on the fact whether the opinion, that the level of protectionism depends on the effects of democratization, is correct. It is also thought that the increase of the deformation of wages depends on and l, while its decrease depends on k. As long as the incomes are obtained from trade protections, those incomes can be handed over to urbanized employees. An important problem in case of urbanized labor force as an interest group with growing strength is the fact that urbanized employees may gain a big share in the division of incomes but the growth of political importance of the capitalists may cause that the shared incomes, handed over to the labor force in regulated sectors of economy will become smaller (Banerji and Ghanem, 1997).

There is no doubt that it is easier for wealthy rather than poor societies to choose democracy (Helliwel, 1992). Since those wealthier societies at the same time have a tendency to a bigger openness, the direction of cause-result events may run from the openness of society to the political system, and not, as was suggested earlier, in the opposite direction. The research showed also that the level of education plays an important role in this respect. The countries with a higher level of education of labor force are more open.

On the basis of the earlier considerations, one can come to the conclusion that authoritarian systems have a tendency towards a broader application of protectionism than democratic systems, and that, in turn, the trade restrictions accompany significant deformations of wages on the labor market. This opinion may be justified on the basis of the observations of the situation in a number of countries in the seventies, eighties and nineties.

Freedom of association is one of the elements of good management and the necessary condition for development. The authoritarian governments do not respect, however, the freedom of association, which is connected with the policy of trade restrictions and with the deformations on the labor markets. One cannot state, however, that improper or ineffective policy on the labor market belonged exclusively to authoritarian regimes or that authoritarianism automatically generates this kind of policy. There are a number of examples of authoritarian countries that do not conduct policies of that kind. The works of such authors as Fields or Freeman show that the repressions against the labor force are not necessary, if one wants to achieve a required economic growth (Fields, 1994; Freeman, 1993).

Finally, it should be pointed out that there exists a close relation between democracy and an economic growth, There are well known examples of open societies that stimulate the economic growth. This is true mainly in case of highly developed and strongly urbanized countries. In the countries with a developed democracy, the pressure groups have a bigger opportunity for acting. The research shows that the presence of trade unions helps to accelerate the economic reforms (Devarajan, Ghanem, Thierfelder, 1997). The benefits resulting from liberalization of the international trade are bigger when the trade unions exist in the sector of the economy under protection. The growth of import abilities leads to the decrease of wage pressures, and when the trade unions agree to that, such a situation allows for a better allocation of labor force in the economy. This is true both in the case of active and passive trade unions, although the effects are better in case of active trade unions.

The Influence of Trade Unions on the Course of Multilateral Trade Negotiations

The trade unions active in an urbanized labor market had a significant influence on the decisions of governments, in the course of multilateral trade negotiations within GATT/WTO. It was especially evident in the negotiations on lowering customs duties and non-tariff measures in steel, shipbuilding, textile and clothing industries, and in coal mining. In the so-called "sensitive" industries, which, for example, in the European Union were under special trade protection, the position of trade unions was very strong.

From the proposal of a textile agreement, which is an element of negotiations within the Uruguay Round, it was evident that a number, or probably most, restrictions in an international textile and clothing trading (existing on the basis of MFA decisions) will not be abolished before the year 2003. Taking into account a possibility of conflicts in that area, the European Union and the United States proposed, for the reduction of restrictions, a transitional period of 10 - 15 years. Major textile and clothing experts from developing and from new industrialized countries express the opinion that 6,5 years would be enough for that purpose. This caused some intensification of the conflict between the United States and the European Union (Langhammer, 1991).

During the Uruguay Round the conflict between the United States and the European Union involved also the steel industry, the industry that suffered serious development troubles. For a number of years the demand for steel was going down, old steel mills were being liquidated and the unprofitable divisions of steel mills were being closed down. The worsening condition of the American steel industry impelled the representatives of that industry to start, the anti-dumping procedures and the actions against the subsidies applied by the European exporters of steel bars and rolled steel, among others against Usinor-Sacilor, and against another French company Ascométal, which was considered by the European Union to be "the steel war". The European Commission expressed regret over that new interventionist offensive on the steel market, especially when the United States broke the well going negotiations within the Uruguay Round, the negotiations on the multilateral agreement on steel products trade.

In the course of the last Uruguay Round, there arose also conflicts involving the area of services, especially banking. Multilateral negotiations on trading services are very complicated considering the complexity of exchange in that field. So far, there is no one explicit theory of service exchange, which is the result of the great variety of forms of services. The thesis saying that the liberalization of service exchange would bring similar benefits, as a free good exchange has not been convincingly proved yet. Therefore, it is not clear whether those classic GATT/WTO norms, such as lack of discrimination, or mutual benefits, could be applied in exchanging services. The situation would become even more complicated in case of the detailed rules, especially if we consider the fact that even the identification of the barriers is a very complex task. Thus, the negotiations can be conducted in a selective way, only in those service sectors in which the potential benefits from the liberalization of exchange are most obvious (Gray, 1993).

During the Uruguay Round the United States accused the European Union that 75% of financial and telecommunication services in their mutual exchange was inadmissible, and that the European Union drew significant profits out of this exchange. The USA justified their position in this respect with the incapacity to satisfy the offers of other parties, especially those from the developing countries. At the same time, they hinted that they could change their position in this matter. The European Union, however, always insisted on a global character of negotiations, and had no guarantees that they would be conducted in this way. Trade unions, to a significant extent, were influencing the position of the European Union. That position in some cases could accelerate and in others retard the course of negotiations on the liberalization of international trade.

Pressure Exerted by Food Producers on the Position of Governments in Major Trade Conflicts

The biggest conflicts between the United States and the European Union within GATT/WTO were caused by agricultural problems. The conflict between the United States and the European Community intensified during the Uruguay Round. The governments of the two economic powers were in this time under a very strong pressure of food producers, who had problems with the sale of agricultural products surpluses in the situation of the shrinking world market and lower prices. One should note, however, that previous conflicts between the EC and the U.S. were always ended with a compromise, although the European side had to agree to bigger concessions.

The problem of liberalization of agricultural products trading is linked to the problem of subsidies application. According to the GATT/WTO decisions (art. XVI), exports of the agricultural products, as so-called basic goods, can be subsidized, if this fact does not interfere with the economic interests of other participants of the agreement. Actually, subsidizing exports of agricultural products may have many different forms, starting with a direct subsidy, through variable compensatory fees, and finally through various forms of government guarantees and preferential credits. In the ministers declaration we read only about a better discipline among the members of GATT/WTO. The total prohibition of subsidies would be the simplest course, but it does not seem to be realistic.

The problem of protection of agriculture by the European Union, resulting from the Common Agricultural Policy (CAP) that had been conducted for years, was considered, during the Uruguay Round to be the main reason of the fact that the talks were so difficult. Major food exporters that participated in negotiations decided to force the Union to change its attitude towards agricultural problems. The United States and the group of fourteen biggest exporters of agricultural products, under the name of Cairns, for a certain time were trying to lower the level of interventionism in the agricultural sector of the EU. At the same time, the final general outcome of the round was to depend on satisfying that demand. The European Union was also lagging with its proposals, concerning trading in agricultural products, behind the U.S. and the Cairns Group. The difference of opinions was difficult to overcome, since the agricultural sector remained the only negotiated sphere in which the proposals of GATT/WTO partners on liberalization could be precisely quantified. That was also a reason why this problem could be so openly discussed (Langhammer 1991).

The disputes, within GATT, between the U.S. and the European Union on agricultural problems, especially on oleiferous seeds, could be, this time, called "the fat war". This conflict was much more serious then previous "trade wars" between the U.S. and the EU. Its solution could, in the future, be very important for the countries of Central and Eastern Europe.

In an effort to limit the EU budget expense for subsidizing agricultural products, it was decided, among other things, that in case of fats, the money would be transferred from the processing sector to the production sector. Instead of compensating the industry for higher costs of purchasing more expensive, local raw materials (the prices paid to the growers of rape or sunflower in the EU are much higher than the world prices), it was decided that subsidies would go directly to farmers, and the size of farms was to be the basis for calculations. At the same time, the Union authorities disclosed that they would be trying to reduce gradually those expenses by reducing guaranteed prices.

The conflicts between the United States and the European Union, arising as a result of the introduction by the EU of new rules in agricultural policy concerning oleiferous plants, caused the U.S. to want to finish the negotiations on subsidizing the agricultural exports, within the Uruguay Round, as quickly as possible. The

U.S. was afraid that they would have to spend more money on subsidizing the exports, if they wanted to compete successfully with the EU on the world market.

This reform was the first in which the attempt was made to eliminate the structural surpluses, the surpluses that had been disorganizing the EU agricultural market and the international trade for many years. It is worth pointing out here that the direct result of announced changes in the agricultural policy of the EU may not be favorable for the countries of Central and Eastern Europe. The simplest form of compensation for farmers is usually the restrictions for the suppliers from abroad. The agricultural lobby in France is especially active in this area. As a result of its activity and the pressure exerted on the government the agricultural goods from abroad have been successfully blocked from the EU market. The position taken by that agricultural lobby influenced also the position of the EU representatives in the debates on the agricultural questions during the multilateral trade negotiations.

In spite of the trade conflicts, most clearly visible in the U.S. - the EU relations, all the countries participating in the international trade were interested in the successful completion of the Uruguay Round. The reduction or the elimination of trade restrictions stimulates significantly the growth of the world trade exchange, while the foreign trade, in turn, is an important factor of the economic growth of individual countries.

Mutual consultations between the representatives of the European Union and the United States resulted, on November 20th 1992, in an agreement (known as Blair House agreement) on the reduction of production of oleiferous plants by the European farmers. Concessions made by both sides prevented a transatlantic trade war. According to the agreement the Union would reduce the subsidies for farmers by 21%, and, during the following years, it will reduce by 36% the subsidies for the exports of agricultural goods. Also the size of the area where oleiferous plants were grown would be reduced, which would reduce their production from 13 million tonnes annually to the maximum of 9.7 million tonnes.

This compromise was considered to be of historical significance. And not only because it helped to avoid a trade war. The success was seen in the resumption of the talks on the international trade liberalization during the Uruguay Round. This Round itself was finished on December 15th 1993, with the agreement on lowering the customs duties for industrial goods by 1/3 on an average, to 3.2%, and with establishing the World Trade Organization (WTO) which was to replace GATT. The agreement on ending the Uruguay Round was ratified by 117 countries on April 15th 1994 in Marrakech, Morocco, and became operative on January 1st of 1995.

There followed a reduction of trade protection in the area of industrial products, further significant reduction of customs tariffs, and decisions to consider important non-tariff barriers - such as Voluntary Exports Restraint Arrangement (VERA) or Multifibre Agreement (MFA) - as illegal. In spite of this success, it is worth noticing that individual countries can still use, for protection purposes, anti-dumping procedures and the mechanism of protection clauses – "safeguards", the rules of which were not significantly changed during the Uruguay Round. Notable successes were reached, however, in the area of agricultural goods and services trading. In case of agricultural goods it was agreed that the reduction of trade protection would result from the reduction of non-tariff measures and from substituting them with customs duties (Martin and Winters, 1995). Thus, there was a renaissance of customs duties, especially in the trade of agricultural products, and once more they became most important for trade protection.

The successful results of negotiations will certainly lead to the growth of the international trade and will help to overcome the development difficulties of the world market participants. The Uruguay Round will bring the growth of the global income by 200 billion dollars annually, starting with 1995. It is estimated that in 2005 the value of the world trade will grow by 230 billion dollars. So, the agreement will result in more investments, more jobs and higher incomes as the function of economic growth. The economic powers will benefit most, however the countries of Central and Eastern Europe, and the developing countries, will get an easier access to new markets for their commodities.

Conflicts Between the Tendencies to International Trade Liberalization and Environmental Protection

The tendencies to liberalize the international trade often stand in clear conflict with the protection of the natural environment that, during the intensification of production, found itself in the center of attention. The process of pollution was one of the negative results of scientific-technological revolution. Many countries introduced special legal regulations in order to protect the environment against pollution. Ecological organizations of different types were established, and also the pressure groups, especially in industrialized countries, interested in the use of trade restrictions by governments for protection of the environment.

The pressure groups acting for natural environment protection see the trade policy in two aspects: as the way of improvement the standards of environmental protection in individual countries and over their borders, and as the instrument for persuading those countries to sign the international agreements on environmental protection. The imports restrictions against the producers coming from the countries with low standards of environmental protection may lead to the improvement of production standards by the local companies resulting from fighting with low competitiveness, and from the attempts to compete with foreign firms (Anderson, 1997).

The application, in trade policy, of discriminating means in relation to the environment, which happened in the countries of Western Europe, is in accordance with the article XX of WTO, and it testifies to the fact that trade barriers are used for the protection of the environment. Thus, the activities related to environmental protection are in conflict with the tendencies leading to international trade liberalization, and with higher investments. From the theoretical point of view, we cannot say that trade liberalization may help the environmental protection, especially when serious steps have to be taken in order to protect this environment against further degradation (Chichilnisky, 1994; Copland and Taylor, 1995;

Corden, 1996). On the other hand, when some government find itself in a difficult situation, the trade reforms will be much more advantageous for that government than the actions in the environmental protection area (Bhagwati and Srinivisan, 1996). That is why the pressure groups connected with the environmental protection are against the international trade liberalization.

The actions of those groups on WTO forum, and their regional activity against the reduction of trade barriers, have three reasons: 1) free trade means the growth of production and income, which, in turn, leads to the degradation of the environment, 2) free trade and growing investments cause the growth of transport activity and encourage companies to transfer the production to the countries with low ecological standards, which from the environmental point of view is wrong, 3) freedom for foreign investments discourage local companies to develop the technologies favorable for environmental protection (Anderson, 1996). The problems of environmental protection, considering their antagonistic nature in relation to the liberalization of international trade, were noticed by GATT/WTO at the beginning of the seventies. A Working Group on Environmental Measures and International Trade was formed. However, its first meeting took place as late as 1991. Since then, the meetings of the group members have been more frequent, and it should be pointed out here that a number of Uruguay Round agreements included the clauses on the environmental protection.

The question of reaching some form of an agreement between the problems of international trade liberalization and the protection of natural environment became an important task for the WTO. Managing the work on trade and environmental protection can be found in a preamble to an agreement on establishing a new trade organization. The program of WTO activities, worked out in the final stage of the Uruguay Round included:

- the relations between the means used in trade and in environmental protection
- the relations between multilateral trade systems and the environmental protection means, applied for protection of the environment
- the influence of the effects of environmental protection on the liberalization of international trade
- the relations between the mechanisms leading to compromises within WTO and within the multilateral agreements on environmental protection (Martin and Winters, 1995).

Reaching the effective agreements on the international trade liberalization and on environmental protection is considered to be both very difficult and very delicate question. The problems of environmental protection have become most important issues. Therefore, it is evident that the international market has to take them into account. The key problem is to make a proper choice: is the introduction of restrictions on international trade the best solution, or will the benefits from environmental protection (as applied by a multilateral trade system) be higher than the costs?

It is necessary also to emphasis that if the rules of international trade are clear – and if they are perceived to be supportive of important environmental values – then their legitimacy will be much greater. Over the long term public support for the WTO depends on a perception that it is balanced and fair (Esty, 1998). Efforts to address the issues identified above could greatly enhance the WTO's reputation. Competing trade and environmental principles could best be balanced through creation of an interpretive statement that focuses on how the "exceptions" spelled out in Article XX would be implemented, rather than through full-blown renegotiation of the environmental elements of the trading system (Esty, 2000).

Finding ways to address the environmental issues that inescapably arise in the context of deeper economic integration must be seen as an important trade policy priority, as a matter of WTO commitment to under girding the trade regime with sound economic theory, and as a matter of political necessity. Building a trading system that is more sensitive to pollution control and natural resources management issues is mandated by the growing degree to which these realms intersect with trade and environmental policies mutually reinforcing are also advisable to the extent that the presence of trade rules that internalize externalities will prove to be more economically efficient over time. Institutionalizing the links from the trade regime to environmental actors and other elements of civil society will also pay dividends. A culture of openness within the WTO is likely to generate policies that the public accepts and that therefore become more useful and durable (Esty, 2000).

In the end of nineties the environmentalists with labor unions and consumer groups will launch a petition demanding a halt to efforts to launch a new round of trade liberalization talks within WTO. It says that Uruguay Round agreements have functioned principally to prise open markets for the benefit of transnational corporations at the expense of national economies; workers, farmers, other consumers and the environment too (Suzman, 1999). The petition urges and end to any effort to expand the powers of the WTO through a new comprehensive round of trade liberalization and calls for a formal review of the international trading system to make it more accountable.

The failure of the Seattle trade ministerial in December 1999 to launch a new round of multilateral trade negotiations dealt a major blow to the WTO. The Seattle meetings exposed significant policy differences among the WTO member countries as well as shortcomings in the way the WTO conducts its business and interacts with other international and nongovernmental organizations (Schott, 2000). The lesson from the Seattle is the need for increased cooperation and coordination among major trading partners (Arai, 2000).

The WTO needs to establish a small, informal steering committee (20 or so in number) that can be delegated responsibility for developing consensus on trade issues among the member countries. Such a group would not undercut existing WTO rights and obligations nor the rule of decision-making by consensus are not advocating proportional or weighted voting. Each member would maintain the ultimate decision to accept or reject such pacts.

Table 8.1. Value of Trade, 1996 (billions of dollars)

	Country	USD (bln)
1	European Union[a] (extra EU)	2.065
2	United States[a]	1.805
3	Japan[a]	914
4	Canada[a]	446
5	Hong Kong, China[a]	369
6	Republic of Korea[a]	331
7	People's Republic of China[b]	326
8	Singapore[a]	299
9	Switzerland[a]	231
10	Mexico[a]	207
11	Malaysia[a]	170
12	Australia[a]	158
13	Thailand[a]	155
14	Brazil[a]	116
15	Norway[a]	113
16	Indonesia[a]	104
17	India[a]	97
18	Turkey	94
19	Poland[a]	78
20	Israel	67
21	South Africa[a]	66
22	Czech Republic[a]	63
23	The Philippines[a]	60
24	Argentina[a]	55
25	Venezuela	40

(a) At present, likely participant in green room. Other likely current participants not shown include Chile ($39 billion), New Zealand ($37 billion), Hungary ($35 Billion), Egypt ($34 billion), Colombia ($32 Billion), and Pakistan ($25 billion).
(b) PRC was included as its accession was imminent.

Source: Compiled from World Bank, World Development Report 1998/99, Balance of Payments Current Account and International Reserves; behind, J.J. Schott and J. Watal, 'Decision Making in the WTO', in J.J.Schott (ed.), *The WTO after Seattle, Institute for International Economics*, Washington DC, 2000, p. 287.

Participation should be representative of the broader membership and based on clear, simple, objective criteria:

- absolute value of foreign trade (exports and imports of goods and services), ranked by country or common customs region, and
- global geographic representation, with at least two participants from all major regions.

A group of countries, based on existing regional arrangements or formed on ad hoc basis, would be encouraged to pool resources and share representation (just as the Nordic countries did for many years during GATT negotiations). In fact, several groups of developing countries have already done so in preparing for the new round (for example, the Mercosur and Caribbean Regional Negotiating Machinery). The formation of groups would be voluntary, each group would be select its representative for a particular meeting from among its membership based on the interests of its members and the expertise of their WTO delegates (Schott and Watal, 2000). The value of trade and global geographic representation would be the two more important chosen criteria of the WTO decision-making. This is both objective and relevant to decision making in the WTO.

The European Union and the New Conditions for Globalization

At the turn of the century, the European Union clearly showed its will to eliminate the trade and investment barriers. This was particularly visible in case of direct foreign investments (DFI). For obvious reasons, this was connected with the introduction, at the beginning of 1999, of the uniform European currency EURO, and with the planned, 4th enlargement of the EU, this time to the East. It was emphasised that the trade liberalization has a special positive significance in the global context (Cohn, 2000). Due to technical progress and to the growth of economic ties between particular countries, participants in the world economy, the benefits resulting from liberalised international trade and from the freedom of movement of direct foreign investments become bigger not only for the industrialised countries but also for the so-called "emerging markets", that is, the countries that find themselves on the stage of the accelerated development, which means also the economies of the Central and Eastern Europe.

At the beginning of this century the exchange of goods between the European Union members and the countries of the Central and Eastern Europe was, to a significant degree, liberalised on the basis of the European Treaties that established the association between the partner countries. In the area of industrial goods exchange these treaties arranged for the creation of the free trade zones, that is, for the elimination of customs and non-tariff restrictions. This purpose has been, to a significant degree, accomplished. The European Union, which, asymmetrically, started the process of liberalization earlier than the countries of Central and Eastern Europe, eliminated, at the beginning of 1998, the last obstacles on the way to its market for the goods from Central and Eastern Europe (these restraints were in the form of quotas and involved some textile and clothing products; the last customs duties were eliminated as early as 1997). The countries of Central and Eastern Europe that practically started to remove the obstacles in the industrial goods imports from the European Union at the beginning of 1995, also significantly opened their own markets. On January 1st, 1999, the last group of customs charges was eliminated (in 1998, an average level of customs duties in the imports of the discussed group of goods did not exceed 2,9 per cent). Customs duties were to remain only for the imports of cars, for which a ten-year long period of liberalization was established. They are being, however, gradually reduced and at the beginning of 2002 will disappear completely.

Although in case of industrial goods trading we have to do with the broadest liberalization, still we cannot declare that the access of the goods from the Central and Eastern Union to the European Union market is completely free, that it can be compared, in this respect, to the rights of the Union member states. There are still certain obstacles resulting from the technological barriers in the area of the natural environment protection, sanitary-hygienic norms, packaging, labelling and marking of merchandise, etc. Also the border controls are in force, since for some products there are still customs duties, while other goods from Central and Eastern Europe have to be checked in order to ensure that they meet the requirements obligatory in the EU market.

On January 1st 2000, the next round on the liberalization of the international trade, especially on trading in agricultural products and in services, was to begin in Seattle, in the United States, this time under the auspices of WTO. Beside the two mentioned areas, it was supposed to cover the classic aspects of the international trade liberalization, such as customs tariffs for industrial products, the problems of public markets and public investments, as well as the general issues of trade, competition and investments. The European Union expressed vivid interest in the new round. In the official Union circles the coming negotiations were described as the "new millennium cycle", which was supposed to emphasise its significance (Cohn, 2000).

In the course of the ministerial session of the WTO members, which was held in the end of November and in the beginning of December 1999, in Seattle (USA), serious protests against the new negotiations on the international trade liberalization, mostly coming from non-governmental, ecological, leftist and anarchic organisations, took place. As a result, on January 1st, the new round of the trade negotiations, called earlier the millennium round, did not start.

It is worth considering what was the root of those protests against the liberalization of trade. One has to notice here that the issues of the free trade exchange are connected with the continuously growing processes of globalisation of the world economy, which has its advocates as well as its opponents. At the same time those globalist and separatist tendencies are, in a sense, linked and they incite each other. It is obvious that the war that is being conducted against any form of dependence, against technology, mass culture and common markets would be impossible without global communication.

It is not easy to find a world centre of antiglobalists. However, one has to observe here that the organisations co-ordinate their actions or, at least, inform one another about them. Internet, the most global medium of all contemporary world media, has become their basic means of communication.

While observing the considerations on the new developmental conditions, one notices that the emphasis is being put on the necessity of adjusting the economic strategies of large concerns to a man and to society, on the necessity of stopping treating them only as consumers. The concurrence of such an attitude with the new social doctrine of the Catholic Church, expressed mainly in the encyclical of John Paul II, "Centesimos annos" is quite striking. Pope John Paul II points out that in order to solve the problems of the contemporary world and to create the proper perspectives for the development of mankind, in the situation of globalisation, the solidarity between people is especially important.

Farmers form one of those social groups that are consistently anti-globalist. In Europe, the French farmers are especially active in that respect. Beside the Peasant Confederation Bove, the Coordination for Citizen Control of the World Trade Organisation (CCCWTO) is particularly radical. Both organisations were active in Seattle and in Davos, and both demand "the imposition of the new, more just concept of the international trade", co-operating at the same time with the leftist groups. The European farmers are supported by the associations of American farmers, owners of those family farms that are not able to cope with the price and productivity competition of so-called agro businesses. In fact, however, what drives the farmers' protests on both sides of the Atlantic is the fear of competition and the fear of the loss of high subsidies as a result of growing, under the auspices of WTO, liberalization in trade exchange and consequently broader opening of markets. This is particularly well seen within the European Union, where the reform of the Common Agricultural Policy, initiated during the Uruguay Round, is taking place (Rowiński, 2000). In consequence, the Common Agricultural Policy is moving in the direction of a bigger liberalization.

In the developing countries the desire to keep, at any price, the existing social relations, lies at the root of the protests against globalisation. In some cases the fundamentalist regimes are ready to do anything, including the destabilisation of their own countries, in order to stop integration and the beginnings of the co-operation with other countries. President of Mexico, Ernesto Zedillo, called the movement of WTO opponents "the opportunistic alliance of the extreme left, the extreme right, the green and the trade unions lobbyists". In his opinion they see their common goal in "saving the developing countries from development"("*Wprost*", February 20, 2000). This is, however, a simplification which is going too far and which has been provoked by the noisy actions of extremists. In fact, just that type of noisy groups makes the objective debate on real problems of globalisation very difficult. The non-governmental organisations, possessing well worked out techniques of lobbying, express their discontentment with that situation.

Globalisation, being an objective and all the time more and more universal phenomenon, should not develop in a spontaneous way. The financial crises that took place at the end of the nineties, especially in the new industrialised countries of the Far East, confirm that opinion. Therefore, the control over the transnational corporations is necessary, especially the control carried on by such international organisations as WTO and International Monetary Fund.

The education of less educated societies is very important in the context of the globalisation process development. The experience shows that the trans-national corporations are much more effective in the countries with a better educated population. This was especially clear when the comparisons of effectiveness were made between the countries of the Far East and of Africa. It turned out that the results achieved in Africa, that is, in the countries with the weakest education in the world, were much lower than in the Far East. Consequently, one can form a conclusion that the foreign capital, especially of international character, is not inclined to invest in the countries with low level of education. In the globalisation situation, education - along with capital, land, organisation, management, and a human factor - is becoming a very important factor of the economic growth.

After the terrorist attacks on the World Trade Center in New York and on the Pentagon in Washington the question arose: how will these attacks influence the perspectives of globalisation? In most general terms, this question may be answered by the statement saying that the actions directed against terrorism will slow down globalisation and make it more costly (*"Business Week"*, October 22, 2001). It will be so because the terrorist threat will certainly result in bigger sums spent on all kinds of safety precautions. This is especially true in case of the safety of the managing staff of foreign firms, and in case of the free flow of people and goods that may decrease and ultimately influence the efficiency of the economic activity. Since the cost of the investment capital will be high, the return to the high levels of investments from the period of economic boom will be very difficult. In short, the golden years of American prosperity and of its influence on global economic growth passed their zenith on September 11th, 2001.

Table 8.2. Deepening of the already slower economic growth before and after September 11th 2001

	USA		Europe		Japan		Latin America		Asia without Japan	
Estimated GDP	2001	2002	2001	2002	2001	2002	2001	2002	2001	2002
Before Sept. 11	1.3	2.7	1.8	2.5	-0.8	0.2	1.3	3.3	4.5	5.8
After Sept. 11	0.9	1.0	1.6	1.5	-0.9	-1.0	0.7	0.7	3.6	4.5

Source: Business Week, October 22, 2001, p. 23.

Before September 11th 2001, the liberalization tendencies involving the flow of goods, services, capital and labour force helped the development of global trade and global investments, while the elimination of barriers influenced, in a beneficial way, the economic growth in the second half of the previous decade. The open global market stimulated the fast growth of the international trade, which increased from 18% in 1990 to 26% in the year 2000 ("*Business Week*", October 22, 2001). The globalisation stimulated the development of the investment capital, of technologies and enterprising Low prices for consumers' goods were helping entrepreneurs to increase productivity, creating supply effects similar to those that appeared after the introduction of silicon to Silicon Valley in the United States.

The new conditions for globalisation certainly will not bring about the disappearance of the world markets, the markets that are already quite well integrated. Nevertheless, the effects of the economic growth model, the one with high productivity and low inflation, characteristic for the nineties, will weaken. This will be caused by the fact that many firms will be forced to cover higher costs concerning the insurance and safety precautions for their overseas staff. Thorough border controls may seriously slow down international transport, at the same time forcing the firms to implement all kinds of stock taking ("*Business Week*", October 22, 2001). Also there may arise the fears of higher political risk, which might significantly narrow the new investment horizons for the firms. What previously caused the fast expansion of international trade and of capital flow may presently become substantially weaker, since the situation created conditions for raising obstacles and barriers that might cause real tectonic changes in the global economic landscape.

In this situation, the actions of the World Trade Organisation are important. The fundamental purpose of the summit that started on November 9th, 2001 in Doha, the capital of Qatar, was to organise the new global round of negotiations on further development of international trade in the situation of the existing and future border obstacles. After the terrorist attacks, the biggest trade powers showed lots of determination in starting the negotiation for the first time within the WTO framework.

It should be emphasised that in the nineties the situation for open trade was ideal. However, at the beginning of the twenty first century it was safety that has become paramount. It has become the fundamental problem and future global prosperity depends on it. After six days of negotiations, the member countries of WTO reached an agreement. The representatives of 144 countries, together with China, which joined WTO on November 10th 2001, and with Taiwan, accepted one day later, on November 11th, as China-Taipei, passed a declaration about starting a new, ninth round of trade negotiations on the liberalization of international trade. The success of the talks was an important matter for WTO. If the new round on lifting the restrictions on the international exchange could not start, it would mean that WTO would not function as a forum for world trade.

Conclusion

International trade has been strongly affected by the forces of globalization. The changes are evident in the growing importance of international trade to national economies and to domestic groups within those economies, in the closer linkages between trade and other international issues, and in the increased membership of countries in WTO (Cohn, 2001). International firms have a major stake in an open trading system today because of their reliance on multinational operations, exports, imports and intrafirm trade. The WTO today is addressing a wide range of nontrade issues such as foreign investment, intellectual property, labor standards, and the environment, which have become closely intertwined with trade issues. Foreign direct investment and trade, for example, are highly complementary because about one-third of trade today is conducted among affiliates of international firms (Cohn 2001).

Both liberals and realists point to important trends in the global trade regime. On the one hand, trade interdependence has been increasing, and there are strong pressures for further trade liberalization. On the other hand, this growing interdependence and the decline of U.S. trade hegemony have led to increased competitiveness and greater temptations to resort to strategic trade policy. Nevertheless, if one considers the role of domestic and transnational (i.e., nongovernmental) actors today, it would seem that the forces for trade liberalization are inexorable. These internationalist firms have played a major role in pressing for trade liberalization at both the global and regional levels (Cohn, 2001).

At the end of 2001 the WTO countries sent a strong signal to the world economy meaning that the long lasting impasse on the new trade negotiations was finally overcome. Agreeing to a new round of negotiations, the representatives of the member countries let it be understood that they support economic growth all over the world. At the same time, everybody was aware that it was only the beginning of a long process of eliminating the barriers to international trade, as well as the new barriers that appeared after September 11th, 2001. One can assume, however, that the new round of negotiations on the liberalization of international trade will last at least several years and it will take time before its effects will be clearly visible.

References

Anderson, K. (1997), 'Environmental Standards and International Trade', in *Annual World Bank Conference on Development Economics 1996*, M. Bruno and B. Pleskovic, (eds), The World Bank, Washington D.C., January, p. 319.

Appolon, D., O.-B. Fure and L. Svasand, (2000), 'Approaching a new millennium. Lesson from the Past – Prospects for the Future', Bergen (Norway).

Arai, H.(2000), 'Some Reflections on the Seattle Ministerial: Toward the Relaunching of a New Round', in J.J. Schott (ed.), *The WTO after Seattle*, Washington, DC.

Institute for International Economics, p. 64.
Banerji, A. and H. Ghanem, (1997), 'Does the Type of Political Regime Matter for Trade and Labor Market Policies?', *The World Bank Economic Review*, Volume 11, January, No 1, p. 173.
Bhagwati, J.N. and T. N. Srinivisar, (1996), ' Trade and the Environment: Does Environmental Diversity Detract from the Case for Free Trade' in J. N. Bhagwati and R. E. Hudec, (eds.), *Fair Trade and Harmonization: Prerequisites for Free Trade?* Cambridge, Mass.: M IT Press.
Blackhurst, R. N. Marian, J. Tumlir, (1977), 'Trade Liberalization, Protectionism and Interdependence', *GATT Studies in International Trade*, Geneva, No 5. Burenstam - Linder, S.(1980), 'How to avoid a New International Economic Disorder', *World Economy*, November, No. 3, vol. 3.
Business Week, (2001), October 22.
Chichilnisky, G.(1994), 'North South Trade and the Global Environment', *American Economic Review* 84 (4), pp. 851-874.
Cohn, T.H. (2000), 'Global Political Economy. Theory and Practice', New York., pp. 214 - 217.
Copland, B.R. and M. S. Taylor, (1995), 'Trade and Transboundary Pollution', *American Economic Review* 85 (4), pp. 716–737.
Corden, W.M. (1996), 'The Environment and Trade Policy', in W. M. Corden, (ed.), *Trade Policy and Economic Welfare*, Oxford: Clarendon Press.
Devarajan, S., H. Ghanem, K. Thierfelder, (1997), 'Economic Reform and Labor Unions: A General Equilibrium Analysis Applied to Bangladesh and Indonesia', *The World Bank Economic Review*, Volume 11, January, No 1, pp. 145-170.
Drozdowicz, Z., Z.W. Puślecki , (eds.), (2000), 'Przezwyciężanie barier w integrującej się Europie', Poznań.
Drucker, P.F. (1986), 'The Changed World Economy', *Foreign Affairs*, (Springs)
Dunkel, A.(1986), Das GATT - Hüter des globalen Wettbewerbs, Die Herausforderung an die Uruguay – Runde', *Neue Zürcher Zeitung*, 1987. 10. 31., No. 352, GATT - Information, 1393, Geneva.
Esty, D.C. (1998), *NGOs at the World Trade Organization*: Cooperation, Competition, or Exclusion, Journal of International Economic Law 1, no.1: 123.
Esty, D.C., (2000), 'Environment and the Trading System: Picking up the Post-Seattle Pieces', in J.J. Schott (ed.), *The WTO after Seattle*, Washington, DC. Institute for International Economics, pp. 250-251.
Fields, G. (1994), 'Changing Labor Market Conditions and Economic Development in Hong Kong, Singapore and Taiwan', Cornell University, Ithaca, New York, Processed.
Freeman, R. (1993), 'Does Suppression of Labor Contribute to Economic Success? Labor Relations and Markets in East Asia', Harvard University. Cambridge, Mass. and London School of Economics, London. Processed.
Giersch, H. (1984), 'Euro sclerosis, the Malaise that Threatens Prosperity', *Financial Times* from January 8.
Goldstein, J.S. (2001),'International Relations'. Fourth edition, New York.
Gray, H.P. (1983), 'A Negotiating Strategy for Trade in Services', *Journal of World Trade Law* No 5, p. 383.
Grossman, G. and E. Helpman, (1994), 'Protection for Sale', *American Economic Review* 84 (4), pp. 833-850.
Helliwel, J.F. (1992), 'Empirical Linkages between Democracy and Economic Growth',

Working Paper 4066. National Bureau of Economic Research, Cambridge, Mass. Processed.

Hsieh, C. (1973), 'Measuring the Effects of Trade Expansion on Employment', A Review of some Research, *International Labor Review*, January.

Kaweck-Wyrzykowska, E. (1983), 'Protekcjonizm w polityce handlowej Stanów Zjednoczonych', Warsaw.

Langhammer, R.J. (1991), Nachsetzen der Uruguay - Runde: zu viele Streitpunkte zu wenig Ergebnisse', Institut für Weltwirtschaft, Kiel, p. 7.

Martin, W. and L.A. Winters, (1995), 'The Uruguay Round: Widening and Deepening the World Trading Systems', *World Bank Policy Research, Bulletin,* November – December Volume 6, No 5, pp. 1, 3.

Puślecki, Z.W. (2000), 'The Central and Eastern European Countries between Integration with European Union and Globalization of the Processes of Economic Development', in D. Appolon, O.-B.Fure and L.Svasand, *Approaching a new millenium. Lesson from the Past – Prospects for the Future,* Bergen (Norway).

Puślecki, Z.W. (1994), 'Ochrona handlowa Wspólnoty Europejskiej', Poznań, p. 161.

Puślecki, Z.W. (2001), System środków kontroli handlowej Unii Europejskiej w warunkach globalizacji, Poznań.

Puślecki, Z.W., (2000), Usuwanie barier w handlu międzynarodowym integrującej się Europy a presje protekcjonistyczne, in Z. Drozdowicz, Z.W. Puślecki, (eds.), *Przezwyciężanie barier w integrującej się Europie*, Poznań, pp. 153-187.

Rowiński, J. (2000), 'Wspólna Polityka Rolna Unii Europejskiej', Instytut Ekonomii Rolnictwa i Gospodarki Żywnościowej. Warsaw, pp. 3-14.

Schott, J.J.(ed.), (2000), 'The WTO after Seattle', Washington, DC. Institut for International Economics.

Schott, J.J. and J. Watal. (2000), 'Decision making in the WTO', in J.J. Schott, (ed.), *The WTO after Seattle,* Washington, DC. Institute for International Economics, pp. 287-292.

Stonehouse, G., J. Hamill, D. Campbell, T. Purdie, (2000), 'Global and Transnational Business. Strategy and Management', Chichester, New York, Weinheim, Brisbane, Toronto, Singapore.

Suzman, M. (1999), 'Coalition in drive to stop trade talks', *Financial Times,* September 15, p. 5.

Chapter 9

Critiquing Traditional Responses to Cocaine and Heroin Trafficking

Joseph E. Vorbach III[1]

Introduction

The elevation of transnational problems like drug trafficking to the status of 'security threat' in national and international policy making circles has been a double-edged sword for governments. Raising the rhetoric has helped to increase awareness of the manner in which the security environment has been transformed, but, at the same time, it has virtually ensured that government responses will be contained largely within state-centric frameworks reserved particularly for "security" challenges. This begs the question of whether or not strictly state-centric approaches to transnational threats are inherently flawed. To explore that question in the context of a specific transnational threat, this chapter analyzes state-centric, U.S.-led responses to cocaine and heroin trafficking. In the United States, the goal of counter-trafficking strategies has been to reduce the availability of the drugs. Success in those endeavors has been measured typically by monitoring price and availability in U.S. illegal drug markets. If the overall effort of governments in the face of the trafficking of illegal drugs had been successful, then the substances would be less available and more expensive in the United States. The available data suggests that the opposite is true.

The Commission on Narcotic Drugs (CND) of the United Nations Economic and Social Council (ECOSOC) reported in late 1999 that 'Despite wide price ranges between different communities, markets and countries in the United States and Western Europe, the average price of cocaine and heroin, at both wholesale and retail levels, has declined in recent years'.[2] Further, The National Narcotics Intelligence Consumers Committee Report (NNICCR) of 1997, an interagency report published by the U. S. Drug Enforcement Administration (DEA), reported that 'the nationwide average purity for retail heroin from all sources was 38.5%, much higher than the average of seven percent reported a decade ago'.[3] This data from the late 1990s is even more discouraging when aligned with official reporting on the lack of success of counter-drug efforts from from earlier in the decade. In 1991, the General Accounting Office was reporting that U. S. intelligence agencies saw no decline in the volume of drugs entering the United States, despite the expenditure of $2.7 billion that year.[4] Having expended $13 billion cumulatively through 1991, there was no indication to that point that the amount of cocaine available in the United States had been reduced.[5] Things were bad in the early 1990s after more than a decade of investing in the drug war and there is little or no evidence that the situation has improved ten years later.

At the same time, the current expenditure by the United States alone of $16 billion annually in the 'War on Drugs' has contributed to the evolution of some unintended negative consequences. As the recent history is unfolded in this paper, two of those harmful outcomes rise clearly to the surface:

- the tendency of the state-centric response merely to displace rather than eradicate the drug trafficking challenge, and
- the tendency of state-centric approaches to militarize societies as they pursue drug traffickers.

Consideration of the first point includes the displacement of illegal drug crops within the geographical confines of one producer nation, displacement from one source country to another, displacement of trafficking patterns by the smugglers in response to law enforcement, and displacement of non-commercial smuggling efforts into legitimate commercial cargoes, also in response to law enforcement. Evaluating the second tendency reveals harmful effects on civil society that have manifested themselves in Peru, Colombia and Burma when the armed forces have taken prominent roles in the counter- trafficking effort.

This chapter begins to build the case for new responses to transnational threats to security that move beyond state-centric models by evaluating the recent history of U.S. and international responses to the challenges posed by the illegal smuggling of cocaine and heroin. It documents the limits of attacking a transnational threat with largely state centric models. Further, it highlights the patterned emergence of unintended consequences in the wake of these state centric approaches, a costly phenomenon that bolsters the argument for new approaches to the problem.

Cocaine

While the United States has long advocated strict source country controls over the raw materials used to manufacture illicit narcotics, its heightened interest in coca production in South America began in the 1970s when dynamics in the market for illegally smuggled marijuana changed and cocaine trafficking became more attractive to the bold and increasingly influential Colombian cartels. Jamaican and Mexican crack-downs on marijuana contributed to the development of Colombian drug cartels that filled voids in the marijuana market in the late 1960s and then shifted to cocaine in the early 1970s.[6] On the supply side, cocaine could be concealed more easily, was less perishable, and provided more profit by volume. On the demand side, it has been suggested that a number of variables contributed to the shift toward cocaine consumption in the United States. These include: the fact that cocaine did not have to be smoked or injected, the fact that early reports suggested that the drug was less addictive than other options, and, finally, the fact that lawmakers in the United States were placing greater emphasis on controlling amphetamines and synthetic drugs.[7]

The United States has since at least 1911 pursued policies with respect to cocaine that emphasize tight controls in source countries.[8] For a number of reasons, however, serious efforts by the United States to address the production of coca in South America were not undertaken until the Nixon Administration.[9] While the 'Special Action Office' created in the White House worked 'to coordinate research, treatment and educational efforts,' it was politically prudent to identify the international supply of illicit narcotics as the most serious aspect of the problem.[10] This tendency to look beyond U.S. borders for solutions was operationalized in two important ways—crop eradication efforts in source countries and counter-trafficking efforts in what have been referred to as the "transit zones".

Source Country Coca Crop Eradication in South America

Peru At the moment in mid-2001, the majority of coca leaf available for processing into cocaine-HCl is being grown in Colombia, but this is a relatively recent development. For at least 20 years from the late 1970s through the late 1990s, most coca leaf was grown in Peru and Bolivia and that is where U.S. crop eradication efforts were directed. In 1981 in Peru, the government, working with the United States, began to eradicate forcibly all unregistered or illegal coca and by 1986, the annual level of U.S. support for both positive (crop substitution) and negative (law enforcement) efforts was more than $23 million.[11] There was no evidence by this time, however, that the joint Peruvian/U.S. effort, which included voluntary and compulsory eradication efforts, crop substitution incentives, and tougher enforcement of drug laws, was having any effect. Of the 60,000 hectares of coca planted in the Upper Huallaga Valley in 1986, only 12,000 were eradicated, and this figure was rendered less significant by the fact that peasants began growing coca in even more remote areas in the Valley.[12]

Efforts by Peru and the United States to deal with coca production in the Upper Huallaga Valley (UHV) were complicated by the presence and influence of the Marxist revolutionary movement 'Sendero Luminoso' (Shining Path)[13] in the same remote region of the country. Heavy handed eradication efforts balanced poorly by ineffectual crop substitution plans drove peasants naturally toward alternative sources of protection and support. The general in charge of the counter-insurgency effort against Sendero in the UHV from spring until Christmas of 1989, Brigadier General Alberto Arciniega Huby, commented 'If we repress 50,000 coca farmers, we create 50,000 recruits or collaborators for Sendero'.[4] This perspective informed Arciniega's approach to the counter-insurgency effort when he arrived in the UHV in the wake of a bloody battle between Sendero forces and local police, one that had ended ignominiously for the police when their base at Uchiza was captured by the insurgents. A week after he arrived, he prevented the reestablishment of the police base at Uchiza because the local peasants claimed the police were harassing them.[15]

As he carried out his counter-insurgency effort through the summer of 1989, Arciniega relied upon the financial support of the local economy to finance his military operations, support that was derived from drug trafficking revenues. For this reason, he was closely scrutinized by the Peruvian police (who received the bulk of U.S. counter-drug assistance to Peru) and the U. S. government. Before he had served a full year in his post, he was reassigned to Lima. This despite a successful counter-insurgency campaign that included, in November of 1989, an Armed Forces Day ceremony in the same square in Uchiza where Sendero had routed the police a year earlier.[16]

General Arciniega's dilemma[17] highlights the difficulty of confronting the corrosive challenge of narco trafficking in a country that lacks well-established institutions for state control on a number of levels. The military had no hope of containing the insurgency if it simultaneously pursued a campaign against the traffickers and their coca plants. The military and the police in Peru worked at cross purposes with the result being a militarization of society without a demonstrable reduction in either the level of success of the insurgency or the amount of coca produced. The U.S., which was assisting Peru in its responses to both challenges, but which took a greater interest in the drug problem because of its domestic effects in the U.S., contributed to this militarization.

Up until late 1993, the combination of Sendero Luminoso and the drug traffickers continued to present the Peruvian government and the United States with a substantial challenge. The Upper Hualaga Valley remained a relatively ungovernable region of Peru and the Marxist rebel group was, in the early 1990s, able to restrict the mobility of Peruvian drug control officers by forcing them to operate only out of so-called 'secure bases'.[18] The leader of Sendero, Amibael Guzmán, was captured by the government in 1992 and on 5 April of that year, President Alberto Fujimori suspended constitutional democracy in the country. The crippling of the command structure of Sendero in the 1993-94 time period explains in part some significant reductions in coca leaf production that were accomplished at that time, although 'aging plants and a destructive fungus'[19] also contributed. Further dramatic reductions, to be revisited in greater detail below, can be attributed to greater success with eradication and alternative development efforts in the UHV after the elimination of the insurgent threat. A linchpin of the efforts undertaken between 1995 and 2000 has been the 'air bridge denial' program which focuses on making air smuggling of coca and coca base out of Peru more difficult. Success in this area creates a glut of raw coca in Peru, lowering prices and making alternative licit crops more attractive. A review of the State Department's International Narcotics Control Strategy Reports from 1996-2000 reveals the U.S. government's belief that this particular program has yielded positive results in recent years.[20]

Bolivia In Bolivia, U.S. efforts in the 1980s to coordinate aggressive crop eradication with the national government were substantial. With the concurrence of then President Paz Estenssoro (but without the necessary pre-approval of the Bolivian Chamber of Deputies),[21] the United States initiated operation Blast

Furnace in 1986, an effort to destroy the by then growing number (possibly as many as 5,000) coca paste production laboratories in the country. It was believed that eliminating the labs would reduce the in-country demand for coca leaf, deflate the value of the raw material, and thus cause farmers to turn away from growing it. This effort was to be buttressed by USAID alternative crop programs.

In the short term, the effort succeeded in causing the 'temporary shutdown of most, if not all of the laboratories', which caused the price of coca leaves to drop to between $14 and $25 per hundred weight, well below the estimated $30 believed necessary to make a profit.[22] The problem, however, was that the operation was not continued through a dry season that ended in October of 1986 and into the rainy season that would last through the middle of 1987, an oversight that allowed traffickers to regroup and prevented USAID efforts from taking hold.[23] Thus, the introduction of a significant U.S. presence into Bolivia, while producing the desired results in the short term, did not eliminate the ability of traffickers to acquire and process coca leaf over the longer term.

Still, perhaps buoyed by the evidence that the problem could be eradicated through a sufficient application of force, the United States continued to press the Bolivian government. An important bilateral agreement signed in February of 1987 tied U.S. aid to progress on crop substitution.[24] Also in 1987, the U. S. began a program known as 'Operation Snow Cap' that involved Drug Enforcement Administration (DEA) officers, the U. S. Border Patrol, U. S. Navy Seals, and U. S. Coast Guard maritime law enforcement experts performing missions in Bolivia.[25] The U. S. presence in the country was increasing and the Bolivian government under President Paz Zamora after 1989, committed itself to using the armed forces in the fight against coca growing and processing in the country despite substantial domestic protests.[26] Notwithstanding the significant effort, the results were unremarkable. Between 1987 and 1991, Bolivian farmers voluntarily eradicated more than 18,000 hectares of coca in response to cash incentives provided by the government. At the same time however, they planted more than 26,000 new hectares in different areas of the country.[27]

In summary, U. S./Bolivian efforts to control coca production and processing in Bolivia up through the early 1990s were relatively unsuccessful. The summary data provided later in this paper illustrates clearly that the production of coca in Bolivia changed very little (increasingly slightly) between 1992 and 1996. Dramatic reductions have been achieved since 1997, the year of the election of President Hugo Banzer,[28] but they must be understood within the regional context of massive cultivation increases in Colombia (see table 1.1).

Colombia Throughout the 1980s, Colombia was the place where Peruvian and Bolivian coca was transported for processing and preparation for shipment. Colombian cartel leaders coordinated regional networks that responded to demand in the United States and Western Europe. While the country accounted for only 10-15% of the global coca leaf production at the beginning of the 1990s, 'at least 70% of the cocaine sold in international markets originated from refineries in Colombia' at that time.[29] Several important factors help to explain the dramatic increase in the amount of coca leaf produced in Colombia over the past decade, particularly in the past five years.

First, the Peruvian government's successful containment of the Sendero Luminoso movement allowed it to focus attention on reducing the amount of coca leaf grown in the Upper Hualaga Valley. This development led to a dramatic reduction in the amount of Peruvian coca available for processing and placed pressure on trafficking groups to develop new sources of supply.

Second, President Hugo Banzer's government in Bolivia wed itself closely to the United States' source country crop eradication strategies and has been successful in substantially curtailing coca leaf production in that country.

Third, the guerilla movements FARC (Fuerzas Armadas Revolucionarias de Colombia) and ELN (Ejército de Liberación Nacional) have increased the geographic area within Colombia outside the control of the central government. In those areas, the revolutionary guerillas and drug trafficking organizations, alone and in concert, have dramatically increased the amount of coca leaf produced inside Colombia.[30]

Fourth, the paramilitary organizations, principally the United Self-Defense Forces of Colombia [AUC], that have formed in Colombia to counter the FARC and ELN have seen fit, despite the obvious inconsistency of the policy, to fund their counter-revolutionary efforts with drug money.[31] This development helps fuel the production of the coca leaf.

All of these variables help to explain the current reality—a more than 50% increase in the amount of coca leaf being produced in Colombia between 1996 and 2000.[32] Table 9.1 illustrates effectively the magnitude of the regional shift.

Table 9.1 Estimated net cultivation of coca leaf in hectares

Year	Peru	Bolivia	Colombia	Total	Total
1992	129,100 (after no eradication)	45,500 (after 3,152 eradicated)	37,100 (after 959 eradicated	211,700	4,111
1996	94,400 (after 1259 eradicated)	48,100 (after 7,512 eradicated)	67,200 (after 5,600 eradicated)	209,700	14,371
2000	34,100 (after 6,200 eradicated)	14,600 (after 7,653 eradicated)	136,200 (after 47,000 eradicated)	184,900	60,853

Source: extracted from estimates in U.S. State Department International Narcotics Control Strategy Report 2000 (accessed 10 March 2001); available from http://www.state.gov/g/inl.

While the estimates indicate that there has been an overall 12% reduction in the amount of raw coca available for processing in South America, that decrease was only possible at the cost of having to eradicate over 47,000 hectares in Colombia.

Further, the data on Colombia provide at least a snapshot of how troubling the situation is in that country.

While the United States has been interested in drug-related developments in Colombia for more than three decades, policy makers have shown renewed interest over the past 18 months as the magnitude of the challenge posed by the Marxist rebels and drug traffickers has been made clear. In the summer of 2000, the United States committed $1.3 billion to support Colombian President Pastrana's 'Plan Colombia.' The U.S. aid includes $1 billion earmarked for the delivery of 18 HH-60 "Black Hawk" helicopters and 42 'Huey' helicopters as well as the training needed to properly man them.[33] The focus of the renewed effort being supported by the U. S. is in the Putamayo region of Southern Colombia where a good deal of the illegal coca crop is cultivated and where armed insurgents are operating.

The links between the drug trade and the insurgents in Colombia, combined with the intense scrutiny that the Colombian government's counter-drug efforts receive in the United States, have meant a growing intensification of the Colombian military's involvement in the counter-drug arena. Worse, where the government has been unable to establish order in the face of the revolutionary challenge posed by the FARC and the FLN, paramilitary groups have emerged to provide security for those who can afford it, and/or to establish order using anti-democratic means. These groups, symbolic of the state's failure to ensure law and order, will make it that much harder for the current Colombian government to eradicate the challenges to its legitimacy. One Colombian scholar of the civil war believes that increasing support for the right wing paramilitary groups is likely in a society seeking relief from an unstable status quo.[34]

Nevertheless, the Colombian government has relatively few choices and the United States, for both immediate and long-term reasons, wants its effort to restore order and security to be successful. Thus, the struggle to deal with an internal conflict, one that has already elicited an intense reaction from the coercive arm of the sovereign government, will undergo a further intensification with the support of other interested actors in the hemisphere. For the insurgents and drug traffickers being confronted by this intensification, one option offering temporary refuge is to move out of Colombia. Anticipating that possibility, Brazil has deployed a force along its common border with Colombia to guard against southerly incursions of guerillas or traffickers.[35] Ecuador has already experienced a change in the nature of border interaction with Colombia since the quasi-civil war there has intensified in recent months. In the border town of Lago Agrio, Ecuador, it is reported that right-wing paramilitary fighters and leftist guerilllas on leave from the fighting in Colombia are routinely killing one another in street fighting.[36] It has been suggested that from, 'Panama to Bolivia, governments and armies are girding for the worst by strengthening their defense forces in every way they can'.[37]

Interdicting Smuggled Cocaine in the Americas

When cocaine became the product of choice for the then nascent Colombian drug cartels beginning in the mid-1970s, the trafficking methods employed were relatively unsophisticated and it is reported that some of the biggest cartel names of the 1980s personally carried amounts of cocaine to the United States.[38] Later, when U.S. demand increased, the traffickers began to employ large airplanes and a whole range of waterborne craft with secret compartments. For law enforcement officials, rising demand and greater organizational sophistication in the cartels meant growing challenges. But, as documented above, the U.S.-led counter-trafficking effort was substantial and included initially a significant effort to identify and intercept vessels and aircraft transiting north from Colombia toward the United States.

Within the Caribbean region during the 1980s and into the 1990s, traffickers and law enforcement officials played a game of cat and mouse that had the traffickers constantly adjusting air and sea routes. In the maritime realm, the traffickers would attempt nearly due-north transits toward Florida, or adjust to the east or west based on their perceived understanding of the law enforcement presence at the time. Some illegal transits ventured to the east of the Antilles islands while others chose to skirt the Central American and Mexican coasts on their way north. In support of air trafficking, smugglers bribed officials in Cuba[39] and Haiti to secure necessary landing and overflight rights. They made airdrops along the coast of Hispaniola and throughout the Bahamas.[40]

For the past 15 years, and particularly since 1989 when the Department of Defense has been engaged more directly in the counter-drug effort by providing assets to detect and monitor suspected drug traffickers, the United States has led an aggressive effort to prevent drug trafficking through the Caribbean. It was for this reason primarily that the traffickers began to look for alternate smuggling routes during the 1990s, a decision that has led to Mexico's emergence as the primary transshipment point for South American cocaine destined for the illegal U.S. market—an estimated 55% of the cocaine sold in the U.S. transits through Mexico.[41] It is alleged that a Mexican trafficker like Juan Carlos Abrego could command a payment of 40-50% of a cocaine shipment for providing transshipment service of Colombian cocaine through Mexico.[42] Within Mexico, this development has had far reaching effects, including the expenditure by trafficking organizations of more than $500 million in bribery money annually, a figure that exceeds the budget of the Mexican Attorney-General's office.[43] From the U. S. perspective, the challenge of interdicting Colombian cocaine has become more complex both practically and diplomatically.

Understanding the potential flow of cocaine across the nation's southwest border requires reliable intelligence about the volume of cocaine being transported from Colombia into Mexico by air, by sea, and over land. Further, the effort demands effective binational engagement with Mexico with respect to Mexican criminal organizations and their border activities. Drug trafficking has long been a particularly challenging issue in the complex relationship between the United States and Mexico. In September of 1969, the Nixon Administration launched 'Operation Intercept' and searched every person and vehicle crossing the border from Mexico. This brought cross-border commerce to a standstill and caused a temporary but serious deterioration in U.S./Mexican relations over the course of the seventeen days that the operation ran.[44] The flow of Mexican marijuana and heroin trafficked across the southwest border that continued throughout the 1970s and 1980s kept the drug issue at the forefront of the bilateral relationship.

In February of 1985, the tenuous nature of the relationship was fully exposed when an U.S. DEA agent, Enrique Camarena, was kidnapped, tortured and murdered in Mexico. In January of the following year, elements of the U.S. DEA, looking for justice, took matters into their own hands by sponsoring "the kidnapping of René Verdugo Urquídez to U.S. territory for his alleged involvement in the assassination of Camarena".[45] Within two weeks of the Camarena murder, the U.S. implemented what became known as Operation Intercept II, an intensification of border inspections that mirrored the 1969 effort. In April of 1990, the DEA sponsored the kidnapping to the U.S. of a second Mexican citizen believed to be involved in the Camarena murder, Dr. Humberto Alvarez Macháin. In the wake of this kidnapping, a Mexican magazine, presumably with information provided by someone inside the Mexican government, published the list of DEA agents present in Mexico at that time.[46] All of these developments related to the Camarena murder highlight the extent to which the drug trafficking problem has the potential to infect the bilateral relationship between the U.S. and Mexico.

The fallout from the Camarena murder did not change the sense that vigilance in the face of the drug trafficker's efforts was imperative. While Mexican frustration with perceived U.S. inattention to demand reduction efforts at home and U.S. law enforcement consternation with the corrosive effects of corruption in Mexico both remain, bilateral cooperation on drug control continues as an important component of the cross-border relationship. The geographic realities of a 2000 mile-long border, one that has been growing ever more open since early 1993 with the implementation of the North American Free Trade Agreement (NAFTA), make this imperative. During fiscal year 2000 (October 1999 through October 2000), 293 million people, 89 million cars, 4.5 million trucks and 572,583 rail cars crossed the southwest border.[47]

In the face of these volumes, the United States responds with as many of its 20,000 customs agents as it can afford to divert from other areas. But when one considers the magnitude of the border control challenge in the southwest and elsewhere, it becomes apparent quickly that there are limits to what can be accomplished by governments alone. Former Director of National Drug Control Policy Barry McCaffrey asserted in testimony in the fall of 1998 that 1.09 million of the 3.5 million trucks crossing the Southwest border in 1997 were inspected by U.S. law enforcement officials.[48] The result of these inspections was the discovery of 16 trucks with cocaine in them.[49]

It has been reported that it takes five inspectors three hours to conduct a thorough inspection of one 40-foot shipping container.[50] Using that estimate, one can analyze truck activity at the busy Otay Mesa border crossing near San Diego, CA. There, 2500 trucks enter the U.S. (on average) each day. There are presently a total of 68 Customs agents available to deal with that volume from 6:00 AM to 6:00 PM each day. Even if all 68 agents were available to work 12 hours each day, only 56 of the 2500 trucks could be thoroughly inspected each day (or a mere 2%

of the volume).[51] When one considers that it takes only 13 truckloads of cocaine to satisfy U.S. demand for one year,[52] the magnitude of the border control challenge is clarified even more.

In 1997, the U.S. interdiction focus was the southwest border, but by 1998, General McCaffrey and others were hedging, mindful of indicators that traffickers had shifted back to the Caribbean or were exploiting the Eastern Pacific maritime route. In September of 1998, McCaffrey cautioned Senators:

> We cannot leave the Caribbean unguarded. We have a major initiative going on there. However, the raw interdiction dollars had to follow the threat [to Mexico].[53]

When McAfferey was in Mexico City in February of 2000, his public statements warned that 'They're switching back. There's a lot more now showing up in the Haiti, Dom Rep (Dominican Republic), Jamaica axis. Haiti is the problem'.[54] While he was meeting with Mexican counterdrug officials, U.S. enforcement agents in Miami seized 198 pounds of cocaine found aboard a Haitian freighter, a catch that they would add to the over 3,000 pounds of cocaine that were seized aboard Haitian vessels in the two weeks before McCaffrey's Mexico trip.[55]

In the Pacific, maritime seizure statistics have gone up dramatically between 1999 and 2001, suggesting a current effort by traffickers to exploit that vast maritime domain. In the fiscal year from October 1999 through October 2000, the U.S. Coast Guard seized 126,000 pounds of cocaine and 80% of it was found in the Eastern Pacific, a figure that is up from 38% of the total in 1999.[56] Some of the seizures have been dramatic: 10.5 tons (the second largest maritime seizure in history) found on a fishing vessel off the Mexican coast in late September 1999,[57] 2.6 tons off the coast of Acapulco in December of 1999,[58] 8.8 tons found on another fishing vessel off of Mexico on March 4, 2001,[59] 1.5 tons tossed from a go-fast boat 200 miles off the west coast of Colombia on May 9, 2001,[60] and in early May, 13 tons of cocaine (the largest maritime seizure of cocaine in U.S. history) 1,500 miles south of San Diego.[61]

Although the Coast Guard and other law enforcement agencies have reacted to that shift by the traffickers, the Commander of the Coast Guard's Pacific Area command noted in an interview, 'There is a limit to how much I can throw out there, and [the traffickers] have unlimited resources'.[62] The guarded pessimism of the operational commander for the Pacific area has been echoed in recent comments by the United States Interdiction Coordinator (also the Commandant of the Coast Guard) Admiral James M. Loy who suggested in testimony before the Senate Caucus on International Narcotics Control on May 15, 2001 that traffickers were keeping pace with intensified interdiction efforts:

> Despite a strong effort and extensive interagency and international cooperation, we were unable to meet our 13 percent seizure rate [per cent of available cocaine actually seized] target in 2000.[63]

These are not encouraging signs for a National Drug Control Strategy that aims to bring the seizure rate above 20% before the end of the current decade.

Heroin

The French Connection

President Nixon's initial 'War on Drugs' was more about heroin and marijuana than it was about cocaine. He wanted, among other things, to arrest the flow of morphine base made of Turkish poppy that was transshipped out of Lebanon, processed by criminal groups in Marseilles, France, and brought to market on the eastern seaboard of the United States. This focus was motivated by the fact that, in 1972, 80% of the heroin that entered the United States followed this route.[64] In his comprehensive study, Alfred McCoy described the activities of the Corsican criminals:

> Protected by their national and local patrons...worked through criminal subcontractors to import [Turkish] morphine from Lebanon, process it into heroin in Marseilles' laboratories, and then export high-grade powder to American Mafia distributors through criminal associates in Canada and the Caribbean.[65]

Nixon's assault on this pipeline bore significant results. Under pressure from the U.S., Turkey announced in 1972 that it would no longer produce opium. At roughly the same time, joint U.S./French law enforcement efforts broke up the Corsican drug syndicates in Marseilles.[66] In the short term, the desired goal of making heroin less available on the streets of the U. S. was accomplished.[67] The state-centric approach to the heroin problem, via bilateral efforts with Turkey and France, appeared to have worked. In the long term, however, the criminal syndicates affected a shift in raw material production that ensured the global volume of illicit poppy continued to rise. The bulk of new production began in Asia's Golden Triangle.

The Golden Triangle

The term 'Golden Triangle' refers to a region that begins in the Shan states of northeastern Burma, continues through northern Thailand, and extends finally into the regions of northern Laos inhabited by the Hmong tribesmen. There existed in this region, prior to 1950, a 100-year tradition of state opium sales, a tradition that was gradually eliminated between 1951 and 1960 under international pressure.[68] Undermining this development, however, was the willingness of government intelligence agencies, often working with the U.S. Central Intelligence Agency (CIA), to allow paramilitary organizations to control what was now an illegal activity. Dominant among these groups was the nationalist Chinese army (Kuo Min Tang or KMT) located initially in Burma. McCoy points out that the KMT presided over an increase in the production of poppy in the Shan state region of Burma from about 18 tons in 1958 to estimates that ranged between 400 and 600 tons in 1970.[69] Clearly, the region had the capacity to respond to disruptions caused by law enforcement efforts in other parts of the world

Still, to replace the refining capacity lost as a result of the breakup of the criminal operations in Marseilles, laboratories that could produce high-grade no. 4 heroin were needed in Southeast Asia. The market incentive for developing those labs was the presence of large numbers of relatively affluent American soldiers deployed in South Vietnam in the 1960s. These refineries began to come online in 1969 when expert chemists from Hong Kong arrived in the region to help service the emerging market.[70] Under Nixon's 'Vietnamization' program, however, U. S. soldiers were ordered home in large numbers in the 1970 to 1972 timeframe. Without really missing a beat, and relying to an important extent on connections between Corsican criminal elements in France and Vientienne, Laos, the no. 4 heroin began to be shipped directly to the United States.[71]

The Nixon Administration was intent on preserving the successes of the French Connection breakup and so it responded quickly when it became clear that increasing percentages of the heroin being seized in America's major cities came from Southeast Asia. A team of 30 DEA agents was deployed to Thailand along with $12 million to assist that Thai government with its counter-narcotics efforts.[72] By the end of 1975, the Southeast Asian share of the U. S. heroin market was back down to 8% from a high of 30% in 1973. The immediate criminal reaction to the Thai/U.S. effort was a dramatic increase in the amount of Mexican heroin supporting the U.S. market—from 39% in 1972 to 90% in 1975.[73] But refining of opium poppy in northern Thailand remained a problem, a phenomena that can be explained by tracing the flight of the KMT.

After 1962, the KMT (as constituted in the 1950s) was no longer a factor in the Shan region as it had been forced to flee in January of 1961 when attacked by the combined force of the Burmese Army and the Communist Chinese. The KMT fled to Laos where many were repatriated to Taiwan with the assistance of the United States. But as many as 2,000-3,000 remained in Laos and eventually moved into Thailand and continued to prosper in the opium trade, moving raw opium poppy out of the Shan region in Burma and processing it in northern Thailand.[74] These remnants of the KMT, fragmented into three components after relocation to Thailand, and a Shan warlord based in Thailand known by the name Khun Sa, were the dominant actors in the Golden Triangle heroin business for most of the period between the mid-1960s and 1990.

There is a great deal of detail to the story of heroin in the Golden Triangle that goes beyond the scope of this research,[75] but the specific interest here is in the responses of governments to the problem of heroin production and trafficking in and from the Golden Triangle region. Of particular interest is the continued success of opium drug lords in producing heroin in Burma and getting it to markets despite determined efforts by regional states, particularly Thailand with assistance from the United States and the international community, to prevent it. The focus in the remainder of this section is on the regional and international political factors that isolated the Shan area as the production and refining point for Golden Triangle heroin during that same period, on Burma's continued difficulty governing the Shan region that made the isolation possible, and on the trafficking patterns from that region over the past two decades that have ensured markets for the heroin despite the efforts of governments.

The Shan region of Burma shares borders with China, Laos and Thailand. Between roughly 1970-1990, the opium produced in the Shan state was taken by caravan to northern Thailand where it was processed into high-grade no. 4 heroin and then shipped to Bangkok, Hong Kong and Manila for further shipment to affluent markets. Strict anti-drug enforcement by the communist regime in China prevented the flow of heroin across that border. As for Laos, while it is clear that the government was involved in heroin trafficking during the 1960s, the ability of the Pathet Lao to establish a unified national liberation movement distinguished that country from Burma in the 1970s. Northern Thailand was the refuge for the KMT remnants between 1962 and the early 1980s when those groups weakened and Khun Sa began to exercise greater control of the region. The willingness of the Thai government to allow this state of affairs on its northern border can be explained two ways. First, the rise of the Burmese Communist Party (BCP) in the Shan states during the period from 1970-1978 raised concern in Thailand about the possibility of collaboration between communist groups in Thailand and the BCP.[76] The second issue was the existence of drug-related corruption at the highest levels of the Thai government.

Northern Thailand was the base of operations for the drug lord Khun Sa from 1974 when he was released from captivity in Burma until he was routed out of the country and back into Burma by Thai forces in January of 1982.[77] The exercise of Thai muscle against Khun Sa came in the wake of revelations about corruption in the military government that seemed, in the early 1980s, to turn the attitudes of a previously apathetic public against a government with such overt associations with the drug trade. This clear shift in policy toward opium refining on the northern border was complimented by a successful crop eradication program that reduced illicit opium production from 145 tons in 1970 to only 24 tons in 1992.[78]

In Burma after 1982, Khun Sa[79] reassembled quickly his dominance over opium flow through the Shan region, although the Burmese Communist Party continued to control heroin in some parts of the region too. But two important developments in Burma in the late 1980s changed the face of the opium situation there. In the late summer of 1988, pro-democracy demonstrations erupted throughout Burma and the fierce, brutal reaction of the military government drove many of the participants to the country's border regions inhabited by the CPB and the ethnic insurgents. The situation became more complicated in the spring of 1989 when mutinies within the CPB led to the break-up of that body into four ethnically based insurgent armies: The United Wa State Army (UWSA), The Myanmar National Democratic Alliance Army (MNDAA), The National Democratic Alliance Army, Eastern Shan State, and the New Democratic Army.[80]

The military government in Rangoon, a junta established in 1988 and renamed the State Law and Order Restoration Council (SLORC), was concerned about the possibility that these new groupings would collaborate amongst themselves or with the pro-democracy groups. It decided, gradually, to enter into agreements with each of the former segments of the CPB. These deals offered the groups the opportunity to engage in whatever business they chose to sustain themselves in exchange for promises that they would not attack the government and would break off ties with the ethnic rebel groups. Not surprisingly, the rebel entrepreneurs chose opium cultivation and heroin production as their means of support. In addition to the factions broken off from the former CPB, a number of smaller, ethnically based separatist groups gave up their struggles against the government in exchange for similar deals with military government in Rangoon.

The SLORC counter-insurgency strategy tacitly accepted drug trafficking activities within Burma's borders in contravention of international treaties to which Burma is party. The result for the Golden Triangle region has been an upsurge in the amount of opium poppy produced in northeast Burma during the 1990s. In 1988, Burma produced 1,280 tons of opium and by 1996, only eight years later, that figure had more than doubled to 2,560 tons—more than two-thirds of world production and enough to manufacture 250 tons of heroin.[81] The SLORC (now referred to as the "State Peace and Development Council" or SPDC), already under intense criticism for its human rights record, has been chastised severely for its failure to confront the drug challenge within its borders.

Even attempts by the SLORC/SPDC to provide some symbolic evidence of success against the opium threat have been exposed as corrupt. In 1993, government forces encircled the Möng Tai Army of Khun Sa, cutting off his ability to carry out narcotics trafficking operations.[82] Three years later, Khun Sa elected to surrender to state authorities and move to Rangoon in exchange for a level of autonomy in business matters not unlike that offered to the former leaders of the CPB. A month after his arrest, ten new businesses with strong links to him were created in Rangoon and he was seen driving around Rangoon in a four-wheel drive vehicle, escorted by army officers.[83] Further, Thai intelligence sources reported that shortly after Khun Sa's surrender, an estimated $24 million was transferred to Rangoon from financial institutions in Thailand.[84] In the interest of preventing the consolidation of anti-government power under communist or pro-democracy leadership, the SLORC/SPDC risked international condemnation and made deals with its opponents that effectively legalized the heroin industry in the Shan region during the 1990s. Meanwhile, conflict in another corner of Asia facilitated the emergence of an opium state that would soon rival Burma in productivity.

A serious drought in the Golden Triangle between 1978 and 1980 coincided with the December 1979 Soviet invasion of Afghanistan. During the 10 year war between the Afghan mujaheddin and the Soviet Army, the exigencies of the conflict and the Cold War politics that drove U. S. support for the Afghan warriors, contributed to the development of a war economy in which opium production and trafficking played a major role. Opium production in Afghanistan rose from about 100 tons in 1971 to 300 tons in 1982.[85] The rise of the Taliban in the early 1990s and the continued internal struggle for control of the country have meant a perpetuation of the war economy conditions, a state of affairs that has been exploited by all sides in the conflict and led to a mushrooming of opium production. By 1992, estimates of the opium yield coming from Afghanistan were up to 640 metric tons and by 2000 an astronomically high 3656 metric tons.[86]

The developments in Afghanistan have increased the flow of heroin from Southwest Asia into Europe. Still, despite enforcement efforts in Thailand, Bangkok and Hong Kong remain important distribution points for the flow of Golden Triangle heroin. Further complicating matters has been the maturation of connections between the ethnic breakaway groups of the former Burmese Communist Party and Chinese criminal 'Triads' moving heroin out of Burma, into Yunnan in Southern China and then out to ports on China's southern coast.[87]

Interdicting Heroin

At different times over the past two decades when Golden Triangle heroin has made up a significant percentage of the heroin being consumed in major US markets (i.e. between 1984 and 1990—a period when Khun Sa dominated opium production and trafficking on the Burma/Thai border—Southeast Asian heroin grew from 5% to 80% of the street supply in New York City),[88] but the current state of affairs indicates that most heroin in the United States comes from South America. In 1997, 75% of the heroin seized in the United States came from South America.[89] This can be explained by the effectiveness of South American traffickers squeezing the Asian criminal groups out of U.S. markets and the fact that growing markets in Asia are more alluring to those local criminals.[90] Still, given the continued dominance of Burma as a source for raw poppy and the demonstrated flexibility of the criminal elements involved in moving the heroin out of Asia, the potential for surges like the one experienced in the late 1980s exists. In recent years, Thai law enforcement officials have discovered heroin bound for North America concealed in bronze statues and major trafficking groups are suspected of secreting large quantities of heroin in commercial cargo where it is shipped through Singapore to Europe or the United States.[91]

For the purposes of this chapter, what is most noteworthy about U.S. efforts to interdict Golden Triangle heroin (and for that matter its contribution to eradication efforts in Thailand and Burma over the years) is the extent to which they have contributed to the creation of a more complex diffusion of heroin trafficking around the globe. This diffusion made the heroin problem that much more difficult to conquer in any comprehensive way. McCoy has put the problem this way:

> Like opium in the nineteenth century, heroin has become a world market commodity and supplies not absorbed in one market found their way into another. Interdiction simply acted as an informal tariff barrier and encouraged syndicates to seek alternative markets in nations with less stringent international enforcement efforts.[92]

Elusive Success and Unintended Consequences

These brief histories of U.S. and international efforts to deal with the production and trafficking of cocaine and heroin unveil two tendencies that repeat themselves with regularity. First, government efforts to either eradicate raw material or to interdict drugs in transit have been frustrated repeatedly by the ability of drug organizations to move production or to change routes. Second, the methods employed by governments to pursue eradication and/or the interception of drugs in transit frequently has had serious negative impacts on civil society in the countries where the eradication and interdiction efforts have been focused. These two phenomena are explored below.

Displacing the Problem, Not Solving It

In an international legal environment in which the vast majority of governments have agreed that the production and trafficking of certain narcotics is illegal, it is hardly surprising that some of the most remote and historically difficult to govern spaces on the planet have emerged as sources of raw material for the illicit production of cocaine and heroin. In the Andean region, Peru, Bolivia and Colombia have all struggled to exercise sovereignty over the entirety of their national territory. In those regions where governance has been most difficult, separatist movements and criminal organizations have flourished. While geography alone cannot explain problems in governance in any country, it is clear that rugged isolation in the Andes, as well as in the Golden Triangle and Afghanistan, have contributed to the difficulties experienced by central governments in those regions.

In the cases of Peru and Bolivia, forced and voluntary eradication programs have moved production of coca leaf within the respective borders of those countries, a phenomenon which helps to explain increases in coca production despite aggressive eradication efforts in the late 1980s and early 1990s. Still, with the application of aggressive eradication programs, made possible in part by the suspension of democratic government in Peru and by continued massive infusions of U.S. aid in both Peru and Bolivia, those countries have dramatically reduced the amount of coca being produced. These developments would encourage optimism were it not for the fact that the absence of effective governance in the Putamayo region of Colombia has resulted in drastic increases in the amount of coca being produced there. Overall, the return on the United States' investment in eradication has been minimal, almost negligible. Today, given the latest massive infusion of U.S. counter drug aid to Colombia that is coincident with the President Fujimori's scandal-ridden departure from Peru, one can imagine a decline in Colombian and a rise in Peruvian coca leaf production over the next few years.

The displacement phenomenon has also been readily evident in Southeast Asian heroin production. The cultivation of heroin poppy has largely been consolidated into Burma as a result of more effective efforts in Thailand to govern the problem and political realities in China, and to a lesser extent Laos, which have prevented poppy production from being as significant in those two countries.

The results of government interdiction strategies in both the Americas and Asia have also been limited by the displacement effect in trafficking routes. U.S. law enforcement efforts in the Caribbean, along the southwest border, and in the Eastern Pacific have resulted in increasing volumes of seized cocaine, but not to the extent believed necessary to keep pace with the growing volumes being trafficked. While it is harder to establish direct cause/effect links between recent U.S. contributions to the interdiction effort against Southeast Asian heroin, part of the reason for that is the Nixon administration's early responses to the Golden Triangle heroin threat and the global diffusion of heroin trafficking that resulted.

The final aspect of the displacement phenomenon is the most difficult to quantify and is therefore, admittedly, somewhat speculative. That is the displacement of illicit drug shipments into the flow of legitimate commerce when law enforcement efforts achieve some success against the non-commercial methods.[93] It is conceivable that traffickers might boost their efforts to exploit legitimate cargoes when large non-commercial loads become too vulnerable. For example, it might be the case that traffickers will take such a course in response to the numerous high volume seizures that have taken place in the Eastern Pacific during the first half of 2001. Definitively detecting such a shift and tracking it to specific commercial shipments is a never-ending challenge for law enforcement. Given the small percentages of both air and maritime commercial shipments that are inspected by the U. S. Customs service, it can be argued that the extent of trafficker exploitation of commercial cargoes is not fully known and therefore not fully understood.

The Impact on Civil Society

The displacement of the drug trafficking threat poses a clear challenge to state-centric approaches to drug trafficking. It is an unintended consequence of an enforcement effort that targets illegal activity in the territory of only one state or in only one region. It ensures unintended, but not entirely unpredictable outcomes. The affects of state-centric counter drug efforts on civil societies in countries where they are applied are less predictable and arguably more insidious over the long term.

The efforts of the United States to attack the drug problem at the source in South America by working with the Andean countries have contributed to the pitting of governments against citizens. The pressure applied by the United States is compelling when development assistance is linked to counter-drug performance objectives defined by the U.S. The annual certification process carried out by the U.S. State Department is the marker by which countries throughout the world are judged worthy of U.S. assistance. The emphasis on drug eradication has led to more heavy-handed tactics by the police, increased use of the military in the fight against drugs, and in some cases, as was at least in part the case in Peru, the suspension of democratic government. In Colombia, the linkages between the Marxist rebels and the narcotics trade combine, given the U.S. commitment to protecting and expanding democracy around the globe, to create a dual incentive for U.S. engagement. But that engagement introduces advanced warfighting capability into a complicated domestic scenario. A society already racked with violence faces an intensification of the fighting between the government and the FARC and ELN. At the same time, the AUC and other paramilitary groups will challenge the Marxist rebels, funding these efforts by collecting protection money from drug producer and trafficking groups.

The U.S. and Colombia find themselves in the current state of affairs, in part, because of the success of the Fujimori-led eradication effort in Peru. The full extent to which Peruvian civil society was eroded while that effort was ongoing during the Fujimori era remains to be seen. Still, revelations of the anti-democratic activities of Fujimori's intelligence chief, Vladimiro Montesinos (including accusations that he may have secreted as much as $70 million in a foreign bank account), when matched with the high levels of support given by the United States during the 1990s, suggest an unfortunate link between U.S. counter-drug aid and the corrupt practices of the Fujimori government.

Finally, in Southeast Asia, Burma represents a sort-of worst case scenario, a politically isolated nation where a military government is complicit in the production of opium poppy that supplies a large percentage of global demand for heroin. An autocratic and corrupt regime suppresses individual freedom while profiting from a trade that is illegal in the eyes of the international community. Bilateral counter-drug engagement between the U.S. and Burma is not the cause of Burma's role in the international heroin industry, but state-centric approaches taken in Thailand with U.S. support (in particular) can be said to have helped isolate the production of heroin in the Shan state region.

This discussion of unintended consequences cannot provide direct cause and effect relationships between particular bursts of U.S. counter-drug assistance and evidence of displacement or militarization. Nevertheless, there are clear patterns that illustrate in a macro-sense that state-centric approaches to the drug problem often bring unintended side effects. These side effects may be deemed, jointly or unilaterally, acceptable in the short term given the serious attention that is given to the drug threat internationally. But in the long term, without a plan to prevent the displacement of the drug trade or to return civil society to a normal state after a brief period of militarization, these side effects are alarming. They are particularly so given their tendency to repeat in different places around the globe and given the absence of any evidence that the cocaine and heroin problems are being brought under control. In other words, since the production and flow of drugs continues without significant interruption while these negative side effects develop, there is a case to be made for considering what other approaches, outside the realm of the state-centric, might be usefully applied to the international drug threat and other transnational threats to security like it.

Conclusion

This chapter established both the ineffectiveness of state-centric approaches to the cocaine and heroin threats, and the occurrence of unintended consequences that flow regularly from these efforts. These findings appear to support the pursuit of initiatives that might augment or in some cases replace the more traditional, state-centric approaches. Research into innovative, non-traditional approaches to the drug trafficking problem that endeavor to increase the capacity of the international system to deal with the threat but that reach beyond the bilateral and multilateral engagement of nation-states to do so, is warranted. In this vain, and particularly in light of the terrorist events of September 11, 2001, governments and legitimate private sector actors ought to be coming together around their shared interest in the question of how to weed out transnational threats to security while maintaining the vitality of the global economy. Drug traffickers, organized criminals engaged in human trafficking and money laundering, and terrorists all share common transnational characteristics and they all exploit an international system wherein the military/law enforcement response relies principally on interactions between and among nation-states. While the capacity of the international system to respond to these threats must inevitably continue to rely on the work of governments, it would appear that those efforts alone will be insufficient. The study of recent responses to cocaine and heroin trafficking builds the case for the consideration of non-traditional approaches to these problems.

Notes

[1] The views expressed herein are those of the author and are not to be construed as official or reflecting the views of the Commandant or of the U.S. Coast Guard.

[2] United Nations Economic and Social Council, Commission on Narcotic Drugs, 43rd session, Vienna, 6-15 March 2000, "World Situation with Regard to Illicit Drug Trafficking and Action Taken by Subsidiary Bodies of the Commission on Narcotic Drugs" (E/CN.7/2000/5), 4.

[3] U. S. Department of Justice, Drug Enforcement Administration, National Narcotics Intelligence Consumers Committee Report 1997 (DEA-98036), November 1998, Executive Summary, page xi.

[4] Alfred W. McCoy and Alan A. Block, "U. S. Narcotics Policy: An Anatomy of Failure", in Alfred W. McCoy and Alan A. Block, *War on Drugs: Studies in the Failure of U.S. Narcotics Policy* (Boulder: Westview Press, 1992), 3.

[5] Ibid.

[6] Paul B. Stares, *Global Habit: The Drug Problem in a Borderless World* (Washington, DC: Brookings Institution, 1996), 30.

[7] Ibid, 30.

[8] For a brief but useful synopsis of the United States' policy toward cocaine in the Americas during the first half of the 20th century, see William O. Walker, "The Bush Administration's Andean Drug Strategy in Historical Perspective", particularly pp. 5-14, in Bruce M. Bagley and William O. Walker III, *Drug Trafficking in the Americas* (Miami: North-South Center Press, 1996), 1.

[9] Ibid, 6-8. Walker points out that greater concern about opiates and concerns about hemispheric security in the years leading up to WWII affected the US perspective.

[10] William B. McAllister, *Drug Diplomacy in the Twentieth Century: An International History* (New York: Routledge, 2000), 235.

[11] Sewall H. Menzel, *Fire in the Andes: U.S. Foreign Policy and Cocaine Politics in Bolivia and Peru* (New York: University Press of America, 1996), 121.

[12] LaMond Tullis, *Unintended Consequences: Illegal Drugs & Drug Policies in Nine Countries* (Boulder: Lynne Rienner, 1995), 97.

[13] Menzel, 121. According to Menzel, Sendero Luminoso had begun its campaign to ultimately overthrow the government of Peru in the late 1960s and had only a small base in the early 1970s, but expanded rapidly and became a destabilizing force in Peruvian Society in the early 1980s.

[14] Patrick L. Clawson and Rensselaer W. Lee III, *The Andean Cocaine Industry* (New York: St. Martin's Press, 1996), 182.

[15] Ibid.

[16] David Scott Palmer, "Peru, Drugs and Shining Path", in Bruce M. Bagley and William O. Walker III, eds., *Drug Trafficking in the Americas* (Miami: North-South Center Press, 1996), 184.

[17] Clawson and Lee, 183. One credible report mentioned by these authors indicates that General Arciniega now lives a very modest life in exile, seeming to indicate that he did not profit personally from drug proceeds while serving as a military commander in Peru.

[18] Ibid, 71.

[19] LaMond Tullis, *Unintended Consequences: Illegal Drugs & Drug Policies in Nine Countries* (Boulder: Lynne Rienner, 1995), 98.

[20] Review conducted by author, 05 June 2001; available from http://www.state.gov/g/inl/narc

[21] Menzel, 16. Menzel, who was the United States' Army-Navy Attaché at the Embassy in La Paz at the time recalls that the Bolivian President, perhaps believing that a failure to go along might jeopardize a U.S. aid program, told the U. S. Ambassador he could do "anything [he wanted] to do!"

[22] Menzel, 20.

[23] Ibid.

[24] Eduardo A. Gamarra, "U.S. Bolivia Counternarcotics Efforts During the Paz Zamora Administration: 1989-1992", in Bruce M. Bagley and William O. Walker III, *Drug Trafficking in the Americas* (Miami: North-South Center Press, 1996), 220.

[25] Ibid.

[26] Ibid, 228 and 239.

[27] Tullis, 101.

[28] Banzer is a curious figure in the drug war story. The military dictator of Bolivia from 1971-1978, he is reported to have profited from the cocaine trade during that period. Since his political resurgence in 1997 (he received only 23% of the popular vote and runs and awkward coalition government), he has worked closely with the United States. His eradication efforts have not been without controversy. In the fall of 2000, peasants in the Chapare region protested a government plan to build 3 military bases in the area to support the counter-drug effort. The protests succeeded in getting the government to back down on the plan. For a critical assessment of Banzer, see George Ann Potter and Linda Farthing, "In Focus: Bolivia: Eradicating Democracy", Foreign Policy in Focus, 5, no. 38 (October 2000), (accessed 13 March 2001); available from https://www.cc.colombia.edu/sec/dlc/ciao/pbei/fpif/ang01.html

[29] Rensselaer W. Lee III, "Colombia's Cocaine Syndicates", in Alfred W. McCoy and Alan A. Block, *War on Drugs: Studies in the Failure of U.S. Narcotics Policy* (Boulder: Westview Press, 1992), 95.

[30] Gabriel Marcella, *Plan Colombia: The Strategic and Operational Imperatives* (Washington, DC: Strategic Studies Institute, 2001), 4. Marcella points out that estimates of the amount of drug money earned annually by the insurgent groups run as high as $500 million.

[31] Ibid. Marcella asserts that the leader of the paramilitary claims a 70% reliance on drug money to fund his activities.
[32] U. S. State Department, Bureau for International Narcotics and Law Enforcement Affairs, International Narcotics Control Strategy Report 2000 (INCSR 2000), (accessed 10 March 2001); available from http://www.state.gov/g/inl
[33] Ellen Nakashima and Matthew Vita, "Clinton Clears Aid Package for Colombia", *Washington Post*, 23 August 2000, A01.
[34] Marcella, 2. For an enlightening interview of the leader of one of the major paramilitary groups in the country, Carlos Castano of the United Self-Defense Forces of Colombia, see Scott Wilson, "Interview with Carlos Castano, Head of the United Self Defense Forces of Colombia", *Washington Post*, 12 March 2001, (accessed 30 May 2001); available from http://www.washingtonpost.com/wp-dyn/articles/A47019-2001Mar9.html. Castano resigned his position as head of the AUC on the same day that the Wilson interview with him was published in the Post. See this follow up article: Scott Wilson, "Colombian Paramilitary Leader Quits", *Washington Post*, 01 June 2001, A28.
[35] Larry Rohter, "Latest Battleground in Latin Drug War: Brazilian Amazon", *New York Times*, 30 October 2000.
[36] Rohter, "Ecuador Afraid as a Drug War Heads Its Way", *New York Times*, 08 January 2001, (accessed 10 January 2001); available from http://www.nytimes.com /2001/01/08 /world/ 08ECUA.html
[37] Rohter, "Latest Battleground".
[38] Clawson and Lee, *The Andean Cocaine Industry*, 37.
[39] Ibid, 44. It is alleged that between April 1987 and 1989, 6 tons of cocaine were smuggled through Cuba's Varadero Airport, an effort that earned a Department of the Cuban Ministry of Interior an estimated $3.4 million dollars.
[40] This airdrop strategy continues today. In the fiscal year that ended on September 30, 2000, a U.S.-led effort known as Operation Bahamas and Turks and Caicos (OPBAT), established in 1987, seized 22 aircraft and vessels, $500,000 cash and 6500 kgs of cocaine by targeting drug trafficking through the Bahamas. See: "15 Million Dollar Cocaine Airdrop Foiled by Operation Bahamas and Turks and Caicos," *Coastline*, (accessed 05 June 2001);available from located online at http://www.uscg.mil/d7/d7dpa/coastline/octnov /6a.htm on 05 June 2001.
[41] U. S. State Department, Bureau for International Narcotics and Law Enforcement Affairs, International Narcotics Control Strategy Report 2000, "Mexico", (accessed 27 May 2001); available from http://www.state.gov/g/inl/rls/nrcrpt/2000/index.cfm?docid=888
[42] Clawson and Lee, 22.
[43] Peter Andreas, "The Political Economy of Narco-Corruption in Mexico," *Current History* 97, no. 618, (April 1, 1998), 162.
[44] Stares, *Global Habit*, 27.
[45] Jorge Chabat, "Drug Trafficking in U.S.-Mexican Relations: What You See is What You Get", in Bagley and Walker, *Drug Trafficking in the Americas*, 378.
[46] Chabat, 381.
[47] Department of the Treasury, U. S. Customs Service, "FY00 Windows of Opportunity for Drug Smuggling (Southwest Border)" (accessed 29 May 2001); available from http://www.customs.ustreas.gov/enforcem/hardline/intoow.htm
[48] Congress, Senate, *U. S. Anti-Drug Interdiction Efforts and the Western Hemisphere Drug Elimination Act: Joint Hearing before the Caucus on International Narcotics Control and the Committee on Foreign Relations*, 105th Cong., 2nd Sess., 16 September 1998, 17.
[49] Ibid.

[50] Stephen E. Flynn, "Beyond Border Control", *Foreign Affairs* 79, no. 6 (November/December 2000), 59.
[51] Data used to make these calculations about the Otay Mesa border crossing obtained from Stephen E. Flynn, Senior Fellow, Council on Foreign Relations who toured the border crossing with U.S. Customs officials during the week of 8-12 January, 2001.
[52] "Drug War Facts", Common Sense for Drug Policy website (accessed 19 May 2000); available from http://www.csdp.org/factbook/interdic.htm. CSDP cites the following sources for this "fact": G. Frankel, "Federal Agencies Duplicate Efforts, Wage Costly Turf Battles", *The Washington Post*, 8 June 1997, A1 and CIA World Factbook 1998.
[53] Congress, Senate, Caucus on International Narcotics Control and Committee on Foreign Relations, (Senate Hearing 105-844), 16 September 1998, 15.
[54] Michael Christie, "Traffickers Moving Back to Caribbean - US Drug Czar", *Reuters*, 10 February 2000.
[55] Ibid.
[56] Ben Fox, "Drug Runners Increasingly Turn to Pacific as Smuggling Route", *San Francisco Chronicle*, 25 January 2001.
[57] Leslie Fulbright, "Coast Guard Seizes 10 Tons of Coke", *Oakland Tribune*, 01 October 1999.
[58] U.S. Newswire as posted on Mexican Embassy, Washington, DC website (accessed 14 December 1999); available from http://www.embassyofmexico.org
[59] James W. Crawley, "Catch of the Day—Drugs; Eight tons of cocaine, fishing boat seized by Coast Guard, Navy" *San Diego Union-Tribune*, 04 March 2001, B1.
[60] Department of Transportation, U.S. Coast Guard, Pacific Area Public Affairs Media Release 09-01, "Coast Guard, Navy Seize More Than 1,600 lbs. of Cocaine", 10 May 2001.
[61] Tony Perry, "Huge Drug Haul Shows Smuggling's New Trends", *Los Angeles Times*, 15 May 2001, Part 2, 8.
[62] Molly Moore, "Cocaine Seizures by U.S. Double in the Pacific Ocean", *The Washington Post*, 03 September 2000, A24.
[63] George Gedda, "DEA Reviewing Caribbean Arrest Rates", *Associated Press*, 15 May 2001 (accessed 15 September 2001); available from Lexis-Nexis Universe
[64] Paul B. Stares, *Global Habit: The Drug Problem in a Borderless World* (Washington: The Brookings Institution, 1996), 25.
[65] Alfred W. McCoy, *The Politics of Heroin: CIA Complicity in the Global Drug Trade* (Brooklyn: Lawrence Hill Books, 1991), 63.
[66] Stares, 27.
[67] McCoy, 73. The amount of heroin seized in the United States in 1973 was less than half of the amount seized in 1971.
[68] Alfred W. McCoy, "Coercion and Its Unintended Consequences: A Study of Heroin Trafficking in Southeast and South West Asia", *Crime, Law & Social Change* 33, no.3 (April 2000), 203.
[69] Ibid, 204.
[70] McCoy, *The Politics of Heroin*, 286.
[71] Ibid.
[72] McCoy, "Coercion and Its Unintended Consequences", 205.
[73] McCoy, *The Politics of Heroin*, 392.
[74] Ibid, 349. The section of McCoy's work that begins on this page develops the story of the KMT in Thailand in greater detail.

[75] McCoy's *The Politics of Heroin* provides detailed historical analysis. It is a controversial work because of its coverage of the activities of the CIA in and around Vietnam during the 1960s.
[76] Ibid, 425.
[77] Ibid, 420.
[78] McCoy, "Coercion and Its Unintended Consequences," 208.
[79] McCoy, *The Politics of Heroin,* 425-426. It is important to not that Khun Sa was not the first or only "drug kingpin" of the Golden Triangle. Between the period of Khun Sa's defeat at the hands of the KMT in 1967 followed by his solitary confinement from 1969-1974, Chinese warlord Lo Hsing-han became, for a time, the most significant opium trafficker in the region.
[80] Bertil Lintner, "Drugs and Economic Growth: Ethnicity and Exports", in Robert I. Rotberg, ed., *Burma: Prospects for a Democratic Future* (Washington, D.C.: Brookings Institution Press, 1998), 168.
[81] Alan Dupont, "Transnational Crime, Drugs, and Security in East Asia", *Asian Survey*, 39, no. 3 (May/June 1999), 440.
[82] Lintner, "Drugs and Economic Growth", 166.
[83] Lintner, "Narcopolitics in Burma" *Current History*, vol 95 (December 1996), 437.
[84] Lintner, "Safe at Home: Drug Lords are Keeping Their Cash in the Country", *Far Eastern Economic Review*, 14 August 1997, 19.
[85] Alfred W. McCoy, "Heroin as a Global Commodity: A History of Southeast Asia's Opium Trade", in Alfred W. McCoy and Alan A. Block, eds., *War on Drugs: Studies in the Failure of U.S. Narcotics Policy* (Boulder: Westview Press, 1992), 264.
[86] Department of State, International Narcotics Control Strategy Report 2000, Southwest Asia Section (accessed 31 May 2001); available from http://www.state.gov/g/inl/rls/nrcrpt/2000/ index.cfm?docid=940
[87] Lintner, "Drugs and Economic Growth", 172.
[88] McCoy, "Coercion and Its Unintended Consequences", 207.
[89] U. S. Department of Justice, Drug Enforcement Agency, NNICC Report (DEA-98036), 40.
[90] U. S. Department of Justice, Drug Enforcement Agency, "Heroin" on agency website (accessed 31 May 2001); available from http://www.usdoj.gov/dea/concern/heroin.htm
[91] NNICC Report 1997, 51 and 53.
[92] McCoy, *The Politics of Heroin,* 396.
[93] Here, "commercial" is intended to mean the normal flow of legitimate cargoes as distinguished from "non-commercial" smuggling efforts like the hiring of a fishing vessel or aircraft for a dedicated drug shipment. While there is undoubtedly a commercial component to the latter example, the distinction is clear.

References

Andreas, Peter. "The Political Economy of Narco-Corruption in Mexico". *Current History*, April 1998, 160-165.

Bagley, Bruce M. and William O. Walker III, eds. *Drug Trafficking in the Americas.* Miami: North-South Center Press, 1996.

Clawson, Patrick L. and Rensselaer W. Lee III. *The Andean Cocaine Industry.* New York: St. Martin's Press, 1996.

Common Sense for Drug Policy. "Drug War Facts". Accessed 19 May 2001. Available from http://www.csdp.org/factbook/interdic.htm

Dupont, Alan. "Transnational Crime, Drugs, and Security in East Asia." *Asian Survey* 39, no. 3 (May/June 99), 433-455.

Flynn, Stephen E. "Beyond Border Control." *Foreign Affairs*, vol. 79, no. 6 (November/December 2000): 57-68.

Lintner, Bertil. "Narcopolitics in Burma." *Current History* 95 (December 1996): 432-437.

_____. "Safe at Home: Drug Lords are Keeping Their Cash in the Country." *Far Eastern Economic Review*, 14 August 1997, 18-19.

Marcella, Gabriel. *Plan Colombia: The Strategic and Operational Imperatives*. Washington, DC: Strategic Studies Institute, 2001.

McAllister, William B. *Drug Diplomacy in the Twentieth Century: An International History*. New York: Routledge, 2000.

McCoy, Alfred W. *The Politics of Heroin: CIA Complicity in the Global Drug Trade*. Brooklyn: Lawrence Hill Books, 1991.

_____. "Coercion and Its Unintended Consequences: A Study of Heroin Traffickin in Southeast and South West Asia". *Crime, Law and Social Change* 33, 191-224.

McCoy, Alfred W. and Alan A. Block. *War on Drugs: Studies in the Failure of U.S. Narcotics Policy*. Boulder: Westview Press, 1992.

Menzel, Sewall H. *Fire in the Andes: U.S. Foreign Policy and Cocaine Politics in Bolivia and Peru*. New York: University Press of America, 1996.

Rotberg, Robert I. ed. *Burma: Prospects for a Democratic Future*. Washington: Brookings Institution Press, 1998.

Stares, Paul B. *Global Habit: The Drug Problem in a Borderless World*. Washington, D.C.: The Brookings Institution, 1996.

Tullis, LaMond. *Unintended Consequences: Illegal Drugs & Drug Policies in Nine Countries*. Boulder: Lynne Rienner, 1995.

United Nations. Economic and Social Council. Commission on Narcotic Drugs. World Situation with regard to Illicit Drug Trafficking and Action Taken by the Subsidiary Bodies of the Commission on Narcotic Drugs (E/CN.7/2000/5). 22 December 1999.

U. S. Congress. Senate. Caucus on International Narcotics Control and the Committee on Foreign Relations. *U. S. Anti-Drug Interdiction Efforts and the Western Hemisphere Drug Elimination Act: Joint Hearing before the Caucus on International Narcotics Control and the Committee on Foreign Relations*. 105th Cong., 2nd Sess., 16 September 1998.

U. S. Department of Justice. Drug Enforcement Administration. *National Narcotics Intelligence Consumers Report 1997: The Supply of Illicit Drugs to the United States* (DEA-98036). Washington, DC: Drug Enforcement Administration, November 1998.

U. S. Department of Justice. Drug Enforcement Administration. "Heroin." Accessed 31 May 2001. Available from http://www.usdoj.gov/dea/concern/heroin.htm

U. S. Department of State. Bureau for International Narcotics and Law Enforcement Affairs. "International Narcotics Control Strategy Report, 2000". Accessed 10 March 2001. Available from http://www.state.gov/g/inl

U. S. Department of Transportation. Coast Guard. Pacific Area Public Affairs Media Release 09-01. "Coast Guard, Navy Seize More Than 1,600 lbs of Cocaine", 10 May 2001. Accessed 05 June 2001. Available from http://www.uscg.mil/pacarea/pcp/newsreleases/list01.htm

U. S. Department of Transportation. Coast Guard. Seventh District. "15 Million Dollar Cocaine Airdrop Foiled by Operation Bahamas and Turks and Caicos". Coastline. Accessed 05June 2001. Available from http://www.uscg.mil/d7/d7dpa/coastline/octnov/6a.htm

U. S. Department of the Treasury. Customs Service. "FY00 Windows of Opportunity for Drug Smuggling (Southwest Border)". Accessed 29 May 01. Available from http://www.customs.ustreas.gov/enforcem/hardline/intoow.htm

Chapter 10

Conclusion: The United States and Europe in a Globalizing World

Daniel S. Papp

Introduction

The trans-Atlantic relationship between the United States and Europe is over 225 years old. Like any relationship that has endured for that long, it has gone through a number of different stages. These stages have been detailed by Howard Hensel in Chapter 1 of this volume.

Driven by new political realities on the ground in Western, Central, and Eastern Europe, new economic situations throughout the world, changing social-cultural conditions in Europe, North America, and elsewhere, and the development of new technology, especially information and communication technologies, the relationship between the United States and Europe is today in transition. What is more, when the transition will end, how it will end, and what the state of U.S.-European relations will be when the transition ends is unclear.

This chapter will briefly examine the driving forces behind the on-going transition in U.S.-European relations. In so doing, it seeks to provide a degree of clarity to the present and future state of the U.S.-European relationship.

The End of an Era

At the outset, it must be emphasized that there never was, is not now, and never will be a single "U.S.-European relationship". U.S.-European relations are composed of an uncountable number of governmental, business, personal, military, social, cultural, and other relationships. As a state, the United States maintains formal diplomatic relations with over 40 European countries as well as the European Union. Thousands of American companies conduct business in Europe, and thousands of European companies conduct business in the United States. And as individuals, millions of Americans and Europeans are engaged with each other in complex webs of relationships that are deeper, richer, and more varied than those that link the residents of any other set of countries and cultures separated by trans-continental distances. The depth, richness, and variety of these webs of relationships provides a virtual guarantee that the United States will long remain vitally involved with Europe, and Europe with the United States.

Nevertheless, U.S.-European relations are in transition in many areas, most clearly and evidently in state-to-state relations. For nearly half a century, from the late 1940s until the late 1980s, the relationship between the United States and Europe was defined by the Cold War. U.S. relations with Western European states, under-girded by the security demands of the Cold War, were generally close and friendly, based on shared political, economic, military, social, cultural, and other values, interests, and institutions.

Conversely, U.S. relations with most of the rest of Europe --the Soviet Union and what were at the time called Eastern European states-- was usually marked by tension and conflict, a derivative of opposed political, economic, and social systems that divided Europe into two hostile armed camps. Like the U.S.-Western European relationship, the U.S-Soviet/Eastern European relationship included political, economic, military, social, cultural, and other dimensions, but they were generally more shallow, less rich, and less diversified than U.S. relations with Western European states.

The rather settled state of U.S.-European relations began to unravel in 1989 when to the surprise of most observers, revolution swept the Soviet Union's satellites in Eastern Europe and communist governments there collapsed. Suddenly, East and West Germany were united. Suddenly, new relationships had to be forged between the United States and Albania, Bulgaria, Czechoslovakia, Hungary, Poland, and Romania. Suddenly, new relationships had to be forged between Western European states and their ex-communist neighbors to the east, and between the Soviet Union and its ex-communist neighbors to the west.

What is more, crucial questions had to be asked and answered about what types of governments, economic systems, and social relationships would replace the discredited ones left by the failed communist experiment in Central Europe. As important, the growing realization that the ex-communist states were not Eastern European states but Central European states introduced a new calculus to European geo-political and geo-strategic affairs.

Two years later, Europe's map, and the U.S.-European relationship, changed once again as the Soviet Union in 1991 disintegrated, unarguably ending the Cold War. Where once there was one state, there now were fifteen, seven of which were unarguably European and eight of which, even though they were not geographically European, wished to one extent or another to maintain a European identity. While the United States, Western European states, and Central European states all were pleased with the Soviet Union's demise, they faced the challenge of formulating and implementing new policies to respond to the new political and strategic dynamics of European and global affairs brought about by the Soviet Union's collapse. Some of the challenges about the future of Russia's relationship with the rest of Europe are skillfully laid out in Chapter 4 by Roger Kanet and Nouray Ibryamova.

The collapse of communism in Eastern Europe and the disintegration of the Soviet Union also raised questions about the future of U.S.-Western European relations, especially the North Atlantic Treaty Organization (NATO). Since the late 1940s, NATO had been a core element of the U.S-Western European trans-Atlantic relationship. Created primarily to deter the Soviet threat, NATO also had other purposes such as keeping the U.S. engaged in Europe; coordinating Western European, Canadian, and U.S. defense policy and planning; and serving as an organization in which West German re-armament could be safely undertaken and managed.

Even so, the collapse of communism in Eastern Europe and the disintegration of the Soviet Union raised questions about NATO's future. With its primary purpose gone, would NATO's other reasons for existing be sufficient to assure its survival? Would new missions be identified for the alliance? Given the new security equation in Europe, would NATO contract as present members opted out, or expand if Central and Eastern European states pushed for membership? The answers to these and other related questions, ably explored in Chapter 3 of this volume by Joyce Kaufman, also raised uncertainty about the future of U.S.-Western European relations.

Questions about the future of U.S.-Western European relations also emerged from another quarter as the European Community (EC) during the 1990s evolved into the European Union (EU). During the 1980s and early 1990s, the EC launched two major initiatives that had potential to change the way state-to-state relations had been conducted in Western Europe for centuries. The first was the 1985 Single European Act, which set 1992 as the date when all tariffs and other barriers on the movement of goods, capital, and people between the EC's then-twelve member states would end. The second was the 1992 Maastricht Treaty, which proposed that the EC's twelve members would join together in a political and economic union, adopt a common currency, share social and domestic policies, and have a common foreign and defense policy. In short, the Maastricht Treaty, whose terms were strengthened by the 1997 Amsterdam Treaty, sought to create a United States of Europe by converting the European Community into the European Union.

The implications of the EU, examined by Yannis Stivachtis in Chapter 2 of this work, for European affairs and for U.S.-Western European relations were immense. What did the EU imply for state-to-state relations and for sovereignty in Europe? Would traditional bilateral relations between the U.S. and individual European states be replaced by a single U.S.-EU relationship? Would the EU become a separate trading zone that excluded U.S. and other non-EU products and investment? Would the development of a separate EU defense and foreign policy identity mean the demise of NATO and the end of trans-Atlantic defense cooperation? Whatever the answers to these and other questions, the creation of the EU and its ensuing success clearly implied that U.S.-Western European relations, just as U.S.-Central European relations and U.S.-Eastern European relations (including Russia) were in transition.

But transition to what? Policy makers, scholars, analysts, and other observers have discussed and debated answers to that question since the early 1990s. They have not yet developed a definitive answer. About the only thing that they agree on is that the transition is continuing.

Clearly, the collapse of communism in Eastern Europe, the disintegration of the Soviet Union, and the creation of the EU meant that an era has ended in U.S.-European relations. The new political realities that exist in Western Central, and Eastern Europe including Russia guarantee that future U.S-European relations will be different than past relations.

In addition, other forces for change are at work in the world that guarantee a new U.S.-European relationship. Beyond the European Union, other regions of the world are also creating free trade areas whose goals, although not as comprehensive as those of the EU, nevertheless have potential to impact U.S.-European relations.

Meanwhile, social-cultural conditions are changing in Europe and the United States. The United States, which has long prided itself on being a diverse society, is becoming more diverse than it has ever been as more and more immigrants from regions other than Europe enter the country. Europe too is becoming more diverse socially and culturally. It is certain that in the twenty first century neither Europe nor the United States will be as "white" as they were in the nineteenth and twentieth centuries; what is not certain is the impact that this reality will have on the trans-Atlantic relationship.

Advances in information and communication technologies in turn will effect all these changes. It is an old but true bromide that the world is becoming a smaller place, due in no small part to Information Age technologies. The impact that Information Age technologies will have on the trans-Atlantic relationship will be sizeable, but again, unpredictable.

An era, then, is over. What emerges from the present period of transition to become the new U.S.-European relationship is not clear, but it will be driven by new political realities on the ground in Western, Central, and Eastern Europe, new economic situations throughout the world, changing social-cultural conditions in Europe, North America, and elsewhere, and the development of new technology, especially information and communication technologies. The remaining pages of this chapter will explore these influences more fully.

New Western, Central, and Eastern European Political Realities

As the twenty first century began, the United States and most states in Europe were struggling to understand the emerging European geo-political and geo-strategic landscape. It was a landscape that was no longer divided into the East and West of the Cold War, and a landscape in which states were no longer the only important international actors.

By the early twenty first century, Europe was again recognized as a complex continent with distinct geographical, political, economic, and organizational regions and sub-regions. Geographically, Europe was at a minimum divided into Western, Central, and Eastern regions, each of which had additional political, economic, and organizational sub-divisions and fault-lines. Thus, in addition to individual states, Western Europe included for example the European Union, the Euro Zone within the European Union, non-EU Western Europe, and NATO

Conclusion

Europe. Central Europe also had its sub-divisions, for example the NATO states of Central Europe, the non-NATO states, and the Balkans. Eastern Europe in turn included the Baltic states, Belarus and Ukraine, and of course Russia. And no one quite knew whether Turkey should or should not be considered a European state.

The maze of Europe's complexity was further complicated by the growing importance of new international governmental organizations (IGOs) such as the Organization for Security and Cooperation in Europe (OSCE), as shown by Maria Raquel Sousa Freire earlier in this volume in Chapter 7, and by the expanding international role of non-governmental organizations (NGOs) such as trade unions, food producers groups, and environmental lobbyists, as discussed by Zdzislaw Puslecki in Chapter 8. This jumble of states, regions, IGOs, and NGOs, joined as well by multinational corporations, made policy formulation and implementation a considerable challenge for all who attempted to think strategically.

In most cases, except for in the Balkans, no real sense of urgency or threat accompanied the struggle to understand the emerging European geo-political and geo-strategic landscape. Rather, a sense of uncertainty extended across the continent as policy makers asked questions that had no definitive answer. Should the EU expand or not, and if so, who should be included? Should NATO expand or not, and if so, who should be included, and what impact would this have on Russia? Should the EU develop a separate defense capability apart from NATO, and if so, how strong should it be, how should it be organized, and what impact would this have on NATO? Should the OSCE be given capabilities that would allow it to engage in preventive diplomacy, crisis management, and post-conflict rehabilitation, and if so, who would provide them and how extensive would they be?

The answers to these and other questions had immense importance for the future of U.S.-European relations. To its credit, the U.S. government - and European governments as well - recognized this, and also clearly understood that the European political landscape was changing rapidly. Thus, the U.S. regularly initiated policies and actions, often in conjunction with European states, to attempt to respond to the changing European political landscape. Even though agreement did not always apparent American and European policies and actions regarding the EU, NATO, and Russia well illustrate the point.

As the European Union emerged from what had been the European Community, the United States and EU member states recognized that a new dimension was being added to U.S.-European relations. Thus, they moved to put the new dimension on a solid foundation, first with the 1990 Trans-Atlantic Declaration and then the 1995 Trans-Atlantic Agenda.

The 1990 Trans-Atlantic Declaration formalized official contacts between the United States and the then-EC. Among other things, it established twice a year consultations between the Presidents of the United States, the European Council, and the European Commission; mandated twice a year foreign policy meetings between the U.S. Secretary of State and the fifteen EC foreign ministers, or the EC Council President acting on their behalf; and declared that representatives of the U.S. Congress and European Parliament would meet twice a year.

The key point here is that under the Trans-Atlantic Declaration, the U.S. formally agreed to deal with the EC as an entity that represented the interests of its member states in certain areas. The U.S. did not withdraw recognition from the sovereign states that were EC members, but in conjunction with those states added another layer, a European layer, to the rich diversity of layers that already made up U.S. relations with Europe.

This process continued in 1995 when the U.S. and EU established the New Trans-Atlantic Agenda (NTA). The NTA was based on four principles: promoting peace, development, and democracy; responding to global challenges; expanding world trade; and building bridges across the Atlantic. Managed by senior officials supported at operational levels by policy experts who are in regular contact with one another, the NTA provides the U.S. and EU a forum in which they can address bilateral and global issues. Under the NTA, the U.S. and EU have developed shared positions or joint policies on economic development and humanitarian assistance in developing countries; limitations on production of precursor chemicals required for illicit drug production; approaches to feared North Korean development of nuclear weapons; promotion of global agreements reducing trade barriers in telecommunications and financial services; agreements on inspecting and certifying products; and providing joint awards for democratization in Central Europe.

Under the NTA, U.S. and EU officials have also abetted trans-Atlantic cooperation in the realm of NGOs, arranging person-to-person conferences for labor officials, consumers, and business people to solidify human ties across the Atlantic. For example, a 1997 conference led to the development of the Trans-Atlantic Information Electronic Services, which provides on-line information (http://www.tiesnet.org) about consumer affairs, education, the environment, and health issues in the U.S. and EU.

This does not mean that the NTA has solved every U.S.-EU disagreement. Differences continue on subsidies to certain industries, regulatory policies, and economic sanctions. But the NTA helps even here, providing a forum in which the U.S. and EU address these issues. The NTA is simply one way that U.S. interests in the EU - and EU interests in the U.S. - can be maintained and strengthened.

The U.S. and European states have also responded to the changed European political landscape by making significant changes in NATO, as detailed by Joyce Kaufman in Chapter 3. These changes will not be repeated here except insofar as to buttress the point that the U.S. and European states have responded and are responding to the changed European political landscape.

For example, as regards mission, NATO was formed to be Western Europe's primary military defense against a Soviet invasion, with NATO members agreeing that an attack against one would be considered an attack against all and that members would respond together against the attacker. This guarantee assured a U.S. military presence in Europe and led to the integration of defense planning of Western European and North American states. It also guaranteed West German participation in Western Europe's defense in a way that did not raise fears about German militarism.

When the Soviet Union collapsed in 1991, the primary reason for NATO's existence disappeared. Even though the other reasons for its existence retained their importance, a critical new reason for NATO's continuation was identified, to help maintain peace and assure stability in the continent as new European political, economic, and social conditions emerged. This changed mission, first intimated in NATO's 1991 Strategic Concept, and was fully accepted in its 1999 Strategic Concept.

Beyond changing its mission, NATO has also responded to Europe's changed political landscape by moving toward a creation of a European leg, adding members, and addressing Russian concerns, though not as completely as Russia would prefer. These changes in NATO have also been addressed elsewhere in this volume, especially by Kaufman in Chapter 3, Kanet and Ibryamova in Chapter 4, and Segell in Chapter 6, and will not be repeated in detail here.

Nevertheless, it is worth noting that as NATO developed its European Security and Defense Identity concept and the EU's Common Foreign and Security Policy evolved in 1999 into a Common European Security and Defense Policy, these transitions were undertaken with an eye to the evolving European political landscape. The same was true for NATO expansion, as it first created the North Atlantic Coordination Council to give former communist countries a connection to NATO, but not too close a connection, by providing a forum in which Europe's evolving security issues could be discussed; moved then in 1994 to form the Partnership for Peace (PFP), under which guidelines were established for military cooperation between PFP members and NATO and the basis was established for joint maneuvers between NATO forces and PFP members, including joint maneuvers between U.S. and Russian troops; and next moved forward in 1999 with its first round of enlargement in which the Czech Republic, Hungary, and Poland joined the alliance. NATO promised other PFP states that this was not the final enlargement and that a second round would follow. This encouraged some PFP states, but at least one, Russia, was far from pleased. Indeed, Russia had strongly opposed any NATO enlargement.

Before NATO enlargement, Russia had cooperated with NATO in several areas, joining NACC, becoming a PFP country, and sending a 2,500 man brigade to Bosnia in cooperation with the NATO-led peacekeeping effort there. Cooperation was sometimes difficult, but on the whole it succeeded.

But NATO enlargement displeased Russia in every respect. Many Russians saw it as a U.S. effort to embarrass Russia. Others considered it a threat to Russia's security. From the perspective of many Russians, the United States had been victorious in the Cold War, and it was now extending its military might via NATO closer to the Russian motherland. Even President Bill Clinton's 1997 assurance that NATO enlargement was not directed against Russia and his promise that NATO would not deploy forces in new NATO countries did not assuage Russian fear and anger.

Nevertheless, Russia made the best of a bad situation. Careful negotiations led on the NATO side by General Secretary Javier Solana and on the Russian side by Prime Minister Yevgeny Primakov led to the 1997 signing of the NATO-Russia "Founding Act on Mutual Relations, Cooperation, and Security". Although not a formal treaty, the Founding Act established a NATO-Russian Joint Council to consider issues such as terrorism, nuclear safety, military doctrine, and peacekeeping.

The Founding Act papered over NATO-Russian disagreements for a time, but as the situation in Kosovo deteriorated in 1998 and 1999, NATO-Russian relations grew stormy. NATO's air assault against Serbian forces in 1999 raised NATO-Russian tensions, and U.S.-Russian tensions, to a higher level than at any time since the Cold War ended. Although tensions eventually eased and Russia agreed to deploy peacekeeping troops in Kosovo once the bombing ended, the deployment almost foundered over conflicts about who would command the Russian troops and where they would be deployed.

Other issues also remained in Russian-U.S. relations and in Russian relations with non-Russian European states. For example, Russia has expressed concern that any EU eastward expansion might deprive Russia of traditional trading partners. At first, Russia also criticized U.S. plans to renounce the Anti-Ballistic Missile Treaty and to deploy a ballistic missile defense system. Conversely, the U.S. and other European states have criticized Russia's war in Chechnya and expressed concern over Russia's slack control over its nuclear materials.

The Russia factor, then, looms large in overall European political affairs. Russia is no longer the enemy, but it is clear that Russian, U.S., and non-Russian European interests in Europe do not always coincide. The questions are "To what extent do they diverge, and can those divergences be constructively and peacefully resolved?"

Bad news and good news for the future of U.S.-European relations therefore emerges from the reality of the changing European political landscape. The bad news is that issues remain between the U.S. and Europe, and that the increased complexity of European affairs means that they must be carefully and consistently dealt with. Many will not be amenable to resolution in the short term. The most significant issues appear to be between Russia and Europe and between Russia and the United States. However, since September 11, 2001, as we will see in the concluding section of this chapter, there have been numerous indications that many of the outstanding issues between Russia and the U.S. may be ameliorated, if not solved.

The good news - and it is good news - is that the U.S. and European states recognize that the landscape has changed and that it is continuing to change rapidly. They also understand that the political landscape is exceedingly complex, and have exhibited an extensive desire to assure the maintenance and even strengthening of a strong and vibrant trans-Atlantic relationship. Even more encouraging, even during the present period of transition, there is also a history of fashioning new policies and modifying old ones that have to this point been successful in coping with most if not all of the issues that have arisen. Challenges remain, but there is nothing to indicates that the new Western, Central, and Eastern European political realities will undermine or weaken the existing trans-Atlantic relationship. Indeed, the new realities provide opportunities to strengthen it, deepen it, and broaden it.

New Global Economic Situations

The new global economic situation presents a somewhat different picture, although not because of an inherent weakness or problem in U.S.-European economic relations. Indeed, economic ties between Europe and the United States, especially between the U.S. and EU states, are a strong and fundamental element of the trans-Atlantic relationship. For example, in 2000, trans-Atlantic trade between the U.S. and Europe accounted for approximately 30 percent of the world's total trade, with more than 20 percent of all U.S. exports and imports going to or coming from Europe.

European Union states are generally the United States most important trade and investment partners in Europe. Although on a country-to-country basis Canada, Mexico, and Japan in 2000 were all larger individual trading partners with the U.S. than any individual European state, the EU as a whole is the United States' most important trading partner. Trade and investment flows between the U.S. and European Union states alone averaged approximately one billion dollars per day, the single largest bilateral trade and investment flow in the world. To be sure, disagreements exist between the U.S. and the EU over agricultural policy, communications issues, and in other areas, but there is no doubt that trans-Atlantic economic relations, especially between the U.S. and EU states, remain strong.

At the same time, not all U.S. trade and investment relationships with European states or within the EU are equal. At least three tiers are evident. Within the EU, American trade with and investment in France, Germany, Great Britain, Holland, and Italy far outstrips U.S. trade with and investment in other EU states. Similarly, American trade with and investment in most other non-EU European states including Russia is as a general rule more limited than American trade with most EU states.

Beyond the tiered-nature of U.S.-European economic relations, there are at least three other factors that may be expected to have a significant impact on U.S.-European relations, the emergence of the European Union, the development of market economies in former communist states, and the creation of regional free trade areas outside Europe. However, it is not clear how these factors collectively will effect U.S.-European relations.

The emergence of the EU illustrates the uncertainty. When the Single European Act was passed in 1985, many prognosticators predicted that its 1992 implementation would lead to a decrease in trans-Atlantic trade as the EU concentrated on eliminating internal barriers to trade and constructing external barriers to trade. This did not occur. Similarly, when the EU introduced the Euro as the single EU currency in 2001, many doomsayers postulated that it would disrupt European and global financial markets and soon challenge the dollar for international supremacy as the preferred currency of exchange. Although at this time the Euro has only a limited historical track record, nothing indicates that earlier fears were founded in fact.

Indeed, if anything, the emergence of the EU as an economic entity appears to have been a boon to both inter-European trade and trans-Atlantic trade. Although some economic dislocations have occurred within the EU and trade disputes occasionally erupt between the United States and the EU over agriculture, communications, and other issue, the emergence of the EU as a prominent international economic actor appears to be a boon both to Europe and to U.S.-Western European relations.

As for the development of free market economies in former communist states, this too appears to have strengthened U.S. ties to Europe. During the Cold War, of course, U.S. economic ties with communist states were limited at most. With the collapse of communism, U.S. and Western European economic interactions with Central European and Eastern European states proliferated. While economic ties between the U.S. and Western European economies on the one hand and Central and Eastern European economies on the other remain much weaker than the U.S.-Western European economic relationship, they are nevertheless much stronger than they were during the Cold War era.

This leads directly to two questions. First, to what extent can either U.S. economic relations with Central and Eastern European states or Western European economic relations with Central and Eastern European states grow? Second, could either U.S. or Western European ties with Central or Eastern European states grow so much that they might undermine U.S.-Western European economic ties? No definitive answer is possible to either question, but given the difficulties that most Central European and Eastern European states continue to encounter as they make the difficult transition from a centralized to a market economy, it appears highly unlikely that either U.S. or Western European ties with Central or Eastern European states will undermine U.S.-Western European economic ties in the foreseeable future.

The creation of free trade areas outside of Europe leads to a less sanguine conclusion. Europe was not the only region that created a free trade area during the 1990s, although the EU went far beyond what other free trade zones envisioned. Indeed, during the 1980s and early 1990s, the United States, Canada, and Mexico concluded the North America Free Trade Agreement (NAFTA); four southern South American states concluded MERCOSUR; and six Southeast Asian states formed the Association of Southeast Asian Nations, which expanded to seven members when Vietnam joined in 1995.

This was just the beginning. In 1994, 18 Asian and American states including Canada, China, Japan, Mexico, and the U.S. signed the Asian-Pacific Economic Cooperation (APEC) agreement, which committed all developed signatory states to remove barriers to international trade between member states by 2010. Signatory developing states had the same objective set for 2020. By 2000, APEC had grown to 21 members which had a combined grow domestic product equal to about half the world's total of $35 trillion and included 42% of the world's trade. Also in 1994, regional integration in the Americas accelerated as 34 of the 35 countries in the Western Hemisphere concluded the Free Trade Area of the Americas (FTAA), which intended to put into operation by 2010 a free trade zone throughout the western hemisphere, Cuba excepted.

What does the development of free trade zones outside of Europe have to do with U.S.-European relations? The answer will probably not be as extreme as that suggested by Glen Segell in Chapter 6 of this volume, a NATO in which there "may be only two members . . . the European Union and NAFTA". But there inevitably will be an impact.

Consider, for example, that the United States is a member of three of the most important operational and planned free trade zones, the already-in-existence NAFTA and the still-to-come APEC and FTAA. NAFTA has already led to a significant expansion in U.S. trade with Canada and Mexico, and assuming that APEC and FTAA overcome the remaining hurdles to their implementation, they may be expected to increase significantly the size and scope of U.S. trade with their member countries. Thus, there is more than a remote possibility that successful free trade zones outside Europe of which the United States is a member may re-orient U.S. economic interests away from Europe toward the Americas and Asia even in the absence of the development of barriers to trade between free trade zones.

The same end result may eventuate from the World Trade Organization's (WTO) efforts to reduce tariff and non-tariff barriers to trade on bilateral and multi-lateral bases. As businesses in the U.S. and other countries identify and are presented with new opportunities to trade, they will follow the profit. And as tariff and non-tariff barriers to trade tumble as the result of WTO and other efforts, doing business with traditional trading partners may not be the best way to make a profit.

The globalization of economic relationships thus has potential to weaken the relative strength of U.S.-European economic relations in comparison with American economic ties with other regions of the world even as U.S. economic ties deepen in Western Europe and broaden in Central and Eastern Europe. To reiterate, this does not imply that there is an inherent problem or weakness in U.S.-European economic relations. Rather, it means that as global business opportunities expand, companies will re-orient their activities to where they can make the most profit. For American companies, that may not necessarily be in Europe, and for European companies, that may not necessarily be in the United States. In a certain sense, then, the expanded role of world trade envisioned by Zdzislaw Puslecki in his closing remarks in Chapter 8 in this volume may lead to a globalization of the economic elements of Yannis Stivachtis' regional international societies, thereby weakening future U.S.-European economic relations.

Changing European and American Social-Cultural Conditions

More than one observer has noted that at root, a fundamental social and cultural identity is the foundation that ties Europe and the United States together. Over the centuries, millions of Czechs, English, Germans, Hungarians, Irish, Italians, Russians, and people from other countries immigrated to the United States from Western Central, and Eastern Europe, creating close social, cultural, and human bonds between the new country in North America and the old countries of Europe.

This identity, it has been argued, is what enabled the U S.-Western European relationship to weather the storms of the Cold War. Others take the argument a step further, maintaining that social, cultural, and human ties between both

Eastern/Central Europe and Western Europe and between Eastern/Central Europe and the United States played a fundamental role in undermining communism.

At the beginning of the twenty-first century, the U.S.-European identity remains strong and vibrant. There are however, three challenges at work that may over time weaken that identity.

The first is immigration. Both the United States and Europe have experienced and are experiencing an influx of significant numbers of new immigrants who over time may modify or re-orient the present U.S.-European social, cultural, and human identity.

In the United States, most recent immigrants are Hispanic. Indeed, according to the U.S. Census Bureau, the U.S. Hispanic population between 1990 and 2000, grew from 22 million people to 35 million people, that is from 9% of the 1990 U.S. population of approximately 247 million to 13% of the 2000 U.S. population of 281 million. The Census Bureau projects that by 2025, the United States' Hispanic population may reach 58 million people, perhaps as much as 20% of the population. Much of the United States' Hispanic population lives in the American South and Southwest, where their social and cultural impact is already well evident.

The question here is the extent to which the growth of this impact will re-orient U.S. identity away from Europe and toward Latin America. Inevitably, at least some re-orientation will occur. At the same time tens of millions of other Americans will retain their social, cultural, and human identity with Europe, thereby assuring a strong future for the U.S.-European identity.

Meanwhile, in Western Europe, significant numbers of new immigrants are arriving from Eastern and Central Europe and from North Africa. Although their numbers and percentages are not as large as those pertaining to immigrants to the U.S. from Latin America, they nevertheless are having a social, cultural, and human impact. The question is once again how large an impact will they have and how extensive a re-orientation of Western Europe's social, cultural, and human identity with the U.S. will occur.

A second challenge that may affect the U.S.-European identity is the successor generation issue. During World War I, World War II, and during the Cold War, millions of Americans served in Europe. Many renewed or developed an affinity for Europe and things European. At the same time, the perils and promises of the Berlin crises, the Hungarian revolution, the Prague spring, and Poland's Solidarity trade union movement assured that the attention of tens of millions of Americans would be riveted on Europe. Most Western Europeans, despite sometime pointed criticism of the United States, were appreciative of U.S. support, while significant numbers of Central and Eastern Europeans outside the Soviet Union quietly hope for a better and different future.

But all that is receding further into the past. No World War I veterans remain alive, tens of thousands of World War II veterans are dying every year, and the memories of Europe of American Cold War veterans are fading. Indeed, the generation of Americans that is presently coming of age knows of the Berlin Wall only from historical documentaries and do not remember Ronald Reagan's stirring appeal, "Mr. Gorbachev, tear down the wall!" Indeed, by the 2000 presidential campaign, it had even become possible for one senior advisor to then-presidential candidate George W. Bush to publicly proclaim that Europe was no longer the United States' primary foreign policy interest.

Conversely, millions of Americans travel to Europe for business and for vacations, and millions of Europeans travel to the U.S. for similar reasons. Nevertheless, some knowledgeable observers are concerned that a successor generation issue is at hand, one in which Americans and Europeans no longer closely identify with one another.

This concern is strengthened by the third challenge, the proliferation of new information and communication technologies. In the context of the U.S.-European identity, the concern here is that as new information and communication technologies provide easier and faster access to more and more societies and cultures, the easier and faster access to more and more cultures will undermine the historical U.S.-European social, cultural, and human identity. The potential impact of Information Age technologies on U.S.-European relations goes far beyond social, cultural, and human relations, however, and will therefore be examined separately in the following section.

Despite these three challenges --immigration, the successor generation issue, and new information and communication technologies-- the fundamental U.S.-European social, cultural, and human identity remains strong. Even with these three challenges, it is likely to remain the foundation of what ties the United States and Europe together.

New Information and Communication Technologies

An immensely dense web of information and communication pathways already ties the United States and Europe to each other. This web is the most extensive in the world, and includes telephony, satellite communications, submarine cables, Internet connections, and other information and communication pathways. Individuals, companies, governments, and other organizations also use this web extensively. For example, according to the International Telecommunications Union (ITU), as much as 50% of the 120 billion minutes of international telephone traffic that people throughout the world used in 2001 was between the U.S. and Europe.

The world's satellite communications presents a similar picture. According to the U.S. Central Intelligence Agency, the United States orient 29 of its 45 Intelsat earth stations toward the Atlantic and 16 toward the Pacific. All five U.S. Intersputnik earth stations serve the Atlantic, as do two of its four Inmarsat earth stations. Canada has five Intelsat earth stations, four devoted to handling trans-Atlantic traffic and one to the Pacific. Both of Canada's Intersputnik earth stations also are devoted to the Atlantic market.

Meanwhile, in Europe, Germany has 14 Intelsat earth stations, twelve concentrating on the Atlantic and two on the Indian Ocean. It also has one Inmarsat station devoted to the Atlantic and two Intersputnik stations divide between the Atlantic and the Indian Ocean. The United Kingdom has 10 Intelsat earth stations, seven serving the Atlantic market and 3 concentrating on the Indian Ocean, with one Inmarsat earth station also covering the Atlantic. France exhibited slightly more diversity, with three Intelsat and one Inmarsat earth stations serving the Atlantic market and two Intelsat stations covering the Indian Ocean.

Clearly, the 94 earth stations that operate in the five largest North American and European telecommunications markets are inordinately devoted to trans-Atlantic traffic. Sixty-seven cover the Atlantic, 19 cover the Pacific, and eight the Indian Ocean.

What is more, everything indicates that new information and communication technologies will strengthen this already strong web of information and communication pathways between the United States and Europe. Using the Internet as an example, one prominent source (http://www.nua.com) reports that as of early 2002, as many as 339 million of the world's 544 million computers that were online were in the U.S., Canada, or Europe. This was 62% of the world's total.

Total Internet bandwidth, which shows the capacity of a network to process traffic such as e-mails and web page browsing and is measured in gigabits per second (gbit/s), presents a similar picture of the extent to which connectivity between the U.S. and Canada on the one hand and Europe on the other supersedes trans-Oceanic connectivity elsewhere in the world. As researched by Telegeography, Inc. and reported by the ITU, bandwidth between the U.S/Canada and Europe in 2001 was 56 gbit/s, between the U.S./Canada and Asia/the Pacific 18 gbit/s, and between the U.S./Canada and Latin America 3 gbit/s. The extent of the dominance of the connectivity between the U.S./Canada and Europe becomes even more apparent when compared to Europe's bandwidth connections with Asia/the Pacific and Latin America, respectively .4 gbit/s and 1 gbit/s.

Together, the existing web of information and communication pathways that connect the U.S. and Europe, the speed with which the U.S. and Europe are bringing new Information Age technologies into use, and the extensive penetration of present and emerging technologies guarantees that the flow of information and communication between the U.S. and Europe will remain robust. Most likely, the trans-Atlantic information and communication pathway will remain the densest trans-oceanic information and communication pathway in the world. This bodes well for the future of U.S.-European relations.

However, new Information Age technologies will also strengthen U.S. information and communication ties with other regions of the world, and they will also strengthen European information and communication ties with other regions or the world. Thus, a relative analysis as well as an absolute analysis must be made.

This reality leads to a critical question: As the globalization of information and communication pathways proceeds, accelerated by new technologies that aid and abet the globalization of business and the globalization of social, cultural, and human contacts and awareness, will information and communication pathways between the U.S. and Europe strengthen more rapidly between the U.S. and Europe than between the U.S. and other regions of the world, and between Europe and other regions of the world? This question cannot be definitively answered, but the answer has critical implications the U.S.-European relationship.

The Impact of September 11

The U.S. clearly has a broad array of interests in Europe, and those interests are evolving across the spectrum of political, security, economic, social-cultural, and technical affairs. But as the horrific events of September 11, 2001, illustrated, single events can also have an immense impact on international affairs and on U.S.-European relations. As we develop conclusions, we would be remiss if we did not briefly examine the impact of September 11 on U.S.-European relations. Three areas deserve special commentary, original reactions, NATO affairs, and the longer-term war on terrorism.

European reaction to the September 11 attacks well illustrated the depth strength of the U.S.-European relationship As news about the catastrophe spread, Great Britain's Prime Minister Tony Blair, whose country had suffered over 100 people killed in the World Trade Center, immediately placed his country's defense forces on highest alert. Declaring that the attacks were "perpetrated by fanatics who are utterly indifferent to the sanctity of human life", Blair promised that Great Britain would help "eradicate this evil completely from the world".

Meanwhile, in Russia, thousands of people lit candles and left flowers in front of the U.S. Embassy in Moscow and the U.S. Consulate in St. Petersburg. Russian President Vladimir Putin promised to provide the U.S. with whatever intelligence Russia had on terrorists and condemned the attacks as a "blatant challenge to humanity" that should unite the international community in the struggle against terrorism. Denmark, France, Germany, Italy, Norway, Spain, and every other European Union state also condemned the attacks and offered condolences.

NATO's response paralleled that of individual European countries. Created primarily to deter a Soviet attack in Europe, NATO after the break-up of the Soviet Union evolved into an organization whose purpose was to maintain peace in Europe and nearby areas. NATO by 2001 had grown into an alliance of 19 countries, with 26 other countries including Russia associated with it in an organization called the Partnership for Peace. Each member of NATO pledged under Article 5 of the North Atlantic Treaty, the document that created NATO, that it considered an "armed attack" against any of NATO's members "an attack against them all", and that it would help defend any member country that is attacked.

With NATO being centered on Europe and having existed for so long primarily to counter the Soviet threat, few people expected that NATO would invoke Article 5 for the first time in defense of the United States. Yet that is exactly what happened. The day after the attack, NATO invoked Article 5 and declared that it would help defend the U.S. It also accelerated the exchange of counter-terrorism information and intelligence, enhanced the defense of U.S. and NATO installations in Europe and stepped up preparations against biological, chemical, nuclear, and radiological attacks.

Importantly, NATO also expanded information exchanges and enhanced anti-terrorist consultations with Partnership for Peace countries. For example, in January and February 2002, NATO and Russian diplomats and military officials met at the NATO Defense College in Rome to discuss civil emergency planning and military cooperation against terrorism.

The response from European states to the war on terrorism initiated by the United States was no different. Every state supported the effort, and some, especially Great Britain, provided armed forces. One measure of the wide support for the war was that every European state that was asked granted the U.S. air transit or landing rights, and all enhanced the sharing of their intelligence information and assets.

Great Britain's Tony Blair was most vocal about his country's support, noting that although "none of the leaders involved in the actions want war ... but we know that sometimes, to safeguard peace, we have to fight. Britain has learned that lesson many times before in our history". Blair also committed British air and ground assets to the war.

Russia's Putin was equally forthright, declaring the U.S. attacks in Afghanistan "necessary". He also worked with Tajikistan and Uzbekistan in Central Asia to assure that former Russian bases there would be made available to U.S. forces. The bases were important for the war against terrorism, and it would have been unthinkable before September 11 for a Russian president to accept, much less work to assure, the presence of American armed forces in Central Asia.

Meanwhile, French Prime Minister Jacques Chirac observed that the fight would be "complex and difficult", that it was "not just a military fight", and that "we are all united". Canada's Prime Minister Jean Chretien sounded a similar note, saying that his country was "part of an unprecedented coalition of nations that has come together to fight the threat of terrorism" and promising that "Canada will be a part of this coalition every step of the way". He too contributed elements of his country's armed forces to the effort. Every other European state on a bilateral basis also expressed support and promised at a minimum to share intelligence with the United States about terrorism.

In all three areas examined here - reaction to the September 11 attacks, NATO's responses, and the attitudes of European states toward the war against terrorism - the depth and strength of the U.S.-European relationship is clear. Indeed, it may even be argued that in some cases, for example with Russia, the September 11 attacks solidified and strengthened the foundation of the U.S.-European relationship.

Conclusions

There is no doubt that U.S.-European relations are in a period of transition, and that the stresses and strains of globalization are increasing both the number and the seriousness of the challenges that confront U.S.-European relations. But if anything, the preceding analysis indicates that the U.S.-European relationship, while uncertain and challenged, is on a solid foundation.

Although an era has ended in U.S.-European relations, the U.S. and most European governments and international governmental organizations appear to be coping well with the challenges presented by the new Western, Central, and European political realities. The challenges presented by the new realities of creating new governments and seizing opportunities for democratization and marketization in most Central and Eastern European states are more regional and local challenges than challenges presented by globalization, but the implications of success or failure in these efforts will be global. Similarly, the challenges of crafting new relationships between the United States and the EU and between the United States and NATO are more regional than global, but the implications of success or failure will be global.

As for the globalization of economic relationships, this, as we have seen, has potential to weaken the relative strength of U.S.-European economic relations in comparison with American economic ties with other regions of the world even as U.S. economic ties deepen in Western Europe and broaden in Central and Eastern Europe. As global business opportunities expand, companies will re-orient their activities to where they can make the most profit. For American companies, that may not necessarily be in Europe, and for European companies, that may not necessarily be in the United States.

U.S.-European social, cultural, and human relations remain solid, but they too are open to challenges from immigration, successor generation concerns, and the impact of emerging information and communication technologies. In all three areas of challenge, countervailing influences are in place, which appear more than sufficient to offset the challenges for the foreseeable future. That having been said, it nevertheless inevitable that the U.S.-European social, cultural, and human relationship will evolve as U.S. and European societies, cultures, and peoples evolve.

Regarding the impact of new information and communication technologies on the overall status of the U.S.-European relationship, there is no doubt that the relationship will be strengthened. The uncertainty is whether information and communication pathways between the U.S. and Europe will grow stronger more rapidly than pathways the U.S. and other regions of the world, and between Europe and other regions of the world.

Finally, the impact of September 11 also appears to have solidified, strengthened, and in some cases even expanded the foundation of U.S.-European relations, as least if European responses to the American tragedy in the three areas examined above are a legitimate representation of European sentiment.

In conclusion, then, globalization and other factors have increased the challenges and strains that exist in the U.S.-European relationship, but at the outset of the twenty first century, no challenge or strain appears significant enough to seriously disrupt or undermine overall U.S.-European relations on either a bi-lateral or a multi-lateral basis. In those areas where serious challenges or strains may exist, for example regarding conflicting U.S. and EU trade policies or disagreement over the expansion of NATO, the U.S. and most European states on either bilateral or multi-lateral basis are taking steps not only to address problems that may develop, but to further cement an already strong relationship

As we saw at the outset, U.S. ties with Europe during the twentieth century were played out through millions of person-to-person contacts and relationships, thousands of business-to-business and organization-to-organization contacts and relationships, and hundreds of government-to-government contacts and relationships. In the later years of the century, these contacts and relationships were further buttressed by developing U.S.-EU contacts and relationships and renewed and expanded in Central and Eastern Europe as communist governments there fell. While globalization and other forces may over time lead U.S. relations with other regions of the world to evolve and develop to rival U.S.-European relations in their depth, complexity, and diversity, there is nothing on the horizon that suggests that U.S. interests in and relations with Europe will diminish significantly in importance.

Index

acquis, and EU enlargement 56-9
Afghanistan
   British role 124
   drug trafficking 218-19
   and NATO 95
Africa, Sub-Saharan, and US national security objectives 35-6
agricultural products, Uruguay Round 190-2
Alaska, acquisition by US 8
Albright, Madeline 111
Amsterdam Treaty (1998) 56, 57, 108, 233
anarchy, and international relations 61, 62-3
Antarctica, and US national security objectives 36-7
ARRC (Allied Command Europe Rapid Reaction Corps)
   and Britain 129-30
   in Kosovo 132
Asia, and US national security objectives 33-5
Atlantic Charter 2

Balkans
   and British defence policy 125, 136
   and EU enlargement 154
   NATO role 79, 81, 82-4
   see also Kosovo; Macedonia; Yugoslavia (former)
Baltic republics, and NATO enlargement 103-4
banking, Uruguay Round 190
Banzer, Hugo, President 210
Bill of Rights, US Constitution 2
Blair, Tony, Prime Minister 95, 125, 246
Bolivia
   coca production

   eradication 208-9
   statistics 210
Bosnia
   and Britain 130
   and Dayton negotiations 85, 92
   and NATO 83, 93, 94
   and the US 84, 85
Britain
   Afghanistan, role 124
   and ARRC 129-30
   Bosnia, role 130
   defence policy
      air force 135
      army 134-5
      the Balkans 125, 136
      force reductions 129-30
      goals 126, 129
      humanitarian issues 125
      independent nuclear deterrent 127-8, 129
      moral dimension 126
      post-Cold War 123-4, 128-9, 130
      post-World War II 126
      Soviet Union 126-7
      Strategic Defence Review 131-7
      and trade 123, 125
      and US support 127
      world role 128
   expeditionary forces, need for 124-6
   Kosovo 131-2
   Macedonia 125
   and September 11 events 245, 246
   Sierra Leone 124, 153
   Strategic Defence Review 124-5
   TLAMs 124, 125, 134
   and UN operations 125
US
   and occupation of Oregon 7, 8
   and US/Canadian border 6-7

and the WEU 129
Zimbabwe, concerns 124
Bull, Hedley
    on the international society 65
    on the international system 64-5
    The Anarchical Society 59
Burma, drug trafficking 216-18
Bush, George W., President 20
Buzan, Barry, *gemeinschaft/gesellschaft* society 59-60, 62

Canada, response to September 11 events 246
CAP (Common Agricultural Policy)
    and EU enlargement 58
    and the Uruguay Round 191
    and the WTO 185
Caribbean, drug trafficking 212, 214
CESDP (Common European Security and Defense Policy) 108, 131
    launch 147, 237
    and NATO 100, 108, 110-13, 147, 153
    role 112, 147-9
    and the WEU 153
CFSP (Common Foreign and Security Policy)
    and ESDI 154
    EU 144, 149-52, 237
    and the European Commission 150
    objective 150, 155
    origins 149
China, Peoples Republic 17
Chirac, Jacques, President 246
Chretien, Jean, Prime Minister 246
Churchill, Winston 2
Clinton, Bill, President 20, 111, 237
coca production
    Bolivia 208-9
    Colombia 209-11
    eradication 207-11
    Peru 207-8
    statistics 210
cocaine
    interdiction 212-14
    trafficking methods 211-12

Cold War
    end, and British defence policy 123-4, 128-9, 130
    and English School of International Relations 62
    and EU enlargement 68-9
    Francis Fukuyama on 61
    and international relations theory 61
    meta-narratives 61-3
    Samuel Huntington on 61-2
    US strategy 12-13, 15
Colombia
    coca production
        eradication 209-11
        statistics 210
    guerilla movements 210
    society, militarization 211
Combined Joint Task Forces, NATO 110
Common European Security and Defense Policy *see* CESDP
Common Foreign and Security Policy *see* CFSP
Common Strategy on Russia, European Council 106, 108
communications technologies, Europe, US 243-5, 247
criminality, international 19
CSCE (Conference on Security and Cooperation in Europe)
    Estonia
        membership 163
        mission to 163-4
    Paris Summit (1990) 159
    see also OSCE
Cuba, US control of 9
culture
    common
        and the EU 70
        European states 69-70
Cyprus, EU membership, reasons for 69
Czech Republic, and NATO enlargement 88, 102, 237

Dayton negotiations, and Bosnia 85, 92
Declaration of Independence (1776) 1-2

democracy, and economic growth 189
Denmark, Maastricht Treaty, rejection 147
developing countries, and globalization 200
Doha meeting, WTO 201
drug trafficking
   Afghanistan 218-19
   Burma 216-18
   Caribbean 212, 214
   countermeasures
      consequences 206, 219-23
      and corruption 221-2
      US 205-6
   Golden Triangle 215-19
   KMT (Kuo Min Tang) 215, 216, 217
   Marseilles 215
   Mexico 212-14
   and militarization of society 208, 211, 219-22
   and national security 205-6
   Pacific 214
   price movements 205
   Thailand 216
   see also cocaine; heroin
drugs policy, Richard Nixon 215, 216
Dunkirk Treaty (1947) 127

East Asia, and US national security objectives 30-1
economic development, Grossman and Helpman model 187-9
economic growth
   and democracy 189
   and September 11 events 200-1
EDC (European Defence Community) 145
EEC (European EconomiC Community) 145
ELN guerilla movement 210
EMU (European Monetary Union), and EU enlargement 58
English School of International Relations, and the Cold War 62
environmental protection
   and trade growth 193-5
   and the WTO 194-5
ESDI (European Security and Defense Identity)
   and CFSP 154
   emergence 152, 237
Estenssoro, Paz, President 208-9
Estonia
   citizenship law 162-3
   CSCE
      membership 163
      mission 163-4
   and the HCNM 165-6
   integration strategy 167-8
   non-citizens 156
   and the ODIHR 166-7
   OSCE mission 164-76
   Russians in 163, 164, 169-70
EU (European Union)
   as an international system 64
   CESDP 100, 108, 110-13, 131, 144, 147-9
   CFSP 144, 149-52, 237
   and common culture 70
   enlargement
      and *acquis* 56-9
      applicants
         motives 68-9
         obligations 56-7, 71
         preparation 57-8
      and the Balkans 154
      and the CAP 58
      and the Cold War 68-9
      and EMU 58
      and identity 71
      implications 58-9
      and national interests 69
      reasons for 68, 69
      and Russia 101, 106, 107, 109-10, 154-5
      significance 66-7, 99
      theoretical framework 60-3
      and the Ukraine 106-7
   General Affairs Council, military bodies 150-2

and globalization 197-201
Helsinki Summit (1999) 124
and NATO 100, 108, 110-13, 143-4, 233
as regional international society 65
and trade liberalization 197-8, 240
Treaty on (1993) 110
US
   agricultural products, conflict 190-2
   relations 236
   steel industry, conflict 189-90
   trade 239
and the WEU 123, 145
Eurasianism, and Russia 107
Eurocorps 132
see also ARRC
Eurocurrency 144
Eurofighter 135
Europe
   common culture 69-70
   common foreign policy 145
   common security policy 145, 155-6
      and the OSCE 160-2
      and the US 152-4
   complexity 234-5
   diversity 234
   expansion 65-7
      reasons 67-8
   identity 70-1
   Kosovo campaign, response 145
   Russia, attitude 107
   US
      communications technologies 243-5, 247
      cultural identity 241-3
      national security objectives 28-9
      relations 231-6, 247-8
      trade 239
   see also EU
European Commission
   'Agenda 2000: For a Stronger and Wider Union' 58
   and CFSP 150
   'Enlargement 2000' 154

European Council, Common Strategy on Russia 106, 108
European Union *see* EU
expeditionary forces, British defence policy 124-6

FARC guerilla movement 210
farmers, and globalization 199
'four freedoms', Franklin Roosevelt 2
Fourteen Points, Woodrow Wilson 2
France
   and Kosovo 85
   response to September 11 events 246
free trade areas
   trade liberalization 240-1
   and the US 240-1
Fujimori, Albert, President 208, 220
Fukuyama, Francis, on the Cold War 61

GATS (General Agreement on Trade in Services) 184
GATT (General Agreement on Tariffs and Trade)
   and trade liberalization 183
   see also WTO
gemeinschaft/gesellschaft, society 59-60, 62, 65
Germany, and Kosovo 85-6
globalization
   and developing countries 200
   economic 18, 247
   and the EU 197-201
   and farmers 199
   Pope John Paul II on 199
   and US/European relations 247-8
Golden Triangle, drug trafficking 215-19
Grossman and Helpman model, economic development 187-9

Hamilton, Alexander, President, and US hegemony 6
Hawaii, acquisition by US 9
HCNM (High Commissioner on National Minorities) 159, 160, 161, 163
   and Estonia 165-6

Helsinki Summit (1999) 124, 132
heroin
 interdiction 219
 trafficking 215-19
Hispanic population, US 242
humanitarian issues and British defence policy 125
Hungary, and NATO enlargement 80, 88, 102, 237
Huntington, Samuel, on the Cold War 61-2

identity
 and EU enlargement 71
 Europe 70-1
information technology, revolution 18
international relations
 theory 60-2
 and the Cold War 61
international society
 definitions 64, 65
 Hedley Bull on 65
 international system, difference 59-60, 64-5
 theoretical approaches 64
international system
 anarchical nature 61, 62-3
 definition 64
 EU as 64
 Hedley Bull on 64-5
 multipolar 17-18
Ireland, Nice Treaty, rejection 146-7
Ivanov, Sergei 104

Jefferson, Thomas, President, and Louisiana Purchase 6
John Paul II, Pope, on globalization 199
Johnson, Andrew, President, Alaska, acquisition of 8
Jospin, Lionel, Prime Minister 95

KFOR troops, Kosovo 86, 132
KMT (Kuo Min Tang), drug trafficking 215, 216, 217
Kok, Wim 146

Kosovo
 ARRC in 132
 European response 145
 and France 85
 and Germany 85-6
 KFOR troops 86, 132
 and NATO 84-6, 92, 94
 and Rambouillet meeting 84-5, 86, 92
 and Russia 104
 and the US 110

Lake, Tony 104
Latin America, US foreign policy 7, 14-15
Louisiana Purchase (1803) 6

Maastricht Treaty (1991) 82, 233
 Denmark, rejection 147
Macedonia, and Britain 125
Marseilles, drug processing 215
meta-narratives, Cold War 61-3
Mexico
 drug trafficking 212-14
 US, war 8
MFA (Multifibre Agreement) 192
MFN (Most Favoured Nation) Clause 185
Middle East, and US national security objectives 33-5
modernisation
 Ottoman Empire 68
 Russia 68
Monroe Doctrine (1823) 7, 8

NAFTA (North Atlantic Free Trade Area)
 creation 240
 and US trade 241
Nasser, Gamal Abdel, President 16
national interests, and EU enlargement 69
national security, and drug trafficking 205-6
NATO
 and Afghanistan 95
 ARRC 129-30, 132

Article 5 invocation 79, 95, 245
Balkans, role 79, 81, 82-4
and Bosnia 83, 93
    lessons 94
and CESDP 100, 108, 110-13, 147, 153
Combined Joint Task Forces 110
enlargement 80, 86-9, 106-10
    Baltic republics 103-4
    costs 87
    Czech Republic 88, 102, 237
    disagreements 87-8
    Hungary 80, 88, 102, 237
    Poland 88, 102, 237
    purpose 105
    and Russia 87, 100-6, 107, 112-13, 237-8
    timetable 88-9
and the EU 100, 108, 110-13, 143-4, 233
formation 145, 232-3
and Kosovo 84-6, 92
    disagreements 85-6
    lessons 94
membership, motives 81
and Operation Deliberate Force 83, 84
PfP program 80, 87, 100, 103, 106, 145, 155, 237
policy-making 80-1
post-Cold War role 79-80, 91-3, 95-6, 100-1, 102, 104-5, 110, 236-7
September 11 events 79, 93-4, 95, 245-6
Serbia, bombing 86, 104
and Soviet Union collapse 80-1
Strategic Concept 1991/1999, compared 81, 89, 90-1
Strategic Concept 1999 92
and UNPROFOR 83, 84
and the US 93-4, 153-4
and the Western European Union 111
and Yugoslavia (former) 81, 82-3, 92, 112, 123
NATO-Russia Founding Act (1997) 103, 104, 105

NATO-Russia Permanent Joint Council 103, 105
New World, and the Old World 1
NGO (Non-Governmental Organizations), and the WTO 185
Nice Treaty (2001), rejection by Ireland 146-7
Nixon, Richard, President, drugs policy 215, 216
NTA (New Trans-Atlantic Agenda) 236
nuclear weapons, Britain 127-8, 129

ODIHR (Office for Democratic Insitutions and Human Rights) 159, 165
    and Estonia 166-7
Old World, and the New World 1
oleiferous seeds, trade negotiations 191-2
Operation Deliberate Force, and NATO 83, 84
opium production, Turkey 215
Oregon, US/British occupation 7, 8
OSCE (Organization of Security and Cooperation in Europe)
    'Charter for European Security' (1999) 160
    Estonia, mission 164-76
    and European security 160-2
    objectives 160
    and Russia 107-8, 161
    see also CSCE
Ottoman Empire, modernisation 68

Pacific, drug trafficking 214
Pacific Basin, and US national security objectives 30-1
pacifism, US 11-12
Palme Commission 145
Panama Canal, construction 9
Partnership and Cooperation Agreement see PCA
Partnership for Peace see PfP
Pastrana Arango, Andres, President 211
PCA (Partnership and Cooperation Agreement) (1994) 108

scope 108-9
Pearl Harbor (1941) 12
Persian Gulf War 82
Peru
  coca production
    eradication 207-8
    statistics 210
  Shining Path movement 207
  society, militarization 208
PfP (Partnership for Peace) program, NATO 80, 87, 100, 103, 106, 145, 155, 237
Phillipines, US acquisition of 9
Poland, and NATO enlargement 88, 102, 237
Primakov, Yevgeny, Prime Minister 237
Prodi, Romano 146
Puerto Rico, acquisition of 9
Putin, President 101-2, 105-6, 112, 245, 246

Rambouillet meeting, and Kosovo 84-5, 86
Reagan, Ronald, President 13
regional international society
  EU as 65
  expansion 65-8
  new members, admittance 69
Roosevelt, Franklin D., President 12
  'four freedoms' 2
Russia
  economy 154
  and Estonia 163, 164
  and EU enlargement 101, 106, 107, 109-10, 154-5
  and Eurasianism 107
  Europe, attitude 107
  foreign policy, principles 108
  and Kosovo 104
  modernisation 68
  and NATO enlargement 87, 100-6, 107, 112-13, 237-8
  and the OSCE 107-8, 161
  and September 11 events 105-6, 108, 245, 246
  US, relations 106, 108
Russians, in Estonia 163, 164, 169-70

Saint Malo Declaration 124, 132, 150
Samoa, US acquisition of 9
Sarajevo, massacre 83, 84
Schroeder, Gerhard 85, 95
Seattle meeting, WTO 195, 198
September 11 events 123
  British response 245, 246
  Canadian response 246
  and economic growth 200-1
  French response 246
  NATO response 79, 93-4, 95, 245-6
  Russian response 105-6, 108, 245, 246
  and US foreign policy 106, 111
  and US/Europe relations 245-6
  see also terrorism
Serbia, and NATO bombing 86, 104
Shining Path movement, Peru 207
Sierra Leone, Britain 124, 153
Single European Act (1985) 233, 239
Solana, Javier 105, 152, 237
Somalia, US forces 130
South America
  coca crop eradication 207-11
  see also Bolivia; Colombia; Peru
Soviet Union
  and British defence policy 126-7
  collapse 17, 232
    and NATO 80-1
  and US containment policy 12-13, 16, 232
  see also Russia
Spaak, Paul-Henry 109
Spanish-American War (1898) 9, 11
steel industry, and the Uruguay Round 189-90

TACIS (Technical Assistance to the Commonwealth of Independent States) 106, 108
terrorism
  international 18-19

war on 95
see also September 11 events
Texas, acquisition by US 8
textiles, and Uruguay Round 189
Thailand, drug trafficking 216
Thatcher, Margaret, Prime Minister 128
Third World, and the US 15-16
TLAMs (Tomahawk Land Attack Missiles), Britain 124, 125, 134
Toynbee, Arnold 62
trade, and British defence policy 123, 125
trade growth
  1996 196
  and environmental protection 193-5
  and the Uruguay Round 193
trade liberalization
  and the EU 197-8, 240
  free trade areas 240-1
  and GATT 183
trade negotiations
  oleiferous seeds 191-2
  and trade unions 189-90
trade unions
  role 186-7
  and trade negotiations 189-90
Trans-Atlantic Declaration (1990) 235-6
Trans-Atlantic Information Electronic Services 236
Turkey
  and EU membership 57
  opium production 215

Ukraine, and EU enlargement 106-7
United Nations
  and Bosnia 83
  operations, and Britain 125
UNPROFOR, and NATO 83, 84
Uruguay Round 183, 184, 185
  and agricultural products 190-2
  banking 190
  and the CAP 191
  conclusion 192
  and the steel industry 189-90
  and textiles 189

  and trade growth 193
US
  Alaska, acquisition of 8
  and Bosnia 84, 85
  Britain
    defence policy 127
    and occupation of Oregon 7, 8
    and the US/Canadian border 6-7
    naval power, early 19c 6-7
  Cold War strategy 12-13, 15
  Constitution, Bill of Rights 2
  Cuba, control of 9
  diversity 234
  drug countermeasures 205-6
    Bolivia 208-9
    Colombia 209-11
    Peru 207-8
  EU
    agricultural products 190-2
    relations 236
    steel industry conflict 189-90
    trade 239
  Europe
    communications technologies 243-5, 247
    cultural identity 241-3
    relations 231-6, 247-8
    trade 239
  and European Security Policy 152-4
  foreign policy
    development 37-41
    and national security objectives 37
    principles 2-3
    problems 38-40
    and September 11 events 106, 111
  and free trade areas 240-1
  as global power 11-17
  Hawaii, acquisition of 9
  hegemony
    and Alexander Hamilton 6
    pursuit of 7-8
  Hispanic population 242
  and Kosovo 110
  Latin America 7, 14-15, 242
  Mexico, war 8

and NAFTA 241
national interests 3-5
national security objectives
   Antarctica 36-7
   East Asia/Pacific Basin 30-1
   Eastern Hemisphere 9-11, 15, 17
   Europe 28-9
   global 13-14, 20-8
   Middle East/SW, Central, South Asia 33-5
   Sub-Saharan Africa 35-6
   Western Hemisphere 6-9, 15, 31-2
and NATO 93-4, 153-4
pacifism 11-12
Panama Canal, construction 9
Phillipines, acquisition of 9
Puerto Rico, acquisition of 9
as regional power 5-11
Russia, relations 106, 108
Samoa, acquisition of 9
and Somalia 130
Soviet Union, containment 12-13, 16, 232
Spanish-American War 9, 11
Texas, acquisition of 8
and the Third World 15-16
and World War I 11
and World War II 12
and the WTO 242

VERA (Voluntary Export Restraint Arrangements) 185, 192
Versailles, Treaty of (1919) 11

Warsaw Pact, collapse (1991) 99, 100, 101, 153
Washington, George, President, and US foreign policy 6
Western Hemisphere, and US national security objectives 6-9, 15, 31-2
Westphalia, Treaty of (1648) 67
Westphalian paradigm 18, 20
WEU (Western European Union)
   and Britain 129
   and CSDP 153
   and the EU 123, 145
   formation 145
   and NATO 111
Wight, Martin 62
Wilson, Woodrow, President, and America as global power 11
   Fourteen Points 2
World Trade Center attacks *see* September 11 events
World War I, and the US 11
World War II, and the US 12
WTO (World Trade Organisation)
   and the CAP 185
   conflicts 185-6
   Doha meeting 201
   and environmental protection 194-5
   and NGOs 185
   opponents of 199
   purpose 184
   Seattle meeting 195, 198
   and US trade 242

Yugoslavia (former), and NATO 81, 82-3, 92, 112, 123

Zamora, Paz, President 209
Zedillo, Ernesto, President 199
Zimbabwe, Britain 124